The Political Economy
of Reform

The Political Economy of Reform

Edited by
Federico Sturzenegger
and
Mariano Tommasi

The MIT Press
Cambridge, Massachusetts
London, England

This book was set in Palatino on the Monotype "Prism Plus" PostScript Imagesetter by Asco Trade Typesetting Ltd., Hong Kong.

Printed and bound in the United States of America.

Library of Congress Cataloging-in-Publication Data

The political economy of reform / edited by Federico Sturzenegger and
  Mariano Tommasi.
    p.   cm.
  Includes bibliographical references and index.
  ISBN 0-262-19400-7 (hardcover : alk. paper)
    1. Developing countries—Economic policy. 2. Economic
  stabilization—Developing countries. I. Sturzenegger, Federico.
  II. Tommasi, Mariano, 1964–
  HC59.7.P5772   1998
  338.9'009172'4—dc21   97-46390
                                                              CIP

Contents

1   Introduction

Federico Sturzenegger and
Mariano Tommasi

Until the basic logic of political life is developed, reformers will be ill equipped to use the state for their reforms.

—George Stigler, as quoted in Milton Friedman (1993)

Economists have always been better at telling policymakers what to do than at explaining why policymakers do what they do. Indeed, many applied economists would consider the second question to lie outside their area of expertise. When pressed to explain why practice so often diverges from prescription, economists instinctively take refuge in the blanket category of "political motives." These two words are highly effective as a conversation stopper: they act as the universal answer to all puzzles related to policymaking, choking off further inquiry.

The experience of developing countries during the 1980s and 1990s (not to mention Eastern Europe) has made this situation increasingly uncomfortable for economists interested in policy. These experiences have made clear that devising successful policies requires an understanding of the forces that govern policymaking.

Consider Argentina, for example. After decades of inflation, stagnation, inward-looking policies, and brief and ineffective attempts at stabilization and liberalization, in the early 1990s a new government dramatically reversed course. A set of radical trade, fiscal, and institutional reforms were implemented, including a currency-board arrangement that linked the currency to the dollar. It is ironic that these reforms were instituted under a Peronist president, Carlos Menem, since Peronism has been virtually synonymous with populism and protectionism. Within a few years, Argentine reforms went further than those adopted over a period of decades in the outward-oriented East Asian countries. While Argentina may be an extreme example, many other countries have gone through similar flip-flops.

The experience of Argentina is a good motivation for what we believe are crucial questions regarding reform. The first question refers to the timing of reforms. Why were reforms implemented only in 1991,[1] after so many years of stagnation and poor economic performance? The second question refers to the way in which reforms are implemented. Why were reforms so widespread and so quick? The third question refers to the identity of reformers. Why was a president with a populist background the one who got market-friendly reforms started? But these are just a subset of the many questions suggested by the reform experience of recent years in Latin America, Eastern Europe, and other places. Other related questions that immediately come to mind are:

• Why are reforms that eventually benefit most segments of society resisted?

• When these reforms are eventually undertaken, what explains the delay?

• Why have many of the Latin American reforms (in Chile, Bolivia, Mexico, Peru, Argentina, and Venezuela) been so radical and gone beyond stabilization policy to include drastic liberalization?

• Why are some reforms subsequently reversed?

• Why do some countries go through cycles—populism followed by orthodox policies, followed in turn by populism yet again?

• How are reforms implemented? Are they carried out in one big wave or are they phased in over time?

• Who are the successful reformers? Are they the traditional supporters of reform or last-minute converts to the cause?

• How does a politician achieve credibility in his or her reform attempt?

This book is a collection of recent papers that have proposed formal models to answer some of these questions. What distinguishes these papers from the previous literature, as well as from the traditional political science literature, is the application of common standards of analytical rigor to economic and political behavior. That is, political agents or groups are assumed to be rational and forward-looking, with expectations that are consistent with the properties of the underlying model. Behavioral rules are derived by solving optimization problems with well-defined objective functions.

The political-economic outcome is derived as a Nash equilibrium in which each individual or group is doing the best it can given the actions of others. Consequently, reforms are viewed as the establishment of institutions that provide incentives for individual decision makers to behave in ways that are collectively desirable.

Intelligent political-economic modeling can sharpen our understanding of the process of policymaking in developing countries, and of economic reforms in particular. Furthermore, it can do much to improve policy advice by understanding the constraints that policymakers and policy-making truly face.

This initial chapter provides an overview of the literature and sets the stage for the rest of the book. The book is ordered around three main questions. First, when and why do reforms take place? Because this deals directly with the feasibility of reform, we spend a considerable fraction of the book—the next nine chapters, which make up part I—trying to understand this. The second question deals with the way in which reforms are (or should be) implemented. This is discussed in part II. Finally, in part III, we tackle the question of the identity of reformers.

"Reform" could mean different things at different times. In order to focus our stories we start with a definition of what we mean by reform. We have in mind: macroeconomic stabilization, trade liberalization, privatization, deregulation, and related market-oriented measures. To avoid definitional quarrels we simply point to the list supplied by John Williamson's (1994) account of the "Washington Consensus," summarized in table 1.1.[2]

Table 1.1
The Washington Consensus on Reform

1. Fiscal Discipline
2. Reorientation of Public Expenditure toward Building Human Capital and Infrastructure
3. Tax Reform: Broaden Base and Cut Marginal Rates
4. Financial Liberalization: End Interest-Rate Controls, etc.
5. Exchange Rates: Unified and Competitive
6. Trade Liberalization: Reduce Tariffs and Eliminate NTBs
7. Foreign Direct Investment: Welcome
8. Privatizations: Do
9. Deregulation: Stop Only for Environmental, Safety or Prudential (Banking) Reasons
10. Property Rights: Secure

Source: Williamson (1994).

The Rocky Road to Reform

Tackling the political economy of reform begs the question of what the political-economic equilibrium was like before reform. In turn, a reform can be thought of as a change in that equilibrium. This section surveys some ideas on such important matters.

The Process of Deterioration

Carlos Diáz Alejandro (1988), no fan of state-led development, wrote about the early days of inward-looking policies in Latin America:

... The 1940s ... witnessed the golden age of import-substituting industrialization in Latin America. Particularly during 1945–52 the economic performance of Latin America outshone not only that of Africa and Asia, but also that of Europe and Japan. The acceleration of industrialization and urbanization started in the early 1930s and continued through the 1940s into the early 1950s. An increasingly confident public sector also continued trends during the 1940s that had started during the preceding decade.

And he also added: "any observer looking around the world during those years could find few areas where the future looked more promising, both economically and politically, than in Latin America."

By the 1980s that future had arrived. But it wasn't what had been expected. Not only was country after country suffering from inflation, real income stagnation, and chronic balance of payments problems; the state itself was at the core of the problem. Rather than building up its confidence it became increasingly weaker, often corrupt, easy prey for interest groups, and eventually incapable of delivering even the most basic public goods and services.

While the cycle of initial-success-followed-by-disaster seems particularly clear for Latin America, similar ups and downs characterized the flirtation with state-led development in places as diverse as Southern Europe, sub–Saharan Africa and South Asia (particularly India). This is certainly not the place to revisit the well-known accounts of economic failure caused by nonliberal policies. The more interesting (and largely neglected) question is why politics became so deadlocked and ineffectual that the useful policies of the 1930s were not updated as circumstances in the world economy changed in the 1960s and afterward. Similarly, one would hope for an account of how Diaz Alejandro's "confident public sector" of the 1940s became the weak and sometimes corrupt entity of the 1970s and 1980s.

The academic literature has provided some (but not many) comprehensive accounts of the relevant dynamics of deterioration. Perhaps best known is the one by Anne Krueger, nicely summarized in her (1993) AER survey. Hers is a story of "vicious cycles": economic policies (such as import protection) lead to economic outcomes (local industrialists make fat profits), which in turn alter the political equilibrium (the import-competing sector gains influence to the detriment of agricultural exporters), which finally causes the strengthening of the initial policies (protection is enhanced).[3] The reliance on planning and controls leads to an analogous vicious cycle. A set of controls that sharply distorts a market creates incentives for people to evade those controls. As people learn, evasion gets worse, which leads the government to enact even more stringent controls, and so on. The global outcome is clear: over time distortions and inefficiencies rise while national welfare (defined in any reasonable way) declines.

Such "Krueger dynamics" are reminiscent of the evolution of interest-group conflict in advanced industrial societies described by Mancur Olson (1982). Both accounts predict that interest groups and distributive coalitions become powerful over time (in Olson, predictably, the emphasis is on the time that it takes to solve collective action problems). Since these groups fail to internalize the deadweight losses created by their rent seeking, eventually "social rigidities" and "stagflation" (in Olson's terminology) set in.

But while these are compelling characterizations of the dynamics of deterioration in different societies, the rationality of individual and group behavior in these situations remains to be established. The basic puzzle is this: if under "Krueger dynamics" the deterioration was propelled by the rent-seeking actions of powerful groups, and these groups could see that they themselves could eventually be made worse off, why did they persevere in such behavior?

Maybe from the vantage point of the 1940s the net present value of payoffs under that rent-seeking strategy was positive (our previous quote from Díaz Alejandro seems to bear this point); but was this also the case from the vantage point of the 1970s or 1980s? As Rodrik (1996) points out, in Krueger's account rent seekers do not seem to anticipate the undesirable consequences of their actions. The same is true, by the way, of many standard accounts of unsustainable populist policies.

This is an important point, particularly because it is not farfetched to hypothesize that in some situations everyone (including powerful rent seekers) ended up worse off than they would have been in some plausible cooperative counterfactual. In the midst of some of the Latin American hyperinflations, even the recipients of large state subsidies would have been well served by the end of both the subsidies and the inflation. Similarly, the proliferation of import-substituting measures in places like India had an ambiguous effect on the effective protection enjoyed by many sectors, which could well have been just as sheltered and suffered less excess burden under free trade. In short, the existence of a Pareto-inefficient equilibrium has to be explained, hopefully without simply assuming myopia on the part of groups.[4] And this explanation must ideally be a dynamic one, in which changes in groups' behavior and welfare over time are accounted for. Some recent papers in the literature provide a more formal and detailed account of this point, and part I of this book concentrates on these dynamics of deterioration.

In the chapters that make up part I, the political economy of a stylized country has the following ingredients: there are powerful pressure groups (sectoral interests like urban industries, trade unions, agricultural producers, public employees, etc.), all of which can influence public policies (subsidies, tariffs, etc.) that redistribute income toward them. Groups interact strategically because they share a common resource constraint, either the government budget or the economy's aggregate resource balance. Finally, there are deadweight losses associated with the redistributive policies. The game among the pressure groups typically has the feature that each sets a policy (demands a net government subsidy, for instance), taking all other groups' demands as given. It is not hard to see how this can lead to a Pareto-inefficient Nash equilibrium: each group would be better off if all groups reduced their demands, but unilaterally restraining one's demands is not rational for each individual player. In a static setting, this is similar to a prisoner's dilemma situation.

Many of these chapters assume that the whole society is organized in groups of comparable size and influence. This is the case of Alesina and Drazen (chapter 4), where two (ex ante) identical groups have to share the cost of stabilization; Mondino, Sturzenegger, and Tommasi (chapter 7), where identical interest groups are involved in a subsidy game; and Velasco (1993 and chapter 8) and Aizenman (chapter 9), where lower levels of government fight for a common pool of resources. Some contributions, on the other hand, emphasize the role of asymmetries between the relevant players. Labán and Sturzenegger (1994 and chapter 5) distinguish between one group that can shield itself from the inflation tax and another that cannot; Tornell (1995), who studies Mexico, assumes that there are two organized and powerful groups that interact strategically, and a large mass of powerless taxpayers. Aizenman and Yi (1995) also present an asymmetric model that focuses on China where they argue a ruling elite dominates the decision-making process. The model in Velasco (1994), motivated by the Chilean experience, is somewhere in between: some groups have access to redistributive policies and some do not, but the latter can gain access over time.

These chapters share some logical structure with the theoretical literature that emerged to explain chronic fiscal profligacy within industrialized countries. For instance, Weingast, Shepsle, and Johnsen (1981) and, more recently, Chari and Cole (1993) have characterized equilibria in which voting by representatives from different districts or constituencies leads to "pork barrel" spending and inefficiently large budgets. This literature —surveyed by Ingberman and Inman (1988) and by Alesina and Perotti (1995)—tends to assume a more explicit representative democracy framework, in contrast to that for developing countries which has focused on interest-group struggles (perhaps understandably, given that the periods under analysis often include military governments).

Raquel Fernandez and Dani Rodrik, in chapter 3, use a majority voting model to explain status quo biases in policy. Reform generates winners and losers. Some of the winners know from the start they will benefit from reform but many other could-be winners are uncertain ex ante. The key point is how the median voter feels. As an illustration, they consider a simple economy with an export sector and two import-competing sectors. The median voter belongs to this last group. Trade liberalization benefits those belonging to the export sector. In addition, after liberalization, a fraction of workers in the import-competing sectors are able to switch successfully to the export sector and share the benefits of reforms. However, it might also be the case that the typical worker in the import-competing sector may expect to lose ex ante (so it may vote the proposal down), even when the reform is socially beneficial in that more than half the population ends up better off.[5]

While these specifications can explain bad policies, they cannot account for reforms, that is, for the reversal of these suboptimal policies. In order to do so, the setup should include some dynamics. In chapter 2, Allan Drazen presents a unifying framework that embeds some of the key papers that attempt such dynamic explanation. Most of those "dynamic" papers focus on macroeconomic variables, for it is there that the destabilizing effects of misguided policies is clearest. A particularly stark example arises when sustained fiscal deficits cause debt to accumulate, which in turn increases the cost of servicing the debt, increasing future deficits. In a highly influential contribution, Alberto Alesina and Allan Drazen (chapter 4) argue that debt is allowed to accumulate because warring fiscal groups do not want to shoulder the cost of fiscal adjustment. In their setup the group that caves in first has to pay a larger share of the stabilization costs. Thus a "war of attrition" occurs, with each group waiting for the other to concede first and accept the burden. As a result, a necessary fiscal stabilization can be delayed.

Raúl Labán and Federico Sturzenegger, in chapter 5, investigate the delays in inflation stabilization for cases where the dynamics are provided by accelerating inflation due to the access to a financial adaptation technology that reduces money demand over time.[6] However, access to this technology is asymmetric; in particular, the rich have better financial alternatives. They show that delayed stabilization can occur, with the poor giving in when the cost of inflation becomes unbearable. What is particularly intriguing about their result is that the poor initially do not accept conditions for stabilization even though they know they will stabilize on worse terms in the future. For this to be the case two conditions have to be met: first, that the costs of stabilization are perceived to be high so that it is not undertaken initially; and second, that the "status quo" deteriorates significantly over time so that it becomes optimal to stabilize later on, even though it is undertaken on less favorable terms.

Another way of accounting for "rational" deterioration focuses on limited information and the dynamics of learning. According to this view (laid out by Harberger 1993 and discussed in Tommasi and Velasco 1996),[7] the key thing about which people have limited information is the way in which alternative policies map into aggregate economic performance. In Latin America, and much of the developing world, there have been roughly two models of the world: one in which extensive state intervention is the best policy, and one in which focused (and minimal) state intervention is the best policy. The former world view tended to lead to inward-looking polices, while the latter often involved an outward orientation. However discredited the former model may be today, it was once (and not long ago) embraced by Western experts and even multilateral financial institutions. Even today, there is not a full consensus among professional economists on which is the best set of policies. If highly trained intelligent people who spend their lives thinking about these problems often disagree, imagine what the situation is like for the average citizen, who only gets sparse (and often biased) information from the mass media, after-dinner conversations and during political rallies.[8]

The informational view, without denying the existence of an under-lying game among interest groups, stresses that, at any point in time, the vector of economic policies is also the result of how much Bayesian learn-ing has taken place about the "correct" model of the world. In this view, the dynamics of deterioration evolve in the following way. At first the world changes—trade grows, technology becomes more important—in such a way that the older model of development becomes less and less adequate. Perceptions about the world also change, but very sluggishly, as the world evolves: people only observe economic outcomes, and cannot readily ascertain whether bad outcomes result from bad policies or simply from adverse random shocks. Learning can only take place over time as a process of gradual updating of beliefs. Finally, even when ideas about what represents good economic policy evolve in the direction of less government intervention and more market-friendly approaches, two key obstacles remain to be overcome. First, those advocating these new ideas must be able to credibly convey them to the population (which could interpret them as just a scheme to favor a particular section of the pop-ulation). Second, market advocates must overcome the formidable opposi-tion of those groups that actually benefit (at least temporarily) from the status quo. As a result, "bad" policies can rationally remain in place for long periods of time, allowing for a gradual but nonetheless painful dete-rioration of economic performance.

Crises and Reform

That economic crises seem either to facilitate economic reforms or to cause them outright is part of the new conventional wisdom on reform and is a key aspect of the Alesina-Drazen and Labán-Sturzenegger specifi-cations discussed above. But while everybody talks about the role of crises, few authors are specific about what exactly is a crisis, and what is the mechanism by which a crisis is supposed to bring about reform.

Let us see what some prominent analysts mean by pre–reform crisis. Bresser Pereira, Maravall, and Przeworsky (1993) argue that "[w]hen pop-ulist leaders in Argentina, Bolivia, Venezuela, Peru and Brazil adopted non-populist policies it was because the crisis in these countries was so deep that even the costs of sticking to populist policies became higher than the costs of adjustment" (57). According to Bates and Krueger (1993):

[i]n all cases, of course, reforms have been undertaken in circumstances in which economic conditions were deteriorating. There is no recorded instance of the beginning of a reform program at a time when economic growth was satisfactory

and when the price level and balance of payments situations were stable. Conditions of economic stagnation (and the recognition that it is likely to continue) or continued deterioration are evidently prerequisites for reform efforts. (P. 454)

Explaining why Australia undertook fewer reforms than New Zealand, Max Corden writes: "[t]he reforms have been less dramatic than New Zealand's because things never got so bad: inflation did not rise so high" (in Williamson 1994, 112).

All of the statements clearly illustrate one notion: things have to get very bad before they get better. This notion is appealing and intuitive, but it is not without problems. Rodrik (1996) provides the most cogent criticisms. First, there is an element of tautology in the explanation: "Reform naturally becomes an issue only when policies are perceived to be not working. A crisis is just an extreme case of policy failure. That reform should follow crisis, then, is no more surprising than smoke following fire." Second, "the hypothesis is virtually non-falsifiable: if an economy in crisis has not yet reformed, the frequently proffered explanation is that the crisis has not yet become 'severe enough.'"

To make sense of the crisis hypothesis, it is necessary to be clear about the mechanisms that link crisis and reform. The game-theory models surveyed in the previous section offer some concrete examples of how the political-economic equilibrium changes to permit reform, and what role crises can play in this context. In all these models, agents (groups) decide what to do by comparing expected streams of payoffs. Typically, the (flow) payoff decreases until the time of reform and, more important, is expected to continue deteriorating if these reforms are not implemented. This deterioration can come about because of exogenous (terms-of-trade and other) shocks, as in Velasco (1994) and Tornell (1995), or because of the endogenous evolution of state variables—financial adaptation in Labán and Sturzenegger (chapter 5), and Mondino, Sturzenegger, and Tommasi (chapter 7), or government debt as in Alesina and Drazen (chapter 4), or Velasco (1993). A reform occurs in this context when the payoff associated with the policy change first exceeds that associated with the status quo.

However, while facilitating reform, crises do have a cost. What is the final verdict when assessing welfare effects? Two chapters deal with the point explicitly. Allan Drazen and Vittorio Grilli, in chapter 6, look at a case in which the cost of inflation increases exogenously and show that by making delay more costly this shock can accelerate the arrival of stabilization. Velasco (1993) shows that an adverse shock to government revenue can cause debt to accumulate more quickly and thereby bring forward in time the occurrence of fiscal reform. More strikingly, both papers show that crises can be "good" for welfare: if the indirect (bene-ficial) effect of reducing delay outweighs the direct (adverse) effect of the crisis, then a "bad" shock can make everyone better off. Notice the second-best nature of the problem: there exists a distortion in the political process that makes the first best unattainable. Because of this, there is room for the crisis to improve welfare. We should also note that the notion of crisis they use is probably not what most observers have in mind: in their models, a crisis entails an increase in the costs of wrong-headed policies that are in force throughout the prereform period, rather than a sharp increase in such costs (e.g., a hyperinflation) shortly before reform takes place. Also, this class of papers relies on dynamic game models that yield multiple equilibria or unique equilibria whose features may not be robust to small modeling alterations. Still, the general point that crises bring forward the timing of reform and therefore have the potential to improve welfare remains an important and useful one.

Economic crises also contribute to Bayesian learning about the "right" model of the world. A period of intense economic disarray leads to a re-assessment of the mapping from policies to outcomes, in particular to a realization of how costly some previous policies were. Harberger (1993) writes:

Practitioners go around with a certain world view in their heads. All sorts of crazy things can happen—like hyperinflations and huge recessions and wrenching debt or exchange rate crises. All of these ... can occur and still leave seasoned practi-tioners unruffled, because their world view already contains sensible explanations for them. Every now and then, however, something happens that does not fit the previous image—something that shakes our Bayesian faith in what we used to think. (P. 16)

The fact that many successful reform efforts under democratic con-ditions were undertaken by populist politicians who had a strategic ad-vantage in transmitting a certain type of information to the public, which is discussed more fully in part III, seems to confirm the view that the dynamics are to some extent informational.[9]

Dynamic Games

In chapters 4, 5, and 6, the delay is endogenous, but the existence of the initial fiscal deficit is not. Mondino, Sturzenegger, and Tommasi (chapter 7) and Velasco (1993 and chapter 8) develop simple dynamic models that can explain such deficit- and inflation-prone fiscal policies.

Guillermo Mondino, Sturzenegger, and Tommasi analyze the dynamics of inflation that arise from fiscal deficits caused by the noncooperative behavior of interest groups who claim subsidies from a common pool of resources. In their specification, the "state" variable is the degree of financial adaptation, which is a proxy for the share of wealth that agents hold in foreign currency or in the underground economy and hence beyond the reach of the tax man. This, in turn, determines the inflation rate that all agents suffer as a consequence of the fiscal deficit. When monetization is high, the costs of inflation are not too large, and interest groups find themselves in a prisoner's dilemma situation where all prefer to ask for subsidies. In the end no group achieves a positive net transfer,[10] however, they all endure the costs of positive inflation. As financial adaptation becomes widespread, the costs of financing a given budget deficit rise. Eventually, inflation is so high that groups find it unilaterally convenient not to demand subsidies, and inflation stops. However, remonetization in the wake of stabilization takes the economy to its starting point where groups once again find it optimal to try to extract rents in the subsidy game. In this context, there can be fully rational cycles of increasing inflation and financial adaptation, followed by stabilization and remonetization. Under some conditions, such cycles can display increasing amplitude over time.

Zarazaga (1993) is another attempt to explain the inflation cycles in countries like Argentina and Brazil. He argues that the "low" inflation stages represent a Nash equilibrium across competing seigniorage units (local governments), and that the hyperinflation bouts are the equivalent of price wars in models of oligopolistic collusion with imperfect monitoring. The simulations of his model are able to replicate inflation patterns within the ranges observed in some "mega-inflationary" experiences.

In chapter 8, Andrés Velasco models fiscal policy as the outcome of a political process in which spending power is in the hands of several decentralized units who represent different interest groups and who behave noncooperatively. The key is that the benefits of spending are group-specific, while the costs (in particular, debt service) are borne by all. In this decentralized system, the benefit from public savings, as perceived by each group, is not the rate of interest, but the rate of interest minus the fraction of government wealth spent by other groups. As a result, incentives are distorted, each group overspends, and debt accumulates over time; in other words, government net assets decline over time. Velasco shows that if these assets fall below a threshold value a new (trigger-strategy) equilibrium can be sustained in which interest groups coordinate on a first-best policy of fiscal restraint and steady debt levels. Shocks to government assets (changes in the international interest rate or terms of trade shocks) can lead to a change in the equilibrium and therefore kick off movements in government debt.

Joshua Aizenman in chapter 9 also presents a model for debt dynamics in a federal system where the central government has limited control over the spending pattern of union members. States have a preference for spending, but if they exceed the targets set by the federal government they risk the possibility of being ousted. At the same time, the higher the overall level of debt, the higher the possibility of voters displacing all state governors in one single stroke. Aizenman's specification delivers a result opposite to that of Velasco. The higher the debt, the lower the possibility of remaining in office (no matter what each governor does), and therefore the higher the incentive to indulge in excessive spending. If the economy starts with such levels of debt, or suffers an income shock that is equivalent to increasing the level of debt, debt dynamics become unstable and a crisis eventually unfolds that requires a change in the nature of the game. This change may involve, for example, shifting more power to the central government.

In the previous section, we talked about the role of crises in triggering economic reform. There is another aspect of crises that is also important. Crises create a sense of urgency. Something needs to be done soon, because the crisis requires an urgent resolution. In the language of some analysts, this creates room for "special politics" for a finite period of time. How exactly does this work? Dani Rodrik, in chapter 10, emphasizes the agenda-setting role of reformist governments. He asks: how could wide-ranging trade and industrial policy reforms be rendered palatable to the interest groups that had been their beneficiaries for so long? How were they persuaded to go along? According to Rodrik, crises enabled reformist governments to package fiscal reforms—which were absolutely crucial for the return to price stability—with trade and industrial policy reforms, which may have been desirable in the longer run but were incidental to the immediate crisis. Policymakers presented domestic interests with a package of both macroeconomic and microeconomic reforms. Since high inflation and macroeconomic instability hurt pretty much everyone across the board, influential interest groups felt compelled to go along.[11] They may have preferred to have only the macroeconomic component of the package, but that was not the choice that they faced.

Still, the question remains: if the agenda-setting game confronted powerful groups with unattractive choices, why did they not choose to change the rules of the game? Why did the powerful minotaurs—in Naím's (1993) wonderful metaphor—agree to behave as paper tigers? Their decision could be rationalized by using insights from the literature on the choice of procedural rules in legislatures.[12] Our reading is that policymaking in developing countries is normally done by "open rule," allowing a say (counter proposals) to a number of key institutional actors, such as trade associations, banking associations, trade unions, rural interests, and so forth. Such a rule is preferred by these powerful interests as long as the costs of the status quo—or of delay—are not too high. In a crisis situation the costs of delay become enormous, and it is then optimal for the key players to move to a closed rule. In a closed rule, an agenda setter makes a proposal that is then accepted or rejected, without room for counter proposals. It is only natural that the agenda setter be the current administration.

Returning to our example of Argentina—where wholesale reforms were implemented in the aftermath of hyperinflation—extraordinary powers were granted to the executive that allowed for across-the-board privatization of public enterprises and government restructuring. Similarly, after the "Tequila Shock" of 1995, the then Finance Minister Domingo Cavallo was able to get through Congress three key and previously almost untouchable issues: caps on pension spending, labor market flexibilization, and privatization of provincial banks.[13] The episode highlights how the threat of financial collapse enabled Cavallo to obtain approval of policies that are only indirectly related to the immediate maintenance of the pegged exchange rate.

What Are the Practical Implications, If Any?

Suppose that we accept the view that the status quo before reform can be thought of as an uneasy equilibrium among competing and imperfectly informed interest groups, with the payoffs that accrue to each changing endogenously over time. Suppose, moreover, that an exogenous shock (a "crisis"), by changing expected payoffs associated with different courses of action, can cause reform to be the "new" equilibrium of the underlying game. What are the practical implications of such a view? Are there any policy lessons lurking within? We discuss three ideas related to this point.

The practical implications of the crisis hypothesis are not easy to ascertain. Even if one believes that little will happen "until conditions are ripe," it is hard to accept the recommendation that advocates of reform simply sit on their hands waiting for the right time to arrive. Much less does one want to advocate the deliberate fabrication of a crisis to accelerate the process—as the Leninists of yesteryear used to do, pushing for the swift decline of capitalism as the surest way to precipitate the advent of socialism. Still, assuming that reformers have limited political and financial capital at their disposal, some attention as to when to spend such capital may well be warranted.

The "informational" view offers an encouraging practical message. It is hoped that the experience of many reforming countries (assuming a modicum of success) will be imitated by others before having to experience themselves a crisis and the associated economic pain. International development agencies have an important role to play in the dissemination of information, and the conveyance of the right policy lessons can costlessly accelerate the reform process and increase welfare. Of course, this possibility hinges on two basic conditions. First, that multilaterals have credibility in the eyes of a yet unreformed country: they must be perceived as disinterested parties, and not as agents of large shareholders whose interests may be opposed to those of the country in question. Second, that they themselves be right about what has to be done. It is still fresh in the mind of many reformers today how multilateral organizations, not long ago, were defenders of industrial policies and subsidized many development projects that allowed for what now would be considered excessive government participation in economic activity.[14]

Perhaps the most relevant finding of this literature is the realization that societies face continued income distribution struggles. How these struggles are resolved and how much damage they will do depends on the "rules of the game"—namely, on the institutional framework with which a society operates. Substantial work remains to be done to find out which institutions are more conducive to the adoption of socially beneficial policies, particularly in developing countries.[15] Bates (1990), North (1990), Calvert (1995), Haggard and Kaufman (1995), Weingast (1995), and Olson (1996) are good points of departure.

Reform Strategies

Once, for one reason or another, a government is willing and able to pursue market-oriented reforms, a whole set of issues arises on how to proceed. Two questions have been at the forefront of the academic and policy discussion: (1) the order in which to implement reforms on different fronts (ordering), and (2) the appropriate speed of reform on each front (for instance, how fast should one remove tariffs and NTBs?). These issues have given rise to heated controversy. Sachs (in Williamson 1994), among others, has passionately argued that going full speed on all fronts is often not just the best, but also the only strategy available to reformers.[16] Skeptics, such as Desai (1995), have argued that shock therapy imposes unbearably high transitional costs and hence weakens political support for reform.[17]

In what follows we survey recent political-economic contributions to the subject. In discussing ordering, we use the terms *big bang* and *unbundling* to refer to situations in which reforms are introduced all at once versus situations in which they are introduced one after the other. In discussing speed, we use the self-explanatory terms *shock therapy* and *gradualism*. Notice that the literature uses many of these terms interchangeably; for instance, gradualism means (depending on the context) going slow on a particular reform or implementing reforms in different sectors one after another rather than simultaneously.

Sequencing

The optimal sequence of reforms depends on both economic and political criteria. The neoclassical economics benchmark is simple: do all reforms immediately and simultaneously. Radical or big bang reform is the first-best reform strategy, as argued by Mussa (1982) early on in the debate. As long as the perceived private costs and benefits correspond to the true social costs and benefits, private economic agents will choose the socially correct pace of adjustment following a full-scale liberalization. The only caveat applies when one can identify a distortion that places the economy in a second-best world; if that is the case, one might be able to design a particular sequencing strategy that can take care of the second-best problem. Put differently, arguments for unbundling must be based on the existence of an unremovable distortion or market failure and of a sequencing second-best solution.

The early literature on the sequencing of economic reforms was spurred by the experience of the Southern Cone of Latin America in the late 1970s and early 1980s. The attempted liberalizations under military rule in Chile, Argentina, and Uruguay eventually led to a series of devaluations and bank panics. One influential view attributed these unfortunate outcomes to mistakes in the order of liberalization (Díaz Alejandro 1985; Corbo and De Melo 1985; and Edwards and Cox Edwards 1987). The need to balance government finances before undertaking other reforms was commonly emphasized. Debate centered on the order of liberalization of the trade and capital accounts, with the majority of authors in favor of opening the former before the latter in order to avoid destabilizing capital flows (Edwards 1984; McKinnon 1991).

Most of the early literature (summarized in Edwards 1992) was informal; the emphasis was on giving policy advice to avoid the difficulties that plagued early efforts at economic reform in Latin America. Subsequent research has been more precise in identifying potential welfare gains or losses associated with different sequences. One possible argument for gradualism is the presence of preexisting distortions in one or several markets that cannot be removed at the time the reform plan is announced. Potential candidates are labor-market interventions, domestic capital–market imperfections, and limits to foreign indebtedness that are not perceived as binding by individual agents (Edwards and Van Wijnbergen 1986; Edwards 1993). In all of these cases, one can imagine circumstances in which the second-best reform strategy will involve some degree of gradualism—for instance, in the sequencing of trade and capital account liberalization.

A related argument by Calvo (1989) emphasizes that imperfect credibility is equivalent to an intertemporal distortion. If the public believes that a trade liberalization will be reversed in the future, quantitative control of the capital account may be called for. The problem with this type of argument is that, in its simplest form, it just assumes the credibility problem. A closer look at its source is necessary to assess the right policy response. For instance, Dani Rodrik suggests in chapter 14 that, if imperfect credibility arises because the public is unsure about the "true preferences" of the government, then overshooting can act as a signaling device.[18]

So far in this discussion exogenous political constraints have sometimes been invoked to claim that a certain distortion cannot be removed, but beyond that, political economy has played no role in determining the optimal sequence. Mathias Dewatripont and Gérard Roland, in chapter 11, provide a political-economic case for unbundling in the implementation of economic reforms. Their basic point is that, when there is uncertainty about the outcome of economic reforms, unbundling has lower experimentation costs than does a big bang. One of their findings is that, contrary to common belief, complementarity of reforms may be a necessary condition for unbundling to be the best strategy. Consider a case in which two reforms have to be implemented and they cannot yield full results unless complemented by each other. Unbundling may help for two reasons. First, because once the first reform is implemented, a refusal to undertake the second will lead to a reversal of the first—both reforms do not stand on their own—and this entails reversal costs. These reversal costs tilt the balance toward full implementation. Second, if the first reforms yield a "favorable" outcome, it builds support for the entire package. If the initial reforms have been a success, people are more willing to accept less popular reforms so as not to lose the gains of the first reforms.

Another argument in favor of unbundling is advanced by Shang-Jin Wei in chapter 12. He argues that gradual sequencing may allow the building of constituencies for reform in the presence of individual-specific uncertainty, as in the framework of Fernandez and Rodrik (chapter 3). Wei's point is illustrated with a simple example that uses the same economy we used to discuss the Fernandez-Rodrik result: one with two import-competing sectors (which comprise the majority of "votes") and an export one. After trade liberalization, a fraction of workers from each of the two import-competing sectors is able to switch successfully to the export sector, which is the obvious beneficiary of reform. While the proposal to remove trade barriers in both import-competing sectors may be opposed by a majority, the removal of barriers on imports in just one sector will have the support of the other two sectors. After some labor has been reallocated from the adversely affected sector to the export industries, it is possible to remove the trade barriers that favored the second import-competing sector. This last move will now enjoy the support of the (now larger) export sector and the import-competing sector hurt by the first reform.

It is interesting to notice that Wei's argument does not need (even though it is not inconsistent with) the assumption of individual-specific uncertainty used by Fernandez and Rodrik. Even if we eliminate ex post heterogeneity (of people coming from the shrinking sectors) and we think of just three types, X, M1, and M2, with reform 1 harming M1 and helping the other two and reform 2 harming M2 and helping the other two, gradualism is still feasible while a big bang is not. In fact, unbundling is equivalent to a divide-and-rule strategy, pitching current majorities against future ones.

On the other side of the debate, César Martinelli and Mariano Tommasi, in chapter 13, argue that political economy considerations suggest implementing all possible reforms simultaneously. Their point is that in societies with powerful interest groups and characterized by a cobweb of redistributive and distortionary policies, "optimal" unbundled plans will be time-inconsistent: winners of early reforms who are hurt by later reforms have an incentive to stop the gradual path in its later stages. Anticipating that the later stages of reform will not succeed, the losers from early reforms will oppose the earlier measures. In such an environment, a big bang is the only way of cutting through the Gordian knot of rents implicit in previous policies. How do we explain the contrasting results in these chapters? Martinelli and Tommasi show that even in cases where gradualism does have lower experimentation costs, the distributional implications of the different reforms can lead to the gradual path being time-inconsistent in a political game. The key difference between chapters 12 and 13 is that Wei's analysis of chapter 12 assumes that majority support is sufficient to guarantee the completion of reforms, while Martinelli and Tommasi in chapter 13 emphasize the presence of veto players.[19] We are not sure which of the two institutional setups best captures the politics of reform in Eastern Europe, but in Latin America (at least until very recently) there are several minotaurs without whose acquiescence no policy is feasible.[20] This suggests that the veto model may be more relevant.

Speed

We now turn from issues of sequencing to issues of speed. Because in the real world adjustment is often costly and time-consuming, it has often been suggested that policy reform should be gradual. Yet the neoclassical benchmark in this area is also stark. As persuasively argued by Mussa (1982), the mere presence of adjustment costs does not imply that policy should adjust gradually. If the private cost of adjustment reflects the true social costs, the optimal policy is to set the distorting policy instruments to zero at the beginning of the planning horizon (the definition of shock therapy in this context) and let rational, forward-looking agents adjust their behavior optimally. Eliminating the distortions gradually would needlessly lead to efficiency losses without any compensating gain. Hence, arguments for gradualism need to be based on the presence of distortions that lead to violations of the first welfare theorem. Note that, following the logic of the second best, this is a necessary but by no means sufficient condition for gradualism to be preferable to the immediate and full elimination of distortions.

The cleanest argument for gradualism along these lines is provided by Gavin (1993), who argues that congestion externalities create too much transitional unemployment (relative to the market optimum) after a big bang. Avoiding the problem may involve gradual restructuring.

Gavin's view implies that people voluntarily choose to change jobs too fast. We are inclined to believe that the evidence does not seem to point in this direction. More likely, the problem is slow job creation, along the lines suggested by Caplin and Leahy (1994).[21] They emphasize informational externalities: firms may be too slow in moving into new ventures, waiting for the revelation of information contained in the moves of other firms. A possible way of dealing with those problems might be to foster information sharing via activities such as government-sponsored visits to other countries by business associations. More generally, the "distortions" can be addressed in two ways: directly (by affecting information flows, for instance) or by tinkering with the speed of reform. Hence, the sole existence of externalities does not constitute a prima facie case for gradualism, especially if other considerations call for rapid action.[22]

More explicitly political-economic arguments for gradualism have been made by Dewatripont and Roland (1991, 1992). They provide a case for gradualism in industrial restructuring that is based on budgetary considerations. They model a reform-minded government facing an inefficient sector with a work force that is heterogeneous in outside opportunities. A move toward allocative efficiency requires a major shift to higher productivity activities and massive layoffs. If outside opportunities are private information, in order to make quick reform politically acceptable, all workers have to be paid the same (high) exit bonus. In such a case, a sequence of increasing exit bonuses (gradualism) may enable restructuring to proceed at a lower fiscal cost.[23]

Finally, Dehejia (1994) looks at a Mussa-like small open labor-abundant economy and adds some political structure to it. There are three types of people: (1) capitalists (the costlessly mobile factor) who lose from trade liberalization; (2) workers in the sector that benefits from reform who are, of course, in favor of reform as fast as possible, and (3) workers in the shrinking sector, who constitute the key players in a majority referendum game. These workers have higher wages to look forward to, but also have to pay retraining costs. If those costs are small enough, they also prefer shock therapy, and Mussa's result is also the political-economic equilibrium. However, when retraining costs are large enough, shock therapy is defeated by majority voting vis-à-vis the inefficient status quo. Dehejia shows that, in such a case, there exists a gradual path of trade liberalization that is preferred to the status quo by the key players (workers in the shrinking sector).

What Are the Policy Lessons, If Any?

Theoretical work on optimal sequencing and speed of economic reforms suggests the following lessons:

(1) Aggregate uncertainty about the outcome of economic reforms (if it gets resolved early enough) makes gradualism less costly than a big bang strategy from the point of view of experimentation and learning costs. This point seems relevant to explaining the long road toward market liberalization followed by countries such as China.[24]

(2) The political rules of the game matter in the choice of big bang versus unbundling. Countries with deeply ingrained distributive conflicts and with powerful interest groups endowed with de facto veto power are well advised to bundle reforms in order to "offer something to everyone" and also avoid time inconsistencies. In cases where majority rule applies, unbundling of reforms might help divide the opposition.

(3) Somewhat surprisingly, the more complementary the reforms (in terms of their sustainability), the better for unbundling strategies. This result can help us understand why successful Latin American cases seem to take a big bang approach, while the picture from Eastern Europe is less clear. In socialist countries, where the basis of a market economy is completely absent, partial reform may be unsustainable in the long run (Murphy, Shleifer, and Vishny 1992); political sustainability then (paradoxically) argues for unbundling. In many developing countries, in contrast, macroeconomic stabilization could in principle be achieved without reforming the trade or regulatory systems; in that case, political approval of the whole package requires that it be bundled.

(4) The theoretical case for gradualism in the implementation of any given reform is mixed. If externalities exist, it may be best to operate on these directly. Under some circumstances gradualism might make reform politically more palatable, but these circumstances seem rather special.

(5) Lack of credibility cuts both ways. Persuading skeptics may require both a big bang of reforms and shock treatment for each policy setting; it may even require going overboard, as argued by Rodrik in chapter 14. But if such extreme therapy proves unconvincing and a lack of credibility remains, having done all the reforms at once (in particular, having opened up the capital account early on) may be the cause of a great deal of trouble.

Tommasi and Velasco (1996) and Rodrik (chapter 10 and 1996) provide evidence that indicates that micro- and macroeconomic reforms have been pursued jointly in many countries, and that trade reforms have tended to be more successful when undertaken wholesale. The evidence on gradualism is more mixed. In the realm of macroeconomic stabilization (particularly if hyperinflation is the initial condition), going fast is common. In the micro realm, and particularly concerning tariff liberalization, slow phase-in periods are often the rule.

We suspect that two rather commonplace factors (on top of the formal ones of special politics and time consistency) tilt the balance in favor of going "cold turkey." The first is fear—fear of what the future may bring. Reforming administrations often face a great deal of uncertainty, and a nontrivial likelihood of being ejected from office. In that situation, the only strategy is "do as much as you can." The second is incompetence: fine tuning of reform requires great technical capabilities and—as Anne Krueger (1992) and Moisés Naím (1993) have convincingly argued—reforming governments seldom have the required personnel and resources. The upshot is similar: keep it simple—and do it soon.

The True Colors of the Reformers

In the previous section, we discussed some papers that look at the problem of credibility from a time-consistency perspective. Another approach to endogenize the credibility of policy (reform) relies on incomplete information. Within this line, some chapters focus on asymmetric information about the preferences of policymakers, while others on asymmetric information about the possible aggregate effect of alternative policies.[25] Chapter 14 by Dani Rodrik, which provides one such application of signaling ideas to the problem of economic reforms, emphasizes the first situation. Chapters 15 and 16 focus on incomplete information about the mapping from policies to outcomes.

Rodrik argues that in order to build credibility about intentions, policymakers may be required to go overboard in reform efforts, doing even more than what would be necessary in a full credibility world. Because deepening the reforms is less costly for the policymaker most favorably disposed to reforming, a sufficient overkill allows him to effectively signal his intentions. This argument is helpful in explaining why reforms have been so radical in some cases; we may interpret in this light the establishment of currency boards in Argentina and the Baltic countries. Bartolini and Drazen (1994) present a similar argument to explain the (costly) early opening of the capital account in several episodes.

One might have conjectured initially that typical free marketeers—that is to say, right-wingers or conservatives of some type—are the most likely to carry out market-friendly reforms. Following this expectation, Williamson (1994) asked his contributors to comment on whether, in their respective countries, market-oriented policies had been creatures of right-wing governments. The summary paper by Williamson and Haggard (1994) reports finding little support for such an association. Indeed, in only three out of thirteen cases was market-oriented reform implemented by what they classified as right-wing governments. Interestingly, these three cases included the two military dictatorships in their sample: Chile and Korea. If anything, the puzzle seems to be the opposite: in many cases "left-wing" politicians have been the ones implementing the reforms. A clear example is that of Carlos Saúl Menem in Argentina. According to Rodrik (1993): "[i]t is ironic that these reforms were instituted under a Peronist president, Carlos Menem, since Peronism has been virtually synonymous with populism and protectionism. Within a year, Argentine reforms had already gone further than those adopted over a period of decades in the outward-oriented East Asian countries" (356).

The recently reelected Alberto Fujimori of Peru is another example of a candidate elected (in 1989) for being to the left of the opposing candidate, Mario Vargas Llosa, yet who nonetheless ended up implementing tough market-oriented reforms. In Bolivia, the orthodox 1985 stabilization was successfully implemented by Victor Paz Estenssoro—leader of the Movimiento Nacional Revolucionario (MNR), an avowedly revolutionary movement with populist leanings, who had pursued inflationary policies in his previous presidency. Conversely, Packenham (1992) argues that the failures of Argentina's Alfonsín and Brazil's Collor de Melo in their reform attempts were partly due to their structural location in the political spectrum: they were not "left" enough.

This puzzle is addressed by Alex Cukierman and Mariano Tommasi in chapter 15, who argue that since voters are not fully informed about the way in which policies map into outcomes, the identity of those proposing a given policy conveys valuable information. This leads to conditions under which policies are more likely to be successful if proposed by "unlikely" characters. The conditions Cukierman and Tommasi identify— asymmetric information and large and rare policy switches, the impact of which will only be fully known far into the future—seem to have been at work in the reform experiences under analysis (as well as in celebrated foreign policy episodes: Nixon and the opening up of China, Begin and the return of Sinai to Egypt, Sadat and the establishment of official ties with Israel, etc.).

Ricardo López Murphy and Federico Sturzenegger use, in chapter 16, a similar imperfect-information framework in which politicians are better able to assess an underlying state of nature that determines the best policy action for the median voter. In such a context politicians' actions affect voters' beliefs about the state of nature. They show that an important variable to explain voter dynamics is the degree of flexibility of a given politician to react to unforeseen events—that is, how much he or she is willing to trade his or her own preference for what the median voter wants.[26] The politician with more flexibility can use this advantage in the political contest in order to manipulate voters' beliefs. As in Cukierman and Tommasi, the most unlikely candidate is in the best position to convince voters of the need for a certain policy action such as structural economic reforms because he or she is better able to transmit the information that those reforms are necessary. The setup provides other interesting results, such as rationalizing a politician who: (1) while in opposition, blocks policies that he or she intends to pursue once in office, and (2) may also move away from electoral promises while retaining high approval rates.

The statement "we have to undertake these tough adjustment measures today in order to improve our future" has more credibility with the working class when heard from the lips of a populist than from the lips of a "Chicago Boy." As argued above, a large part of the dynamics of economic policy reform is informational, and this information tends to flow from above. In cases like Argentina's Menem, his advocacy of market reforms can speed up the adoption of the necessary policies by helping convince the populace about the costliness of staying with the previous policies. Similar reasoning can help us understand some cases where the ordering of reforms was different from the conventional wisdom peddled by international lending institutions. The best feasible (time-consistent) strategy may require that policymakers implement first those measures that hurt their natural base of support (the people with whom they have a stock of credibility), even if there is no economic rationale for that particular ordering. The vigor with which President Patricio Aylwin of Chile pursued fiscal austerity and made it a top priority (often at the expense of public-sector employees who had overwhelmingly voted for him) may be read as an attempt to shore up his credentials as an inflation fighter. The same could be said about the fervor with which President Fernando Henrique Cardoso of Brazil, a former socialist, is advocating wholesale privatization.

Final Comments

Our survey of the recent literature on the political economy of reform is spotty and rather idiosyncratic. The interested reader should glance at the complementary volumes by Blanchard et al. (1991), Frieden (1991), Papageorgiou, Michaely, and Choksi (1991), Przeworski (1991), Lustig (1992), Ranis and Mahmood (1992), Bates and Krueger (1993), Taylor

(1993), Bosworth, Dornbush, and Labán (1994), Bradford (1994), Haggard and Webb (1994), Nelson (1994a), Williamson (1994), Armijo (1995), Dornbusch and Edwards (1991, 1995), and the individual contributions of Asilis and Milesi-Ferreti (1994), Krueger (1992), Harberger (1993), Edwards (1994), Graham (1994), Naím (1994), Nelson (1994b), Hausmann (1994), and Sachs (in Williamson 1994). Many of these references include fascinating country studies, which due to space limitations and division of labor, will not be treated in this book. Tommasi and Velasco (1996) and Rodrik (1996) are overviews of the field close in spirit to this introduction, but with a wider coverage of topics.

As this introduction suggests, there are many unanswered questions in this field. We believe that the collection we present constitutes a promising starting point for further developments. There are three related avenues in which the research agenda should proceed and, in part, is already proceeding.

First, more integration of the work by political scientists and economists is necessary, including a closer integration of theoretical models with empirical work.

Second, more attention needs to be given to the role of political institutions in shaping reform outcomes and vice versa. Coming back one last time to our favorite example, we did not even mention the fact that President Menem's Peronist party had a majority in Congress at the time of reform (an obviously important fact emphasized, for instance, by Haggard and Kaufman (1995) and by Spiller (1995)).[27] Also, the new constraints on the behavior of politicians that the reform process has introduced is reshaping party configurations in some countries such as Venezuela and Argentina (Benton 1997).

Finally, (research and reform) efforts should concentrate on the second stage of reforms, which consists mainly of building state capacity and transforming predatory states into developmental ones (Naím 1994; Tommasi and Velasco 1996).

Notes

We thank Nicolás Gadano and Shawn Wade for useful comments. This introduction draws extensively from Rodrik (1993) and from Tommasi and Velasco (1996).

1. Some measures, such as trade liberalization, started in the late 1980s but 1991 was a clear turning point.

2. Rodrik (1996) points out that it is wise to maintain the distinction between the macro and micro components of that "package" since their economic foundations as well as their "politics" are different.

3. It is not surprising that this view arose from a trade theorist; that policies get locked in is well known in trade theory. See, for example, Bhagwati (1982, 1988) and Krueger (1974).

4. The careful reader may have detected the influence of Bates (1990) in this approach to thinking about policy decisions. There is another interpretation under which some groups are net beneficiaries even at the worst point of the process. In that case one has to explain how can those (presumably small) groups impose their will all along, until the time of reform. See Tornell (1995), and further references below, for initial attempts at such an explanation.

5. This will be the case, for instance, when the export sector is close to 50 percent of the economy.

6. See also Labán and Sturzenegger (1992, 1994).

7. These ideas have yet to be formalized. A natural starting point is the political science literature on rational ignorance in democratic politics. An accessible introduction is Matsusaka (1995). See also Krehbiel (1991), North (1994), Lupia and McCubbins (1995), and references there. Colander and Coats (1989) contains some useful suggestions on how to think about the transmission of economic ideas.

8. Bruno (1993) makes the perceptive point that economists' dissent about "details" can lead to the political system failing to implement even the obvious measures.

9. For a highly innovative explanation—based on regret theory—of why reforms are undertaken in times of economic crises, see Aizenman and Yi (1995, 1996).

10. Because all groups demand the same subsidy in equilibrium, agents end up paying, in inflation tax, an amount identical to the subsidy obtained.

11. Rodrik—as do the authors of many of the other chapters—views macroeconomic adjustment as a win-win proposition. This ignores the cost side of macroeconomic adjustment. It is true that everybody prefers low inflation to hyperinflation, but successful stabilization programs require tough fiscal adjustments that in some cases fall more heavily on some groups (public employees, retirees, sectors benefiting from cheap government credit, etc.). Nonetheless, the main thrust of his argument works even if fiscal adjustment is not Pareto-improving. One of the main points in the agenda is to document the exact distributional impact of each of the reform measures.

12. There is a healthy literature here. See, for instance, Krehbiel (1991, chap. 5).

13. As common to many reform efforts (Edwards 1994), labor-market flexibilization has been one of the most difficult measures to obtain. During Tequila, Cavallo was able to pass a law that lowered hiring and firing costs for small and mid-sized companies. The Argentine executive is still, in 1998, fighting for a wider liberalization of the labor market.

14. It is likely that the story we told about the dynamics of ideas/interests within countries can also explain, in part, the behavior of multilateral organizations.

15. One has, of course, to be very careful in thinking about institutional reforms geared to avoiding socially undesirable outcomes. Institutions do not operate in a vacuum, nor do all societies respond equally to the same institutional framework. Putnam (1993), for example, discusses the different response of the Italian regions to the (common) decentralization process started in the mid seventies. He shows that the (same) seeds of institutional innovation grow differently in different socioeconomic and cultural soils to produce different kinds of institutional plants. See Tarrow (1996) for a critical analysis of Putnam's work.

16. This view is shared in Lipton and Sachs (1990), Aslund (1991), Berg and Sachs (1992), Boycko (1992), Frydman and Rapaczynski (1994), Murphy, Shleifer, and Vishny (1992), Sachs (1993, 1995), and Hausmann (1995), among others.

17. See also Portes (1990, 1991), McKinnon (1991), McMillan and Naughton (1992), Murrell (1992), and Aghion and Blanchard (1994).

18. Similarly, Bartolini and Drazen (1994) argue that opening the capital account in itself may signal the type of government, buying credibility for the whole package. Notice that Calvo was arguing for delaying capital account liberalization because of the (unexplained) lack of credibility.

19. The same assumption (veto players) is implicit in Dewatripont and Roland (1991, 1992). In a model of industrial restructuring that we discuss below, they assume that the government cannot fire workers from the inefficient sectors, but has to bribe them to exit. For a general approach to the role of veto players in the determination of policy, see Tsebelis (1994).

20. Burgess and Stern (1993), in their study of tax reform in a broad sample of developing countries, conclude the following: "reforms facing strong and active opposition cannot be imposed upon countries. For government commitment to tax reform to be credible, the likely behavior of gainers and losers needs to be taken into account and a broad consensus arrived at" (802).

21. Another explanation for slow job creation is the lack of perfect credibility of the reforms emphasized by Guillermo Calvo. Obviously, the solution to such a problem is by no means a gradual tariff reduction. One could also construct an argument by which higher unemployment reduces credibility because of a higher chances of a political backlash. Still, for that to be tied to a policy prescription for gradualism, one needs a good understanding of whether (and why) gradual reform reduces unemployment.

22. Auernheimer and George (1994) show that gradual trade liberalization induces a distortion in consumption-accumulation decisions and results in welfare costs that, if the gradual change is extended over "too long" a period, may even exceed the long-run benefits of liberalization.

23. It is interesting to note the contrast between the assumption in Dewatripont and Roland (1991, 1992) and that in Fernandez-Rodrik and Wei. Workers know their chances of getting a job in the growing sectors all to well in Dewatripont-Roland, while they have no clue in Fernandez-Rodrik and Wei. It would be desirable to try to establish empirically whether the successful movers have some observable distinguishing characteristics (age, employment history, education, location, etc.) to distinguish between these two hypotheses.

24. On the other hand, we believe that the true merits of wide-ranging economic reforms are not fully revealed in the first couple of years. Hence, the arguments that emphasize resolution of uncertainty along the transition path are not that relevant except for cases such as China's where gradualism spans a few decades.

25. The distinction is somewhat artificial, since we know from the literature on signaling that both cases can be reduced to a common theoretical structure through the notion of "types" (see, for instance, Gibbons (1992) and Calvert (1986)).

26. They call "flexibility" the relative weight of the office motive in the politician's objective function.

27. Geddes (1994) is an excellent account of the way in which institutions shape the incentives of government decision makers and of aspirants to that role.

References

Aghion, P., and O. Blanchard. 1994. "On the Speed of Transition in Central Europe." *NBER Macroeconomics Annual.* Cambridge, MA: MIT Press.

Aizenman, J., and S-S. Yi. 1995. "Reforms from Within—The Role of External Factors." Dartmouth College. Mimeo.

Aizenman, J., and S-S. Yi. 1996. "Regret Theory and Policy Reform: It Ain't Broken, But You May Want to Fix It Anyway." Dartmouth College, August. Mimeo.

Alesina, A., and R. Perotti, 1995. "The Political Economy of Budget Deficits." *IMF Staff Papers* (March): 1–32.

Armijo, L. 1995. "Conversations on Democratization and Economic Reform." Working Papers of the Southern California Seminar.

Asilis, C., and G. M. Milesi-Ferreti. 1994. "On the Political Sustainability of Economic Reform." IMF Research Department. Mimeo.

Aslund, A. 1991. "Principles of Privatization." In *Systematic Change and Stabilization in Eastern Europe*, ed. Laszio Csaba, 17–31. Dartmouth, UK: Aldershot.

Auernheimer, L., and S. George. 1994 "Shock versus Gradualism in Models of Rational Expectations: The Case of Trade Liberalization." Texas A&M, August. Mimeo.

Bartolini, L., and A. Drazen. 1994. "Capital Account Liberalization as a Signal." University of Maryland. Mimeo.

Bates, R. 1990. "Marcropolitical Economy in the Field of Development." In *Perspectives on Positive Political Economy*, ed. J. Alt and K. Shepsle, 31–54. Cambridge: Cambridge University Press.

Bates, R., and A. Krueger, eds. 1993. *Political and Economic Interactions in Economic Policy Reform: Evidence from Eight Countries.* Oxford: Basil Blackwell.

Benton, A. 1997. "Explaining Recent Party Instability in Latin America: Combining Insights from Economic and Institutional Based Analyses." Paper delivered at Midwestern Political Science Association Conference, April.

Berg, A. and J. Sachs. 1992. "Structural Adjustment and International Trade in Eastern Europe: The Case of Poland." *Economic Policy* 14 (April): 117–173.

Bhagwati J. 1982. *Import Competition and Response.* Chicago: University of Chicago Press.

Bhagwati J. 1988. *Protectionism.* Cambridge, MA: MIT Press.

Blanchard, O., R. Dornbusch, P. Krugman, R. Layard, and L. Summers. 1991. *Reform in Eastern Europe.* Cambridge, MA: MIT Press.

Bosworth, B., R. Dornbusch, and R. Labán, eds. 1994. *The Chilean Economy: Policy Lessons and Challenges.* Washington, DC: The Brookings Institution.

Boycko, M. 1992. "When Higher Incomes Reduce Welfare: Queues, Labor Supply, and Macro Equilibrium in Socialist Economies." *Quarterly Journal of Economics* 107 (3) (August): 907–920.

Bradford, C., ed. 1994. *Redefining the State in Latin America.* Paris: OECD.

Bresser Pereira L., J. M. Maravall, and A. Przeworsky. 1993. *Economic Reforms in New Democracies: A Social Democratic Approach.* Cambridge: Cambridge University Press.

Bruno, M. 1993. *Crisis, Stabilization and Economic Reform: Therapy by Consensus.* New York: Oxford University Press.

Burgess, R., and N. Stern. 1993. "Taxation and Development." *Journal of Economic Literature* 31: 762–830.

Calvert, R. 1986. *Models of Imperfect Information in Politics.* New York: Harwood Academic Publishers.

Calvert, R. 1995. "The Rational Choice Theory of Social Institutions: Cooperation, Coordination and Communication." In *Modern Political Economy: Old Topic, New Directions,* ed. J. Banks and E. Hanushek, 216–267. New York: Cambridge University Press.

Calvo, G. 1989. "Incredible Reforms." In *Debt, Stabilization and Development,* ed. J. Braga de Macedo, G. Calvo, P. Kouri, and R. Findlay, 217–234. Oxford: Basil Blackwell.

Caplin, A., and J. Leahy. 1994. "Business as Usual, Market Crashes, and Wisdom after the Fact." *American Economic Review* 84 (June): 584–65.

Chari, V. V., and H. Cole. 1993. "A Contribution to the Theory of Pork Barrel Spending." Federal Reserve Bank of Mineapolis Staff Report 156.

Colander D. and A. Coats. 1989. *The Spread of Economic Ideas.* Cambridge: Cambridge University Press.

Corbo, V., and J. De Melo. 1985. "Liberalization with Stabilization in the Southern Cone of Latin America," *World Development* 13 (August): 5–15.

Dehejia, V. 1994. "Income Distribution and the Limits to Policy Reform: Shock Therapy or Gradualism?" Mimeo. Columbia University.

Desai, P. 1995. "Beyond Shock Therapy." *Journal of Democracy* 6(2) (April).

Dewatripont, M., and G. Roland. 1991. "Economic Reform and Dynamic Political Constraints." *Review of Economic Studies* 59: 703–730.

―――. 1992. "The Virtues of Gradualism in the Transition to a Market Economy." *Economic Journal* 102: 291–300.

Díaz Alejandro, C. 1985. "Good Bye Financial Repression, Hello Financial Crash." *Journal of Development Economics* 19: 1–24.

―――. 1988. "The 1940s in Latin America." In *Trade, Development and the World Development: Selected Essays of C. F. Díaz Alejandro,* ed. A. Velasco. Oxford: Basil Blackwell.

Dornbusch R., and S. Edwards. 1991. *The Macroeconomics of Populism in Latin America.* Chicago: University of Chicago Press.

―――. 1995. *Reform, Recovery and Growth: Latin America and the Middle East.* Chicago: University of Chicago Press.

Edwards, S. 1984. "The Order of Liberalization in Developing Countries." Princeton: Princeton Essays in International Finance.

Edwards, S. 1992. "The Sequencing of Structural Adjustment and Stabilization." ICEG Occasional Paper 34.

————. 1993. "Economic Reform, Labor Markets and the Social Sectors: A Latin American Perspective" World Bank. Mimeo.

————. 1994. "Trade and Industrial Policy Reform in Latin America." NBER Working Paper 4772, June.

Edwards, S., and A. Cox Edwards. 1987. *Monetarism end Liberalization: The Chilean Experiment*. Boston: Ballinger Publishing Company.

Edwards, S., and S. Van Wijnbergen. 1986. "Welfare Effects of Trade and Capital Market Liberalization." *International Economic Review* 27 (February): 141–48.

Frieden, J. 1991. *Debt, Development and Democracy: Modern Political Economy and Latin America, 1965–1985*. Princeton: Princeton University Press.

Friedman, M. 1993. "George Stigler: A Personal Reminiscence." *Journal of Political Economy* 101(5) (October): 772.

Frydman, R., and A. Rapaczynski, 1994. *Privatization in Eastern Europe: Is the State Withering Away?* London: Central European University Press.

Gavin, M. 1993. "Unemployment and the Economics of Gradualist Reform." Columbia University. Mimeo.

Geddes, B. 1994. *Politician's Dilemma: Building State Capacity in Latin America*. Berkeley and Los Angeles: University of California Press.

Gibbons, R. 1992. *Game Theory for Applied Economists*. Princeton: Princeton University Press.

Graham, C. 1994. *Safety Nets, Politics and the Poor: Transitions to Market Economies*. Washington, DC: The Brookings Institution.

Haggard, S., and R. Kaufman. 1995. *The Political Economy of Democratic Transitions*. Princeton: Princeton University Press.

Haggard, S., and S. Webb, eds. 1994. *Voting for Reform: Democracy, Political Liberalization, and Economic Adjustment*. New York: Oxford University Press.

Harberger, A. 1993. "Secrets of Success: A Handful of Heroes" *American Economic Review* 83 (May): 343–50.

Hausmann, R. 1994. "Sustaining Reform: What Role for Social Policy." In *Redefining the State in Latin America*, ed. C. Bradford. Paris: OECD.

————. 1995. "Quitting Populism Cold Turkey: The Big Bang Approach to Macroeconomic Balance." IESA. Mimeo.

Ingberman D., and R. Inman. 1988. "The Political Economy of Fiscal Policy." In *Surveys in Public Economics*, ed. P. Hare, 105–160. Oxford and New York: Basil Blackwell.

Krehbiel, K. 1991. *Information and Legislative Organization*. Ann Arbor: University of Michigan Press.

Krueger, A. 1974. "The Political Economy of the Rent Seeking Society." *American Economic Review* 64 (June): 291–303.

————. 1992. *Economic Policy Reform in Developing Countries*. Oxford: Basil Blackwell.

————. 1993. "Virtuous and Vicious Circles in Economic Development." *American Economic Review* 83 (May): 351–55.

Labán, R., and F. Sturzenegger. 1992. "La Economía Política de los Programas de Estabilización." *Coleccion Estudios CIEPLAN 36* (December): 41–66.

―――. 1994. "Distributional Conflict, Financial Adaptation and Delayed Stabilization." *Economics and Politics* 6(3) (November): 257–278.

Lipton, D., and J. Sachs. 1990. "Creating a Market Economy in Eastern Europe: The Case of Poland." *Brookings Papers on Economic Activity*, No. 1.

Lupia, A., and M. McCubbins. 1995. "Can Democracy Work? Persuasion, Enlightenment, and Democratic Institutions." Manuscript. Harvard University Program on Political Economy.

Lustig, N. 1992. *Mexico. The Remaking of an Economy.* Washington, DC: The Brookings Institution.

Matsusaka, J. 1995. "The Economic Approach to Democracy." In *The New Economics of Human Behavior*, ed. M. Tommasi and K. Ierulli, 140–54. Cambridge University Press.

McKinnon, R. 1991. *The Order of Economic Liberalization.* Baltimore: Johns Hopkins University Press.

McMillan J., and B. Naughton. 1992. "How to Reform a Planned Economy: Lessons from China." *Oxford Review of Economic Policy Spring* 8(1): 130–143.

Murphy, K., A. Shleifer, and R. Vishny. 1992. "The Transition to a Market Economy: Pitfalls of Partial Reform." *Quarterly Journal of Economics* 107(3) (August): 889–906.

Murrel, P. 1992. "Conservative Political Philosophy and the Strategy of Economic Transition." *East European Politics and Society Winter* 6(1): 3–16.

Mussa, M. 1982. "Government Policy and the Adjustment Process." In *Import Competition and Response*, ed. J. Bhagwati. Chicago: University of Chicago Press.

Naím, M. 1993. *Paper Tigers and Minotaurs: The Politics of Venezuela's Economic Reforms.* Washington, DC: Carnegie Endowment.

―――. 1994. "Latin America: The Second Stage of Reform." *Journal of Democracy* 5(4) (October): 33–48.

Nelson, J. 1994a. *A Precarious Balance: Democracy and Economic Reforms in Latin America.* San Francisco: ICS Press.

―――. 1994b. "Linkages Between Politics and Economics." *Journal of Democracy* 5(4): 49–62.

North, D. 1990. "A Transaction Cost Theory of Politics," *Journal of Theoretical Politics* 2(4): 355–367.

―――. 1994. "Economic Performance Through Time." *American Economic Review* 84 (June): 359–68.

Olson, M. 1982. *The Rise and Decline of Nations.* New Haven: Yale University Press.

―――. 1996. "Capitalism, Socialism and Dictatorship." Manuscript. University of Maryland.

Packenham, R. 1992. "The Politics of Economic Liberalization: Argentina and Brazil in Comparative Perspective." Stanford. Mimeo.

Papageorgiou D., M. Michaely, and A. Choksi, eds. 1991. *Liberalizing Foreign Trade*. Cambridge: Basil Blackwell.

Portes, R. 1990. "Introduction to Economic Transformation of Hungary and Poland" *European Economy* 43 (March): 11–18.

———. 1991. "The Path of Reform in Central and Eastern Europe: An Introduction." *European Economy* Special Issue, no. 2: 3–15.

Przeworski, A. 1991. *Democracy and the Market: Political and Economic Reforms in Eastern Europe and Latin America*. Cambridge University Press.

Putnam, R. 1993. *Making Democracy Work, Civic Traditions in Modern Italy*. Princeton: Princeton University Press.

Ranis, G. and A. Mahmood. 1992. *The Political Economy of Development Policy Change*. Oxford: Basil Blackwell.

Rodrik, D. 1993. "The Positive Economics of Policy Reform." *American Economic Review* 83 (May): 356–61.

———. 1996. "Understanding Economic Policy Reform." *Journal of Economic Literature* 34 (March): 9–41.

Sachs, J. 1993. *Poland's Jump to the Market Economy*. Cambridge, MA: The MIT Press.

———. 1995. "The Political Challenge of Economic Transition: The Case of Poland." Harvard University. Mimeo.

Spiller, P. 1995. "Regulatory Commitment and Utilities' Privatization: Implications for Future Comparative Research." In *Modern Political Economy: Old Topics, New Directions*, ed. J. Banks and E. Hanushek, 63–79. Cambridge: Cambridge University Press.

Tarrow, S. 1996. "Making Social Science Work Across Space and Time: A Critical Reflection on Robert Putnam's Making Democracy Work." *American Political Science Review* 90(2) (June): 389–97.

Taylor, L., ed. 1993. *The Rocky Road to Reform*. Cambridge, MA: MIT Press.

Tommasi, M., and A. Velasco. 1996. "Where Are We in the Political Economy of Reform?" *Journal of Policy Reform* 1: 187–238.

Tornell, A. 1995. "Are Economic Crises Necessary for Trade Liberalization and Fiscal Reform? The Mexican Experience." In *Reform, Recovery and Growth: Latin America and the Middle East*, ed. R. Dornbush and S. Edwards. Chicago: University of Chicago Press.

Tsebelis, G. 1994. "Decision Making in Political Systems: Veto Players in Presidentialism, Parliamentarism, Multicameralism and Multipartyism." *British Journal of Political Science* 25: 289–325.

Velasco, A. 1993. "A Model of Endogenous Fiscal Deficits, and Delayed Fiscal Reforms." C. V. Starr Center Report 93–94, New York University.

———. 1994. "The State and Economic Policy: Chile 1952–1992." In *The Chilean Economy: Policy Lessons and Challenges*, ed. B. Bosworth, R. Dornbusch, and R. Labán. Washington, DC: The Brookings Institution.

Weingast, B. 1995. "The Political Foundations of Democracy and the Rule of Law." Stanford, February. Mimeo.

Weingast, B., K. Shepsle, and C. Johnsen. 1981 "The Political Economy of Benefits and Costs: A Neoclassical Approach to Redistributive Politics." *Journal of Political Economy* 89 (August): 642–64.

Williamson, J., ed. 1994. *The Political Economy of Policy Reform*. Washington, DC: Institute for International Economics.

Williamson, J., and S. Haggard. 1994. "The Political Conditions for Economic Reform." In *The Political Economy of Policy Reform*, ed. J. Williamson. Washington, DC: Institute for International Economics.

Zarazaga, C. 1993. "Hyperinflations and Moral Hazard in the Appropriation of Seignorage." Working Paper 93-26, Federal Reserve Bank of Philadelphia, November.

I

Why? (The Positive Political Economy of Reforms)

Inaction and Delay

2

The Political Economy of Delayed Reform

Allan Drazen

2.1 Introduction

Economic reform is such a commonly used term among both politicians and economists that a naïve observer might think that designing and implementing reforms is what policymakers actually do. The truth is that enacting a reform program is something done all too rarely. A more accurate description is that the enactment of policy reforms, even the most necessary ones, is often long-delayed.

A standard explanation for the failure to change policy is that policymakers do not know what policy will work better. That is, the problem is one of policy design. Though problems in formulating a new policy can explain some failures to change ineffective current policies, such difficulties cannot explain all such failures. There are numerous examples across a broad range of countries where well-specified reforms which would clearly raise social welfare are just not implemented.[1] The purpose of this chapter is to address this question of why countries often delay the adoption of welfare-increasing reforms. More specifically, I will bring together several recent strands of research on this question in a single, unified framework.

The question of why certain policies which appear to be optimal are not adopted, while other policies which appear to be suboptimal are adopted is, in fact, at the heart of political economy. The starting point of a political economy analysis is the realization that the paradigm of a social planner choosing policies does not describe the way decisions are actually made. Instead, policy choices often reflect the resolution of conflicts of interest between groups with different goals; distortions away from optimality may result from the mechanisms for making collective choices. Recent work on delayed reform thus often starts with the question: why

Originally published in *Policy Reform* 1 (1996): 25–46. Reprinted with permission.

might conflicts of interest and the mechanisms by which such conflicts are resolved lead to a delay in adoption of beneficial reforms?

There are two basic approaches in current research to non-adoption and/or delay of policy change. Each is based on heterogeneity of interest and some sort of uncertainty about net benefits of reform, though in quite different ways. One approach concentrates on distributional conflict, as in the papers of Alesina and Drazen (1991) and Drazen and Grilli (1993). There is a conflict over how the *known* cost of a policy change will be divided among interest groups, so that ex-post heterogeneity (that is, heterogeneity caused by the change in policy) is the key concept. Though each interest group knows the net benefit it would receive from the change under a proposed allocation of costs, each group is uncertain about the net benefits other groups will enjoy and hence about their willingness to pay for the reform.

In the second approach, the key concept is that some interest groups are uncertain about the benefits they themselves will enjoy if a reform is adopted, as in the work of Fernandez and Rodrik (1991) and Rodrik (1993), where non-adoption of beneficial reforms in a static context, rather than delay over time, is the focus. Heterogeneity nonetheless plays a role, in that some groups are certain to benefit from reform, so that there can be reforms which would end up benefitting a majority of the population are not adopted if enough groups are uncertain about net benefits. This "status quo bias" has been extended to explain delay in a dynamic context in the work of Laban and Sturzenegger (1994a,b).

As indicated above, I want to present a simple framework which encompasses both approaches, making them more accessible and allowing comparison with each other, as well as with other explanations of delay. My goals in presenting such a framework are two-fold. First, some of the work is quite technical (such as the war of attrition model of Alesina and Drazen or the dynamic version of status quo bias model of Laban and Sturzenegger) and hence not very accessible. There is therefore an argument for presenting the same results in a simpler framework. Second, one may ask how these different approaches fit together. The framework I will set out may strike many as too abstract and will certainly not convey all the richness of the models it is meant to capture. But I hope the main driving force of each model and the connections between models will be made clear, justifying such a skeletal approach.

I will exposit this approach by considering a sequence of examples concerning a decision of whether or not to purchase a lumpy good. This decision will be interpreted as whether or not to support or implement a reform program, the precise interpretation depending on the specific problem. The formal framework is based on a very simple background problem:

Problem 0: Purchase of a (Lumpy) Private Good

An agent makes a one-time decision of whether or not to purchase a good which costs c. He gets utility u^B if he buys the good and utility $u^N < u^B$ if he does not. The solution to this problem is simple: buy the good if $c \leq u^B - u^N$, otherwise, do not buy.

2.2 Some Roads Not Taken

Before considering these approaches in detail, I want to summarize quickly some explanations of delay in adopting reforms which I consider less than fully satisfactory. The problem is not that they are empirically irrelevant in explaining delay to change policy—in fact, they often play a major role—but that they fail to address adequately the central question of why countries do not adopt reforms when their social benefits are clear. The first explanation for failure to reform is ignorance of how to do so. That is, ineffective policies are not changed because of uncertainty or disagreement about what would be effective. Though it is far from easy to design highly effective policy, so that this argument has empirical importance, it misses the main point I want to consider. When there is uncertainty about what to do, the failure to take action is not surprising; delay is puzzling when there is agreement about what measures must be taken, but nonetheless, nothing is done.[2]

A second explanation is that though there is political agreement on what to do, a country lacks the technical expertise to carry out the desired program successfully: there is a lack of the necessary technicians, managers, or bureaucrats. Though this may be a constraint in some cases, it doesn't explain the failure to carry out many programs, such as deficit reduction.

A third explanation for inaction may be termed "benign neglect": given time, the problem will solve itself, so the response of "mañana" is optimal. To make sense of such a response in a world of rational agents, one may draw the distinction between transitory and permanent conditions. If a problem results from a shock which is perceived to be transitory shock, policy lags mean that doing nothing may be the best response. Any lag in the ability to implement a policy, or in the effects the policy will have once put in place, means that activism may make things worse rather than better. Similarly, if a problem is "on the way" to being solved, so that what we are observing is a transitional period, taking no action may be the optimal action.[3] (One should note, however, that arguing for "benign neglect" may simply be an excuse for unwillingness to act.) Here too, the argument has empirical relevance as an explanation for policy delay, but doesn't answer the question of why there are delays when it is agreed that problems won't solve themselves.

A final explanation for the failure to adopt necessary policy changes is simple irrationality: societies, like individuals, put off making difficult choices, even though they know they must be faced and will only become more difficult with time.[4] As with the previous explanation, irrationality may have some empirical significance in that there are delays which are difficult to reconcile with rational behavior, nonetheless this is not a satisfactory explanation. Our *raison d'être* as economists is to take phenomena which have resisted a logical explanation and explain them in a coherent, consistent framework. In the specific area of political economy, the goal is to show how polices which seem sub-optimal (hence, irrational in terms of basic welfare economics), can in fact be shown to be the result of the political mechanism under which the decisions of rational, self-interested agents are aggregated.

Note that this formalization of problem 0 immediately rules out the arguments considered in this section: the decision of whether to adopt the policy is made rationally; there is no question about what the policy change is; there is no difficulty in implementing it; and the benefits will accrue only if action is taken.

I now turn to this question of rationally explaining seemingly irrational delay in adopting socially beneficial policy reform. In the next two sections I consider static versions of the two main approaches to modelling privately optimal, but socially inefficient delay.

2.3 Distributional Conflict

The conflict-over-distribution approach has as its basis the notion that reform is a public good, so that people may be in favor of reform, but want someone else to bear the cost. I therefore begin with the static problem 0, with the good interpreted as a public good. This is a well-known problem of supply of a public good; the version I present follows Fudenberg and Tirole (1991).

Problem DC-1: The Static Public Goods Game

There are two agents (call them i and j), and the good is a public good: if either agent buys the good, both receive utility u^B; if neither agent buys the good they both receive u^N. The two agents i and j have costs c_i and c_j, where if an agent i purchases the good he receives net utility $u^B - c_i$. Each agent knows his own cost, but not that of the other agent. He only knows the other agent's cost is distributed as $P(c)$ over $[c, \bar{c}]$, where $P(c)$ is common knowledge.

An agent's "strategy" in this game is whether or not to buy the good as a function of his cost c_i. Denote these two actions by 1 and 0. Formally, the strategy of an agent i, $s_i(c_i)$, assigns to each c_i an action 1 or 0. For ease of exposition let $u^B = 1$ and $u^N = 0$. The payoff of an agent i depends on his cost, his strategy (that is, choice of whether to purchase or not), and the other agent's strategy, where j will be used to denote the other agent. Formally, we may write the payoff as

$$u_i(s_i, s_j, c_i) = \max(s_i, s_j) - s_i c_i. \tag{1}$$

Consider an equilibrium in which we solve for a pair of strategies $(\hat{s}_i(\cdot), \hat{s}_j(\cdot))$ for each possible value of c_i and c_j such that each agent's behavior is optimal given the other agent's strategy. The solution to this problem is simple. If we define by z_j the equilibrium probability that player j purchases the good (that is, $z_j = Pr(\hat{s}_j(c_j) = 1)$), the solution is: Player i purchases the good ($\hat{s}_i = 1$) if $c_i \leq 1 - z_j$; player i does not purchase ($\hat{s}_i = 0$) if $c_i > 1 - z_j$.[5]

What the solution indicates is that because of the public nature of the good and the possibility that another agent may supply the good, the individual will not purchase the good if he thinks that the probability that someone else will purchase is high enough, even though the benefit exceeds the cost of private purchase. In the optimal solution, an individual equates not cost and benefit, but cost and expected benefit. In equilibrium if both agents are known to act according to this rule, the equilibrium probability and reservation level of cost can be derived. If $\hat{c}_j$ is j's reservation cost, so that $z_j = Pr(c \leq c_j \leq \hat{c}_j) = P(\hat{c}_j)$, we have

$$\hat{c}_i = 1 - P(\hat{c}_j) = 1 - P(1 - P(\hat{c}_i)), \tag{2}$$

with an identical equation for $\hat{c}_j$. If there is a unique $\hat{c}$ which solves this equation, this is the solution.

To take an example, if $P(c)$ is uniform on $[0, 2]$, we may derive $\hat{c} = 2/3$ and $P(\hat{c}) = 1/3$. Hence, if both agents have costs that lie between $2/3$ and 1, the good will not be supplied in equilibrium, even though each agent would be better off if he supplied the good. Though each agent would benefit, each decides not to supply, given his cost and the probability that the other agent will supply the good. Therefore, in equilibrium the good is not supplied.

In terms of a reform program, if all interest groups believe that there is a high probability that some other group will bear the burden of implementing the program, the reform will not be adopted, even if everyone would benefit. It is this insight which will yield a "war of attrition" in a dynamic game, in which each group plays a waiting game hoping some other group will "surrender" and bear the cost of the reform program. The public good nature of reform is the key characteristic of delayed reform in this approach.

It has been argued that a crucial feature of the static public goods game (and of the war-of-attrition and uncertainty-about-benefits models presented below) is that there is no ex-post compensation of losers by winners, so that the nature of the solution would change if transfers were made. This misses the whole point, which is to study how distributional conflict can lead to delay. That is, we want to study the implications of being able to shift the burden of reform, rather than situations where there is no conflict over distribution of the burden of reform (let's say due to an institutional structure which *mandated* ex-post compensation).

2.4   Uncertainty about Individual Benefits

The second approach to explaining the non-adoption of socially beneficial reforms, and ultimately delay in adopting reforms in a dynamic setting, concentrates on uncertainty about the net benefits which the reforms will yield, rather than conflict over who will bear the cost of reforms whose benefits are known. In a static framework the key paper is Fernandez and Rodrik (1991), which is concerned with the specific issue of trade reform. In a two-sector model, a liberalization will lower wages in one sector, but raise them in the other sector, with the change in wages being known. Workers in the first sector can move to the second sector, but at a cost. The key point is that the cost of moving is not fully known ex-ante, so that the net benefit of higher wages is not known ex-ante. More specifically, the cost of moving has two parts: there is a general cost which is known before the policy change is adopted; and there is an individual specific cost which is known only after the reform program has been put in place. Individuals in the first sector know the distribution of possible costs, but not the cost they will actually face if they decide to move. Individuals in the first sector support the reform program only if they believe their net utility will rise as a result of its being adopted; individuals in the second sector unconditionally support the reform. Reforms are adopted by majority vote, so the passage of a reform requires a majority of voters to expect a net benefit.

The decision facing workers in the first sector may be represented as buying a private good priced with a two-part tariff, where there is uncertainty about the second part of the cost. Formally one has:

Problem UB-1: Uncertainty About Private Benefits

The individual must pay a known fixed cost x before sampling from a known distribution of costs $P(c)$. The individual thus makes two decisions: whether to pay the entry cost x; and, having done so, whether to purchase the good. If he does not pay the entry cost he receives utility u^{SQ}; when he pays the entry cost he receives utilities u^B if he buys and u^N if he does not (where u^N need not equal u^{SQ}).

Here, the decision as to whether to support a reform program is the decision of whether to pay the fixed cost x (which will be called the *adoption* cost); buying the good at cost c (the *adjustment* cost) represents the decision to move sectors. The adoption cost may be thought of as the known dislocation that will accompany a reform program. Uncertainty about c thus represents uncertainty about the net benefit of a reform program, which is central to this approach.

The solution to this two-stage problem is not difficult. In the second stage, having paid the adoption cost x and learned his private adjustment cost c, an individual will buy the good (that is, switch sectors) if $c \leq u^B - u^N$. In the first stage, the individual will pay the adoption cost as long as the expected utility from having adopted the reform exceeds u^{SQ}. (For simplicity of argument, suppose it must be strictly greater; equality implies a preference for the status quo of u^{SQ}.) Using the second-part result, one is in favor of adopting the reform if

$$\int_{c=\underline{c}}^{c=u^B-u^N} (u^B - x - c)\, dP(c) + \int_{c=u^B-u^N}^{c=\bar{c}} (u^N - x)\, dP(c) > u^{SQ}. \tag{3}$$

To take a specific distribution, in the case where (as above) $P(c)$ is uniform over $[0, 2]$, the condition (3) becomes

$$\left(\frac{u^B}{2} - \frac{u^N}{2}\right)^2 + u^N > u^{SQ} + x. \tag{4}$$

The left-hand side is the *expected* benefit from adoption of the reform abstracting from adoption costs, that is, expected utility in the post-reform state. The right-hand side is the cost of adoption, including the opportunity cost u^{SQ}.

Equation (4) makes a number of points clear about the decision of agents who are uncertain whether they will benefit or not. First, even if the worst-case utility from reform exceeds the status quo ($u^N > u^{SQ}$), adoption costs may mean they will not support the program. Note however that an excess of u^{SQ} over u^N is like an adoption cost; therefore, for $u^{SQ} - u^N$ large enough, agents will not support the reform even if $x = 0$. Second, if the gainers (among those who are initially uncertain) clearly benefit, but the losers end up no better off than the status quo ($u^B - c - x > u^{SQ}$, but $u^N = u^{SQ}$), uncertainty about who will be a gainer is crucial. If the losers are actually worse off under a reform, very large gains to the winners may not be enough to offset the effects of this uncertainty.

To take an example, let $u^B = 2$, $u^{SQ} = u^N = 0$. Using (4) one calculates that for $x = 1$ the individual is indifferent between paying and not paying the entry cost—he would be better off 50% of the time paying the cost giving him the option to purchase the good. For x slightly greater than one, no individual would support the program, though almost half would benefit from the reform.[6]

Problem UB-1 and the results derived from it could be thought of as representing the problem of a social planner who maximizes expected utility in a world where ex-post compensation is impossible. If all agents were facing this uncertainty, then a reform would be rejected only if it lowered expected welfare or if less than half of the population would benefit ex-post. Hence, the presence of agents who are certain to benefit is necessary for a socially beneficial reform, that is one which would benefit a majority, to be rejected by majority voting.

To see how this occurs, consider an economy made up of *one* person who is certain to benefit from the reform (e.g., already in the second sector) and a large number of people as described in problem UB-1, that is, unsure of their net benefits. Consider the parameter values in the example where $x = 1$ (so that uncertain voters are indifferent), and assume indifferent voters opt for no change. Thus, a reform which would benefit over 50% of the population ex-post would be voted down almost unanimously! This illustrates a key result of the Fernandez-Rodrik paper.[7] Using problem UB-1, one can easily show that a program which ends up hurting a majority of the population may be adopted if enough people who are hurt ex-post expect ex-ante that they will be gainers. These two results imply a "bias" towards the status quo. Reforms adopted can be reversed (once individuals gain information about the actual benefits), but reforms not adopted even though they would benefit the majority will not later be adopted, since this information cannot be discovered. Hence, strictly speaking, the model will not generate delay. We return to this point in section 2.6.

2.5   Delayed Reform Due to Distributional Conflict

The Alesina-Drazen (1991) model is a dynamic version of the public goods problem discussed in section 2.2. Their model of delayed stabilization considers an economy in which the government is running a deficit due to the failure of interest groups to agree on a deficit reduction program. In the absence of a consensus, only highly distortionary taxes can be used to finance government expenditures, and the revenue from those taxes is insufficient to fully cover expenditures. A fiscal reform program replaces highly distortionary taxes with less distortionary taxes large enough to cover government expenditures and close the deficit. There is disagreement however on how the burden of these higher taxes should be distributed across groups in the economy: each group would like the burden of higher taxes placed elsewhere and refuses to agree to bearing a large fraction of the taxes in the hope that some other group will concede and accept (or no longer block) a fiscal reform placing a high burden on them. As groups can obstruct programs they dislike, fiscal reform requires consensus. Only when a group realizes that it can only do worse by waiting (for example, when they realize their opponents are far more able politically or economically to withstand the distortions of the current tax regime), will they concede and accept a reform with unfavorable distributional implications.

The war-of-attrition approach can be represented by a dynamic version of problem DC-1. One possibility would be to consider a multiperiod discrete-time version of the problem, in which each agent maximizes the discounted sum of expected payoffs, with the single-period payoff being defined as in problem DC-1. Consider, for example, a two-period version of the game. If z_{j2} were independent of what happened in the first period, simply reflecting $P(c)$ as above, optimal behavior would be independent across periods; each period's problem can be solved as above, yielding the same reservation cost in each period, namely $\hat{c}$ as above. What is crucial in a dynamic framework is that the probability of j's supplying the good in period 2, z_{j2}, depends on the action that i took in the first period. Since it is known that the other agent uses a reservation cost rule, observing him *not* buying the good provides information about his cost. If agent i believes that j's equilibrium reservation cost in period 1 is $\hat{c}_{j1}$, observing no supply leads i to update the distribution of possible costs by truncating the distribution $P(c)$ below $\hat{c}_{j1}$. Hence i updates the probability z_{j2}. Knowing that the other agent is solving this inference problem leads each agent to "shade" his reservation cost $\hat{c}_{j1}$ downward in the first period, relative to what he would choose in the absence of such an inference. This lower reservation cost represents the incentive to delay in the hope that the other agent will act.

Closer to the Alesina-Drazen framework would be a continuous-time, infinite-horizon version of the game. In order to present some of the comparative dynamic results of that paper, I broaden the framework slightly.

Problem DC-2: The Continuous-Time Public Goods Game

The set-up in continuous time, including payoffs, costs, and information structure, is identical to that in problem DC-1 for the static game, except that the agent who buys the good pays a fraction α of the cost $(1/2 < \alpha \leq 1)$, with the other agent paying $1 - \alpha$, from the date of supply T onward. (This framework clearly includes the earlier model for $\alpha = 1$.) Each chooses a date $T(c)$ to agree to pay a disproportional share as a function of his cost, where his objective is to maximize discounted expected payoff, where the discount rate is ρ.

To solve this problem, denote the utility of the agent with private cost c who concedes and agrees to pay the fraction α of the cost (the "loser") by

$$
U^L(T,c) = \int_{x=0}^{T} u^N e^{-\rho x}\, dx + e^{-\rho T} \int_{x=T}^{x} (u^B - \alpha c)e^{-\rho(x-T)}\, dx
$$

$$
= \frac{u^N}{\rho}(1 - e^{-\rho T}) + \frac{u^B - \alpha c}{\rho}\, e^{-\rho T} \tag{5}
$$

and the utility of the agent with cost c who pays only the fraction $1 - \alpha$ of the cost (the "winner") by

$$
U^W(T,c) = \int_{x=0}^{T} u^N e^{-\rho x}\, dx + e^{-\rho T} \int_{x=T}^{x} (u^B - (1-\alpha)c)e^{-\rho(x-T)}\, dx
$$

$$
= \frac{u^N}{\rho}(1 - e^{-\rho T}) + \frac{u^B - (1-\alpha)c}{\rho}\, e^{-\rho T}. \tag{6}
$$

To solve for i's optimal behavior, we begin, as in the static public goods game, by summarizing j's optimal behavior in terms of his probability of paying the greater share of the cost of supplying the good ("conceding"). In continuous time, this is represented by a cumulative distribution function $\Gamma(T)$, giving the probability of his conceding at or before T, with an associated PDF $\gamma(T)$. One may then calculate agent i's expected utility as a function of possible concession time T by noting that with probability $1 - \Gamma(T)$ agent i concedes, his infinite-horizon utility being $U^L(T)$, while if j's concession time is $x < T$, the utility of i is $U^W(x)$, that is, it depends on x. Expected utility of agent i as a function of T and his cost c_i may then be written

$$EU(T) = (1 - \Gamma(T))U^L(T, c_i) + \int_{x=0}^{T} U^W(x, c_j)\gamma(x)\,dx. \qquad (7)$$

To calculate optimal T, substitute (5) and (6) into (7), and set the derivative with respect to T equal to zero to obtain[8]

$$\frac{\gamma(T)}{1 - \Gamma(T)}\frac{(2\alpha - 1)c_i}{\rho} = u^B - u^N - \alpha c_i. \qquad (8)$$

This equation has a simple interpretation. Consider first the left-hand side. The first term is the probability that agent j concedes at T, conditional on his not having yet conceded. The second term is the gain in utility to agent i from T onwards if the greater share of supply of good is paid by his opponent rather than himself. It is $U^W(T) - U^L(T)$, which is the lesser share of the cost he must pay, discounted over an infinite horizon. Thus, the left-hand side represents the expected gain to i of waiting another instant to concede. The right-hand side is the cost of waiting another instant to concede, which is the foregone utility associated with not having the good for another instant minus the cost of supplying that he saves over the instant. Hence (8) indicates that agent i concedes and agrees to pay a disproportionate share of the cost when the expected gain from waiting just equals the cost from waiting, that is, the loss in utility from waiting another instant to concede. This solution as represented by the above equation is analogous to the solution to the static public goods game conditional on z_j given after equation (1), namely buy the good if $c_i \leq 1 - z_j$.

The solution to the problem will be the agent's optimal concession time as a function of his cost, denoted $T(c)$, where an agent with no cost would supply immediately ($T(0) = 0$). This boundary condition is obvious, since an agent who has no cost of supplying the good will choose to do so immediately. However, equation (8) cannot be used directly to calculate equilibrium $T(c)$, since the distribution $\Gamma(T)$ is unknown. Analogous to

the discussion of equilibrium in the static game which followed the characterization of optimal behavior conditional on z_j, we must derive equilibrium $\Gamma(T)$. Since agent j is solving the same sort of problem, agent i
assumes he follows a reservation cost rule, where his concession time is
increasing in his cost. As in the static game, let's consider the symmetric
solution, where agent j concedes according to the same function $T(c)$,
where T is increasing in c (and $T(0) = 0$).[9] This implies that the probability that agent j concedes before T is the probability that his c is less
than c_i, namely $P(c_i)$. That is,

$$\Gamma(T) = \Gamma(T(c)) = P(c)$$

so that $\gamma(T)T'(c) = p(c)$. This allows us to replace $\gamma(T)/(1 - \Gamma(T))$ in (8)
by $p(c)/[(1 - P(c))T'(c)]$. Equation (8) becomes

$$T'(c) = \frac{p(c)}{1 - P(c)} \frac{1}{\rho} \frac{(2\alpha - 1)c}{u^B - u^N - \alpha c}, \tag{9}$$

which is relevant for $c < (u^B - u^N)/\alpha$. (Higher cost types would never
find it optimal to supply the good.) This is a differential equation in the
function $T(c)$ which, combined with the boundary condition $T(0) = 0$,
can be solved for the optimal concession time $T(c)$ for each agent. The
solution may be represented by either curve in figure 2.1. With both
agents i and j behaving according to $T(c)$, the expected date of reform T^E
may be calculated as the expected minimum T, which reflects the expected
minimum c. This latter probability is the density multiplied by the probability that no other c is lower. For the case of only two agents one obtains

$$T^E = 2 \int_{x=0}^{\bar{c}} T(x)(1 - P(x))p(x)\, dx. \tag{10}$$

To take an example of a solution, suppose $\alpha = 1$, $u^B = 1$, and $u^N = 0$,
and the distribution of c is uniform over $[0, 2]$, exactly as in the example
for problem DC-1. The differential equation for $T(c)$ becomes

$$T'(c) = \frac{1}{\rho} \frac{c}{(1 - c)(2 - c)}, \tag{11}$$

which has a solution

$$T(c) = \frac{1}{\rho} \ln \frac{(2 - c)^2}{4(1 - c)} \tag{12}$$

so that $T(0) = 0$, $T'(c) > 0$, and $\lim_{c \to 1} T(c) = \infty$.

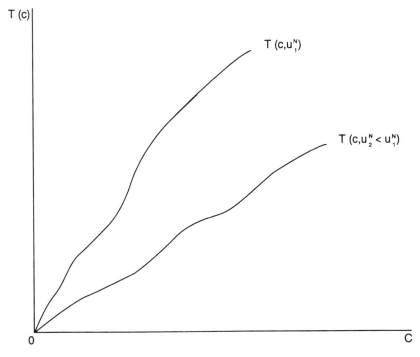

Figure 2.1
Optimal concession time

The solution to problem DC-2 and its implications represents the basic result of the war-of-attrition approach to delayed reform. Interest groups who would benefit from a reform refuse to bear the cost in the hope that someone else who may benefit even more will bear the cost, as in the static public goods game. The dynamic element reflects learning about the net benefit that other groups assign to a reform, or, equivalently, the cost that other groups assign to the distortions associated with the prereform environment. (This is the specific interpretation that Alesina and Drazen give to the relative costs across agents.) Hence, delay reflects a war of attrition, as each interest group tries to "wait out" other groups in the hope that they will concede first. Delay ends and reform takes place when some group realizes that they are relatively weaker than other groups and agree to bear a disproportionate burden of the reform program.

The formalization of the problem allows one to derive the implications for the expected length of delay of changes in some basic parameters. For example, higher pre-reform distortions, as represented by a lower value of u^N, clearly lowers $T'(c)$ in (8). Since the lowest cost type concedes at time

0 for any value of u^N, a smaller slope of the $T(c)$ curve means the new curve lies below the old one (see figure 2.1), so each type chooses to concede earlier. From (10) the expected date of reform is thus earlier.

This result forms the basis of the argument of Drazen and Grilli (1993) on the benefit of crises in inducing policy reform. Since higher pre-reform distortions induce an earlier expected reform, the government, by inducing a crisis, can hasten the expected date of reform. Intuitively, if what is blocking a reform is the inability to gain consensus on how the burden of reform is to be divided among interest groups, a crisis can hasten agreement by increasing the distortion associated with the status quo, thus raising the cost of not agreeing to reform. That is, a crisis can make each interest group more amenable to reform, and hence shorten the expected delay in adopting a reform. (A highly distorted status quo, where these distortions rise over time, will play the central role in the dynamics of policy reform in the model of Labán and Sturzenegger (1994).) In fact, as Drazen and Grilli show, if the expected date of reform is significantly brought forward, lower pre-reform utility implies that expected welfare can actually rise.[10]

By the same reasoning as used for the case of lower u^N, it can be shown that a more unequal sharing of the burden of reform will result in a later expected date of reform. (This follows immediately from the previous result and inspection of (8). When the burden is shared equally ($\alpha = 1/2$), there will be no delay ($T'(c) = 0$, so that $T(c) = 0$): since the "winner" pays the same share as the "loser", any agent for whom the reform is beneficial will immediately agree to pay half of the cost if his opponent will pay the other half.[11] Equal sharing of the burden removes the public good aspect of reform, and therefore removes the basic reason for reform to be delayed. As the disproportionate burden the "loser" pays rises, there is an increase in an agent's gain from waiting to see if his opponent will bear this burden.

2.6   Dynamic Models With Uncertainty About Individual Benefits

Favorable Circumstances

Some situations are more favorable than others to implement a policy reform, and it may be optimal to wait for more favorable circumstances if there is a cost of failure. This argument has been formalized by Orphanides (1993), who applied it to inflation stabilization via exchange rate management, which required a sufficient stock of foreign exchange reserves. The level of reserves is subject to stochastic influences once a reform program is put in place, and too low a level of reserves will require program abandonment. Not surprisingly, the optimal decision on when to undertake a stabilization program is summarized by a reservation level of reserves; if reserves are below that level, waiting is optimal.[12]

The Orphanides problem can be represented by a simple dynamic version of problem 0:

Problem UB-2: Optimal Private Waiting

The agent is infinitely lived and makes a one-time decision to buy the good. Before he purchases, he has utility u^N per period. In period t he draws a cost c_t from a known, given distribution $P(c)$. He can choose to buy the good in that period and receive net utility $u^B - c_t$ in every period $s \geq t$ thereafter. Or, he can wait, receiving u^N in the current period and drawing c_{t+1} next period.

This is an optimal stopping problem, where the solution is obviously a reservation level $\hat{c}$, which depends on the parameters of the problem, including the cumulative distribution function $P(c)$. The agent will purchase the good if $c_t \leq \hat{c}$, and will wait if $c_t > \hat{c}$. In terms of policy change, reform will take place when conditions are favorable, that is when c_t is relatively low. There will be optimal delay of beneficial reforms, in the sense that there can be periods when no reform will take place even though $c_t < u^B - u^N$, since $c_t > \hat{c}$. But, there will be no bias towards delay, in the sense of waiting though times are good.

Hence, this view of delay is sensible (it explains why delays may occur if policymakers believe bad times are transitory and conditions will improve) and it has some empirical relevance. It suggests, however, that difficult reforms should be adopted mostly in good times. In fact, we more often see the opposite: there is delay even though the economic situation is deteriorating and expected only to get worse, with reforms adopted only in a time of crisis. One explanation for this fact is given in the work of Drazen and Grilli (1993), discussed above. Labán and Sturzenegger (1994a,b) present another explanation, which as we shall see, is technically, though not economically, very similar to the Orphanides model.

Before considering that work, one should note how an optimal stopping problem is related to the war-of-attrition approach, problem DC-2. Consider extending the optimal stopping problem to include the other variant of optimal procrastination, namely, "benign neglect" in the expectation that things will get better by themselves. A simple way to do this is to include a probability that in each period the good will be costlessly supplied by nature. This will increase the return to doing nothing. Thus,

as in the war of attrition, in the optimal stopping problem the higher is
the probability that the good will be supplied without my taking any
action, the less likely I am to take action. Delay reflects the hope on the
part of each agent that the good will be supplied without his having to
do so. But, there is a crucial difference between the two problems. In the
optimal stopping problem, this key probability was *exogenous*, so that
delay based on perceiving a very high probability of no need for action
could be judged to be irrational in light of subsequent developments.
In the public goods game the same probability is *endogenous*: with a
small number of agents, the probability that someone else will take action
depends on their beliefs about the probability of my acting; delaying
could therefore be interpreted as a rational attempt to force someone else
to act.

Problem UB-2 could be extended to include the other variant of optimal procrastination, namely, "benign neglect" in the expectation that
things will get better by themselves. Suppose we extend the problem by
including a probability that in each period the good will be costlessly
supplied by nature. This will increase the return to doing nothing. If this
probability is high enough, continual delay may be the optimal solution.

Deteriorating Conditions

Labán and Sturzenegger have applied a dynamic version of the Fernandez-
Rodrik model to the case of inflation stabilization. Thus, they address
precisely the question addressed by Alesina and Drazen, namely, why do
countries delay the fiscal adjustment they realize is necessary for reducing
very high inflation, but present a different answer. Labán and Sturzenegger
consider an economy with two groups, rich and poor. The groups live in
an inflationary environment, reflecting the use of seigniorage to finance
government expenditures in the absence of an agreement on allocating
the burden of non-distortionary taxation. As in Fernandez and Rodrik
(and in contrast to Alesina and Drazen), there is uncertainty about the net
benefits of stabilization.

The dynamics in the two-period, discrete-time model come from the
ability of the rich in the first period to invest in a "financial technology"
which partially shields them from costly inflation (for example, converting
domestic currency assets into assets denominated in foreign currency),
which is unavailable to the poor. "Dollarizing" assets reduces the domestic
monetary base and increases inflation in the second period. Hence, the
failure to reach agreement on a fiscal retrenchment in the first period leads
to an endogenous deterioration in the economy (as the rich increase their

utilization of the financial technology), so that the poor face even higher costs from inflation in the second period.

Labán and Sturzenegger demonstrate that this model driven by uncertainty about the post-stabilization environment can generate delay, with the poor agreeing to unfavorable terms in the second period which are worse than those they rejected in the first period. What is especially intriguing in their result is that the poor reject an agreement in the first period *even though they know* they will suffer an extra period of inflation and then stabilize on even worse terms. To see how this may come about, consider a two-period version of problem UB-1 in which the costs and benefits change over time. To see where the result comes from I will choose parameter values such that the cost of reform increases over time, but not as much as the cost of not reforming.

Problem UB-3: Multiperiod Uncertainty with Deterioration

Consider the set-up of problem UB-1 in a two-period framework. The option of buying the good can be purchased for a fixed cost x_1 in the first period or a fixed cost $x_2 > x_1$ in the second period, where in each case adjustment costs are drawn from a distribution $P(c)$. Assume further that the utility associated with the status quo is falling over time, with $u_2^{SQ} \ll u_1^{SQ}$.

The individual has three possible actions: adopt in the first period, and gain the possible benefits over both periods; wait and adopt in the second period; or, never adopt. The utility associated with each of these decisions are, respectively,

$$(a) \quad (1 + \beta) \left[\left(\frac{u^B - u^N}{2} \right)^2 + u^N \right] - x_1$$

$$(b) \quad u_1^{SQ} + \beta \left[\left(\frac{u^B - u^N}{2} \right)^2 + u^N \right] - \beta x_2 \qquad (13)$$

$$(c) \quad u_1^{SQ} + \beta u_2^{SQ}.$$

For delay with ultimate adoption to dominate either of the other options, (b) much dominate (a) or (c). For (b) to exceed (a) (delayed reform preferred to immediate reform), we must have

$$u_1^{SQ} - \beta x_2 > \left[\left(\frac{u^B - u^N}{2} \right)^2 + u^N \right] - x_1. \qquad (14)$$

Even in the case where there is no discounting of future costs ($\beta = 1$), this would be the case if the excess of u_1^{SQ} over post-reform expected utility (the term in brackets) outweighs the excess of x_2 over x_1. That is, if the current status quo is not too bad, sufficient uncertainty about post-reform utility may make delay optimal, even though the costs of reform will go up with delay. For it nonetheless to be optimal to reform tomorrow, rather then delay still further, (b) must also exceed (c), requiring (in the case of no discounting, so that there is no bias toward delay)

$$\left[\left(\frac{u^B - u^N}{2} \right)^2 + u^N \right] - x_2 > u_2^{SQ}. \tag{15}$$

For this inequality to be consistent with (14), it is sufficient that u_2^{SQ} be small relative to u_1^{SQ}. That is, a large enough deterioration of the status quo will make it worthwhile to adopt a reform program with uncertain benefits in the second period. Thus, postponement is optimal, even though it is known that reform will be undertaken on less favorable terms.[13]

The Labán-Sturzenegger model clearly depends on two general features: sufficiently large uncertainty about the post-stabilization environment to make it worthwhile to put up with the status quo temporarily; and, sufficiently large deterioration in the status quo to make adoption of a program eventually optimal. An analogy would be to the need for a patient whose health is poor and getting worse to undergo a very risky operation. Though his chances of surviving the operation may decrease the longer he waits and though he may know he eventually has no choice, he may prefer to remain in the certain state of poor health and put off taking the chance of an unsuccessful operation as long as possible.

On the technical level, the driving force in the model of multiperiod uncertainty with deterioration is basically the same as in problem UB-2, the Orphanides model of optimal waiting. The difference is that one looks not at the benefit from agreeing to reform net of its cost, but at the net benefit relative to that of *no* reform. In the Orphanides model, the utility associated with the status quo is constant over time and reform occurs when the cost of reform is low. In contrast, in the Laban and Sturzenegger model, the key driving force is the deterioration of the status quo. Though the cost of reform is rising over time, the utility associated with the status quo is falling even faster. Therefore even though reform occurs when the cost is high relative to the benefit u^B (addressing the criticism of the Orphanides model), it could be better characterized as occurring when the net benefit of reform *relative* to the status quo is high.[14]

Though the basic argument as to why a socially beneficial reform is delayed is the same in a technical sense, the underlying economics are quite different. One model has reform occurring at good times, the other at bad times. Moreover, the deterioration is endogenous, rather than reflecting exogenous factors: in Labán-Sturzenegger it is the financial adaptation often seen in high inflation countries. This adaptation is beneficial for the individual, but there is a negative externality in that it further drives up inflation, which is costly to society.[15]

The structure of both models also implies that reform occurs when it is socially optimal, in the sense of maximizing expected welfare. Hence the Labán-Sturzenegger model is more like problem UB-1 than the Fernandez-Rodrik model per se, since, as was noted above, the results of the Fernandez-Rodrik model depended on the existence of another type of agent who benefits from reform with certainty. Adding such agents to the Labán-Sturzenegger model would make it strictly analogous to Fernandez-Rodrik; specifically, a reform that is expected to benefit more than half of the population could be rejected by majority vote.

2.7   Conclusions

The war-of-attrition and uncertainty-about-net-benefits approaches should be viewed as complementary, each stressing different components of rational delay. First, as already indicated, while in the war-of-attrition model an individual who agrees to bear the cost of a reform program knows what his net benefit will be, central to the Fernandez-Rodrik approach is uncertainty about the net benefits an individual will receive from a reform program. (These needn't be mutually exclusive: in the war-of-attrition model, for example, a group could be uncertain about the net benefit from conceding, though know the benefit from conceding is stochastically dominated by the net benefit if one's opponent concedes.) This brings up another difference between the two models. In the war-of-attrition approach, a reform program must have public good aspects, since the whole driving force is the desire to have some other agent bear the cost of a public good. In the uncertainty-about-individual-benefits approach, the "good" in question could be purely private; there need be no public good aspect to a reform program, since the allocation of costs is not the driving force, though in general there will be.

Finally, there is a difference in the decision process by which a reform program is adopted. In the war-of-attrition approach, the consensus nature of the decision to adopt a reform is crucial to the story, with all parties agreeing on how the burden of adjustments is to be divided after one group has "conceded" by agreeing to bear a disproportionate share of the cost. As indicated in the previous section, this may be consistent with several formal models of decision-making. In the uncertainty-about-individual-benefits approach, reforms are adopted by majority vote, modelled possibly in terms of a median voter. Here too, other formal methods of decision-making are possible, with the key point being that individual inputs into decisions depend on the assessment of their own benefits.

In the final analysis, however, it is a similarity of outlook between the two approaches which should be stressed. Both models assign a central role to heterogeneity and the conflict of interests this implies. In the absence of this conflict, there would be no delay or failure in adopting a welfare-improving reform. Both models depend on the inability of fully cooperative behavior among groups (no possibility of equal share of burden in the war-of-attrition model, no ex-post compensatory transfers in the uncertainty about benefits model). This simply reflects the basic insight, namely that inherent conflict of interest in allocating the net benefit or cost of reform is a crucial factor in the failure of countries to enact reforms.

Notes

I wish to thank my discussants Jon Faust and Oleh Havrylyshyn for useful comments.

1. A leading example would be the failure to cut the budget deficit and reduce explosive rates of monetary growth in many episodes of hyperinflation.

2. One should note however that clever (and often not-so-clever) politicians try to avoid taking action when it is clear what should be done by claiming that the correct course of action is in fact far from clear. Hence, pleading ignorance about what needs to be done is often a smokescreen for unwillingness to take actions.

3. In *War and Peace*, the Russian general Kutuzov argues against pursuing Napoleon in his retreat from Moscow on the grounds he has been defeated and further action would be counterproductive, "Patience and time are my warriors,... A lump of snow cannot be melted instantaneously. There is a certain time limit in less than which no amount of heat can melt the snow. On the contrary the greater the heat the more solidified the remaining snow becomes."

4. Akerlof (1991) presents an insightful discussion and modeling of procrastination.

5. Let agent j's decision be characterized by $\hat{c}_j$, such that $\hat{s} = 1$ if $c_j < \hat{c}_j$. Agent i chooses s_i to maximize his expected utility, which can be written

$$EU_i = \int_{c_j=c}^{\hat{c}_j} u_i(s_i, \hat{s}_j = 1, c_i)\, dP(c) + \int_{c_j}^{\bar{c}} u_I(s_i, \hat{s}_j = 0, c_i)\, dP(c)$$

$$= \int (1 - c_i s_i)\, dP(c) + \int (s_i - c_i s_i)\, dP(c)$$

$$= z_j(1 - c_i s_i) + (1 - z_j)(s_i - c_i s_i).$$

It follows that $s_i = 0 \Rightarrow EU_i = z_j$, and $x_i = 1 \Rightarrow EU_i = 1 - c_i$. Therefore $s_i = 1$ if and only if $1 - c_i > z_j$.

6. It is assumed here that individuals view themselves as identical ex-ante, that is, that they have no prior knowledge about the likelihood that they will be among the gainers from the reform.

7. A crucial assumption for this result is the impossibility of ex-post transfers from winners to losers.

8. One may easily verify that the second-order condition holds, so that the solution is a maximum.

9. $T(c)$ monotonically increasing in c follows from the nature of the optimization problem.

10. This argument depends on the specific role that a crisis plays in a war-of-attrition model and should not be taken to imply that crises increase welfare in general in economies where necessary reforms are delayed.

11. If the other agent has a cost above the critical level, so that he refuses to pay, the first agent, with a cost below the critical level, will pay the full amount, since he immediately learns his opponent cannot be induced to pay anything.

12. When programs are multi-stage there is also a stopping rule whereby it is optimal to abandon a program already in place if reserves fall too sharply after a stabilization program has been started.

13. As indicated in the discussion of problem UB-1, $x > 0$ is not necessary to get these results, though rising adoption costs strengthen the crucial role played by deterioration of the status quo in this model.

14. Velasco (1992) presents a model of delayed reform based on agents drawing resources from a common pool, the government. When the government is resource-rich, optimal individual behavior is non-cooperative, and each agent tries to appropriate as much as possible. Over time government debt grows, meaning that there are fewer resources to be appropriated. The loss associated with no cooperation is therefore large and cooperative behavior (leading to reform) can be sustained.

15. Mondino, Sturzenegger, and Tommasi (1994) present a model where dynamic financial adaptation combined with non-cooperative behavior in demanding subsidies (which are covered by inflationary finance) lead to recurrent cycles in inflation acceleration followed by stabilization.

References

Alesina, A. and A. Drazen (1991) "Why are Stabilizations Delayed?" *American Economic Review* 81, December: 1170–88.

Drazen, A. and V. Grilli (1993) "The Benefit of Crises for Economic Reforms," *American Economic Review* 83, June: 598–607.

Fernandez, R. and D. Rodrik (1991) "Resistance to Reform: Status Quo Bias in the Presence of Individual Specific Uncertainty," *American Economic Review* 81, December: 1146–55.

Fudenberg, D. and J. Tirole (1991) *Game Theory*, Cambridge, MA: MIT Press.

Labán, R. and F. Sturzenegger (1994a) "Distributional Conflict, Financial Adaptation and Delayed Stabilization," working paper, forthcoming, *Economics and Politics*.

——— (1994b) "Fiscal Conservatism as a Response to the Debt Crisis," working paper, forthcoming, *Journal of Development Economics*.

Mondino, G., F. Sturzenegger, and M. Tommasi (1994) "Recurrent High Inflation and Stabilization: A Dynamic Game," working paper.

Orphanides, A. (1993) "The Timing of Stabilizations," working paper.

Rodrik, D. (1993) "The Positive Economics of Policy Reform," *American Economic Review* 83, May: 356–61.

Velasco, A. (1992) "A Model of Fiscal Deficits and Delayed Social Reform," working paper.

3

Resistance to Reform: Status Quo Bias in the Presence of Individual-Specific Uncertainty

Raquel Fernandez and
Dani Rodrik

Why do governments so often fail to adopt policies that economists consider to be efficiency-enhancing? This is one of the fundamental questions of political economy. The answer usually relies on what may be called a "nonneutrality" in the way that the gains and losses from the reform are distributed within society: the gainers from the status quo are taken to be politically "strong" and the losers to be politically "weak," thereby preventing the adoption of reform. (Nondistorting transfers would of course short-circuit this problem, but they are usually ruled out as unavailable.) In pressure-group models, this nonneutrality typically expresses itself in the form of differential organizational ability: for example, the gains from the status quo may be concentrated on a small number of individuals while the losses are diffuse, such that free riding hampers the lobbying efforts of the second group to a much greater extent.[1] In voting models, the nonneutrality operates through distributional consequences across individuals, so that the median voter may prefer the status quo to a reform that would increase aggregate real income.[2]

We propose a different source of nonneutrality in this chapter, one that relies on *uncertainty* regarding the distribution of gains and losses from reform. What we will show, specifically, is that there is a bias toward the status quo (and hence against efficiency-enhancing reforms) whenever (some of) the individual gainers and losers from reform cannot be identified beforehand.[3] There are reforms which, once adopted, will receive adequate political support but would have failed to carry the day *ex ante*. Significantly, the result holds even if individuals are risk-neutral, forward-looking, and rational and in the absence of *aggregate* uncertainty regarding the consequences of reform. Moreover, the conclusion does not rely on hysteresis due to sunk costs.

Originally published in *American Economic Review* 81, no. 5 (1991): 1146–55. Reprinted with permission.

While the logic is general, we will use trade liberalization as an example to motivate our approach and the specific model. Trade reform is a particularly interesting example because there is possibly no area in which there is greater consensus among economists.[4] Despite the well-known gains from trade, however, trade liberalization is politically one of the most contentious actions that a government can take. Historically, significant liberalizations have almost always been associated with changes in political regime or else have been undertaken at a point of economic crisis. There is by now a large literature on the political economy of trade policy.[5]

A striking paradox, particularly in developing countries, is that while trade reform typically turns out to be a boon to large segments of the private sector, these same groups are rarely enthusiastic about reform early on. This is a pattern observed in Taiwan and South Korea (early 1960's), Chile (1970's), and Turkey (1980's), the leading cases of trade liberalization in the developing world. In all three cases, reform was imposed by authoritarian regimes and against the wishes of business, even though business emerged as the staunchest defender of outward orientation once the policies were in place.[6] Existing models of trade reform cannot account for such apparently inconsistent behavior. However, the anomaly is consistent with the results of our model. In each of these cases, there existed considerable uncertainty regarding the identity of the eventual beneficiaries (and losers) from the reform. As with any largescale price reform, it was difficult to predict *ex ante* precisely which sectors and which entrepreneurs would be the winners. In such a setting, the nonneutrality identified in this paper comes into play in full force: when individuals do not know how they will fare under a reform, aggregate support for reform can be lower than what it would have been under complete information, even when individuals are risk-neutral and there is no aggregate uncertainty. Moreover, the role of uncertainty in determining the outcomes is not symmetric, since reforms that are initially rejected will continue to be so in the future while reforms that are initially accepted may find themselves reversed over time.

In section 3.1, we provide a simple, diagrammatic exposition which shows the logic of the argument in as transparent a manner as possible. In sections 3.2 and 3.3, we develop a model which embeds the results within standard trade theory and demonstrates that the results can obtain within a general-equilibrium framework. We conclude the chapter with section 3.4.

3.1   The Argument

The maintained assumption in this chapter is that a policy reform is more likely to be adopted the larger is the number of individuals in favor of it. For concreteness, it is convenient to use the language of majority voting (although our argument will also hold for some other social-choice mechanisms).

Figure 3.1A shows schematically an economy in which individuals are aligned uniformly on a continuum between 0 and 1, as represented by the horizontal axis. The midpoint of the axis is indicated by "M." We assume that the economy has two productive sectors, sectors W (for winners) and L (for losers). D represents the demarcation point between the status quo allocation of individuals in the two sectors: individuals in sector L are located to the left of D, and individuals in sector W are to the right of D. As drawn, a majority of the individuals are in the L sector prior to reform.

Now consider a reform that, if adopted, would increase the return to W-sector individuals, lower the return to L-sector individuals, and draw individuals from the second sector to the first. The top panel of figure 3.1A shows the distributional outcome, with the two boxes representing the gains and losses accruing to individuals on different segments of the continuum. The magnitudes of gains and losses are indicated by the numbers corresponding to each box. All individuals already in the W sector naturally gain, but there are also some gainers among individuals who were previously employed in the other sector. Since the reform is taken to enhance efficiency, the gainers' box is larger in area than the losers' box (the net gain is 0.04). Notice that, as the figure is drawn, gainers constitute a majority. In the presence of complete certainty, the reform in question would therefore be adopted: the potential winners in the L sector would join W-sector individuals to pass the reform.

Now suppose that the individuals in the L sector do not know who among them will be winners and who will be losers and that *ex ante* they consider it equally likely that any single one of them will be a winner. All that they know is the aggregate number (or the proportion) of winners. Will there still be a majority in favor of reform? Note that uncertainty renders all L-sector individuals identical *ex ante*. To know which way to vote, they will compute the expected benefit from reform. The expected benefit equals the weighted average of the gains and losses, with the weights equaling the probability of each outcome occurring. The lower panel of figure 3.1A shows that the expected benefit is negative (-0.067 per L-sector individual). Since the L sector represents a majority of the

A.   Majority is better off with reform ex post:

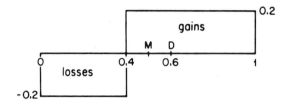

But majority votes against reform ex ante:

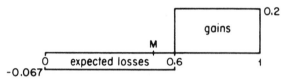

B.   Majority is worse-off with reform ex post:

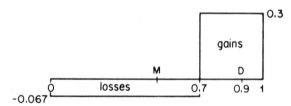

But majority votes for reform ex ante:

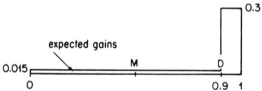

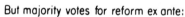

Figure 3.1
Gains and losses from reform

economy at the outset, the proposed reform would not be adopted. The losses to the many are pulling down the gains to the few, leaving an expected loss for all but the individuals already in the W sector. Note that the reform is not adopted even though (i) individuals are risk-neutral, (ii) a majority would vote for the reform *ex post*, and (iii) both (i) and (ii) are common knowledge.

This example establishes that the presence of individual-specific uncertainty can distort aggregate preferences. However, it does not establish that there will necessarily be a bias against reform. One can also construct examples in which this type of uncertainty leads to the adoption of a reform that turns out to be unpopular *ex post*.[7] Figure 3.1B shows such an example. The top panel once again displays the actual outcomes under reform, with only a minority benefiting this time. Under certainty, therefore, this reform would not command majority support. However, when L-sector individuals are all equally uncertain about how they will fare under reform, the outcome could be different. When there is uncertainty, the expected benefit could be positive for all. This is shown in the lower panel of figure 3.1B. The expected gain per L-sector individual can be calculated to be 0.015 in this case: $[(0.3 \times 0.2) + (-0.067 \times 0.7)] \times (0.9)^{-1}$.

There is an important asymmetry between the two cases, however. In the second case (in which a reform is passed and turns out to be unpopular), information is revealed as to how individuals actually fare under the reform. Therefore, if there is ever a second vote or a chance to reconsider, the reform may be repealed. In the other case (in which reform is not passed), no new information is revealed, since the status quo is maintained. This asymmetry between the two cases leads to a status quo bias.

This may appear to be a contrived example with many loose threads. For example, what keeps returns in the two sectors from being equalized in equilibrium, and is that necessary to the argument? What is the source of uncertainty regarding the identities of gainers and losers? As we will show in the next section, it is possible to generalize the example and to place it in the context of a simple general-equilibrium model.

3.2   The Model

Consider a two-sector perfectly competitive economy in which each sector produces a distinct good, X or Y, using one factor of production, labor (L), and with constant-returns-to-scale technology. There is no harm in thinking of X and Y as aggregates made up of individual commodities.

Workers (or individuals) in each sector can by the same logic be interpreted as producing different products. Thus,

$$X = L_x/a_x$$

$$Y = L_y/a_y$$

and

$$L_x + L_y = \bar{L}$$

where $a_j > 0$, $j = x, y$.

Labor cannot relocate between sectors costlessly. The cost to an individual's relocation is modeled as having two components: θ, a known general investment cost incurred prior to switching sectors, and c_i, an individual-specific cost element incurred only upon actually switching sectors. The value of the second component, however, is unknown to the individual and is revealed only if the general investment cost is incurred. Only the distribution of c_i, $f(c)$, is known.[8] The interpretation behind this formulation is that workers have different abilities and productivities and, therefore, that their "net" wages in another sector will differ. Workers cannot know what their true abilities are before sinking the cost θ, which can also be thought of as investment in sector-specific human capital.[9] Alternatively, entrepreneurs may not have the information necessary to be able to determine precisely what their firm's cost structure would be in the new industry. Only after obtaining this information at cost θ is their cost structure revealed. This is a plausible way of capturing the uncertainty that is likely to surround each individual's prospects under reform.

Workers must therefore make two decisions: (i) whether to undertake the general investment cost and, if the first is decided affirmatively, then (ii) whether to switch sectors and thereby incur the cost c_i. To find the optimal choice, we start with the second decision. A worker who has invested θ will choose to switch from industry y to industry x if the difference between wages in the two industries is larger than her c_i. Thus, for any wage difference, there exists a level of c, $\tilde{c}$, such that all workers with $c_i \leq \tilde{c}$ will switch to industry x. Therefore, let

$$\tilde{c} = \tilde{w}_x - \tilde{w}_y \tag{1}$$

where $\tilde{w}_j$ is the equilibrium wage in sector j that results from the reform.

Ex ante, workers are identical and atomistic. Consequently, a worker in sector Y will decide to incur the general investment cost if her expected net benefit from doing so is nonnegative, that is, if

$$F(\tilde{c})\left[\tilde{w}_x - \int_{\underline{c}}^{\tilde{c}} f(c)c\,dc[F(\tilde{c})]^{-1}\right] + [1 - F(\tilde{c})]\tilde{w}_y - \theta \geq \tilde{w}_y \tag{2}$$

where $\underline{c} \geq 0$ is the infimum over the values taken by c_i and $F(c)$ is the cumulative distribution function. The left-hand side represents expected income when θ is incurred, while the right-hand side is the (certain) level of income in the absence of the investment. Rearranging terms, we obtain

$$[\tilde{w}_x - \tilde{w}_y]F(\tilde{c}) - \int_{\underline{c}}^{\tilde{c}} f(c)c\,dc - \theta \geq 0. \tag{3}$$

In order to illustrate our argument most clearly, we consider a country that is small in world markets, so relative prices within each aggregate are fixed by world price ratios. Let this country initially have a tariff of a magnitude such that

$$P^0 = a_x/a_y$$

where $P = p_x/p_y$ is the (tariff-inclusive) relative price of good X in terms of good Y. We normalize the domestic price of the imported good, good Y, to equal 1. Thus, decreases in the value of the tariff have the effect of increasing the relative price of good X. Labor's initial distribution between sectors, L_y^0 and L_x^0, is given by history. Perfect competition in the labor market ensures that

$$w_j = p_j/a_j \qquad j = x, y. \tag{4}$$

Therefore, given the initial tariff level, $w_x^0 = w_y^0$. Note that w_y is invariant with respect to P and equal to $1/a_y$.

Let us analyze the behavior of this economy with respect to changes in the tariff rate commencing at P^0. As the tariff rate falls, $\tilde{w}_x - \tilde{w}_y$ increases, but initially no individual will choose to undertake the general investment cost. Simultaneously, the value of $\tilde{c}$ increases, as $d\tilde{c}/dP = d\tilde{w}_x/dP = 1/a_x$. Note that the left-hand side (LHS) of (3) is increasing with P (i.e., $d(\text{LHS})/dP = F(\tilde{c})/a_x > 0$). Therefore, at a sufficiently high relative price, P^*, all y-sector individuals are indifferent between incurring the investment cost and not. Those individuals who choose to undertake the general investment cost and have a $c_i \leq c^*$ will move to sector x (where c^* is the $\tilde{c}$ associated with P^*).[10] Any further increases in the relative price have all y-sector individuals strictly preferring to incur the general investment cost

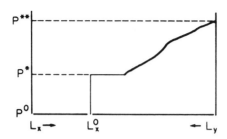

Figure 3.2
Allocation of labor between sectors as a function of relative prices

and, as $\tilde{c}$ and the relative wage of sector x increase monotonically with P, further labor reallocation (see fig. 3.2).

We wish to show that there exist circumstances in which trade reform (in the manner of a tariff decrease) would be voted in under complete certainty as to the *ex post* identity of individuals but would be rejected under uncertainty, despite the fact that individuals are risk-neutral. Consider, therefore, an initiative to change prices in this economy from P^0 to P^* by reducing the tariff level accordingly. Since P^* is the price ratio at which all individuals are exactly indifferent between undertaking the investment cost and not, c^* is exactly that level of $\tilde{c}$ such that

$$\tilde{c}F(\tilde{c}) - \int_{\underline{c}}^{\tilde{c}} f(c)c\,dc - \theta = 0.$$

If asked to vote on whether to undertake this reform, all individuals in sector y would vote against this proposal. To see this, note that the purchasing power of the wage earned by an individual who remains in sector y is unchanged in terms of good Y and is strictly lower in terms of good X. Given that at P^* y-sector individuals are indifferent between undertaking the investment cost (under the assumption that the reform will go through) and not investing and remaining in sector y under the new price system, these individuals' expected real income from the reform must be lower than that resulting from remaining with the status quo. Therefore, if $L_y^0 \geq L_x^0$, this measure would be rejected by majority vote.

If, on the other hand, individuals knew *ex ante* what their identities would be under the new regime (i.e., if each individual knew her c_i) and were then asked if they would be willing to pay $\theta + c_i$ in order to switch sectors, there may now be some y-sector individuals who would be willing to do so and, accordingly, willing to vote in favor of the reform.[11]

That is, it is easy to show that, in general, there exist c_i such that

$$v(P^*, w_x^* - \theta - c_i) > v(P^0, w_y^0)$$

where $v(\cdot)$ is the individual's indirect utility function.[12]

In order to provide a clear example, we further specify some characteristics of this economy: we assume that individuals' preferences are identical, risk-neutral, and given by

$$V(P, I) = v(P)I = \frac{I}{P^\gamma}$$

where I is the individual's income level and $1 \geq \gamma > 0$. The function $f(c)$ is assumed to be distributed uniformly on the interval $[0, \tilde{c}]$, so $f(c) = 1/\tilde{c}$, and thus, $\tilde{c} = (2\theta\tilde{c})^{0.5}$.

Note first that $w_x^* = P^*/a_x = w_y^* + \tilde{c} = w_y^0 + \tilde{c} = (1/a_y) + \tilde{c}$ and, therefore, $P^* = P^0 + \tilde{c}a_x$. Thus, we must show that there exist c_i such that

$$v(P^*)[w_y^0 + \tilde{c} - \theta - c_i] > v(P^0)w_y^0.$$

That is, we must show

$$(P^*)^{-\gamma}[w_y^0 + \tilde{c} - \theta - c_i] > (P^0)^{-\gamma}w_y^0.$$

Noting that P^*/P^0 can be written as $1 - \tilde{c}a_y$ yields

$$1/a_y + (2\theta\tilde{c})^{-0.5} - \theta - c_i > (1/a_y)[1 + a_y(2\theta\tilde{c})^{-0.5}]^\gamma$$

which can be satisfied for many parameter values (e.g., $a_y = \theta = 1$, $\tilde{c} = 2$, $\gamma = 0.5$).[13]

3.3   Dynamic Considerations

The model discussed above establishes that certain reforms that would have been popular *ex post* may not muster support *ex ante*. So far, it does not establish a *bias* toward protection, however. As mentioned in section 3.1, it is possible to come up with instances in which reform is embraced initially, only to prove unpopular once the identities of winners and losers are revealed. In a static setting, the logic of uncertainty works symmetrically, making both cases "equally" likely.

There is good reason to suspect, however, that in practice there will exist an asymmetry in favor of the status quo (protection). The asymmetry arises from the fact that new information is revealed in the case in which a reform is initially embraced and instituted, while no such thing happens when the reform is rejected from the outset. Therefore, if given a second chance, the electorate may reverse a reform that has been "mistakenly" embraced. Moreover, when considering a set of reforms that may possess a short life span due to the fact that it will be overturned in the future, rational forward-looking individuals may vote against reforms that initially appear to benefit them. By contrast, if an electorate initially chooses to reject a reform, the electorate will not change its vote. since no new information is revealed in the latter case, an electorate that has refused reform once will continue to do so no matter how many times it is given an opportunity to reconsider.[14] Thus, there is an important asymmetry between the time consistency of the status quo and the time consistency of certain reforms.

We will now show (i) that reforms, even if instituted with majority support, may be short-lived and (ii) that there is a tendency toward inertia (toward the maintenance of the status quo) in these economies. To introduce dynamic considerations into the framework, we turn to a two-period version of the model. Individuals are able to vote at the beginning of each period on whether to institute (or continue with) the reform during that period. A decision not to continue with a reform that was previously instituted is taken to imply a return to the original relative prices. In each period, after voting, individuals decide whether or not to incur the investment cost θ (paid up front in its entirety) and, as before, whether or not to switch sectors and incur the individual-specific cost. They then earn the corresponding wage in that period. The possible outcomes are exhibited in figure 3.3.

There are four possibilities: (i) reform is first instituted and then reversed because it proves unpopular; (ii) reform is instituted and sustained because it proves popular: (iii) reform is always opposed; and (iv) reform is first

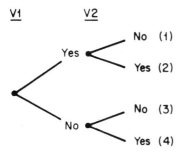

Figure 3.3
Possible outcomes when individuals vote in each of two periods

rejected and then accepted. While (i)–(iii) are possible equilibrium outcomes, (iv) is not if, in this two-period model, the second period is not lengthier than the first.

The problem posed by the existence of a period significantly lengthier than any other is that the possibility of strategic voting is introduced. In our two-period example this would entail all individuals voting against the reform in the first period and in favor of the reform in the second since, foreseeing that once uncertainty is resolved a majority will overturn the reform (case (i)), individuals prefer to reject the reform in the first round in order to institute it in the second round, thereby preserving the reform for a greater length of time. In the more plausible case of periods of equal length, strategic voting of this sort will never occur. Case (iv) will never be an equilibrium, since if voters reject the reform no information is revealed and, consequently, there is no incentive to accept the reform the following period. Since the existence of periods of uneven length is rather artificial, we henceforth rule it out, eliminating (iv) as a possible equilibrium outcome. Apart from this restriction, nothing qualitative in our results depends on the number of time periods or on the finiteness of individuals' horizons. Note, therefore, the bias toward the status quo: reforms that are initially rejected continue to be so, whereas some reforms that were previously accepted cannot be sustained.

To make the preceding discussion a bit more concrete, consider the same example as in the previous section, with identical parameters and with the same set of initial conditions. Suppose that the effect of the reform under consideration is to change relative prices from P^0 to $P' > P^* > P^0$. P' is such that sector-y (and, of course, then also sector-x) individuals would be willing to vote in favor of this reform if they thought that, once instituted, the reform would be permanent. Thus, P' must satisfy

$$v(P')\left\{ [w'_x(1+\delta) - \theta]F(\tilde{c}) - \int_0^{\tilde{c}} cf(c)\, dc + [w'_y(1+\delta) - \theta][1 - F(\tilde{c})] \right\}$$
$$> v(P^0)w_y^0(1+\delta) \tag{5}$$

where w'_j is the equilibrium wage in sector j associated with P'. The terms in the braces constitute the expected income from the reform for an individual initially in sector y, and the expression on the right-hand side of the inequality is a sector-y individual's status quo utility. Note that the wage earnings of an individual are now multiplied by $1 + \delta$, which is the appropriate discounting of wages earned over two periods ($0 < \delta < 1$ is the individual's discount factor).[15] Letting P' be such that $\tilde{c} < \bar{c}$, expression (5) can be rewritten as

$$v(P')\left[\tilde{c}(1+\delta)F(\tilde{c}) - \int_0^{\tilde{c}} cf(c)\,dc + w_y'(1+\delta) - \theta\right] > v(P^0)w_y^0(1+\delta)$$

and $\tilde{c}$ can be expressed as

$$\tilde{c} = \frac{a_y P' - a_x}{a_y a_x}.$$

Recalling that $w_y' = w_y^0 = a_y^{-1}$ and performing the appropriate substitutions yields

$$\left(\frac{(0.5+\delta)[a_y P' - a_x]^2}{[a_y a_x]^2 \tilde{c}} - \theta\right)a_y(1+\delta)^{-1} + 1 > \left(\frac{P'}{P^0}\right)^\gamma.$$

The above condition ensures that all y-sector individuals would vote in favor of a permanent trade reform that changes relative prices from P^0 to P', since their *ex ante* expected utility from this reform is greater than the level of utility enjoyed under the status quo. If, however, $F(\tilde{c})L_y^0 - L_x^0 < [1 - F(\tilde{c})]L_y^0$, then, since the individuals who have remained in sector y now enjoy a lower real wage than before, in the second period the majority of the population will vote against the reform and in favor of a return to the status quo.[16]

It should be noted that, although it may appear that reform would always be supported for a sufficiently large P, this is misleading. The size of the reform is constrained by the initial level of trade restrictions.

Will individuals still vote for the reform in period 1, knowing that there will be a return to the status quo following the second vote? Forward-looking individuals will realize that the first-period vote now presents a choice between the status quo and *temporary* reform. They will vote for the latter only if

$$v(P')\left[w_x'F(\tilde{c}) - \int_0^{\tilde{c}} cf(c)\,dc + w_y'[1 - F(\tilde{c})] - \theta\right] > v(P^0)w_y^0. \tag{6}$$

Notice that second-period wages are equal across sectors (given a return to the status quo).[17] Therefore, y-sector workers will vote for reform only if the expected first-period benefits exceed the costs. Since this condition is more restrictive than that of equation (5), as the differential between w_x and w_y now accrues for one period only, there will be cases in which a reform will be rejected even though it would have been embraced had it been perceived as permanent. Individuals will sometimes find it unprofitable to incur the investment costs for a transitory reform and, hence, will vote against the reform from the outset. However, the lower is δ (i.e., the more the future is discounted or the greater the interval between votes), the more likely it is that a reform that is accepted when permanent will still be accepted when temporary.

3.4   Concluding Remarks

Our framework has a number of interesting features. First, it shows how uncertainty regarding the identities of gainers and losers can prevent an efficiency-enhancing reform from being adopted, even in cases in which reform would prove quite popular after the fact. As the extended version of the model shows, there is a bias towards the status quo. Second, the model suggests that an appropriately large reform will be needed to get individuals to respond in the desired manner.[18] This is a conclusion shared with some other positive models of reform in which either hysteresis asymmetric information plays a role (see Rodrik, 1989a,b). Third, our model helps explain an apparent puzzle: in countries like Korea, Chile, and Turkey, radical trade reforms introduced by autocratic regimes have not collapsed (and indeed have turned out to be popular), even though they had little support prior to reform. Our framework makes clear why *ex ante* hostility to reform and *ex post* support are quite consistent with each other.

It should be clear that our argument does not rest on the assumption of a democratic voting mechanism. One could also, for example, obtain the same qualitative results if decisions were made according to the preferences of a median interest group. What is crucial to our results is that there be no mechanism that costlessly translates the intensity with which individuals favor a proposed reform into outcomes (e.g., frictionless lobbying). Such a mechanism would, of course, implement all reforms that increase efficiency.

The question may arise as to whether feasible transfer schemes exist to institute otherwise unpopular trade reforms by popular support. In most models, the answer would be trivially "yes." Here, there is an important consideration that constrains the use of such "bribing" mechanisms. Any such transfer scheme may be time-inconsistent, providing incentives to the *ex post* majority to renege on the agreement. Of course, such questions can be settled only by examining the equilibria of particular "bribing" games.

It should also be obvious that, while we have selected trade reform as an example, the logic applies to any reform that creates a distribution of gains and losses whose incidence is partially uncertain. Since this is a characteristic of any important policy change one can think of—whether it be macroeconomic stabilization in developing countries, welfare reform in advanced industrial countries, or transition to a market economy in socialist countries—the general principle established here with respect to the obstinacy of the status quo has wide relevance.

An interesting extension which we do not explore in this chapter would be to endogenize the set of reforms that are politically feasible and to allow individuals to choose not only between a specific reform and the status quo, but also among alternative reforms. A model with greater institutional structure would be needed to determine how these reforms are initially selected.

Notes

Raquel Fernandez's work was supported by NSF grant SES 89-08390 and by a Hoover Fellowship. Dani Rodrik's work was supported by the World Bank through a research project on Sustainability of Trade Reform (RPO 675-32) and by an NBER Olin Fellowship. We thank Loreto Lira for research assistance, the Japanese Corporate Associates Program of the Kennedy School for financial support, and Alberto Alesina, Guillermo Calvo, Avinash Dixit, Konstantine Gatsios, Larry Karp, Anne Krueger, Timur Kuran, Marc Lindenberg, Mike Mussa, three referees, and participants at the NBER Conference on Political Economics and at seminars at Boston University, Chicago Business School, Dartmouth College, The Federal Reserve Board, Harvard University, The International Monetary Fund, NBER Summer Institute, and Syracuse University for useful comments.

1. See Rodrik (1986) for another example.

2. We thank Jagdish Bhagwati for suggesting the formulation of our problem in terms of a "nonneutrality."

3. Anne O. Krueger (1989) coins the phrase "identity bias" to describe a somewhat related problem, one that arises from the possibility that the precise knowledge of the losers' identities evokes a more sympathetic response from the general population toward their plight than if their identities were unknown. This is a psychological Schellingesque distinction between statistical and individual-specific information which differs from ours (see Thomas C. Schelling, 1984, chap. 5). See also William Samuelson and Richard Zeckhauser (1988) for a broad discussion of the sources of status quo bias at the level of individual decision-making, and Timur Kuran (1988) for a review and critique of the related literature.

4. Even when the strictly economic case for free trade fails, economists are generally quick to embrace it for the same practical reason that Churchill embraced democracy, namely as the lesser evil among possible alternatives. See, for example, Paul Krugman (1987).

5. See Robert E. Baldwin (1985, chap. 1) and Bhagwati (1988) and the references therein. On median-voter models of trade policy, see in particular Wolfgang Mayer (1984) and Mayer and Raymond Riezman (1987).

6. For more detail on these cases, see our working paper (Fernandez and Rodrik, 1990).

7. Bhagwati (1981), for example, argues that elites in developing countries may sometimes support policy reforms which end up hurting them due to the policy-maker's occasional inability to establish the distributional impact of a reform.

8. For simplicity of exposition, we are assuming that the relocation cost is independent of the sector from which the individual is relocating.

9. However, individuals who desire to switch sectors are not free to do so without incurring both costs (i.e., were they to do so, it is assumed that their marginal product would be zero).

10. This zero-one behavior with respect to undertaking the general investment cost is a product of the linearity of technology. A decreasing marginal product of labor, as in the Ricardo-Viner model, would exhibit a continuously increasing proportion of individuals willing to incur the general investment cost as a function of relative prices.

11. We have confined our attention to a positive analysis of status quo bias. While the reforms that we consider are efficiency-enhancing, they are not Pareto-efficient, given the assumed absence of lump-sum transfers.

12. Throughout this discussion, in order to further simplify exposition, we assume that tariff revenue is distributed solely among those workers originally located in sector x.

13. Note that if $\gamma = 1$ (i.e., individuals only consume good X), then the above inequality can never be satisfied, since the wage increase in sector x would leave individuals with the same real wage as prior to the reform, and moreover, the individual would have paid the general and individual-specific investment cost.

14. This statement is subject to a caveat, as will be made clear in the exposition of the argument.

15. As expressed in (5), c_i is only incurred in the first period. We could have considered c_i to be incurred in each period without altering any of our conclusions.

16. A necessary condition for this phenomenon to occur is $\tilde{c} < \hat{c}/2$.

17. This allows us to bypass the question of whether sector-x individuals who have relocated in sector y must incur any costs if they wish to return to sector x.

18. However, this is no longer true if individuals are risk-averse; a large reform would magnify the uncertainty and could solidify the preference for the status quo on account of the greater risk.

References

Baldwin, Robert E., *The Political Economy of U.S. Import Policy*, Cambridge, MA: MIT Press, 1985.

Bhagwati, Jagdish, "Need for Reforms in Underdeveloped Countries" (Comment on Gunnar Myrdal), in Sven Grassman and Erik Lundberg, eds., *The World Economic Order: Past and Prospects*, New York: St. Martin's Press, 1981, pp. 526–33.

————, *Protectionism*, Cambridge, MA: MIT Press, 1988.

Fernandez, Raquel and Rodrik, Dani, "Why Is Trade Reform So Unpopular? On Status Quo Bias in Policy Reforms," NBER (Cambridge, MA) Working Paper No. 3269, 1990.

Krueger, Anne O., "Asymmetries in Policy Between Exportables and Import-Competing Goods," NBER (Cambridge, MA) Working Paper No. 2904, March 1989.

Krugman, Paul, "Is Free Trade Passé?" *Journal of Economic Perspectives*, Fall 1987, *1*, 131–44.

Kuran, Timur, "The Tenacious Past: Theories of Personal and Collective Conservatism," *Journal of Economic Behavior and Organization*, September 1988, *10*, 143–71.

Mayer, Wolfgang, "Endogenous Tariff Formation," *American Economic Review*, December 1984, *74*, 970–85.

———— and Riezman, Raymond, "Endogenous Choice of Trade Policy Instruments," *Journal of International Economics*, November 1987, *23*, 377–81.

Rodrik, Dani, "Tariffs, Subsidies, and Welfare with Endogenous Policy," *Journal of International Economics*, November 1986, *21*, 285–99.

————, (1989a) "Promises, Promises: Credible Policy Reform via Signalling," *Economic Journal*, September 1989, *99*, 756–72.

————, (1989b) "Policy Uncertainty and Private Investment in Developing Countries," NBER (Cambridge, MA) Working Paper No. 2999, June 1989; *Journal of Development Economics*, forthcoming.

Samuelson, William and Zeckhauser, Richard, "Status Quo Bias in Decision Making," *Journal of Risk and Uncertainty*, March 1988, *1*, 7–59.

Schelling, Thomas C., *Choice and Consequence*, Cambridge, MA: Harvard University Press, 1984.

4   Why Are Stabilizations Delayed?

Alberto Alesina and
Allan Drazen

Countries often follow policies which are recognized to be infeasible in the long run for extended periods of time. For instance, large deficits implying an explosive path of government debt are allowed to continue even though it is apparent that such deficits will have to be eliminated sooner or later. A puzzling question is why these countries do not stabilize immediately, once it becomes apparent that current policies are unsustainable and that a change in policy will have to be adopted eventually. Delays in stabilization are particularly inefficient if the longer a country waits the more costly is the policy adjustment needed to stabilize and if the period of instability before the policy change is characterized by economic inefficiencies. Fiscal imbalances are often associated with high and variable inflation; fiscal stabilization also stops inflation. This chapter studies the politico-economic determinants of delays in the adoption of fiscal adjustment programs.

The literature on the prestabilization dynamics implied by an anticipated future stabilization (e.g., Thomas Sargent and Neil Wallace, 1981; Drazen and Elhanan Helpman, 1987, 1990) assumes that the timing of the future policy change is exogenous.[1] Since in these models the long-run infeasibility of current policy is known from the beginning, what is missing is an explanation of why the infeasible policy is not abandoned immediately. Explanations of the timing of stabilization based on irrationality, such as waiting to stabilize until "things get really bad," are unconvincing: since the deterioration in the fiscal position can be foreseen, the argument depends on countries that delay stabilization being more irrational than others. Explanations that give a key role to exogenous shocks leave unexplained both why countries do not stabilize as soon as unfavorable

Originally published in *American Economic Review* 81, no. 5 (1991): 1170–88. Reprinted with permission.

shocks occur and why stabilizations that are undertaken often do not seem to coincide with significant observable changes in external circumstances.[2]

This chapter argues that the timing of stabilizations and, in particular, their postponement cannot be easily understood in terms of models in which the policymaker is viewed as a social planner maximizing the welfare of a representative individual. On the contrary, heterogeneity in the population is crucial in explaining these delays. In many cases, the process leading to a stabilization can be described as a war of attrition between different socioeconomic groups with conflicting distributional objectives. Delays in stabilization arise due to a political stalemate over distribution; stabilizations occur when a political consolidation leads to a resolution of the distributional conflict.

More specifically, even though it is agreed that stabilization requires a change in fiscal policy to eliminate budget deficits, there may be disagreement about how the burden of the policy change is to be shared. When socioeconomic groups perceive the possibility of shifting this burden elsewhere, each groups may attempt to wait the others out. This war of attrition ends, and a stabilization is enacted, when certain groups "concede" and allow their political opponents to decide on the allocation of the burden of the fiscal adjustment. Concession may occur via legislative agreement, electoral outcomes, or ceding power of decree to policy-makers.

We present a simple model of delayed stabilization due to a war of attrition and derive the expected time of stabilization as a function of characteristics of the economy, including parameters meant to capture, in a rough way, the degree of political polarization. For example, the more uneven is the expected allocation of the costs of stabilization when it occurs, the later is the expected date of a stabilization. Hence, if unequal distribution of the burden of taxation is an indicator of political polarization, more politically polarized countries will experience longer periods of instability.[3] More institutional adaptation to the distortions associated with instability also implies later expected stabilization, while partial attempts to control the deficit prior to a full stabilization may make the expected time of full stabilization either earlier or later. We also show that, if it is the poor who suffer most in the prestabilization period, they bear the largest share of the costs of stabilization. The distribution of income is also related to the timing of stabilization. Conditions are derived under which a more unequal distribution of income implies either an earlier or later stabilization.

Our approach is related to the literature on dynamic games between a monetary and a fiscal authority with conflicting objectives (Sargent, 1986;

Guido Tabellini, 1986, 1987; Michael Loewy, 1988). In that literature, a war of attrition is played between the fiscal and monetary authorities: an unsustainable combination of monetary and fiscal policies is in place until one side concedes.[4] Our shift in emphasis to a game between interest groups has several justifications. First, the assumption that the monetary authority is independent of the fiscal authority is unrealistic for most countries with serious problems of economic instability. Second, the difference in the objective functions of different branches of government may be related to their representing different constituencies; here, we tackle issues of heterogeneity directly.[5]

The chapter is organized as follows. Section 4.1 summarizes some regularities observed in a number of stabilizations which suggest using a war of attrition as a model. Section 4.2 presents a stylized model of stabilizations based on the empirical observations and shows how delays result from individually rational behavior. Section 4.3 presents comparative-static results on how the expected date of stabilization will differ in economies with different characteristics. The final section suggests extensions.

4.1 Delayed Stabilization as a War of Attrition

No single model can explain every episode of delay in enacting a macroeconomic stabilization. Historical and current evidence suggests, however, that in many cases of instability due to severe fiscal imbalances, it was disagreement over the allocation of the burden of fiscal change that delayed the adoption of a new policy. We begin by noting common features of the stabilization process across several episodes, features which suggest modeling stabilization as a war of attrition.

1. There is agreement on the need for a fiscal change but a political stalemate over how the burden of higher taxes or expenditure cuts should be allocated. In the political debate over stabilization, this distributional question is central.

Sharp disagreements over allocating the burden of paying for the war were common in the belligerent countries after World War I (Alesina, 1988; Barry Eichengreen, 1990). For example, in France, Germany, and Italy, the political struggle over fiscal policy was not about the need for reducing enormous budget deficits or the debt overhang, but over which groups should bear higher taxes to achieve that end. Parties of the right favored proportional income and indirect taxes; parties of the left proposed capital levies and more progressive income taxes (Robert Haig, 1929; Charles Maier, 1975).

In particular, France in the first half of the 1920s is a textbook example of a distributional war of attrition. The period 1919–1926 is marked by a high degree of polarization of the political debate and by large swings in the composition of the legislature. After it became clear, in the early 1920s, that the German war reparations would not have solved the French fiscal problem, the Chamber of Deputies was deadlocked for several years because of lack of agreement on feasible fiscal plans. For instance, in the fall of 1922 the centrist Minister of Finance proposed a 20-percent across-the-board increase in the income tax. The proposal was not approved in the Chamber, because of the opposition of both the Conservatives and the Socialists. The former proposed an increase in indirect taxes, which relied mostly on the poor (Maier, 1975) and a reduction in the progressivity of the income tax. The latter proposed a capital levy, a more progressive income tax, and reduction in indirect taxation. The lack of a compromise led to an 18-month period of complete fiscal inaction, which implied a sharp rise in the inflation rate, capital flight, and speculative attacks against the franc. A conservative tax bill was not approved until March 1924. This attempted fiscal stabilization was, however, only temporary. The election of an internally divided "cartel des gauches" in the spring of 1924 initiated an additional period of fiscal instability. An endless debate within the leftist coalition on the imposition of a capital levy and the consequent fiscal inaction implied a further deterioration of the floating-debt problem.

Britain after the war also faced a large budget deficit; however, in contrast to the experience of France, Germany, and Italy, the dominant position of the Conservatives led to a rapid stabilization by means that favored the Conservatives' traditional constituencies.

Fiscal imbalances reappeared in the 1930s, as a result of the Great Depression. France, once again, provides an excellent example of a political stalemate due to distributional conflicts.[6] After a period of relative political and fiscal stability (1926–1932), the effects of the economic depression on fiscal revenues generated large budget deficits (after six years of surpluses) leading to the reappearance of a large stock of floating short-term debt (Julian Jackson, 1985); in contrast to the 1920s, budget deficits in the 1930s occurred in a deflationary situation. After six years of Conservative control of government, the left reported an electoral victory in 1932; however, the center-left radicals refused to form a coalition with the Socialists. From 1932 to 1936 a series of short-lived centrist (or center-left) governments failed to adopt a coherent fiscal policy because of the opposite political pressures from the Conservatives and the Socialists. The former were firmly committed to the gold standard and argued for a sharp deflation of nominal wages and prices with cuts in government spending and increases in indirect taxation to eliminate the deficit. The Socialists opposed wage cuts, argued in favor of public investment to sustain aggregate demand, and proposed, as in the 1920s, an increase in the level and progressivity of income taxation and various forms of capital taxation to eliminate the fiscal imbalance (Jackson, 1985). The long debate over a proposal (opposed by the Socialists and favored by the Conservatives) for a cut of 20 percent of the salaries of public employees is emblematic of the political stalemate. In 1936, the Popular Front gained office, and a few months later the franc was devalued. Divisions within the coalition and lack of confidence in the business community led to a further economic deterioration and to the fall of the government, in 1938. A newly elected Conservative government attempted a fiscal stabilization; it is hard to say whether it would have succeeded or not because of the outburst of the Second World War. Eichengreen and Jeffrey Sachs (1985) argue that, because of the delay in abandoning the gold standard and the incoherence and inaction of French economic policy in the 1930s, this country suffered particularly severe consequences of the Great Depression.

Current examples of delayed adjustments of fiscal imbalances due to political stalemate can be found in both OECD and LDC countries. Several authors have suggested that the recent increase in the debt/GNP ratios in several OECD economies is due to the failure of weak and divided coalition governments to agree on fiscal-adjustment programs.[7] The cases of Belgium, Ireland, and Italy, the three OECD countries currently with the highest debt/GNP ratio are good examples of this point of view. In several Latin American countries, and particularly in Argentina, the failure to stabilize in the face of endemic inflation has gone hand in hand with continued political polarization and instability and the failure of any group to consolidate its power effectively (Rudiger Dornbusch and Juan Carlos DePablo, 1988). Similarly, in Israel in the 1980s, once the need for sharply restrictive aggregate demand policies to end the inflation was widely accepted, there was still disagreement over how the burden of restrictive policies would be distributed between labor and business.

2. When stabilization occurs, it coincides with a *political* consolidation. Often, one side becomes politically dominant. The burden of stabilization is sometimes quite unequal, with the politically weaker groups bearing a larger burden. Often this means the lower classes, with the burden of a successful stabilization being regressive.

The successful stabilizations in France (1926) and Italy (1922–1924) coincided with a clear consolidation of power by the right. In both cases, the burden fell disproportionately on the working class (Maier, 1975). Poincaré's 1926 program included increases both of indirect taxes and of the income tax on the lower middle class. Except for a very mild "once and for all" tax on real estate, no capital levies were introduced. On the contrary, tax rates on the wealthiest fraction of taxpayers were substantially reduced, as documented by Haig (1929), who concluded that, when the fiscal crisis came to an end, "the remedy was sought in lightening the burden on rich taxpayers and by increasing the levy on those of moderate means" (p. 164).

The German stabilization of November 1923 followed a new Enabling Act giving the new Stresemann government power to cut through legislative deadlocks and quickly adopt fiscal measures by decree. Though the government that took power in August was a "Great Coalition" of the right and the left, by autumn "the far right was more dangerous and powerful than the socialist left," and government policy reflected the perceived need to appease conservative interest groups (Maier, 1975, p. 384).

Giavazzi and Pagano (1990) document that the successful Danish fiscal adjustment, started in 1982, was made possible by the election of a conservative government with a solid majority. This ended period marked by a series of minority coalition governments, unable to stop the growth of government debt.

3. Successful stabilizations are usually preceded by several failed attempts. Often a previous program appears to be similar to the successful one.

In a war of attrition, the cost of waiting means that the passage of time will imply concession on the same terms that a player earlier found "unacceptable." The components of the successful Poincaré stabilization of 1926 are quite similar to his program of 1924. Several unsuccessful attempts in Germany appear to be quite similar *ex ante* to the November 1923 program (Dornbusch, 1988). Many aspects of the July 1985 stabilization in Israel had been previously proposed but rejected by the government.

In summary, the central role of conflict over how the burden of stabilization is to be shared, the importance of political consolidation in the adoption of a program, and the fact that programs that were previously rejected are agreed to after the passage of time, suggests modeling delayed stabilization as arising from a war of attrition between different socioeconomic groups.

In the basic war-of-attrition model from biology (John Riley, 1980), two animals are fighting over a prize. Fighting is costly, and the fight ends when one animal drops out, with the other gaining the prize. Suppose that the two contestants are not identical, either in the costs of remaining in the fight or in the utility they assign to the prize. Suppose further that each contestant's value of these is known only to himself, his opponent knowing only the distribution of these values. The individual's problem is then to choose a time of concession based on his type (i.e., the value of his costs and payoffs), on the distribution of his opponent's possible type, and on the knowledge that his opponent is solving the same problem. In equilibrium, the time of concession is determined by the condition that, at the optimal time, the cost of remaining in the fight another instant of time is just equal to the expected gain from remaining, namely the probability that the rival drops out at that instant multiplied by the gain if the rival concedes.

For a war of attrition between heterogeneous individuals to give expected finite delay in concession under incomplete information, two obvious features are important. First, there must be a cost to remaining in the fight, that is, to not conceding. Second, the payoff to the winner must exceed that to the loser. In the next section, we show how stabilizations may be modeled with these features in mind.

4.2   The Model

We consider an economy as in Drazen and Helpman (1987, 1990) in which the government is running a positive deficit (inclusive of debt service) implying growing government debt.[8] Stabilization consists of an increase in taxes which brings the deficit to zero, so that government debt is constant. We assume that, prior to an agreement on how to share the burden of higher taxes, the government is limited to highly inefficient and distortionary methods of public finance. In particular, monetization of deficits, with the associated costs of high and variable inflation, is often a main source of government revenue prior to a fiscal stabilization. The level of distortionary financing and, hence, the welfare loss associated with it rise with the level of government debt, where welfare losses may differ across socioeconomic groups.[9]

A second type of cost to continuing in a war of attrition is political. For a group to prevent the burden of a stabilization being placed on it, it must mobilize and use resources for lobbying activities to influence the outcome of the legislative process. Different groups may differ in their political influence and therefore in the level of effort needed to continue fighting. In the development of the model, the first interpretation of prestabilization costs is stressed, but we will return to political interpretations in the concluding section.

The benefit of stabilization derives from the move away from highly distortionary methods of financing government expenditures. In this respect, stabilization benefits everybody. The differential benefits reflect the fact that the increase in nondistortionary taxes is unequally distributed.

Concession in our model is the agreement by one side to bear a disproportionate share of the tax increase necessary to effect a stabilization. As the examples in the previous section illustrate, effective concession may be reflected in a formal agreement between the various sides (as in the Israeli case), in the formation of a new government that is given extraordinary powers (as in the French or German cases), or in the outcome of elections in which one side gains a clear majority and opposing groups decide not to block their program any longer.[10]

More formally, consider a small open economy which issues external debt to cover any deficits not covered by revenues. The economy is composed of a number of heterogeneous interest groups which differ from one another in the welfare loss they suffer from the distortions associated with the prestabilization methods of government finance.

Until $t = 0$, the government budget is balanced, with external government debt constant at level $b_0 \geq 0$. At $t = 0$ a shock hits, reducing available tax revenues. From $t = 0$ until the date of stabilization, a fraction $(1 - \gamma)$ of government expenditure (inclusive of interest payments) is covered by issuing debt, and a fraction γ is covered by distortionary taxation. What is important is not that γ is fixed, but that it is positive. Calling g_0 the level of expenditures from $t = 0$ until a policy change, debt $b(t)$ evolves according to

$$\dot{b}(t) = (1 - \gamma)[rb(t) + g_0] \tag{1}$$

where r is the constant world interest rate. Taxes before the date of stabilization are thus

$$\tau(t) = \gamma[rb(t) + g_0]. \tag{2}$$

Equation (1) may be solved to yield

$$b(t) = b_0 e^{(1-\gamma)rt} + \frac{g_0}{r} (e^{(1-\gamma)rt} - 1). \tag{3}$$

This implies that (2) may be written as

$$\tau(t) = \gamma r \bar{b} e^{(1-\gamma)rt} \tag{4}$$

where $b \equiv b_0 + g_0/r$, which can be shown to be the present discounted value of future tax payments for any nonzero values of γ before and after stabilization.

A stabilization consists of an increase in taxes sufficient to prevent further growth in the debt. Hence, taxes to be levied from the date of stabilization T onward are

$$\tau(T) = rb(T) + g_T \tag{2'}$$

where g_T is the level of expenditures after a stabilization. If we assume, for simplicity, that $g_T = g_0$, (2') becomes

$$\tau(T) = r\bar{b} e^{(1-\gamma)rT}. \tag{4'}$$

Equations (3) and (4) imply that, before the stabilization, both the debt and the distortionary taxes grow exponentially. From the time of stabilization onward, the level of debt is constant. At time T, taxes jump upward to the level given in (4') and remain constant afterward.

An agreement to stabilize is an agreement on how the taxes $\tau(T)$ are to be apportioned between different interest groups. For simplicity, assume that there are only two groups.[11] The "loser" assumes a fraction $\alpha > \frac{1}{2}$ of the tax burden at T, the "winner" a fraction $1 - \alpha$. The fraction itself is not bargained on: it is a given parameter meant to capture the degree of polarization in the society. A value of α close to 1 represents a high degree of polarization or a lack of political cohesiveness.

Taxes after an agreement on a stabilization are assumed to be nondistortionary. What is important is that they are *less* distortionary than taxes before a stabilization; otherwise, there would in general be no incentive to concede, that is, to stabilize.

Infinitely-lived groups differ from one another in the utility loss they suffer due to distortionary taxes. We will index groups i's loss by θ_i, where θ is drawn from a distribution $F(\theta)$, with lower and upper bounds $\underline{\theta}$ and $\bar{\theta}$; θ_i is known only to the group itself, other groups knowing only the distribution $F(\theta)$. For simplicity, we assume that the utility loss from distortionary taxes, K_i, is linear in the level of taxes, namely,[12]

$$K_i(t) = \theta_i \tau(t). \tag{5}$$

The prestabilization distortionary tax can be viewed as the inflation tax. Obviously, the treatment of inflation in this nonmonetary model is very stylized; what is crucial in this model is the problem of fiscal adjustment, not the monetary dynamics per se.[13]

Flow utility depends on consumption (c), government spending (g), and the cost (K). Though we leave the dependence of utility on government expenditure implicit (since g is constant over time), this dependence is important below in treating problems of feasibility. The level of income, y, is assumed for most of the paper to be constant across individuals. The possible effects of distribution of income on the timing of a stabilization are considered below. The flow utility of groups i is linear in consumption and of the form

$$u_i(t) = c_i(t) - y - K_i(t). \tag{6}$$

Subtracting y in the utility function is simply a normalization. The level of income is assumed to be high relative to the interest payments on the debt; the importance of this assumption will be made precise below. After a stabilization, $K_i = 0$, as taxes after a stabilization are nondistortionary. Henceforth, to simplify matters, the subscript on the function u_i is suppressed.

Each group maximizes expected present discounted utility by choice of a time path of consumption and a date to concede and agree to bear the share α of taxes if the other group has not already conceded. We denote flow utility before a stabilization by $u^D(t)$ and the lifetime utility of the loser and the winner from the date of stabilization onward by $V^L(T)$ and $V^W(T)$, respectively. If stabilization occurs at time T, lifetime utility of the winner and of the loser may then be written as

$$U^j(T) = \int_0^T u^D(x) e^{-rx}\, dx + e^{-rT} V^j(T) \qquad j = W, L \tag{7}$$

where the discount rate equals the interest rate r. Expected utility as of time 0 as a function of one's chosen concession time T_i is the sum of $U^W(X)$ multiplied by the probability of one's opponent conceding at X for all $X \leq T_i$ and $U^L(T_i)$ multiplied by the probability of one's opponent not having conceded by T_i. If we denote by $H(T)$ the distribution of the opponent's optimal time of concession (this is, of course, endogenous and will be derived below) and by $h(T)$ the associated density function, expected utility as a function of T is

$$EU(T_i) = [1 - H(T_i)]U^L(T_i) + \int_0^{T_i} U^W(x)h(x)\,dx$$

$$= [1 - H(T_i)]\left[\int_0^{T_i} u^D(x)e^{-rx}\,dx + e^{-rT_i}V^L(T_i)\right]$$

$$+ \int_{x=0}^{x=T_i}\left[\int_0^x u^D(z)e^{-rz}\,dz + e^{-rx}V^W(x)\right]h(x)\,dx. \tag{8}$$

The time path of consumption and T_i are chosen to maximize (8).

With linear utility, any consumption path satisfying the intertemporal budget constrain with equality gives equal utility. Denote by c^D, c^L, and c^W consumption before a stabilization, after a stabilization for the loser, and after a stabilization for the winner, respectively. Assuming that each of the two groups pays one-half of taxes before a stabilization, we have the lifetime budget constraints:

$$\int_0^T c^D(x)e^{-rx}\,dx + \int_T^\infty c^L(x)e^{-rx}\,dx = \int_0^T (y - \tfrac{1}{2}\gamma r\bar{b}e^{(1-\gamma)rx})e^{-rx}\,dx$$

$$+ \int_T^\infty (y - \alpha r\bar{b}e^{(1-\gamma)rT})e^{-rx}\,dx \tag{9}$$

$$\int_0^T c^D(x)e^{-rx}\,dx + \int_T^\infty c^W(x)e^{-rx}\,dx = \int_0^T (y - \tfrac{1}{2}\gamma r\bar{b}e^{(1-\gamma)rx})e^{-rx}\,dx$$

$$+ \int_T^\infty (y - (1-\alpha)r\bar{b}e^{(1-\gamma)rT})e^{-rx}\,dx. \tag{10}$$

The following consumption path is then clearly feasible:[14]

$$c^D(t) = y - \frac{\gamma}{2}r\bar{b}e^{(1-\gamma)rT} \qquad 0 \le t < T \tag{11a}$$

$$c^L(t) = y - \alpha r\bar{b}e^{(1-\gamma)rT} \qquad t \ge T \tag{11b}$$

$$c^W(t) = y - (1-\alpha)r\bar{b}e^{(1-\gamma)rT} \qquad t \ge T. \tag{11c}$$

Flow utility before a stabilization is the following:

$$u_i^D(t) = -\frac{\gamma}{2}\,r\bar{b}e^{(1-\gamma)rT} - K_i \tag{12}$$

$$= -\gamma r(\tfrac{1}{2} + \theta_i)\bar{b}e^{(1-\gamma)rt}$$

which is the income effect of taxes plus the welfare loss arising from taxes being distortionary.

With constant consumption after a stabilization, discounted utility V^j ($j = W, L$) is simply constant flow utility for each group divided by r. Using (11) and (6) (where $K_i = 0$ after a stabilization), one immediately obtains

$$V^W(T) - V^L(T) = (2\alpha - 1)\bar{b}e^{(1-\gamma)rT} \tag{13}$$

which is the present discounted value of the excess taxes that the loser must pay relative to the winner.

The optimal concession time for a group with cost θ_i, T_i, can now be determined.[15] We will first derive the solution for the case in which the problem of debt service exceeding income is ignored and then show how this solution is modified when the issue of feasibility is explicitly considered.

We further assume, for the time being, that $\underline{\theta} > \alpha - \frac{1}{2}$. We discuss the economic meaning of this assumption below. Since the distribution $H(T)$ is not known, equation (8) cannot be used directly. However, by showing that T_i is monotonic in θ_i, we can derive the relation between $H(T)$ and the known $F(\theta)$, namely $1 - H(T(\theta)) = F(\theta)$.

LEMMA 1 $T_i'(\theta_i) < 0$.

(See the appendix for a proof.)

We now want to find a symmetric Nash equilibrium in which each group's concession behavior is described by the same function $T(\theta)$. In this equilibrium, if all other groups behave according to $T(\theta)$, group i finds it optimal to concede according to $T(\theta)$. Thus, the expected time of stabilization is the expected minimum T, with the expectation taken over $F(\theta)$. There may be asymmetric equilibria (i.e., where groups behave according to different $T(\theta)$) even though each group's θ is known to be drawn from the same distribution $F(\theta)$. For example, there are equilibria in which one group concedes immediately. We do not investigate such equilibria, since our interest is in demonstrating that this type of model can yield delay.[16]

PROPOSITION 1   There exists a symmetric Nash equilibrium with each group's optimal behavior described by a concession function $T(\theta)$, where $T(\theta)$ is implicitly defined by

$$\left[-\frac{f(\theta)}{F(\theta)} \frac{1}{T'(\theta)} \right] \frac{2\alpha - 1}{r} = \gamma(\theta + \tfrac{1}{2} - \alpha) \tag{14}$$

and the initial boundary condition

$$T(\bar{\theta}) = 0. \tag{15}$$

(See the appendix for proof.)

The right-hand side of (4) is the cost of waiting another instant to concede. The left-hand side is the expected gain from waiting another instant to concede, which is the product of the conditional probability that one's opponent concedes (the hazard rate, in brackets) multiplied by the gain if the other groups concedes. Concession occurs when the (group-specific) cost of waiting just equals the expected benefit from waiting.

The role of the assumption $\underline{\theta} > \alpha - \frac{1}{2}$ should now be clear. If a groups has a cost θ such that $\theta + \frac{1}{2} < \alpha$, the group would always prefer to wait than to concede, since the cost of living in the unstabilized economy and bearing half the tax burden would be less than the cost associated with being the "loser." That is, the group's $T(\theta)$ would be infinite. The above assumption means that stabilization occurs in finite time with probability 1 (ignoring any feasibility issues, to be discussed below).

Equation (14) is also useful in understanding the evolution of the war of attrition from the viewpoint of one side. Consider a group with $\theta < \bar{\theta}$. At time 0, there is some probability that its opponent has $\theta = \bar{\theta}$ and will concede immediately. If no one concedes at time 0, both sides know that their opponent is not type $\bar{\theta}$. At the "next" instant the next-highest type concedes and so on, so as time elapses each side learns that its opponent does not have a cost above a certain level. When the conditional probability of an opponent's concession in the next instant (based on what the group has learned about his highest possible cost) is such that (14) just holds, it is time to "throw in the towel."

Let us now consider the issue of feasibility. From equation (11b), it follows that a stabilization in which one groups pays a share α of taxes is not feasible after $T = [1/(1 - \gamma)r] \ln(y/\alpha r\bar{b})$. Indicate this value with T^* and let θ^* be the associated cost defined by $T(\theta^*) = T^*$. Suppose, therefore, that if no concession has occurred by T^* the government closes the budget deficit by a combination of expenditure cuts and distortionary taxes which imply very large loss of utility. If the utility loss is sufficiently high, a group with $\theta < \theta^*$ would prefer to concede at T^* than to have the distortionary solution imposed. The government's threat thus implies that the distribution of concession times will have a mass point at T^*, with concession occurring at that point with probability 1 if it has not occurred before. If both groups concede at T^* a tie-breaking rule is used: a coin is flipped, with the loser bearing the share α of nondistortionary taxes.

To close the argument, the existence of a mass point at T^* means that groups with costs close to but above θ^* (i.e., groups that would have conceded *before* T^* under strategy $T(\theta)$ if there were no mass at T^*) will now find it preferable to wait until T to concede under the tie-breaking rule. Define $\tilde{\theta} > \theta^*$ as the cost when a group is indifferent between being the stabilizer at $\tilde{T} = T(\tilde{\theta})$ and waiting until T^* to be the stabilizer with probability $\frac{1}{2}$. The addition of the government's threat at T^* will therefore not affect optimal strategy for groups with $\theta \geq \tilde{\theta}$. Since T^* is increasing in y and $\tilde{T}$ is increasing in T^*, $\tilde{T}$ would be increasing in y. Thus, as y increases, the fraction of the distribution of groups whose behavior is described by $T(\theta)$ in Proposition 1 rises. Put another way, for fixed y arbitrarily high, the time until the solution in Proposition 1 holds can also be made arbitrarily long.

If we relax the assumption that $\underline{\theta} > \alpha - \frac{1}{2}$, it is possible that no group concedes, and stabilization takes place only due to intervention as above. This seems to be consistent with historical experience. Maier (1975) argues that inflation stabilization in Germany and France in the 1920s was possible only because the costs of living with inflation were perceived as too high by participants in the political process. In contrast, the budget imbalances in France in the 1930s, which were not accompanied by high inflation, were not resolved until the Second World War broke out. That is, the costs of the fiscal crisis may not have been perceived as sufficiently high to induce any group to "concede."

Given concession times as a function of θ, the expected date of stabilization is then the expected minimum T, the expectation taken over $F(\theta)$. With n players the probability that a given θ is the maximum (so that $T(\theta)$ is the minimum) is its density $f(\theta)$ multiplied by the probability that no other θ is higher, namely $[F(\theta)]^{n-1}$, multiplied by n. With $n = 2$, the expected value of minimum T (i.e., the expected time of stabilization T^{SE}) is thus

$$T^{\text{SE}} = 2 \int_{\underline{\theta}}^{\bar{\theta}} T(x)F(x)f(x)\,dx. \tag{16}$$

As long as all participants in the process initially believe that someone else may have a higher θ, stabilization does not occur immediately. The cumulative distribution of stabilization times T is therefore 1 minus the probability that every group has an θ lower than the value consistent with stabilization at T. With two groups, this is

$$S(T) = 1 - [F(\theta(T))]^2 \tag{17}$$

where $\theta(T)$ is defined by $T(\theta) = T$.

Two observations are useful in helping to explain the key role of heterogeneity. Suppose, first, that all groups are identical, as in a representative-agent model. If we interpret this as there being a single agent, he knows with probability 1 that he will be the stabilizer. Since u^D is negative, equation (8) implies that expected utility is maximized by choosing T_i equal to 0, that is, by stabilizing immediately. Intuitively, if an individual knows that he will end up bearing the cost of a stabilization, a cost to waiting implies that it is optimal to act immediately.

Heterogeneity alone is not sufficient, however, to delay stabilizations. There must also be uncertainty about the cost to waiting of other groups. If it is known to all that a group has higher costs than anyone else, optimal behavior will imply that this group concedes immediately. Intuitively, stabilization is postponed because each interest group believes the possibility that another group will give up first.

In addition, it is interesting to compare the sense in which stabilization becomes "inevitable" in this chapter with that used in Sargent and Wallace (1981) and Drazen and Helpman (1987, 1990). In those papers, a positive deficit (exclusive of debt service) implies that government debt is growing faster than the rate of interest, so that its present value is not converging to 0. The failure of this transversality condition to hold (and hence the long-run infeasibility of the path) is what makes the stabilization inevitable. Here, the war of attrition ends in finite time with a stabilization, even if debt grows more slowly than the rate of interest. Hence, our approach indicates why countries whose policies are technically feasible (in the sense that the present discounted value of the debt goes to zero) will eventually stabilize if current policies involve welfare loss.

4.3 Why Do Some Countries Stabilize Sooner than Others?

We can now ask how different parameter values affect the expected time of a stabilization. Our goal is to see whether observable characteristics of economies explain why some countries stabilize sooner than others. These results are presented in several propositions and explained intuitively. The proofs are in the appendix. We proceed under the assumption that $\underline{\theta} > \alpha - \frac{1}{2}$.

Distortionary Taxes or Monetization

PROPOSITION 2 When the utility loss from distortionary taxation is proportional to the level of taxes, financing a greater fraction of the prestabilization deficit via distortionary taxation (a higher γ) implies an earlier date of stabilization.

This result may seem surprising, for it says that an attempt to control the growth of government indebtedness may actually hasten the date of stabilization. A higher γ on the one hand implies a greater distortion for a given deficit, inducing earlier concession. However, making more of an effort to reduce the deficit implies that government debt grows more slowly, and hence the distortions which induce stabilization also grow less fast. The first effect dominates because our proportional specification in (5) implies that both the gain from being the winner and the loss from no stabilization are proportional to the size of the debt, so that a slower growth of the debt does not in itself change their relative magnitudes.[17] Higher monetization has the effect of raising the cost of the distortions in the unstabilized economy relative to the gain from having another group stabilize *at each point in time*. This result is consistent with the idea that it is easier to stabilize hyperinflations than inflations that are "only" high.[18]

Costs of Distortions

PROPOSITION 3   An increase in the costs associated with living in an unstable economy, for an unchanged distribution of θ, will move the expected date of a stabilization forward.

Countries with institutions that lessen the utility loss from distortionary financing of government expenditures (such as indexation) will, *other things equal*, be expected to postpone stabilization longer.[19] If the utility loss is an increasing (perhaps convex) function of inflation, a sharp acceleration of inflation will lead to a stabilization. This would explain the timing of the French and German stabilizations.

Political Cohesion

PROPOSITION 4   If $\alpha = \frac{1}{2}$, stabilization occurs immediately; the larger is α above $\frac{1}{2}$, the later is the expected date of stabilization.

The difference in the shares of the burden of stabilization, α, could be interpreted as representing the degree of political cohesion in the society. Countries with α close to $\frac{1}{2}$ can be characterized as having high political cohesion, since the burden of stabilization is shared relatively equally, while those where the burden is very unequal, so that α is close to 1, are more polarized or less cohesive. When the relative burden of a stabilization is unequally distributed, the gain from waiting in the hope that one's opponent will concede is larger. Hence, each group holds out longer.

This intuitive result suggests a relationship between measures of political stability and macroeconomic outcomes. Roubini and Sachs (1989a,b) argue that governments composed of large, short-lived, and uncohesive coalitions are associated with large budget deficits. They construct an index of political cohesion and stability in the government and show a strong correlation between that index and budget deficits after 1973 in several industrial countries. One explanation of this finding that is consistent with our model concerns the decision-making process within the coalition. Large coalitions of politically diverse parties find it particularly hard to reach agreements on how to allocate tax increases or expenditure cuts among the constituencies represented by coalition partners. In the absence of such an agreement, deficits grow. Alex Cukierman et al. (1990) argue that the level of inflation in a cross-section of countries is inversely related to measures of political stability.

Income Dispersion and Longer Delays in Stabilizing

Finally, we consider the implications of dropping the assumption that all groups have the same income. Greater dispersion in the distribution of income can affect the timing of stabilization if a group's cost is a function of its income. As emphasized above, delays can only occur if relative costs are unknown to each group. If relative costs depend upon relative income levels, this implies that delays are observed only when relative positions in income distribution are unknown.

An increase in income inequality may make relative income levels more apparent, leading to an immediate stabilization. Consider instead a mean-preserving spread in the distribution of income, maintaining the assumption of uncertainty about relative incomes. Intuitively, one may conclude that this should also lead to an earlier stabilization, since it means that some group will have a higher cost and this concede earlier. Such reasoning is incomplete, for it ignores the change in behavior (i.e., in the function $T(\theta)$) induced by the change in the distribution of costs. The fatter upper tail for costs means that each group perceives a higher likelihood that its opponents' costs have increased. This perception would lead it to hold out longer.

PROPOSITION 5   If the utility loss due to distortionary taxes is a decreasing, convex function of income and if income is unobservable, a mean-preserving spread in the distribution of income $G(y)$ that keeps the expected minimum of the y's constant implies a later expected date of stabilization.

Note that if $\theta'(y) < 0$, it is the "poor" who lose the war of attrition, since the "rich" suffer less from the prestabilization distortions and can hold out longer.

The assumption of uncertainty about relative incomes is perhaps more realistic under the second interpretation of the costs provided in Section II, namely, as resources that must be devoted to the political process to avoid bearing a disproportionate share of the burden of stabilization. In this case, the level of group-i income, y_i, would then be interpreted as the resources available for political purposes. With uncertainty both about the relative political skills of groups and about what fraction of their total income they are willing to devote to the political struggle, assuming uncertainty about relative "income" is more realistic.

An empirical finding consistent with Proposition 5 is presented by Andrew Berg and Sachs (1988), who find a correlation between the degree of income inequality and the frequency of debt rescheduling: countries with a more unequal income distribution have experienced more difficulties in servicing their external debt. Although this evidence is not directly related to the timing of stabilizations, it is consistent with the idea that countries with more income inequality will, at a given level of debt, find it more difficult to adopt policies necessary to insure solvency.

4.4 Summary and Extensions

Delayed stabilizations can be explained in a model of rational heterogeneous agents. However, in contrast, the same model with a rational representative individual would yield immediate stabilization. Since many of the results are summarized in the introductory section, we conclude by discussing some generalizations and by touching on some issues that the model did not address but which are important in explaining stabilization.

First of all, even though we considered the example of a delayed budget adjustment, our argument is much more general. Any efficient policy change with significant distributional consequences can be delayed by a "war of attrition": trade and financial liberalizations are additional examples of this type of policy reform.[20]

Second, for simplicity, no changes in external circumstances following the original shock were considered. More generally, during a war of attrition, a change in the environment (including aid or foreign intervention) may lead to a change in agents' behavior and rapid concession by one side. Even (or especially) when this change is foreseen, the war of attrition is crucial in the delay of stabilization until the external change.

A third generalization involves a more precise formalization of the political process. In particular, this would lead to a more satisfactory characterization of the political costs involved in sheltering oneself from bearing the burden of stabilization. As in the model above, such costs may increase with the size of the outstanding debt: as the difference between payoffs of winners and losers rises, as a result of the growing level of debt, each side should be willing to spend more time and resources in lobbying activities to induce its rivals to concede. Since different groups differ in their political influence or access to resources, such direct political costs will be central to the timing of concession.

A political model also suggests alternative interpretations of some of our results. For example, in Proposition 3, the effect of a shift in the distribution of θ could be interpreted as follows. Countries with political institutions that make it relatively more difficult for opposing groups to "veto" stabilization programs not to their liking will stabilize sooner. In addition, we have not explicitly considered important political events such as elections, the timing of which may be related to the timing of stabilizations. An electoral victory of one side may make it more difficult for the opponents to block its program and shelter themselves from the burden of stabilization. Thus, one might expect successful stabilizations following elections with a clear winner. In the terminology of our model, an electoral landslide may be an important signal of the distribution of the relative strength of different groups.

Finally, we note some issues that we did not discuss. The first is credibility. Delays in successfully stabilizing an economy are related to what determines the probability of success, where the "credibility" of a program has come to be seen as a crucial ingredient of success. One notion of credibility is simply whether or not the economics of a program "make sense." For example, the Brazilian Cruzado Plan of 1986 was not seen as credible. While technical feasibility is necessary for success, it is clearly not sufficient, as the failure of apparently well-designed programs indicates. This notion of credibility thus lacks predictive power, as Dornbusch (1988) argues, since successful and unsuccessful programs often appear to be quite similar *ex ante*. As an example, he refers to the great similarity between Poincaré's successful 1926 program and the failed 1924 attempt as well as several unsuccessful attempts in Germany prior to the November 1923 program.

A second notion of credibility concerns the degree of commitment of a policymaker to the plan, in that he is unlikely to give in to pressure to abandon fiscal responsibility and revert to inflationary finance.[21] This has been formalized in terms of "strong" and "weak" policymakers with different objective functions. A weak policymaker, after a period of mimicking the strong one, abandons policies of monetary restraint. If the public is uncertain about the degree of commitment of the policymaker to fiscal responsibility, success is less likely. In these models, the policymaker's "type," which is crucial, is both exogenous and unobservable. For this reason, credibility as commitment also lacks predictive power.

Our model suggests that successful stabilizations need not be associated with a sharp change in external circumstances, nor does the program being implemented need to look sharply different from what had previously been proposed. The credibility and success of a program reflects the political support it can muster. A main message is that necessary changes in the level of political support may simply result from the passage of time, so that a program that was unsuccessful at one point in time may later be successful. In the war of attrition, passage of time and the accumulation of costs lead one group to give in and make a previously rejected program economically and politically feasible. This may come via the political consolidation of one "group" which forces its opponent to "throw in the towel" in the war of attrition. The role of political consolidation as an element of "credibility" is also emphasized by Sargent in his discussion of hyperinflations and in his comparison of Poincaré and Thatcher (Sargent, 1982, 1984).

Second, in reality, successful stabilizations are not one-shot affairs. One component of success is the design of how the adjustment process should be spread out over time. Our notion of timing emphasizes the beginning of a successful program, not the timing of its stages once it has begun. Theoretically, these different notions of timing can be separated, with this paper addressing the question of why significant policy changes, multistage or otherwise, are delayed. In fact, since stabilization takes time, programs often appear to be successful for a period of time, only to fail subsequently. Hence, the issue of delayed stabilization should ideally be considered simultaneously with issues of both partial and multistage stabilizations.

Appendix

Proof of Lemma 1 Differentiating (8) with respect to T_i, one obtains

$$\frac{d\,\text{EU}}{dT_i} = e^{-rT_i}\left\{ h(T_i)[V^W(T_i) - V^L(T_i)]\right.$$

$$\left. + [1 - H(T_i)]\left[u_i^D(T_i) = rV^L(T_i) + \frac{dV^L(T_i)}{dT_i}\right]\right\}. \tag{A1}$$

Using the definitions of $V^W(T)$, $V^L(T)$, and $u_i^D(t)$, (A1) becomes

$$\frac{d\,\text{EU}}{dT_i} = e^{-rT_i}\left\{ h(T_i)(2\alpha - 1)\bar{b}e^{(1-\gamma)rT_i}\right.$$

$$\left. + [1 - H(T_i)]\left[\gamma r\left(\alpha - \frac{1}{2} - \theta_i\right)\bar{b}e^{(1-\gamma)rT_i}\right]\right\}. \tag{A2}$$

Differentiating with respect to θ_i, we obtain

$$\frac{d^2\,\text{EU}}{dT_i\,d\theta_i} = \{-[1 - H(T_i)]\gamma r\bar{b}e^{(1-\gamma)rT_i}\}e^{-rT_i} < 0. \tag{A3}$$

Equation (A3) means that, when others are acting optimally, $d\,\text{EU}/dt$ is decreasing in θ_i. Optimal concession time T_i is therefore monotonically decreasing in θ_i.

Proof of Proposition 1[22] Suppose that the other interest group is acting according to $T(\theta)$, the optimal concession time for a group with utility cost θ. Choosing a time T_i as above would be equivalent to choosing a value $\hat{\theta}_i$ and conceding at time $T_i = T(\hat{\theta}_i)$. After the change in variable, equation (8) becomes

$$\text{EU}(\hat{\theta}_i, \theta_i) = F(\hat{\theta}_i)\left[\int_{\hat{\theta}_i}^{\bar{\theta}} -u^D(x)e^{-rT(x)}T'(x)\,dx + e^{-rT(\hat{\theta}_i)}V^L(T(\theta_i))\right]$$

$$+ \int_{x=\hat{\theta}_i}^{x=\bar{\theta}}\left[\int_x^{\bar{\theta}} -u^D(z)e^{-rT(z)}T'(z)\,dz + e^{-rT(x)}V^W(T(x))\right]f(x)\,dx. \tag{A4}$$

Differentiating with respect to $\hat{\theta}_i$ and setting the resulting expression equal to zero, we obtain (dropping the i subscript)

$$\frac{d\,\mathrm{EU}}{d\hat{\theta}} = f(\hat{\theta})[V^{W}(T(\hat{\theta})) - V^{L}(T(\hat{\theta}))] + F(\hat{\theta})\left[u^{D}(\theta,\hat{\theta}) - rV^{L} + \frac{dV^{L}}{dT}\right]T'(\hat{\theta})$$

$$= 0 \tag{A5}$$

which becomes, after substitutions,

$$\frac{d\,\mathrm{EU}}{d\hat{\theta}} = -f(\hat{\theta})(2\alpha - 1) - F(\hat{\theta})\gamma r\left(\theta + \frac{1}{2} - \alpha\right)T'(\hat{\theta}) = 0. \tag{A6}$$

Now, by the definition of $T(\theta)$ as the optimal time of concession for a group with cost θ, $\hat{\theta} = \theta$ when $\hat{\theta}$ is chosen optimally. The first-order condition (A6) evaluated at $\hat{\theta} = \theta$ implies (14). (Substituting $T'(\theta)$ evaluated at $\hat{\theta}$ from (14) into (A6), one sees that the second-order condition is satisfied, since (A6) then implies that $\mathrm{sign}(d\,\mathrm{EU}/d\hat{\theta}) = \mathrm{sign}(\theta - \hat{\theta})$.)

To derive the initial boundary condition, note first that, for any value of $\theta \leq \bar{\theta}$, the gain to having the opponent concede is positive. Therefore, as long as $f(\bar{\theta})$ is nonzero, groups with $\theta < \bar{\theta}$ will not concede immediately. This in turn implies that a group with $\theta = \bar{\theta}$ (i.e., a group that knows it has the highest possible cost of waiting) will find it optimal to choose $T(\bar{\theta}) = 0$.

Proof of Proposition 2   A higher fraction of prestabilization deficits financed by taxation corresponds to a higher value of γ. Comparing the optimal time of concession as a function of θ for $\tilde{\gamma} > \gamma$, we have

$$T'(\theta) = \frac{f(\theta)}{F(\theta)}\frac{(2\alpha - 1)/r}{\gamma(\theta + \frac{1}{2} - \alpha)} \tag{A7}$$

$$\tilde{T}'(\theta) = -\frac{f(\theta)}{F(\theta)}\frac{(2\alpha - 1)/r}{\tilde{\gamma}(\theta + \frac{1}{2} - \alpha)}. \tag{A7'}$$

Since $V^{W} - V^{L}$ is the same in both cases, the initial boundary condition is the same for γ and $\tilde{\gamma}$, that is, $T(\bar{\theta}) = \tilde{T}(\bar{\theta}) = 0$. Inspection of (A7) and (A7') indicates that $\tilde{T}'(\theta) > T'(\theta)$ for all values of θ. Combining these two results, we have that $T(\theta) > \tilde{T}(\theta)$ for $\theta < \bar{\theta}$. Equation (16) then implies that $\tilde{T}^{\mathrm{SE}} < T^{\mathrm{SE}}$.

Proof of Proposition 3   A multiplicative shift in θ has an identical effect to an increase in γ in Proposition 2. By an argument analogous to the one used in that proof, $T(\theta)$ will shift down, and hence T^{SE} will fall.

Proof of Proposition 4   When $\alpha = \frac{1}{2}$, $V^{W} = V^{L}$. Since there are costs to not conceding, it is optimal to concede immediately. To prove the second part of the proposition, the same argument as in Proposition 2 shows that $T(\bar{\theta}) = \tilde{T}(\bar{\theta}) = 0$ for $\tilde{\alpha} > \alpha$. Since the right-hand side of (14) decreases with an increase α, $\tilde{T}'(\theta) < T'(\theta)$ for all values of θ. Using the same reasoning as in Proposition 2, we have that $\tilde{T}(\theta) > T(\theta)$ for $\theta < \bar{\theta}$. Equation (16) implies $\tilde{T}^{SE} > T^{SE}$.

Proof of Proposition 5   Suppose $\theta_i = \theta(y_i)$ with $\theta' < 0$, where a group's income y_i is unobservable. Let $G(y, \sigma)$ be the distribution of income with bounds $\underline{y}$ and $\bar{y}$, where increases in σ correspond to a more dispersed income distribution. Increasing σ corresponds to a mean-preserving spread of income if for some $\tilde{y}$

$$G_\sigma(y, \sigma) \geq 0 \qquad \text{for } y \leq \tilde{y}$$

$$G_\sigma(y, \sigma) \leq 0 \qquad \text{for } y > \tilde{y}.$$

The expected minimum value of y can be written as

$$E(y_{min}) = 2 \int_{\underline{y}}^{\bar{y}} [1 - G(x, \sigma)] g(x, \sigma) x \, dx \tag{A8}$$

which by integration by parts equals $\int_{\underline{y}}^{\bar{y}} [1 - G(x, \sigma)]^2 \, dx$. Constant expected y_{min} implies

$$\int_{\underline{y}}^{\bar{y}} [1 - G(x, \sigma)] G_\sigma(x, \sigma) \, dx = 0. \tag{A9}$$

Equations (A9) and (16) imply

$$T^{SE}(\sigma) = 2 \int_{\underline{y}}^{\bar{y}} T(x, \sigma) [1 - G(x, \sigma)] g(x, \sigma) \, dx. \tag{A10}$$

Repeated integration by parts implies that (A10) can be written as

$$T^{SE}(\sigma) = \frac{2\alpha - 1}{r\gamma} \left\{ \frac{-\frac{1}{2}}{\theta(\underline{y}) + \frac{1}{2} - \alpha} + \frac{1}{2} \int_{\underline{y}}^{\bar{y}} (1 - G(x, \sigma))^2 \left[\frac{1}{\theta(x) + \frac{1}{2} - \alpha} \right]^2 \theta'(x) \, dx \right\} \tag{A11}$$

If the change in σ does not affect the lower bound $\underline{y}$ and if $(d^2\theta/dy^2) \geq 0$, we have

$$\frac{dT^{SE}(\theta)}{d\sigma} = -\frac{2\alpha - 1}{r\gamma} \int_{\underline{y}}^{\bar{y}} [1 - G(x, \sigma)] G_\sigma(x, \sigma) \left[\frac{1}{\theta(x) + \frac{1}{2} - \alpha} \right]^2 \theta'(x) \, dx$$

$$\geq -\frac{2\alpha - 1}{r\gamma} \frac{\theta'(\tilde{y})}{[\theta(\tilde{y}) + \frac{1}{2} - \alpha]^2} \int_{\underline{y}}^{\bar{y}} [1 - G(x, \sigma)] G_\sigma(x, \sigma) \, dx = 0. \tag{A12}$$

Notes

We thank Barry Eichengreen, Raquel Fernandez, Stephan Haggard, Elhanan Helpman, Peter Kennen, Barry Nalebuff, Dani Rodrik, Howard Rosenthal, Jeffrey Sachs, two referees, and participants of several seminars for very helpful comments. Substantial revisions of this paper were performed while Alesina was an Olin Fellow at the NBER; he thanks the Olin and Sloan Foundations for financial support. Drazen's research was supported by National Science Foundation Grant No. SES-8706808.

1. In Sargent and Wallace (1981) and Drazen and Helpman (1987), the timing of stabilization is deterministic and exogenous; in Drazen and Helpman (1990), the timing is stochastic, but the distribution of the time of stabilization is exogenous.

2. See Athanasios Orphanides (1989) for a model in which a rational government delays a stabilization program to take advantage of more favorable exogenous circumstances.

3. The effects of political instability on the path of government debt is studied in a different framework by Alesina and Guido Tabellini (1989, 1990), Torsten Persson and Lars Svensson (1989), and Tabellini and Alesina (1990).

4. David Backus and John Driffill (1985a,b) and Tabellini (1988) discuss a war of attrition between trade unions and a central bank, leading to periods of inefficient outcomes. An additional application of the war-of-attrition model is in the labor-strike literature; for a survey see John Kennan and Robert Wilson (1988).

5. Kenneth Rogoff (1985) suggests that it may be optimal to appoint a central banker with preferences that do not coincide with social preferences. In this case, however, the central bank's preferences are known by the public, while a war of attrition requires uncertainty about an opponent's characteristics.

6. We are grateful to Barry Eichengreen for pointing out to us this example.

7. See Nouriel Roubini and Jeffrey Sachs (1989a,b) for statistical evidence on post-1973 OECD democracies, Francesco Giavazzi and Marco Pagano (1990) on Denmark and Ireland, and Giavazzi and Luigi Spaventa (1988) on Italy.

8. Since we are considering an economy with constant output, this is equivalent to a rising debt/GNP ratio.

9. The view that the utility loss from living in an unstabilized economy flows from the use of distortionary financing of part of the government deficit raises an obvious question: why not simply accumulate debt until an agreement can be reached on levying less distortionary taxes? We suggest that there may be constraints on the rate of growth of the debt, especially if it is external, but do not model this here.

10. Elections may also give one side a clear mandate not because its opponents have conceded on their distributional objectives, but because a majority of voters see that side as more *competent* to handle an economic crisis. The issue of competency is not considered here.

11. This may be generalized easily to more than two groups if we keep the assumption of exogenously fixed shares: if one group agrees to pay a share $\alpha > 1/n$, each other group pays $(1 - \alpha)/(n - 1)$ of the burden. A more general approach is that once one group concedes, the $n - 1$ groups remaining engage in a "second-round" war of attrition, and so on. This may lead to similar results, but it is a much more complex problem, which we have not explored.

12. We could adopt a more general specification for K_i, such as

$$K_i(t) = \theta_i[\tau(t)]^{1+m} \qquad m > 0.$$

The qualitative features of our results do not change with this more general specification. The differences will be emphasized in what follows.

13. The technical difficulty in developing an explicitly monetary model in this framework is the following. Money demand should depend on expected inflation. The latter, in turn, is a function of the perceived probability that a stabilization program is adopted in each period. While in Drazen and Helpman (1990) this probability is exogenous, in this chapter it is endogenously determined and will depend on utility and, therefore, on expected inflation. Hence, equilibrium would mean a fixed point in this probability function. Thus, it appears to be technically infeasible to derive endogenously this probability distribution in a model in which the distribution itself affects utility via the decision about money-holding.

14. We impose a condition below which insures that consumption is not negative in every period.

15. This derivation follows Christopher Bliss and Barry Nalebuff (1984).

16. Of course, if different groups' endowments are perceived to be drawn from different distributions, each group will have a different $T_i(\theta)$. See, for example, Drew Fudenberg and Jean Tirole (1986).

17. When the utility loss from distortionary taxation rises more than proportionally with the level of taxes (as in footnote 11), the effect of slower growth of the deficit may dominate. It can be shown (details are available from the authors upon request) that low-θ groups will concede later, so that if it happens that both groups have low θ, increased γ will mean a later date of stabilization.

18. Drazen and Vittorio Grilli (1990) use a war-of-attrition model to investigate how an economic "crisis," defined as a period of high (and thus costly) inflation, actually raises total welfare by inducing agreement over a policy change.

19. The caveat here is that increased indexation may induce greater monetization or higher prices for a given level of monetization.

20. Raquel Fernandez and Dani Rodrik (1990) suggest a different explanation for the postponement of the adoption of trade reform, based on a bias in favor of the "status quo" with majority voting. Our approach and theirs are not inconsistent.

21. Rodrik (1989) studies trade reforms from this perspective. Backus and Driffil (1985a,b), Robert Barro (1986), and Tabellini (1988) study monetary policy.

22. This proof closely follows Bliss and Nalebuff (1984).

References

Alesina, Alberto, "The End of Large Public Debts," in F. Giavazzi and L. Spaventa, eds., *High Public Debt: The Italian Experience*, Cambridge: Cambridge University Press, 1988, pp. 34–79.

Alesina, Alberto and Tabellini, Guido, "External Debt, Capital Flight, and Political Risk," *Journal of International Economics*, November 1989, 27, 199–220.

————, "A Positive Theory of Fiscal Deficits and Government Debt," *Review of Economic Studies*, July 1990, 57, 403–14.

Backus, David and Driffill, John, (1985a) "Rational Expectations and Policy Credibility after a Change of Regime," *Review of Economic Studies*, April 1985, 52, 211–22.

————, (1985b) "Inflation and Reputation," *American Economic Review*, June 1985, *75*, 530–8.

Barro, Robert, "Reputation in a Model of Monetary Policy with Incomplete Information," *Journal of Monetary Economics*, February 1986, *17*, 1–20.

Berg, Andrew and Sachs, Jeffrey, "The Debt Crisis: Structural Explanations of Country Performance," *Journal of Development Economics*, November 1988, *29*, 271–306.

Bliss, Christopher and Nalebuff, Barry, "Dragon-Slaying and Ballroom Dancing: The Private Supply of a Public Good," *Journal of Public Economics*, January 1984, *25*, 1–12.

Cukierman, Alex, Edwards, Sebastian and Tabellini, Guido, "Seignorage and Political Instability," Centre for Economic Policy Research (CEPR) Working Paper No. 381, February 1990.

Dornbusch, Rudiger, "Notes on Credibility and Stabilization," NBER (Cambridge, MA) Working Paper No. 2790, 1988.

———— and DePablo, Juan Carlos, "Argentine Debt and Macroeconomic Instability," NBER (Cambridge, MA) Working Paper No. 2378, 1987.

Drazen, Allan and Helpman, Elanhan, "Stabilization and Exchange Rate Management," *Quarterly Journal of Economics*, November 1987, *52*, 835–55.

————, "Inflationary Consequences of Anticipated Macroeconomic Policies," *Review of Economic Studies*, January 1990, *57*, 147–67.

Drazen, Allan, Helpman, Elanhan, and Grilli, Vittorio, "The Benefit of Crises for Economic Reforms," NBER (Cambridge, MA) Working Paper No. 3527, 1990.

Eichengreen, Barry, "The Capital Levy in Theory and Practice," in R. Dornbusch and M. Draghi, eds., *Public Debt Management: Theory and History*, Cambridge: Cambridge University Press, 1990, pp. 191–220.

Eichengreen, Barry and Sachs, Jeffrey, "Exchange Rates and Economic Recovery in the 1930s," *Journal of Economic History*, December 1985, *45*, 925–46.

Fernandez, Raquel and Rodrik, Dani, "Why Is Trade Reform So Unpopular? On Status Quo Bias in Policy Reforms," NBER (Cambridge, MA) Working Paper No. 3269, February 1990.

Fudenberg, Drew and Tirole, Jean, "A Theory of Exit in Duopoly," *Econometrica*, July 1986, *54*, 943–60.

Giavazzi, Francesco and Pagano, Marco, "Can Severe Fiscal Contractions Be Expansionary? Tales of Two Small European Countries," in Olivier Blanchard and Stanley Fischer, eds., *NBER Macroeconomic Annual 1990*, Cambridge, MA: MIT Press, 1990, pp. 75–111.

Giavazzi, Francesco, Pagano, Marco, and Spaventa, Luigi, *High Public Debt: The Italian Experience*, Cambridge: Cambridge University Press, 1988.

Haig, Robert, *The Public Finance of Postwar France*, New York: Columbia University Press, 1929.

Jackson, Julian, *The Politics of Depression in France*, London: Cambridge University Press, 1985.

Kennan, John and Wilson, Robert, "Strategic Bargaining Methods and Interpretation of Strike Data," unpublished manuscript, New York University, 1988.

Loewy, Michael, "Reaganomics and Reputation Revisited," *Economic Inquiry*, July 1988, *26*, 253–64.

Maier, Charles, *Recasting Bourgeois Europe: Stabilization in France, Germany, and Italy in the Decade After World War II*, Princeton: Princeton University Press, 1975.

Orphanides, Athanasios, "The Timing of Stabilizations," unpublished manuscript, Massachusetts Institute of Technology, 1989.

Persson, Torsten and Svensson, Lars, "Why a Stubborn Conservative Would Run a Deficit: Policy with Time Inconsistent Preferences," *Quarterly Journal of Economics*, May 1989, *104*, 325–46.

Riley, John, "Strong Evolutionary Equilibrium and the War of Attrition," *Journal of Theoretical Biology*, February 1980, *82*, 383–400.

Rodrik, Dani, "Promises, Promises: Credible Policy Reforms Via Signalling," *Economic Journal*, September 1989, *99*, 756–72.

Rogoff, Kenneth, "The Optimal Degree of Commitment to an Intermediate Monetary Target," *Quarterly Journal of Economics*, November 1985, *100*, 1169–90.

Roubini, Nouriel and Sachs, Jeffrey, (1989a) "Government Spending and Budget Deficits in the Industrial Democracies," *Economic Policy*, April 1989, *8*, 100–32.

———, (1989b) "Political and Economic Determinants of Budget Deficits in Industrial Democracies," *European Economic Review*, May 1989, *33*, 903–33.

Sargent, Thomas, "The Ends of Four Big Inflations," in R. Hall, ed., *Inflation*, Chicago: University of Chicago Press, 1982, pp. 41–98.

———, "Stopping Moderate Inflations: The Methods of Poincaré and Thatcher," in R. Dornbusch and H. Simonsen, ed., *Inflation, Debt and Indexation*, Cambridge, MA: MIT Press, 1984, pp. 54–96.

———, "Reaganomics and Credibility," in T. Sargent, ed., *Rational Expectations and Inflation*, New York: Harper and Row, 1986, pp. 19–39.

Sargent, Thomas and Wallace, Neil, "Some Unpleasant Monetarist Arithmetic," *Federal Reserve Bank of Minneapolis Quarterly Review*, January 1981, *5*, 1–17.

Tabellini, Guido, "Money, Debt, and Deficits in a Dynamic Game," *Journal of Economic Dynamics and Control*, December 1986, *8*, 427–42.

———, "Central Bank Reputation and the Monetization of Deficits," *Economic Inquiry*, April 1987, *25*, 185–201.

———, "Centralized Wage Setting and Monetary Policy in a Reputational Equilibrium," *Journal of Money, Credit, and Banking*, February 1988, *20*, 102–18.

——— and Alesina, Alberto, "Voting on the Budget Deficit," *American Economic Review*, March 1990, *80*, 37–52.

5

Fiscal Conservatism as a Response to the Debt Crisis

Raúl Labán and
Federico Sturzenegger

5.1 Introduction

During the 1980s inflation in Latin America was to a great extent the product of the debt crisis which abruptly shut off all sources of voluntary external finance and imposed a need for costly adjustment processes. The postponement of these adjustments led to a decade of high inflation, as governments financed the payments of interests on foreign debt through inflation taxation rather than through increases in legislated taxation or expenditure cuts.

In this chapter we simultaneously address two issues. First, we explain why there was a delay in implementing the required adjustments needed to confront the debt crisis. Second, we characterize how the existence of such a delay affects the measures which the economy finds politically acceptable when stabilization is finally attempted. When faced with a shock which implies the need for fiscal adjustment, groups have to bargain over a fiscal reform package; while inflation is low and its costs are not so high, groups may decide to postpone the costs of such an inflation stabilization. If this happens some agents begin to evade the inflation tax, so that inflation imposes an increasing burden on agents without access to capital flight, financial adaptation and other means of inflation tax evasion. The economy suffers a period of high and accelerating inflation which leaves those agents with restricted access to the financial sector in an increasingly worse position. Eventually, these groups are willing to accept adjustment programs which impose on them a high share of the adjustment costs. Because low income groups are the ones most likely to have restricted access to the financial sector the inflation process will induce a fall

Originally published in *Journal of Development Economics* 45 (1994): 305–24. Reprinted with permission.

Table 5.1
Government Spending and Inflation[a]

Year	Argentina G	Argentina π	Peru G	Peru π	Venezuela G	Venezuela π	Mexico G	Mexico π
1980	13.36	101	11.72	50	11.74	21	10.40	29
1981	14.07	104	11.96	67	12.64	16	11.23	27
1982	12.22	165	13.06	80	12.76	10	11.30	57
1983	14.23	344	13.16	100	12.16	6	9.39	102
1984	12.00	641	11.59	111	10.67	12	9.98	65
1985	11.11	667	12.50	163	10.82	11	9.70	58
1986	12.86	87	12.04	78	11.46	12	9.63	86
1987	6.71	133	13.30	86	10.51	28	8.98	132
1988	6.21	343	10.00	666	10.84	30	8.69	114
1989	6.33	3079	9.91	3399	9.97	84	10.95	20
1990	4.45	2314	6.12	7481	8.81	41	11.69	27

Source: World Bank (1992). Numbers are in percentages.
[a] G denotes government spending/GDP. π denotes the inflation rate.

in the amount of transfers to these groups, i.e., a process of increasing "fiscal conservatism."

Table 5.1 shows data on government consumption and inflation rates for Argentina, Peru, Venezuela, and Mexico. The table shows a clear pattern in which an increase in the inflation rate is accompanied by a strong reduction in government spending. If government consumption is a measure of the provision of services to low income groups, the table indicates a decline in this group's (bargaining) power to sustain a given level of transfers as inflation accelerates.

Table 5.2 provides additional evidence on the increasingly regressive nature of fiscal policies in those countries that delay stabilization. The table shows the annual percentage change in real government spending per capita on education and health services for four highly-indebted countries which delayed their adjustment—Chile, Costa Rica, Mexico, and Morocco. It also shows data for two "early adjusters," namely Korea and Turkey. The table suggests that delayed adjustment seems to be accompanied by a decline in spending.

It is only now, ten years after the onset of the crises, that adjustment programs are finally being implemented successfully in most of Latin America. (See Bruno and Fischer, 1991; Dornbusch and Edwards, 1995.)[1] Four main explanations are usually presented for why only now do we see programs of structural reform in Latin America: (a) That reforms

Table 5.2
Change in Real Government Expenditure Per Capita

	Education			Health		
	1970–80	1981–84	1985–87	1970–80	1981–84	1985–87
Late Adjusters						
Chile	3.1	−3.4	−3.4	2.2	−4.8	−2.9
Costa Rica	8.6	−9.7	7.3	117.6	−7.0	1.7
Mexico	11.4	−1.8	−13.8	1.4	−4.8	−9.0
Morocco	8.1	−2.1	−1.9	1.8	−6.7	0.5
Early Adjusters						
Korea	10.8	8.7	6.9	13.2	10.6	29.9
Turkey	10.0	2.6	3.8	5.7	−25.7	12.0

Source: Nelson (1992).

are the pragmatic response to the exhaustion of a given economic model. (See Frieden, 1991; Vial, 1992.) (b) That swings in ideology induced by external events have affected the political landscape making adjustment programs politically viable. The collapse of the Soviet block, for example, may have been an important force in inducing or generating the political support for recent reforms. (c) That reforms in Latin America are largely due to the success of the adjustment programs in Chile and Mexico. This "demonstration effect" may have convinced other policy makers that structural adjustment effectively works, and finally (d) that the role of the IMF or the World Bank has been important in inducing such a common pattern of adjustment (see Stallings, 1992; Kahler, 1992).

In the real world, all elements play a role in explaining what happens, and while exogenous shocks to ideology have certainly occurred in recent years, we believe that what is politically acceptable is mainly the result of the endogenous evolution of the economic conditions in a given country. These economic conditions are what we want to analyze in this paper.

It has been argued that even though from an economic point of view an early stabilization may be preferred, at moderate levels of inflation there is not enough political support for adjustment since many individuals visualize the results as negative *for them*.[2] Early attempts to stabilize are often blocked by different interest groups. As inflation reaches higher levels, the total disruption of normal economic life may generate the required political support that will be the basis of a successful stabilization program. The importance of economic crisis in building up the necessary support for introducing major reforms are also discussed in Drazen and Grilli (1993), Hirschman (1985), Haggard and Kaufman (1992), and Cardoso and Helwege (1992). This line of argumentation suggests that an economic crisis (e.g., a hyperinflation) may in fact be necessary in order for stabilization to be attempted.[3]

But if inflation is increasing and stabilization will eventually take place, does there exist a rationale for delaying stabilization? Delayed stabilizations have been formalized in Alesina and Drazen (1991) using a war of attrition between two groups, where the agent that first agrees to the stabilization program pays a higher fraction of the stabilization costs. Delay arises because there is asymmetric information regarding the degree to which inflation affects each player so that each group waits in the hope that his opponent will give in first. Velasco (1992) derives a story for deficit financing and delays based on a dynamic game in which different government agencies obtain, at a cost, resources from a common pool of government funds. While the paper is written in terms of deficit financing it applies equally well to inflation stabilization. At low inflation rates the unique equilibrium is to extract resources from this common pool even though this increases inflation through time. Once inflation becomes high enough an equilibrium can be supported in which everybody agrees not to extract further resources from the common pool.[4] Labán and Sturzenegger (1994) use a dynamic framework with post-stabilization payoff uncertainty, risk aversion, costly policy reversion and distributional conflict to generate delays. In that model delays exist because, while inflation is low, agents may not be willing to incur the risk associated to the partially irreversible stabilization attempt.

An additional characteristic of many adjustment programs is that some of the groups end up accepting conditions that earlier they found unacceptable. For example, Israel's stabilization of mid-1985 was different from earlier failed attempts in that a heavier burden was placed on workers. In Argentina, during the second Peronist government, the successive stabilization attempts during 1974–76 were increasingly biased against the lower income classes (see DiTella, 1983). Alesina and Drazen (1991) emphasize the coincidence of stabilization with a political consolidation of the right. They refer to the Poincaré stabilization of 1926 and Italy's stabilization of 1922–24 to argue that the lower income classes suffer the largest burden of stabilizations. A similar pattern for the stabilization programs in the 1980s is documented in Geddes (1993). Our model, as will be discussed later, endogenizes the change in relative bargaining positions for different groups over time and accounts for this increased consolidation of the right.

In this chapter, we emphasize the role played by the existence of stabilization costs in deciding when to stabilize. These costs may arise from a contractionary impact of stabilization on output (i.e., real wage cuts and/or employment losses) among other sources. In the presence of less than fully credible reforms, there may be uncertainty on how fast private investment (Rodrik, 1989; Dornbusch, 1991b) and/or net exports (Labán, 1991) would react to offset (at least partially) the negative impact on output induced by a fiscal contraction. Dornbusch (1991a) incorporates a cost of stabilization into the evaluation of the ex-ante benefits of stabilization or economic reform. Fernandez and Rodrik (1990) introduce costs at the individual level by assuming agents are not certain about their post-reform economic standing. We show that the interplay of stabilization costs and distributional conflict may generate delays as well as change the conditions of stabilization through time even in the presence of fully informed and rational agents. In the initial stages of the inflation episode it may be an equilibrium strategy for both groups not to reach an agreement to stabilize, since the costs of inflation may not compensate the benefits of postponing stabilization (these benefits arise from the fact that the delay shifts the stabilization cost to the future). The persistence of positive inflation will trigger a process financial adaptation (i.e., a flight from money), which will increase the rate of inflation and therefore the incentives to stabilize for both groups but will also concentrate the burden of inflation on the poor (Cardoso, 1992; Nelson, 1992; Sturzenegger, 1992). This redistribution of costs induces them to accept conditions that they were not prepared to accept before. If the financial adaptation process is deep enough in that it leads to extremely high rates of inflation associated with high welfare costs stabilization becomes optimal. Thus, we formalize the two main findings of tables 5.1 and 5.2: that stabilization will be delayed until "things get really bad," and that extreme inflation will tend to reduce the level of government spending.

5.2   The Model

We assume a discrete time economy, populated by two types of infinitely lived agents organized in two socio-political groups which maximize the expected utility of their representative agent. Each group is composed of a continuum of agents distributed on the unit interval with total aggregate unitary mass. We call these groups poor (p) and rich (r), as they differ in that the rich have access to a financial adaptation technology which allows them to evade a distortionary (inflation) tax. For the poor this technology is assumed not available or too costly to implement.[5]

Each poor and rich individual receives at the beginning of every period an endowment of size e. Agents are assumed to consume all their net endowment in each period. Prior to the debt crisis, we assume that the government finances a program of transfers to the poor by foreign borrowing. In addition, the interest on such debt is also paid through further external indebtedness. Thus, during this period the stock of public external debt evolves according to

$$b_t = (1 + r)b_{t-1} + g, \qquad (1)$$

where b_t is the stock of external debt at t, r is the (constant) interest rate on foreign borrowing, and g is the level of resources transferred to the poor in each period.

Let us assume that at the beginning of period T_0 the economy is subject to a (debt) shock, which abruptly shuts off all sources of external financing. Before there is political support for stabilization—tax reform and expenditure cuts which balance the budget—the government finances its interest payments and the pre-shock level of transfers through distortionary taxation levied on both agents. Thus, in the pre-stabilization economy the budget constraint for the government in each period is given by

$$rb_{T0} + g = \frac{\pi_t}{1 + \pi_t}(2e - F_t) \qquad (2)$$

under the assumption that no debt reduction takes place. F_t denotes the aggregate level of financial adaptation chosen by the rich group in period t, which represents the fraction of their endowment that is exempt of distortionary taxation. Thus, the tax rate π is endogenous and depends on the aggregate level of tax evasion. Even though ours is a non-monetary economy we interpret the tax as inflationary financing, where g represents seigniorage collection, π the inflation rate, and the tax evasion technology is interpreted as a process of financial adaptation or currency substitution.[6] Without loss of generality in what follows we assume that $b_{T0} = 0$.

At the beginning of each period, both groups decide whether or not to attempt stabilization and bargain on the conditions of the fiscal reform package to be implemented. Stabilization requires agreement between both groups.

While stabilization is not implemented the rich decide, every period, the share of their endowment to be protected against inflation taxation.

The use of this financial adaptation technology is not without costs. We assume that each rich agent faces a cost of investing an amount f_t in this technology in period t equal to $c(f_t, K_t)$, where $K_t = \sum_{z=0}^{t-1} F_z$ denotes the aggreate level of knowledge regarding financial adaptation accumulated at the beinning of period t. This stock of know-how increases with the use of these technologies. This learning process may represent either a process of "learning by doing" or the development of a wider menu of financial and transaction institutions. An increase in the stock of experience on how to use these technologies is assumed to reduce the marginal cost of engaging in this process. Additionally, we assume that for any given stock of knowledge, an increase in the holdings of tax-free assets faces convex costs. Thus, the previous setup is captured by assuming that: $c_f > 0$, $c_{ff} > 0$, $c_{fff} > 0$, $c_K > 0$ and $c_{fK} > 0$. We also assume that $c(0, K_t) = c_f(0, K_t) = c_K(0, K_t) = 0$. Even though any individual agent cannot affect the aggregate level of financial adaptation in equilibrium we must have $f_t = F_t$ for all t.

In the absence of stabilization the poor pay a proportion θ_t of the distortionary taxation in period t and the rich bear a fraction $(1 - \theta_t)$, where

$$\theta_t = \frac{e}{2e - F_t}. \tag{3}$$

Inflation also has distortionary effects which generate welfare losses. These effects have been emphasized in the literature since Bailey (1956), but may include changes in the overall efficiency of the economic system as formalized by Tommasi (1992). Here, we assume these costs can be represented by an additive reduction in the endowment for each agent equal to $\phi(\pi)$, with $\phi'(\pi) > 0$ and $\phi''(\pi) > 0$.

In sum, pre-stabilization, the flow of utilities for poor and rich in period t are given by

$$U_t^p = e - \phi(\pi_t) + (1 - \theta_t)g, \tag{4}$$

$$U_t^r = e - \phi(\pi_t) - (1 - \theta_t)g - c(f_t, K_t), \tag{5}$$

i.e., the endowment minus the costs of inflation plus net transfers. The rich in addition pay the real cost of financial adaptation. If stabilization is implemented, we assume for simplicity that legislated taxes fall completely on the rich. The level of post-stabilization redistribution of income g^s is the result of a bargaining between the two groups, so flow utilities will equal $U_t^p = e + g^s$ and $U_t^r = e - g^s$ for poor and rich, respectively.

Figure 5.1
The bargaining process

If stabilization is implemented, a cost Q has to be paid by both groups. This cost is motivated, as discussed in the introduction, by the contractionary effects or fall in real wages induced by the stabilization. We assume that Q is a constant and that both groups pay an equal share of the stabilization costs.[7]

Figure 5.1 helps to build intuition regarding the bargaining process which takes place during a stabilization. The real line represents all possible transfers which may be agreed upon. The poor will accept all post-stabilization transfers which give them a higher utility level than that attained by not stabilizing this period and behaving optimally ever after. Thus if we denote that value by g^p in figure 5.1 the poor will accept all transfers greater or equal to this amount. The rich, on the contrary, will only accept making transfers lower or equal to those which give a utility level equal to waiting, i.e., they will accept all post-stabilization transfers of g^r or less. The position of these cutoff demands will depend on time, the costs of inflation and the extent of the financial adaptation process. The difference between both values will depend on the benefits of stabilization versus the benefits of delaying. In the figure, we have assumed that $g^r \geq g^p$. In this case we say that there are gains to trade or that a mutually beneficial arrangement between both groups can be achieved. Stabilization is delayed whenever both groups cannot reconcile their demands, i.e., whenever $g^p > g^r$. In what follows we prove two propositions which build up to our main result regarding the existence of delays. Only then do we turn to an evaluation of how the optimal agreements change through time.

PROPOSITION 1   Provided that the assumptions on $U(.)$ and $c(f, K)$ are satisfied, for the stable monetary equilibrium while stabilization is not achieved we find:

(a) $f_t^* > 0 \ \forall \ t$ (positive equilibrium level of financial adaptation),

(b) $f_t^* > f_{t-1}^*$ (increasing equilibrium level of financial adaptation),

(c) $\pi_t > \pi_{t-1}$ (inflation endogenously increases),

(d) $\theta_t > \theta_{t-1}$ (regressive impact of financial adaptation).

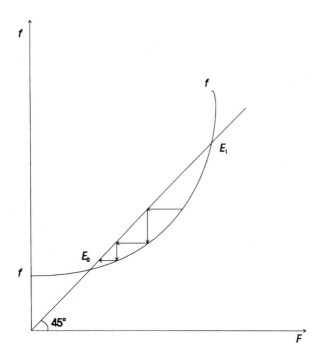

Figure 5.2
Stable and unstable monetary equilibria

Proof   See appendix. □

The monetary equilibria for this economy are depicted in figure 5.2. The individual level of financial adaptation depends positively on the aggregate level because a higher aggregate level of financial adaptation induces a higher inflation rate. This relation is depicted as curve *f-f* in figure 5.2. Monetary equilibria are defined as those points where individual and aggregate decisions coincide, i.e., where *f-f* crosses the 45° line. Depending on the size of the pre-stabilization transfers and the stock of financial adaptation know-how, the economy may have zero, one, or two equilibria. The dual monetary equilibria in figure 5.2 are a reflection of the Laffer curve—the same amount of seigniorage collection may be obtained at either a low or high inflation rate. Contrary to Bruno and Fischer (1990), the low inflation equilibrium is stable while the high inflation equilibrium is unstable. If the amount of investment on the financial innovation technology by the rich were equal to zero our problem would be stationary and thus delays would not be possible. But in choosing the optimal level of financial adaptation (f^*), the agent equalizes the marginal benefits of investing in this technology (given by the inflation rate) to its marginal cost. Because this cost is low for small increases in financial adaptation (recall that $c_f(0, K) = 0$) the agent always finds it optimal to invest a strictly positive amount. Over time the economy experiences a process of learning due to the simultaneous use of financial adaptation technology by many agents in previous periods (graphically this shifts the f-f curve upwards) which induces additional investments in this technology. This, for the stable equilibrium, increases the rate of inflation.

Proposition 1 allows to compute the inflation path while stabilization is not implemented. This path is necessary in order to compute the optimal strategies for both groups. We first derive the maximum amount the rich are willing to pay (g_t^r) and the minimum the poor are willing to receive (g_t^p) at the beginning of each period in order to support the implementation of a stabilization program. Using these cutoff demands we derive the conditions that must be satisfied in order for there to be an area of possible agreement $(g_t^r \geq g_t^p)$. We then characterize this area over time and determine the precise moment when stabilization is actually implemented.

In order to characterize this area consider the amount of transfers the rich and the poor are willing to accept in order to avoid delaying stabilization by J periods. For the rich this amount g_t^r is defined by

$$\sum_{i=t}^{t+J-1} \delta^{i-t}\{e - (1 - \theta_i)g - \phi(\pi_i) - c(f_i^*, K_i)\} + \sum_{i=t+J}^{\infty} \delta^{i-t}\{e - g_{t+j}^s\} - Q\delta^J$$

$$= \sum_{i=t}^{\infty} \delta^{i-t}\{e - g_t^r\} - Q, \tag{6}$$

where g_t^s represents the level of government transfers agreed upon if stabilization is implemented in period t. The first term in the left-hand side represents the present discounted value of utility during the $J - 1$ initial inflationary periods. The second term is the present discounted value of utility thereafter, and the last term represents the present discounted value of the stabilization cost. This must equal the present discounted value of utility, net of stabilization costs, obtained by stabilizing in period t. Similarly for the poor the amount g_t^p is defined by

$$\sum_{i=t}^{t+J-1} \delta^{i-t}\{e + (1 - \theta_i)g - \phi(\pi_i)\} + \sum_{i=t+J}^{\infty} \delta^{i-t}\{e + g_{t+j}^s\} - Q\delta^J$$

$$= \sum_{i=t}^{\infty} \delta^{i-t}\{e + g_t^p\} - Q. \tag{7}$$

To stabilize in period t, given that otherwise stabilization will be attempted J periods hence, we must have $g_t^r \geq g_t^p$ or equivalently that $A(t,J) = g_t^r - g_t^p \geq 0$. Manipulating Eqs. (6) and (7) we find that

$$A(t,J) = \sum_{i=t}^{t+J-1} \delta^{i-t}[2\phi(\pi_i) + c(f_i^*, K_i)] - (1 - \delta^J)2Q, \tag{8}$$

where the function $A(t,J)$ denotes the welfare gain from stabilization in period t instead of in period $t + J$. It depends positively on the costs of inflation incurred by both agents, $2\phi(\pi)$, and the deadweight costs of financial adaptation, $c(f_i^*, K_i)$. It depends negatively on the returns to delaying stabilization, which are represented by the reduction in the cost of adjustment induced by discounting.

The solution to the problem of timing the stabilization can be obtained by evaluating the function $A(t,j)$ when J takes its equilibrium value J^*. For notational ease we define the function $\psi(t) = 2\phi(\pi_t) + c(f_t^*, K_t)$, which is assumed to be an increasing function of the inflation rate.

PROPOSITION 2 Assume that there exists a T such that $A(T,J) > 0 \; \forall J$. Then $A(t,J^*)$ is an increasing function for all $t < T$.

Proof See the appendix. □[8]

The proposition shows that the gains to stabilization are monotonically increasing over time and, therefore, that there exists a unique T^* for which the gains from stabilization become positive. Stabilization takes place for the smallest integer t such that $t \geq T^*$, where T^* solves

$$2\phi(\pi_{T^*}) + c(f_{T^*}^*, K_{T^*}) = (1 - \delta)2Q, \tag{9}$$

and corresponds to the time period in which the agreement area becomes nonnegative. An important feature of equation (9) is that it does not depend on the distributional parameter θ, the decision to stabilize depending only on the aggregate costs and benefits of delaying the adjustment.[9]

Equation (9) delivers several intuitive results regarding the stabilization date. First, that the larger the stabilization costs the longer will be the delay. Second, that the greater the discounting (small δ) the longer will be the delay. These two terms appear jointly on the right-hand side of (9) because the benefits of delaying are given by the fall in the real cost of stabilization induced by transferring the stabilization cost towards the future. If there is no discounting nothing is gained by waiting and therefore there will be no delays. Third, that the more costly is inflation or financial adaptation the shorter will be the delay. These two terms add up to the costs of delaying stabilization.

The existence of delay looks strikingly counterintuitive. If everybody knows the future evolution of the economy and anticipates that stabilization will be implemented, it seems natural to think that stabilization will be undertaken right away as doing so would avoid all the inflation costs incurred during the delay. The intuition for delay in this model relies on the fact that discounting affects the relative costs of stabilizing today versus tomorrow. As time goes on, the process of financial adaptation increases inflation if no agreement is reached, therefore the burden of not stabilizing increases. Eventually, the costs of inflation are not compensated by further delays.

We now ask the question of how the path of inflation would look like in the presence of a central planner. Given a path for the process of financial adaptation a central planner who appropriately weighs the utility of the two groups would also delay stabilization, as benefits and costs are the same as for the individual groups. The main difference relies on the fact that a central planner would never engage in the process of financial adaptation as it only redistributes income between the groups in addition of inducing net deadweight losses. Once the dynamics of money demand are eliminated the inflation rate will be constant and delays are not possible—either stabilization is implemented in the first period or never.

It is common in political rhetoric to hear that tough measures are never implemented since no policy maker wants to pay the costs of stabilization without enjoying the benefits. In part we have captured this intuition, as in our setup a high discount factor makes it very attractive to shift the stabilization costs to the future. Finally, we find that stabilizations are implemented only when things get out of hand, i.e., when inflation has reached very high levels. In this sense we formalize the idea that governments react only when things have gotten "really bad," or when no alternatives are left.

5.3 Conservative Governments

In this section we discuss the increasingly conservative nature of stabilization efforts in the presence of delays. The existence of such a regressive bias in the stabilization programs as shown in tables 5.1 and 5.2 is interesting, because even though it is anticipated by the poor, i.e., they know that the delay will 'hurt' them in the long run, they are still unwilling to reduce their demands to make them compatible with those of the other group.[10]

In order to show how the stabilization agreement depends on the length of the delay, suppose, just to fix ideas, that two economies differ in their stabilization costs Q so that they will stabilize at different dates. In this section we ask how this affects the fiscal arrangement agreed upon.[11] We show that the longer the delay, and consequently the higher the inflation rate attained before stabilization, the smaller the level of transfers that groups will agree upon when stabilization is implemented.

Consider that stabilization takes place in period t. From (6) and (7) we have[12]

$$g_t^p = (1 - \delta)[(1 - \theta_t)g - \phi(\pi_t)] + \delta g_{t+1}^s + (1 - \delta)^2 Q, \tag{10}$$

and

$$g_t^r = (1 - \delta)[(1 - \theta_t)g + \phi(\pi_t) + c(f_t^*, K_t)] + \delta g_{t+1}^s - (1 - \delta)^2 Q. \tag{11}$$

Due to the linearity of the utility functions, the Nash bargaining outcome is given by the average of both group's demands,

$$g_t^s = \frac{g_t^r + g_t^p}{2}. \tag{12}$$

It is easy to see from (10), (11) in (12) that

$$g_t^s = (1 - \delta)\left\{(1 - \theta_t)g + \frac{c(f_t^*, K_t)}{2}\right\} + \delta g_{t+1}^s, \tag{13}$$

and similarly for $g_{t+i}^s \ \forall i > 0$. Note that the post-stabilization level of transfers depends on the net transfers observed in the pre-stabilization economy and that the term between brackets in (13) is an average of the transfers received by the poor, $(1 - \theta_t)g$, and the transfers plus costs of financial adaptation paid by the rich, $(1 - \theta_t)g + c(f_t^*, K_t)$. The larger the amount of transfers received by the poor in the pre-stabilization economy the larger the post-stabilization transfer obtained under a Nash bargaining solution. Integrating (13) forward we obtain[13]

$$(g_{t+1}^s - g_t^s) = \frac{(1 - \delta)}{2} \sum_{i=t}^{\infty} \delta^{i-t}\{c(f_{i+1}^*, K_{i+1}) - c(f_i^*, K_i) - 2g(\theta_{i+1} - \theta_i)\}\forall t. \tag{14}$$

We now show that the level of transfers in a Nash bargaining solution, g_t^s, decreases over time.

PROPOSITION 3   For the economy described in section 5.2, and for g_t^s defined by (12) we have that $g_{t+1}^s - g_t^s < 0 \ \forall t$.

Proof   See the appendix. □

Proposition 3 results from the fact that the net transfers received by poor agents fall steadily if inflationary financing of transfers is maintained. Inflation induces financial adaptation, and because financial adaptation shifts the burden of the inflation tax towards them, poor agents find that the net transfers they receive fall over time. Rich agents choose how much to financially adapt (though at cost $c(.)$) so it is natural to believe that they will engage in financial adaptation only if this increases their welfare. As long as the costs of financial adaptation do not increase too much in equilibrium, the rich agents' *relative position* will improve. Proposition 3 shows that this is always the case. This change in relative bargaining positions induces a steady decline in the level of transfers in the post stabilization agreement, thus formalizing the outcomes observed in tables 5.1 and 5.2.[14]

5.4   Conclusions

This chapter shows that it is possible to understand delays in policy implementation as the result of distributional conflict between different interest groups in the presence of costly stabilization. Initially inflation is moderate and the costs of inflation are small. Groups cannot match their relative demands, and stabilization is not agreed upon. As time goes by, the use of financial innovation increases the equilibrium rate of inflation and redistributes the burden of inflation taxation to the poor. The increase in the level of inflation raises the costs of not reaching an agreement and stabilization is therefore more likely to occur.

Two well-recognized stylized facts concerning delayed stabilizations are accounted for by our model. First, that things have to get "bad" before any action is taken. Hyperinflation, wars and political crises are usually a catalytic for change. Our model provides a very simple framework which allows an understanding of why this may be so without having to rely on irrational behavior of economic agents or imperfect information. Secondly, that as the rate of inflation increases, the relative position of the poor worsens. They are willing to accept progressively less favorable conditions in order to stabilize. The contribution of this paper is to show that the knowledge of the future deterioration in their relative position may not be strong enough to change their present demands to a point in which stabilization is immediately achieved. The model therefore gives a rationale for economic policies in Latin America since the outset of the debt crisis. Initially the economies resorted to inflation financing, as no consensus for reform existed. After a decade of high and increasing inflation the economies implemented strongly conservative stabilization programs.

In the political debate we often hear comments regarding the delay such as: *nobody wants to pay the costs if the benefits come in the future*, and *adjustment is only attempted by governments which have long horizons*. We believe that the role of the discount factor in (9) captures the intuition behind these statements. The timing of stabilization is essentially a decision as to when to pay the adjustment cost. Policymakers (or economies) which heavily discount the future find very beneficial to shift this cost into the future and will thus delay adjustment more. Regarding the current implementation of structural reform programs, the political rhetoric includes statements like: *the reforms today are the consequence of the exhaustion of an economic model*, or that, *reforms today take place because governments have no alternatives*. The exhaustion of an "economic model" takes place in our setup when inflation has increased to such levels that further delays are no longer optimal.

A central planner would never experience delays, as he would never engage in the process of financial adaptation, thus removing time dependency from the model and ruling out delays. The centralized economy could get stuck in a low inflation equilibrium with the central planner not risking stabilization, but where things do not worsen through time. The decentralized economy would, on the other hand, through the financial innovation process increase the rate of inflation, perhaps to the point where stabilization is finally implemented. While the process of extreme inflation may then be beneficial for the economy because it triggers the political support for radical reform, it is also true that it will have lasting and important income distribution effects.

An obvious extension includes the possibility of understanding inflation cycles. Kiguel and Liviatan (1991) document the fact that inflation may be highly variable, with periods of high inflation superseded by transitory stabilization attempts. Our model has potential for explaining these facts. Assume for example that the stabilization cost Q is an unknown random variable. After each stabilization attempt, agents update their beliefs about this stabilization cost. If there is the possibility of reversing the stabilization attempt, then agents may decide to backtrack if the cost of stabilization turned out to be higher than initially expected. While this would explain the possibility of a collapse, it can also explain why inflation will have to increase to higher levels until stabilization is once again implemented: agents will now update upwards their beliefs on the stabilization costs and therefore for stabilization to be an equilibrium inflation will have to reach even higher levels. Furthermore, as the economy retains, at least to some extent, the expertise in the use of alternative financial instruments, inflation acceleration in the wake of the failed stabilization attempt takes place more rapidly.

Because the possibility of collapses will depend on the realization of the costs of stabilization, we may see similar countries with very different inflation experiences. Some will fall into a pattern of inflation-stabilization cycles. Some will have a successful initial stabilization and some will be able to stabilize only after several failed attempts. What our model suggests is that the dynamics of money demand are such that all economies eventually stabilize. Not surprisingly, the periods of high monetary instability are relegated to brief spans of time where several countries experience extreme inflation at the same time. Such was the case of Central Europe in the 1920s and of Latin America in the 1980s. The early 1990s show that the transformation of the Latin American economies had reached a point where further inflationary financing was neither politically acceptable nor economically viable.

Appendix

Proof of Proposition 1   To decide on the optimal level of financial adaptation, the rich maximize the following objective function:

$$\max_{\{f_t\}_{t=0}^{\infty}} \sum_{t=0}^{\infty} \delta^t \left\{ e - \frac{\pi_t}{1 + \pi_t}(e - f_t) - \phi(\pi_t) - c(f_t, K_t) \right\}, \tag{A.1}$$

taking π_t and K_t as given and $\delta < 1$ the discount factor. The first-order conditions are

$$\left[\frac{\pi_t}{1 + \pi_t} - c_f(f_t, K_t) \right] \leq 0, \quad \text{and} \quad = 0 \text{ if } f_t > 0 \ \forall t > 0. \tag{A.2}$$

For $f_t = 0$ to be a solution to this maximization problem, the first-order condition should be non-positive. Thus (a) follows from the fact that $\pi_t > 0 \ \forall t$ and $c_f(0, K_t) = 0$.

Eq. (A.2) defines the optimal level of tax evasion chosen by a rich agent in each period as a function of the aggregate level of financial adaptation for a given stock of knowledge and seigniorage collection. This relationship is represented by the locus f-f in figure 5.2, which from Eq. (2)

and (A.2) is upward sloping $(df/dF = (g/(2e - F)^2 c_{ff}^2) > 0)$ and convex $(d^2f/dF^2 = g[(2(2e - F)c_{ff} + c_{fff}/c_{ff})/(2e - F)^4 c_{ff}] > 0)$. Equilibrium will be attained when $f = F$.

As from (A.2) we have $df/dK = -c_{fK}/c_{ff} > 0$, an increase in the level of financial adaptation know-how will shift the locus f-f upwards. Computing the change in the *equilibrium* level of financial adaptation as a consequence of a change in K, we have $df^*/dK = -c_{fK}/[g/((2e - F)^2 - c_{ff})]$, which proves (b) for the stable equilibrium where $df/dF = g/(2e - F)^2 c_{ff} < 1$.

Finally, since $f_t^* = F_t^* > f_{t-1}^* = F_{t-1}^* > 0 \; \forall t$ from (a) and (b), (c) follows from (2) and (d) follows from (3). $\square$

Proof of Proposition 2   We work the solution backwards from T. From the fact that $A(T, J) > 0 \; \forall t$ we know that in period $T - 1$ we will have $J^* = 1$; therefore, the optimal strategy is derived by computing the value of $A(T - 1, 1)$, which from (8) equals

$$A(T - 1, 1) = \psi(T - 1) - (1 - \delta)2Q. \tag{A.3}$$

From (A.3) it is evident that two cases arise, one in which $A(T - 1, 1) > 0$ and the other in which $A(T - 1, 1) < 0$. Consider the case in which $A(T - 1, 1) > 0$. This implies that when evaluating $A(T - 2, J)$, the equilibrium J in period $T - 2$ is again equal to 1 (because stabilization is an equilibrium in period $T - 1$). But then

$$A(T - 2, 1) = \psi(T - 2) - (1 - \delta)2Q < \psi(T - 1) - (1 - \delta)2Q$$

$$= A(T - 1, 1), \tag{A.4}$$

which is true from the fact that ψ is increasing in inflation which, in turn, is increasing through time from proposition 1.

In the case in which $A(T - 1, 1) < 0$ we must show that this implies that $A(T - 2, 2) < A(T - 1, 1)$, as in period $T - 2$ agents realize stabilization will only come in two periods if it is not implemented in the current one. Using the definition for $A(.)$, we must show that

$$A(T - 2, 2) = \psi(T - 2) + \delta\psi(T - 1) - (1 - \delta^2)2Q$$

$$< \psi(T - 1) - (1 - \delta)2Q = A(T - 1, 1), \tag{A.5}$$

but the above inequality can be rewritten as

$$\psi(T - 2) - \psi(T - 1) + \delta[\psi(T - 1) - (1 - \delta)2Q]$$

$$= \psi(T - 2) - \psi(T - 1) + \delta A(T - 1, 1) < 0, \tag{A.6}$$

which is satisfied from ψ being increasing in time and $A(T-1,1) < 0$. The result now follows for previous periods by induction. $\Box$

Proof of Proposition 3   Rewite the expression between brackets in (14) as

$$L = c(f_{i+1}^*, K_{i+1}) - c(f_i^*, K_i) - g(\theta_{i+1} - \theta_i) - g(\theta_{i+1} - \theta_i). \tag{A.7}$$

We want to show that $L < 0 \forall t$. Add and subtract g to rewrite (A.7) as

$$L = [c(f_{i+1}^*, K_{i+1}) + (1 - \theta_{i+1})g] - [c(f_i^*, K_i) + (1 - \theta_i)g] - [(\theta_{i+1} - \theta_i)g], \tag{A.8}$$

which represents the difference in the net change in the costs of inflation paid by the rich and the poor. Because (A.8) is expressed in differences we can approximate it by computing how the total cost of inflation for the rich and for the poor change with K. I.e., we need to show that $\partial L'/\partial K < 0$ where

$$L' = c(f, K) + (e - f)\frac{\pi}{1 + \pi} - e\frac{\pi}{1 + \pi}.$$

Similarly we need to show that

$$\partial[c(f, K) + (e - f)\pi/(1 + \pi)]/\partial K < \partial[e\pi/(1 + \pi)]/\partial K. \tag{A.9}$$

Computing these derivatives at equilibrium values (when $f = F$) and using the first-order conditions of the maximization problem of proposition 1, (A.9) reduces to

$$c_K + (e - f)\frac{d\pi/(1 + \pi)}{df}\frac{df}{dK} < e\frac{d\pi/(1 + \pi)}{df}\frac{df}{dK},$$

or

$$c_K < f\frac{d\pi/(1 + \pi)}{df}\frac{df}{dK}.$$

But from (2) and the result of proposition 1, the right-hand side is positive. Therefore the inequality is true. $\Box$

Notes

This chapter was written while at CIEPLAN, Santiago, Chile. We thank Josef Perktold, Héctor Schamis and an anonymous referee for useful comments, and Michael Barnes for editorial assistance.

1. As of 1992 most Latin American countries had inflation rates under 35%. The exceptions were Ecuador and Peru (with inflation rates under 100%), Uruguay (with an inflation rate of around 100%) and Brazil which continued to exhibit monthly rates above 15%.

2. See, for example, Alesina and Drazen (1991) and Dornbusch et al. (1990).

3. Maier (1975) discussing the German stabilization of the 1920s recognizes the importance of the high welfare costs associated with extreme inflation in inducing different groups to agree upon stabilization. The same has been argued with respect to the Bolivian experience of the 1950s (Eder, 1968), its hyperinflation episode of the 1980s (Morales, 1991), and the Argentinean experience in the 80s (Heymann, 1991).

4. For a related story that also allows for policy cycles see Mondino et al. (1992).

5. If we allow this technology to be available, at higher cost, for the lower income group, the results of this chapter will still hold. This assumption is made here only for simplicity of exposition.

6. The setup we have in mind is that of a cash-in-advance constraint economy with two imperfect substitutes assets. Rich agents decide on the optimal portfolio of these two assets to carry their wealth between the moment they receive their endowment and the moment consumption takes place.

7. Nevertheless, it is possible that the cost of stabilization may be related among other things to the level of inflation. As inflation accelerates the costs of stabilization may increase. As we approach a hyperinflation these costs may fall, as all prices become indexed to the exchange rate. It is also possible to allow one group to pay a higher fraction of the stabilization costs or for the costs of inflation to affect both groups differently. These extensions in no way jeopardize the results of the model.

8. The assumption indicates that there exists a level of financial adaptation (hence inflation) large enough that stabilization is always an equilibrium. Because high inflation can induce high levels of welfare costs this is not a restrictive assumption.

9. On the contrary, as will be shown in section 5.3, the level of post stabilization transfers will depend critically on the distributional parameter θ.

10. They will be "hurt" in the sense that the long-run level of transfers will be lower than what would have been obtained under an earlier stabilization. Nevertheless, because agents choose their cutoff demands, they must still be better off by delaying stabilization.

11. The same result holds for comparative statics on any of the elements which affect the optimal stopping time.

12. From proposition 2 we know that, because the costs of delaying are monotonically increasing, the optimal cutoffs are computed by assuming that if stabilization does not take place in this period it will take place in the following one (i.e. that $J^* = 1$).

13. The transversality condition is automatically satisfied as both cutoff demands converge to zero as inflation increases.

14. Note that g^s does not depend on the costs of inflation, $\psi(\pi)$. This derives from the assumption that inflation affects both groups equally. If this were not the case the increase in the inflation rate would have effects on the post-stabilization level of transfers in addition to those induced through financial adaptation. We leave these extensions to the reader.

References

Alesina, A. and A. Drazen, 1991, "Why are stabilizations delayed?" *American Economic Review* 81, no. 5, 1170–1188.

Bruno, M. and S. Fischer, 1990, "Seigniorage, operating rules, and the high inflation trap," *Quarterly Journal of Economics* 105, 353–347.

Bruno, M. et al., eds., 1991, *Lessons of economic stabilization and its aftermath* (MIT Press, Cambridge, MA).

Cardoso, E., 1992, "Inflation and poverty," Working paper no. 4006 (NBER, Cambridge, MA).

Cardoso, E. and A. Helwege, 1992, *Latin America's economy: Diversity, trends and conflicts* (MIT Press, Cambridge, MA).

DiTella, G., 1983, *Argentina's experience under a labour based government* (Macmillan, New York).

Dornbusch, R., 1991a, "Credibility and stabilization," *Quarterly Journal of Economics* 106, 837–850.

Dornbusch, R., 1991b, "From stabilization to growth," *World Bank Review*.

Dornbusch, R. and S. Edwards, eds. 1995, *Reform, recovery, and growth in Latin America and the Middle East* (University of Chicago Press, Chicago, IL).

Dornbusch, R., F. Sturzenegger and H. Wolf, 1990, "Extreme inflation: Dynamics and stabilization," *Brookings Papers on Economic Activity* 2, 1–84.

Drazen A. and V. Grilli, 1993, "The benefits of crisis for economic reforms," *American Economic Review* 83, no. 3, 598–607.

Eder, G. J., 1968, *Inflation and development in Latin America: A case history of inflation and stabilization in Bolivia* (The University of Michigan Press, Ann Arbor, MI).

Fernandez, R. and D. Rodrik, 1990, "Why is trade reform so unpopular? On status quo bias in policy reforms," *American Economic Review* 80, no. 5, 1146–1155.

Frieden, Jeffry, 1991, *Debt, democracy and adjustment in Latin America* (Princeton University Press, Princeton, NJ).

Geddes, B., 1993, Democracy, labor and structural adjustment, Mimeo. (UCLA, Los Angeles, CA).

Haggard S. and R. Kaufman, 1992, "The political economy of inflation and stabilization in middle-income countries," in S. Haggard and R. Kaufman, eds., *The politics of economic adjustment* (Princeton University Press, Princeton, NJ).

Heymann, D., 1991, "From sharp disinflation to hyperinflation, twice: The Argentina experience 1985–1989," in M. Bruno et al., eds., *Lessons of economic stabilization and its aftermath*, 103–141 (MIT Press: Cambridge, MA).

Hirschman, A., 1985, "Reflections on the Latin America experience," in L. Lindberg and C. Maier, eds., *The politics of inflation and economic stagnation*, Theoretical Approaches and International Studies (The Brookings Institution, Washington).

Labán, R., 1991, Coordination failures and the costly transition from stabilization to growth, Mimeo. (MIT, Cambridge, MA).

Labán, R. and F. Sturzenegger, 1994, "Distributional conflict, financial adaptation and delayed stabilizations," *Economics and Politics* 6, no. 3, 255–274.

Mahler, M. 1992, "External influence, conditionality, and the politics of adjustment," in S. Haggard and R. Kaufman, eds., *The politics of economic adjustment* (Princeton University Press, Princeton, NJ).

Maier, C., 1975, *Recasting bourgeois Europe: Stabilization in France, Germany, and Italy in the decade after World War I* (Princeton University Press, Princeton, NJ).

Miguel, M. and N. Liviatan, 1991, "The inflation–stabilization cycles in Argentina and Brazil," in M. Bruno et al., eds., *Lessons of economic stabilization and its aftermath*, 191–239 (MIT Press: Cambridge, MA).

Mondino, G., F. Sturzenegger and M. Tommasi, 1992, "Recurrent and high inflation: A dynamic game," Mimeo. (UCLA, Los Angeles, CA).

Morales, J. A., 1991, "The transition from stabilization to sustained growth in Bolivia," in M. Bruno et al., eds., *Lessons of economic stabilization and its aftermath*, 15–47 (MIT Press: Cambridge, MA).

Nelson, Joan, 1992, "Poverty, equity and the politics of adjustment," in S. Haggard and R. Kaufman, eds., *The politics of economic adjustment* (Princeton University Press, Princeton, NJ).

Rodrik, D., 1989, "Policy uncertainty and private investment in developing countries," Working paper no. 2999 (NBER, Cambridge, MA).

Stallings, B., 1992, "International influence on economic policy: Debt, stabilization, and structural reform," in S. Haggard and R. Kaufman, eds., *The politics of economic adjustment* (Princeton University Press, Princeton, NJ).

Sturzenegger, F., 1992, "Inflation and social welfare in a model with endogenous financial adaptation," Working paper no. 4103 (NBER, Cambridge, MA).

Velasco, A., 1992, "A model of fiscal deficits and delayed fiscal reforms," RR 92.06 (C.V. Starr Center for Applied Economics, New York University, New York).

Vial, 1992, *Hacia donde va Latino-America?* (CIEPLAN eds., Santiago, Chile).

World Bank, 1992, *World tables* (The World Bank, Washington, DC).

6

The Benefit of Crises for Economic Reforms

Allan Drazen and Vittorio Grilli

When expenditures consistently outrun revenue the resulting inflation may have the effect of convincing the public and government that taxes must be raised to finance public investment. In the advanced industrial countries income taxation, and big spurts in taxation generally, have become possible only under the impact of major emergency and crisis, mostly in wartime. In a number of developing countries inflation has acted as an equivalent of war in setting the stage for more forceful taxation.
—Albert Hirschman, "Reflections on the Latin American Experience"

Standard economic theory, not to mention common sense, suggests that economic welfare is usually maximized when distortions are minimized. The preference for nondistortionary taxes to finance government spending provides a leading example. Similar reasoning is used to support gradualism in the introduction of policies in order to minimize the distortions or instability which sharp policy reversals may induce.

A very different point of view is represented in the above passage from Albert Hirschman. The welfare losses associated with economic distortions and crises enable societies to enact measures that would be impossible to enact in less distortionary circumstances. In other words, distortions and crises may raise welfare if they are the only way to induce necessary policy changes. For example, this argument has been used to explain how hyperinflations are ended. In many cases, an agreement among political groups to take painful measures to end inflation was achieved only because of the very high welfare costs associated with extremely high rates of inflation. (We discuss some examples in the conclusions.) This suggests that the heavy costs of extremely high inflation and the situation of emergency associated with it were necessary to force the adoption of stabilization programs.

Originally published in *American Economic Review* 83, no. 3 (1993): 598–607. Reprinted with permission.

In this chapter we explore the argument that, from a dynamic pro-spective, crises and emergencies may be welfare-improving and hence de-sirable. When ongoing social conflict implies that an economy has settled in a Pareto-inferior equilibrium, radical changes are often needed to break the stalemate and put the economy on a welfare-superior path. The necessary introduction of drastic measures, which may involve sharp tax increases and expenditure cuts, is usually unpopular and forcibly resisted because of distributional concerns. The distress associated with living through an economic crisis often makes these measures acceptable. The extreme welfare loss that each agent suffers in a crisis dwarfs the loss he may associate with an unfavorable distribution of the burden of a major policy change. The destabilization of the economy, therefore, may facili-tate the transition to a welfare-superior equilibrium.

Formalizing the argument that crises may be welfare-improving makes clear the importance of the distributional implications of large policy changes; that is, it makes clear that drastic but necessary policy changes are resisted because economic participants believe someone else can be forced to bear the burden of the change. The argument that distributional conflict between groups can explain the failure to adopt necessary policy changes was suggested by Alberto Alesina and Drazen (1991) and has been used in the sociological literature. Here we argue that the "benefit of crises" view is a normative implication of this positive argument.

A further advantage of formalizing the "benefit of crises" argument is that it enables us to reexamine other arguments about the desirability of mitigating the costs of inflation. Stanley Fischer and Lawrence Summers (1989), for example, argue that policies meant to reduce the cost of in-flation, such as indexation, lead governments to follow more inflationary policies and thus may ultimately lower welfare.[1] In the specific dynamic model we consider, however, we find that indexation, while raising the rate of inflation, leaves expected welfare unchanged. Fischer and Summers consider a steady-state model where indexation leads to higher perma-nent inflation, whereas we consider a dynamic process for inflation in which the choice of higher current inflation will induce an earlier shift to noninflationary financing. Assessing the welfare effects of a policy such as indexation requires considering not only its current possibly inflationary effects, but also the effects on the future path of inflation via endogenous government policy.

Our argument can be seen as an example of the theory of the second best, albeit a nonstandard one. The "preexisting distortion" is the nature of the policy-making process; given the political constraints, a distortionary policy must be introduced to enable adoption of a major policy reform. Hence our result is in a sense one level removed from the standard application of the theory of the second best to policy choice, being concerned with constraints on the policy-choice mechanism itself.

For the story to be complete, we also need an explanation of how an economy may find itself in a suboptimal equilibrium. While this aspect is not explicitly modeled in this chapter, in our approach the mechanism responsible for the suboptimal state of the economy is the same one that makes crises potentially useful. In a society composed of socioeconomic groups with conflicting interests, where there exists no consensus over economic policy and the distribution of the benefits and costs associated with policy change, welfare can be well below the first-best optimum. In such a situation, the economy can proceed for a long time, and potentially indefinitely, on paths that are well below its potential.

The plan of the chapter is as follows. In the next section we present a model of individual behavior in agreeing to changes in policy, focusing on the role of inflation in inducing agreement. This leads to an expression for expected social welfare as a function of the rate of inflation. In Section 6.2 we solve the model via simulation, deriving the optimal rate of inflation and the expected date of policy change. The main result of the optimality of a period of high inflation (and the associated distortion) emerges. In the conclusion, we interpret this as well some other nonintuitive results and consider general lessons of the simulations.

6.1   Setup of the Model

Our general argument is that highly distortionary financing can be welfare-improving if the government must finance some portion of its expenditures in a distortionary way. This argument can be applied to any type of distortionary taxation in a model of endogenous policy change. Here we apply it to inflation raising welfare by inducing tax reform. Consistent with the historical experience of many countries, we consider an economy in which monetization is due to the inability to reach agreement about the distribution of nondistortionary (or less distortionary) taxes. That is, the government budget can be fully financed by nondistortionary taxes only when it is agreed how to allocate taxes between different individuals or social groups. In the interim, at least part of the budget must be covered by printing money.

The shift to nondistortionary financing requires consensus on the allocation of tax burdens, usually requiring groups to bear higher taxes than they would have originally liked. The failure to adopt a non-distortionary tax package therefore is due to each individual or social group attempting to wait the other out in the attempt to bear a lower share of taxes, with interim use of the inflation tax imposing costs on the whole society.

Operationally, we model problems of agreement and the implied delay in tax reform as a "war of attrition" between two individuals, seen as representative agents of two conflicting groups. We follow Alesina and Drazen (1991), where it was argued that the war of attrition is an appropriate way to model delay in adopting policy changes when conflict over the distributional consequences of the policy change is important.

The Government Budget and Monetization

For simplicity, we assume that all of the government budget is covered by taxation, at least part of which is distortionary (here, the inflation tax). This implies that government debt is constant, and for simplicity, we set it equal to zero. To understand the role of this assumption, remember that our argument requires there to be some distortionary finance in the absence of an agreement on the distribution of the burden of nondistortionary taxation. What about the possibility that government expenditures are *fully* covered by bond issuance to avoid any current distortion? Fully covering expenditures by bond finance implies that debt is growing faster than the rate of interest, so that such a path is infeasible in the long run. Distortionary finance cannot therefore be avoided in the absence of agreement. Once one accepts the fact that a path with deficits and bond financing cannot be distortion-free, the size (or even presence) of a deficit does not qualitatively affect our argument. If bond-financing were used and current bond issuance were covered by nondistortionary taxes in the future, our setup would capture the choice between distortionary and nondistortionary taxation that a model with the choice between monetization and bond issuance would imply.

Denote by γ the fraction of expenditures covered by seigniorage before an agreement over a nondistortionary tax package is reached ("agreement"), the remainder covered by lump-sum taxes. As indicated above, the key to the benefit-of-crises view is the assumption that, in the absence of an agreement, some part of the budget must be financed by distortionary means (i.e., by inflation). Formally, this means that γ is constrained to be no less than some $\bar{\gamma} > 0$.

The government budget constraint prior to an agreement at time T is then

$$i(t)m(t) + \tau(t) = g \qquad t < T, \tag{1}$$

where i is the nominal interest rate, m is real money balances, τ is total nondistortionary taxes, and g is government expenditure.[2] The government's choice is over a rate of monetary growth which yields a level of seigniorage. This choice of how to finance expenditures can be summarized by

$$i(t)m(t) = \gamma g \qquad \text{with } \gamma \geq \bar{\gamma}. \tag{2}$$

If γ is constant over time, τ and $i(t)m(t)$ will be constant over time as well.

After an agreement at T, the government budget is simply

$$\tau(t) = g \qquad t \geq T. \tag{1'}$$

In addition to specifying the total level of taxes, we must specify how tax burdens are divided between the two individuals. Since the distribution of the cost of stabilization is the crucial element, what is important is that agreement entails that one side bears a larger fraction of total taxes after agreement has been reached than before. In general, any distribution of taxes after T where one side agrees to bear a fraction $1 \geq \alpha > \frac{1}{2}$ of the tax burden will yield a delay in reaching an agreement. For simplicity we assume that taxes are divided half–half before a stabilization and fall entirely on one individual after a stabilization (i.e., $\alpha = 1$). None of the conclusions depends on this last assumption.

Individual Behavior

We imagine the economy to be populated by two different representative individuals (or social groups). At each point in time, utility for each individual is a positive function of consumption c and a negative function of inflation π. The utility cost of inflation is group-specific and may be written $w(\theta, \pi(t))$, where θ indexes the cost of inflation to each of the two groups. Let instantaneous utility of the representative individual with cost θ be

$$u^\theta(t) = c^\theta(t) - w(\theta, \pi(t)). \tag{3}$$

This specification of utility could be derived from an underlying utility function over consumption and real money balances. The utility from money balances is implicit in the cost of inflation $w(\theta, \pi(t))$.

At the beginning $(t = 0)$, the group-specific component θ is independently drawn from a distribution $F(\theta)$ with lower and upper bound $\underline{\theta}$ and
$\bar{\theta}$. The group-specific θ is known only to the group itself, while the other
group only knows the distribution $F(\theta)$. For $w(\theta, \pi)$, we consider a simple
function of the form

$$w(\theta, \pi) = a + b\theta\pi^n, \tag{4}$$

where, a, b, and n are constants.

In order to compute the equilibrium level of inflation, we need to specify the aggregate demand for real balances. In this type of heterogeneous-
agent model it is difficult to derive aggregate money demand starting
from utility maximization. Therefore, we make the reasonable assumption
that aggregate money demand is given by

$$m^d = ke^{-\alpha i_t/(1+i_t)}, \tag{5}$$

which has been shown to be compatible with individual maximization (see
Guillermo Calvo and Leonardo Leiderman, 1992).

Substituting (5) into (2) and assuming a constant real interest rate r, we
have

$$(r + \pi)ke^{-\alpha(r+\pi)/(1+r+\pi)} = \gamma g, \tag{2'}$$

which implicitly defines the equilibrium level of inflation as a function of
γ, denoted $\pi(\gamma)$.

The infinitely-lived individual's objective is to maximize expected present discounted utility by choice of a time path of consumption and a date
(T_i) to agree to bear the high tax burden if the other individual has not
already volunteered. Let us denote by $S(T)$ the distribution of the opponent's optimal concession time, and by $s(T)$ the associated density function. [These will of course depend on $F(\theta)$ and on his strategy.] Expected
utility as a function of chosen concession time (T_i) can then be written as

$$EU(T_i) = [1 - S(T_i)]\left[\int_0^{T_i} u^P(x)e^{-\rho x}\,dx + e^{-\rho T_i}V^H(T_i)\right]$$

$$+ \int_0^{T_i}\left[\int_0^x u^P(z)e^{-\rho z}\,dz + e^{-\rho x}V^N(x)\right]s(x)\,dx, \tag{6}$$

where ρ is the discount rate, u^P is the flow utility prior to agreement, V^H
is the present discounted utility from the time of stabilization onward of
the individual who agrees to bear high taxes, and V^N is the present discounted utility from the time of stabilization onward of the individual

who bears low taxes. The first term represents the expected utility if the agent will be the one to concede (at time T_i), while the second term represents the expected utility deriving from the possibility that the other agent will concede before T_i (at time x).

The assumption that instantaneous utility is linear in consumption means that any feasible consumption path yields the same utility. We therefore assume that individuals simply consume their current income, net of regular and inflation taxes. Consumption may then be written as

$$c^P = y - \frac{im + \tau}{2} = y - \frac{g}{2}$$

$$c^H = y - g$$

$$c^N = y, \tag{7}$$

where y is current pretax income, c^P is consumption prior to agreement, c^H is consumption of the individual who bears heavy taxes, and c^N is the consumption of the individual who bears light taxes (in this specific example, no taxes).

To find the optimal time that an individual of type θ agrees to bear the high tax burden if his opponent has not already conceded, denoted $T(\theta)$, we solve (following Alesina and Drazen [1991]) for a symmetric Nash equilibrium where, if the other individual is behaving according to $T(\theta)$, it is optimal to behave according to $T(\theta)$. In the Appendix we prove that the $T(\theta)$ function defined by the following equation is such an equilibrium:

$$T'(\theta) = -\left(\frac{f(\theta)}{F(\theta)}\right) \frac{g/\rho}{w(\theta, \pi) - g/2}, \tag{8}$$

where $T(\bar{\theta}) = 0$. That is, if the group is characterized by the maximum possible cost of inflation, it will concede immediately. Also note that $T(\theta)$ is monotonically decreasing in θ, so that high-cost groups concede first.

To understand the nature of the optimal strategy we may write (8) as

$$-\left[\left(\frac{f(\theta)}{F(\theta)}\right) \frac{1}{T'(\theta)}\right] \frac{g}{\rho} = w(\theta, \pi) - g/2. \tag{8'}$$

The right-hand side is the cost of waiting another instant to concede, that is, the difference between the utility loss due to inflation and the increase in taxes implied by the stabilization to the individual who concedes. The left-hand side is the expected gain from waiting another instant to concede, which is the product of the conditional probability that one's opponent concedes (the hazard rate, in brackets) multiplied by the gain if the other group concedes (i.e., the present discounted value of the future government expenditures). Concession occurs when the cost of waiting just equals the expected benefit from waiting.

We will work with the case where $f(\theta)$ is uniform over $[\underline{\theta}, \bar{\theta}]$, that is, $F(\theta) = \theta - \underline{\theta}/\bar{\theta} - \underline{\theta}$, so that $-f(\theta)/F(\theta) = 1/\underline{\theta} - \theta$. Under this assumption, using (8), $T(\theta)$ is given by

$$T(\theta) = \int_{\underline{\theta}}^{\theta} \frac{-g/\rho}{(\theta - \underline{\theta})(w(\theta, \pi) - g/2)} \, d\theta, \tag{9}$$

where, we recall, $w(\theta, \pi) = a + b\pi(\gamma)^n$. Using the method of partial fractions and integrating, we obtain the optimal time of concession of an individual of type θ, namely,

$$T(\theta) = -\frac{-g/\rho}{w(\underline{\theta}, \pi(\gamma)) - g/2} [\ln(\theta - \underline{\theta}) + \ln(\bar{\theta}, \pi(\gamma)) - g/2)] + C_0,$$

where the constant C_0 is defined by the condition that the highest-cost type concedes immediately, that is, $T(\bar{\theta}) = 0$. We thus have

$$T(\theta) = -\frac{-g/\rho}{w(\underline{\theta}, \pi(\gamma)) - g/2} \left[\ln[(\theta - \underline{\theta})/(\bar{\theta} - \underline{\theta})] + \ln \left[\frac{w(\bar{\theta}, \pi(\gamma)) - g/2}{w(\theta, \pi(\gamma)) - g/2} \right] \right]. \tag{10}$$

Equation (10) is used to derive the expected date of stabilization, which is the expected minimum T, the expectation taken over $F(\theta)$. One may show that the expected date of stabilization is decreasing in γ, which is why inflation can have a positive effect on welfare. (Details of the derivation of the expected date of stabilization can be found in Alesina and Drazen [1991]).

Social Welfare

We consider a social planner who weights each of the two individuals equally. Ignoring for a moment the direct dependence of individual utility on θ (in contrast to its dependence via T), if agreement comes at time T and the monetization parameter until T is γ we may write social welfare as

$$L(T; \gamma) = \int_0^T u^P(z; \gamma)e^{-\rho z} \, dz + e^{-\rho T} \frac{V^H + V^N}{2} \tag{11}$$

where we use the fact that V^H and V^N are independent of both T and γ. Expected social welfare is then the expectation of $L(T; \gamma)$ taken over the distribution of possible agreement dates, namely,

$$\text{ESW}(\gamma) = \int_0^\infty L(T; \gamma) g(T) \, dT \tag{12}$$

where $G(T)$ is the cumulative distribution of someone conceding by time T and $g(T) = dG(T)/dT$. To calculate this and to take into account the dependence of utility on an individual's type, we must express the distribution in terms of θ and integrate individual lifetime utility $L(\cdot)$ over the distribution of θ.

First we calculate $g(T)$. Using the characteristics of $T(\theta)$, we have that the probability that no one concedes by T is $1 - G(T(\theta)) = [F(\theta)]^2$. Differentiating we find the probability that someone concedes at T, namely, $g(T) = dG(T)/dT$, is

$$g(T) = -2[T'(\theta)]^{-1} F(\theta) f(\theta). \tag{13}$$

Using (13) and the fact that $dT = T'(\theta) \, d\theta$, after a change in variables, expected social welfare becomes

$$\text{ESW}(\gamma) = 2 \int_{\underline{\theta}}^{\bar{\theta}} L(T(\theta, \gamma), \gamma) F(\theta) f(\theta) \, d\theta. \tag{14}$$

Substituting (10) into (11) and the resulting expression into (14) gives the expected-social-welfare function to be maximized. We note that γ enters (14) only through the dependence of social welfare on individual utility and the dependence of individual utility [via $w(\theta, \pi)$] on γ.

6.2 Optimal Monetization and Inflation

We can now ask whether positive inflation can be welfare-increasing. The reason why this may be true should, by now, be clear. Higher inflation, by raising the cost of living in the economy prior to stabilization, will shorten the delay in reaching agreement. There is thus a trade-off, with higher inflation lowering welfare until an agreement is reached, but inducing an earlier time of agreement on use of nondistortionary financing. There should therefore be a positive but finite level of inflation which maximizes expected utility.

To show that positive inflation is in general optimal in inducing a policy change, we consider simulations. (Simulations not presented here

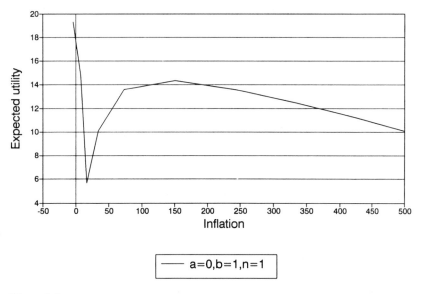

Figure 6.1
Inflation and expected utility

are in Drazen and Grilli [1990].) We fix the level of the real interest rate and the discount rate at 4 percent, and we choose a value of $\alpha = 3$, which we take from the estimate in Guillermo Calvo and Leonardo Leiderman (1992). The ratio of government expenditure to output was set at 50 percent and $k = 0.12$, so that money balances are 10 percent of output at zero inflation. We present the case in which $a = 0$ and $b = n = 1$. In figure 6.1 we plot the expected level of utility as a function of the rate of inflation. The simulation on which this figure is based reveals that the first best is one in which Friedman's rule prevails (when the rate of inflation is equal to $-r$, i.e., -4 percent).

The first best is relevant only when nondistortionary taxes could fully cover government expenditure ($\bar{\gamma} = 0$), so that seigniorage revenues are not needed. That is, it is relevant only after an agreement has been reached on how to allocate the burden of nondistortionary taxes. Before such agreement is achieved, the use of inflation is necessary for revenue purposes and $\gamma \geq \bar{\gamma} > 0$. Figure 6.1 makes clear that low levels of inflation are not always the optimal (second-best) choice. In this example, if the level of expenditures that has to be financed by distortionary taxation exceeds 2.2 percent of output, it is preferable to finance a much larger fraction of expenditure (5.8 percent of output) by seigniorage and thus

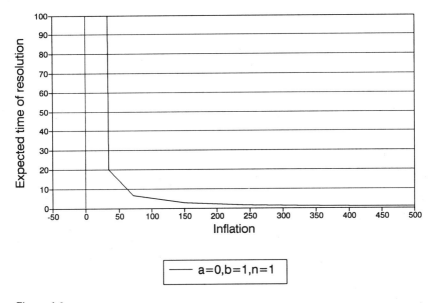

Figure 6.2
Inflation and time of resolution

induce a much higher level of inflation (133 percent) than the one strictly necessary for static budgetary reasons.

Figure 6.2, where we plot the expected time of resolution as a function of inflation, clarifies the nature of the trade-off. As expected, the time of resolution is a decreasing function of inflation. The interesting aspect is the particular shape of this function. The reduction in the time of resolution is concentrated at relatively small values of inflation. At high levels of inflation, the current utility loss outweighs the benefits deriving from a quicker stabilization.

Change in the costs of inflation could be represented by changes in the parameters a, b, and n in the cost function (4). Here we only discuss some of the results, without presenting the specific simulations. A main result is that changes that tend to increase the cost of inflation reduce the need for a high level of inflation (e.g., for $b = 3$ optimal inflation falls to 46 percent). Conversely, economies that have high degrees of protection against inflation (e.g., because of pervasive indexation) will be characterized by high levels of optimal inflation. While our model is different from the one used by Fischer and Summers (1989), it produces the same result, that increasing indexation increases inflation. A key difference, however, is that changes in the parameters of the cost-of-inflation function have no effect on expected utility.

How can one explain the invariance of expected utility to changes in the costs of inflation? Here, it is due to inflation affecting social welfare only through its effect on the utility of the groups engaged in the war of attrition. There is a social-welfare-maximizing level of realized w, the cost of inflation. Changes in the parameters of the function $w(\cdot)$ change the level of inflation that achieves this, but not the resultant level of expected utility. The result is related, for example, to one on the ineffectiveness of automobile safety regulation (Sam Peltzman, 1975): drivers have a chosen level of safety, so that mandatory seat-belt regulation will induce them to drive faster until their net level of safety is unchanged.

The general message is that there is an optimal level of utility loss or suffering. If all the effects of inflation are internalized by the agents involved in choice of policy, then structural changes will not affect this optimal level of utility loss, and expected social welfare will be invariant to structural changes.

This suggests that the invariance result will *not* hold if inflation affects social welfare in ways which agents involved in policy-making do not internalize (as would be the case if we had explicitly considered political parties with narrow constituencies). We further expect that, in such a case, decreases in the cost of inflation to agents involved in the war of attrition which are not shared by other (i.e., noninvolved) groups will decrease maximized social welfare, as higher inflation will be needed to induce agreement. This result is analogous to Peltzman's argument that faster driving will reduce *aggregate* safety, as pedestrians will be put at greater risk.

6.3   Conclusions

Our analysis may be seen as a formalization of the view that policies which reduce (but do not eliminate) either inflation or the costs associated with inflation may be counterproductive, since they make it more difficult to gain agreement on undertaking painful policy steps to eliminate inflation. Our results suggest that countries may have to suffer some significant inflation if they are to adopt fiscal policies consistent with a long-run low-inflation path. More generally, our analysis suggests that endogenizing the choice of tax policy may lead to a novel application of the theory of the second-best, whereby distortionary taxation is preferred to nondistortionary taxation.

An interesting aspect of stabilization induced by high inflation is that inflation does not need to be a deliberate choice of the policymaker. In fact, it is often the case that when there exists lack of social consensus, monetization and thus inflation are used as the last resort to avoid public bankruptcy. In this case, the mechanism described above operates without an explicit decision to do so.

A number of historical episodes can be interpreted in this way. After the end of World War I several European countries faced serious fiscal problems. Very large debt had been accumulated during the war; revenues were insufficient to cover current expenditures, let along repay the outstanding war debt. While fiscal adjustments were necessary, a social consensus on the sharing of the burden of stabilization programs was difficult achieve. Only after inflation was out of control, or threatened to become so, was agreement finally achieved and new tax packages introduced.

Two well-known examples are Germany and France during this period. In Germany, fiscal and monetary reforms sufficient to end extreme monetization of deficits were introduced only in October 1923, after the hyperinflation reached 29,000 percent. In France, stabilization occurred only with the appointment of Raymond Poincare in 1926, after serious inflationary pressure and periods of intense speculation against the franc. Two less well-known examples are perhaps Czechoslovakia and the Netherlands. In Czechoslovakia, the agreement on the introduction of a new capital levy in 1920 was reached only after two years of heavy reliance on seigniorage. Similarly, in the Netherlands, sufficiently large increases in capital taxes were passed in 1919 after several years of high inflation. Additional evidence may be found in Alesina and Drazen (1991) and in Barry Eichengreen (1990).

While in the model above we assumed that the government equally weighted the welfare of the two interest groups, in reality this may not be the case. If the policymaker is biased in favor of one of the two groups, he could use distortionary taxes not just to induce agreement, but also to produce an outcome in favor of his constituency. The social desirability of crises, in this case, becomes questionable.

Appendix

To derive (8) we begin with the individual's expected utility (6). Differentiating with respect to T_i and θ, one can show that $d\text{EU}/dT_i$ is decreasing in θ, which implies that optimal concession time $T(\theta)$ is monotonically decreasing in θ: a group with a higher cost will concede earlier. Suppose the other interest group is acting according to $T(\theta)$, the optimal concession time for a group with utility cost θ. Choosing a time T_i as above would be equivalent to choosing a value $\hat{\theta}_i$ and conceding at time $T_i = T(\hat{\theta}_i)$. Expected utility can then be written as equation (A1).

$$EU(\hat{\theta}_i, \theta_i) = F(\hat{\theta}_i)\left[\int_{\hat{\theta}_i}^{\bar{\theta}} -u^P(x)e^{-\rho T(x)}T'(x)\,dx + e^{-\rho T(\hat{\theta}_i)}V^H(T(\hat{\theta}_i))\right]$$

$$+ \int_{\hat{\theta}_i}^{\bar{\theta}}\left[\int_x^{\bar{\theta}} -u^P(z)e^{-\rho T(z)}T'(z)\,dz + e^{-\rho T(x)}V^N(T(x))\right]f(x)\,dx.$$

$$(A1)$$

Differentiating with respect to $\hat{\theta}_i$ and setting the resulting expression equal to zero, we obtain (dropping the i subscript)

$$\frac{dEU}{d\hat{\theta}} = f(\hat{\theta})[(V^H(T(\hat{\theta})) - V^N(T(\hat{\theta}))]$$

$$+ F(\hat{\theta})\left(u^P(\theta, \hat{\theta}) - \rho V^H + \frac{dV^H}{dT}\right)T'(\hat{\theta}) = 0. \qquad (A2)$$

After substitutions, this becomes

$$\frac{dEU}{d\hat{\theta}} = -f(\hat{\theta}) - F(\hat{\theta})\gamma r(w - g/2)T'(\hat{\theta}) = 0. \qquad (A3)$$

Now, by the definition of $T(\theta)$ as the optimal time of concession for a group with cost θ, $\hat{\theta} = \theta$ when $\hat{\theta}$ is chosen optimally. The first-order condition (A3) evaluated at $\hat{\theta} = \theta$ implies (8). [Substituting $T'(\theta)$ evaluated at $\hat{\theta}$ from (8) into (A3), one sees that the second-order condition is satisfied, since (A3) then implies that sign $dEU/d\hat{\theta} = \text{sign}(\theta - \hat{\theta})$.]

To derive the initial boundary condition, note first that for any value of $\theta \leq \bar{\theta}$, the gain to having the opponent concede is positive. Therefore as long as $f(\bar{\theta})$ is nonzero, groups with $\theta < \bar{\theta}$ will not concede immediately. This in turn implies that a group with $\theta = \bar{\theta}$ (i.e., one that knows it has the highest possible cost of waiting) will find it optimal to concede immediately. Thus, $T(\bar{\theta}) = 0$.

Notes

We thank seminar participants at Princeton and Yale Universities for helpful comments.

1. Laurence Ball and Stephen Cecchetti (1991) further explore the Fischer-Summers model.

2. Here we use $i(t)m(t)$ as a measure of seigniorage revenues. Our argument, however, does not depend on the particular definition of seigniorage.

References

Alesina, Alberto and Drazen, Allan, "Why Are Stabilizations Delayed?" *American Economic Review*, December 1991, *81*, 1170–88.

Ball, Laurence and Cecchetti, Stephen, "Wage Indexation and Discretionary Monetary Policy," *American Economic Review*, December 1991, *81*, 1310–19.

Calvo, Guillermo and Leiderman, Leonardo, "Optimal Inflation Tax Under Precommitment: Theory and Evidence," *American Economic Review*, March 1992, *82*, 179–94.

Drazen, Allan and Grilli, Vittorio, "The Benefits of Crises for Economic Reforms," National Bureau of Economic Research (Cambridge, MA) Working Paper No. 3527, 1990.

Eichengreen, Barry, "The Capital Levy in Theory and Practice," in Rudiger Dornbusch and Mario Draghi, eds., *Public Debt Management: Theory and History*, Cambridge: Cambridge University Press, 1990, pp. 191–220.

Fischer, Stanley and Summers, Lawrence, "Should Nations Learn to Live with Inflation?" *American Economic Rievew*, May 1989 *(Papers and Proceedings)*, *79*, 382–7.

Hirschman, Albert, "Reflections on the Latin American Experience," in Leon Lindberg and Charles Maier, eds., *The Politics of Inflation and Economic Stagnation: Theoretical Approaches and International Studies*, Washington, DC: Brookings Institution, 1985, pp. 53–7.

Peltzman, Sam, "The Effects of Automobile Safety Regulation," *Journal of Political Economy*, August 1975, *83*, 677–725.

Dynamics

7   Recurrent High Inflation and Stabilization: A Dynamic Game

Guillermo Mondino,
Federico Sturzenegger, and
Mariano Tommasi

7.1   Introduction

Many Latin American countries have suffered from high and variable inflation rates. This variability can be characterized by frequent attempts to stabilize which succeed in rapidly bringing inflation down but which are gradually abandoned. The resulting price patterns for Argentina and Brazil during the 1980s are shown in figure 7.1. Most of these stabilization efforts are supported by the population at their inception, but support eventually dwindles away. In this chapter, we provide a model in which this pattern develops and is repeated through time.

A possible hypothesis is that governments (societies) have a number of different goals. For instance, there may be demands on the government for redistribution, which can easily be met by printing money. At low inflation, those goals/demands become salient and policies are implemented that sooner or later lead to high inflation. At that stage the inflation problem becomes salient and stabilization is attempted.

In this chapter, we take a political economy approach to the question of inflation, trying to explain the observed patterns within an individually optimizing setting. We model an economy consisting of (atomistic) agents who organize into pressure groups in order to request transfers from the government. These groups maximize the welfare of their constituents, affected positively by the transfers received, and negatively by inflation. The government accommodates the demand for subsidies from the pressure groups by printing money which ultimately results in inflation. We apply Bentley's (1908) hypothesis that government behavior is endogenous to underlying conflicts of interest, and hence do not endow it with

Originally published in *International Economic Review* 37, no. 4 (1996): 1–16. Reprinted with permission.

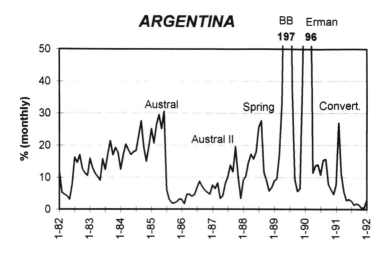

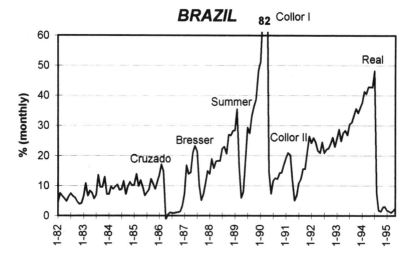

Figure 7.1
Inflation cycles: Argentina and Brazil

independent goals. To borrow political science jargon, we take a "society-centered" approach.[1]

The stage-game between groups alternates between a prisoners' dilemma and a coordination game. The dynamics arise from the optimal financial response of individuals. Agents conduct transactions either with currency or with costly alternatives that hedge them against inflation. These alternatives include indexed checking accounts, non-fiat money, barter, and foreign currency. We refer to the use of these alternatives as *financial adaptation*.

One of the equilibria the model generates takes the following form. Suppose the economy starts with low inflation and low financial adaptation. Each interest group weighs the advantages it can derive from receiving a subsidy from the government with the costs it understands will follow: the inflation and financial-adaptation costs forced upon its members in the current and future periods. Under some conditions, demanding the subsidy is optimal for the group and this leads to inflation. In response to the resulting inflation and given the technological constraints, the process of financial adaptation deepens over time. Under the accelerating inflation and widespread financial adaptation, the groups perform anew their intertemporal calculations. Eventually, demanding a subsidy would result in such a high inflation that it is optimal to accept a stabilization program that cuts subsidies. Since dealing with alternative financial instruments is expensive, stabilization leads to a process of remonetization which brings the economy back to the initial state. At that point pressure groups demand transfers once again, and inflation resumes.

The equilibrium just described seems to explain the three stylized facts introduced above: high average inflation, variability of the inflation rate over time, and periodic stabilization attempts that are "successful" only for a short time. The results are due to the presence of elements of both conflict and commonality of interests. The equilibrium strategy is state-dependent, including cooperation at high inflation and conflict at low inflation. Our formalization is consistent with the view of Havrilesky (1990, p. 714): "Inflation increases over time until it reaches a critical level where ever-rising, collectively-shared costs and zero long-run benefits force interest groups to coalesce and to demand the implementation of monetary restraint."

The equilibrium conditions we derive are suggestive of the type of structural reform necessary to permanently support price stability. In order to settle "distributional conflicts" in a permanent manner, reforms must take place to either change the payoffs of the game or to somehow induce more cooperative play. Recent successful stabilization programs in Latin America and Israel have been accompanied by "institutional" reforms. Institutional reforms that increase the costs of inflation (de-indexation), that allow for unrestricted use of financial adaptation, or other changes that render more difficult a transitory redistribution of income, could turn low inflation into a permanent equilibrium.

The model in this chapter relates to some recent work on political economy. In particular, Fernandez and Rodrik (1991) show the possibility of *policy inaction* in the context of trade liberalization. They show how a positive sum game may not take place if interest groups do not, ex ante, know the distribution of gains and losses. Alesina and Drazen (1991) show the possibility of *policy delay* in the context of inflation stabilizations when parties, uncertain about the other's tolerance for pain, debate over the distribution of costs of the program. Guidotti and Vegh (1992) show the possibility of *policy reversals*: a stabilization program that has brought down the inflation rate may collapse if a balance of payments crisis occurs before the war of attrition over fiscal adjustment is over. All these papers assume some uncertainty or asymmetric information over the pay-offs of the other party. Once the relevant information is revealed, struggles are resolved immediately and permanently, eliminating the possibility of re-peated inflation and stabilization cycles. In our model we integrate in a single framework the possibility of inaction, delays, and policy reversals while providing an explanation for the underlying inflation problem, without resorting to uncertainty or asymmetric information.

The rest of the chapter is organized as follows. Section 7.2 introduces the economy's technology, preferences, and rules of engagement. Section 7.3 describes the conditions necessary for the existence of oscillating and of stable inflation equilibria. Section 7.4 analyzes some extensions. Section 7.5 discusses possible policy implications and interpretations of the model.

7.2   Description of the Economy

The economy is inhabited by a continuum of infinitely-lived agents, who receive an endowment e every period. These agents are identical in every respect but for a characteristic that we index by $i \in [0, 1]$ that differentiates them from a collective-action point of view. The agents are organized into two politically active groups, $A = [0, 1/2]$ and $B = [1/2, 1]$.[2] These groups demand transfers s_t^A and s_t^B from the government, which are financed via inflation. Individuals, knowing s_t^A and s_t^B, decide their level of financial adaptation based on their expectations of inflation.

Let $f_t(i)$ be the amount of the endowment that individual i transacts outside the domestic currency circuit. The payoff function is

$$\sum_{t=0}^{\infty} \delta^t [e + s_t(i) - \pi_t(e - f_t(i)) - \phi(\pi_t) - T(f_t(i))], \tag{1}$$

where e represents the endowment, $s_t(i)$ is the subsidy the individual receives (which equals either s_t^A or s_t^B, depending on which group he belongs to), $\pi(e - f)$ is the inflation tax, $\phi(\ )$ are the costs of inflation, and $T(\ )$ is the cost of operating with financial alternatives.

Costs of Inflation

$\phi(\pi)$ captures the costs of inflation above and beyond those involved in substituting away from money (discussed below). It includes menu costs, distortions caused by relative price variability, misallocations of human capital, and credit market effects.[3] To observe stabilizations we require that groups eventually stop requesting transfers. They will find it optimal to do so when the costs of inflation grow larger than the benefits of government transfers. For this to happen, we require the cost of inflation function not to be too concave.[4] To simplify the presentation, we assume here the linear case $\phi(\pi) = \alpha\pi$.

Financial Technology

Following the empirical evidence on the dynamics of money demand reviewed in appendix 2 of Mondino, Sturzenegger, and Tommasi (1993; see note 4 below) we impose three conditions on the financial (transactions) technology which deliver a money demand function which responds to changes in inflation as in the data:

(1) Agents need to hold enough domestic currency *or* alternative means of transactions in order to purchase goods. In each period, agent i trades $(e - f_t(i))$ in domestic currency and $f_t(i)$ in "foreign" currency.[5] These latter transactions are exempt from the inflation tax.

(2) The process of changing f_t over time is restricted by the presence of *adjustment* costs. To keep the analysis simple and tractable we use the stark version of the convex adjustment cost model depicted in figure 7.2: f can be increased at no cost by steps of size J, and can be reduced for free. Mathematically,

$$f_{t+1} \in \{0, J, 2J, \ldots, f_t, \min[f_t + J, e]\}. \tag{2}$$

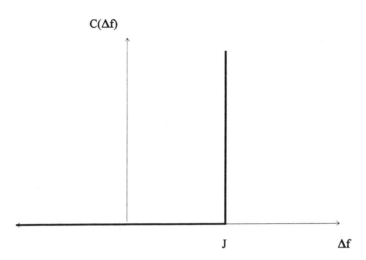

Figure 7.2
Cost of financial adaptation

This stark formulation enables us to generate (under some conditions) inflation cycles, as shown in Proposition 1. In section 7.4 we discuss two generalizations of this formulation which deliver inflation escalation (Proposition 2) and permanent stabilizations (Proposition 3). These generalizations may be more appropriate descriptions of the dynamics of money demand and are easily accommodated within our framework.

(3) *Operating* in inflation-shielded assets is also costly. The cost arises from the inconvenience of exchanging currencies, gathering information on exchange rates, legal constraints to the use of foreign currency, and so on. The existence of such costs is necessary to obtain a demand for domestic currency. It is empirically clear that once inflation is brought down, the demand for domestic currency increases, indicating that operation in alternative technologies is relatively inefficient. Even more remarkable is the fact that during hyperinflations there is always a residual demand for domestic cash.[6] To keep the structure of the model as simple as possible we assume the costs of operating in financial alternatives to be proportional to the stock of "financial adaptation." Yet, to insure that domestic money remains valued at very high inflation rates, we add a large cost for completely substituting away from domestic money. Formally,

$$T(f_t) = \begin{cases} \tau f_t & \text{for } f_t < e \\ \tau f_t + K & \text{for } f_t = e, \end{cases} \tag{3}$$

where we assume the operation costs to be higher at the point where the level of financial adaptation equals the endowment. To further simplify the exposition, we assume $K > S$ in what follows.

Individual Choice

Individuals must choose sequences $\{f_t\}_{t=0}^{\infty}$ to maximize (1) for given sequences $\{\pi_t\}_{t=0}^{\infty}$, subject to (2), the law of motion for f_t.

Groups

As mentioned in the introduction, the political structure is such that individuals can only access government subsidies through group pressure. Group decisions can be reached by any voting mechanism since we always have group unanimity. Each group's action set is $\{S, 0\}$ in every period; that is, it either requests (and gets) a transfer of size S for each of its members, or refrains from doing so. (As explained later, the main results also obtain with a convex action set $[0, S]$.) s_t^A and s_t^B denote the actions of groups A and B at time t. They choose strategies that maximize discounted utility (1) of their members. Note that in so doing, they internalize the inflation costs paid by their members but not the costs imposed on the other groups.

Government

As said, the government's role is the provision of subsidies financed by the inflation tax. We restrict the taxation choices to highlight the importance of inflation taxes as a short-term instrument, assuming that regular taxation is not very flexible in the short run. The nature of the subsidies is left unspecified. Cash transfers, cheap credit, monetary accommodation of price and wage increases, and devaluations can all be thought of as group subsidies that have inflationary effects.

The equilibrium in the money market once we substitute the government budget constraint gives

$$\tfrac{1}{2}[s_t^A + s_t^B] = \pi_t(e - F_t), \tag{4}$$

which determines the inflation rate. Notice that here total subsidies equal revenue from the inflation tax. Additionally, the unitary measure of agents implies that the aggregate endowment equals individual endowment, e, which is constant over time. $F_t = \int_0^1 f_t(i) \, di$ represents aggregate financial adaptation.

7.3   Equilibrium

An equilibrium to our economy is a set of sequences $\{\pi_t, s_t^A, s_t^B, f_t, F_t\}_{t=0}^{\infty}$ such that: (i) individuals choose $\{f_t\}_{t=0}^{\infty}$ to maximize (1) subject to (2) given $\{\pi_t\}_{t=0}^{\infty}$, (ii) $f_t = F_t$ for all t, and (iii) the sequences $\{s_t^A, s_t^B\}_{t=0}^{\infty}$ constitute an equilibrium to the game between sectors, given (4), (i), and (ii).

The game between sectors is a dynamic one, in that stage payoffs are dependent upon past actions through financial adaptation and hence inflation. Introducing general strategy profiles in such games is complicated. For that reason, we restrict the equilibrium concept to Markov Perfection (Fudenberg and Tirole 1991, chap. 13). A Markov Perfect Equilibrium (MPE) is a profile of Markov strategies that yields a Nash equilibrium in every proper subgame. "Markov" or "state-space" are strategies where the past influences current play only through its effect on a state vector which summarizes the direct effect of past information on the current environment. In our game, the proper state variable is the degree of aggregate financial adaptation F. However, we refer to the inflation rate π as our state variable to aid the intuition of the results in terms of a publicly known and easily observable variable.

In the proposition below we characterize all Symmetric Markov Perfect Equilibria (SMPE), in which both groups follow the same strategy.[7] Using (4) and the fact that there is a unit mass of agents, we see that in a SMPE inflation can take values 0, $\pi_1 = S/e$, $\pi_2 = S/(e - J)$, and $\pi_3 = S/(e - 2J)$.

PROPOSITION 1   (1) Inflation Cycles. (1a) Cycles of High Inflation. An equilibrium in which inflation oscillates from 0 to π_3 exists for $\tau < [S/2(e - 2J)]$ and $\alpha < (e - 2J)$. (1b) Cycles of Low Inflation. An equilibrium in which inflation oscillates from 0 to π_2 exists for $S/2(e - J) < \tau < S$ and $S/2 > \tau J + \alpha S[1/(e - J) - 1/2e]$.

(2) Steady Low Inflation. An equilibrium in which $\pi_t = \pi_1 \; \forall t$, exists for $\tau > S/e$ and $\alpha < e$.

(3) No Inflation. For $\alpha > e$, or $\tau < S/2(e - J)$ and $\alpha > (e - J)[1 - 2J\tau/S]$, equilibrium implies $\pi_t = 0 \; \forall t$.

COROLLARY   High inflation implies cyclical inflation ($\pi_2 \; \forall t$ and $\pi_3 \; \forall t$ are not equilibria).

The proposition is proven in the appendix. Figure 7.3 illustrates the possible combinations of τ and α that generate the different types of equilibrium discussed in the proposition.[8]

As the proposition indicates, inflation cycles result when the costs of operating in a financially adapted economy (τ) are relatively low and

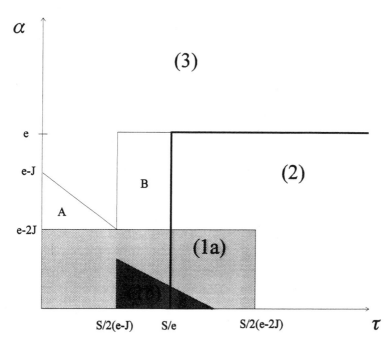

Figure 7.3
Equilibria

when the marginal costs of inflation (α) are also low. The equilibrium (Markov) strategies that generate inflation cycles consist of demanding subsidies when past inflation (and hence, financial adaptation) is low, and not demanding subsidies when last-period inflation is high. In general, the inflation-cycle strategies take the form

$$s_t^j = \begin{cases} 0 & \text{for } \pi > \bar{\pi} \\ S & \text{for } \pi \leq \bar{\pi} \end{cases} \quad \text{for } j = A, B. \tag{5}$$

where $\bar{\pi} = 0$ in the case of two-period cycles, as in Proposition 1, and $\bar{\pi} > 0$ in the more general case explored in section 7.4, where inflation will escalate before a stabilization takes place.[9]

The intuition behind the inflation-cycle equilibria is simple. Assume that the economy was operating under low inflation. Since the marginal costs of inflation are low ($\alpha < e - 2J$) and since the level of financial adaptation is relatively low (as no incentives existed to keep it high) the groups will find it optimal to request subsidies. Since individuals understand that a subsidy request has to be financed via the inflation tax, they engage in some financial adaptation (in fact, they try to dollarize as much as they can). The resulting macroeconomic equilibrium will then show an abandonment of fiscal discipline and an acceleration of the inflation rate together with a deepening of the financial adaptation of the economy. Next period, inflation will have already been high and financial adaptation widespread. Hence, the choice is for groups to ask for subsidies again (forcing further financial adaptation and hence a further increase in the inflation rate) or to refrain from demanding a subsidy. Suppose that adaptation was already very high (case (1a)) last period. If the groups demand subsidies, given the already high level of dollarization and the new possibility for further adaptation, the inflation rate will explode. Fearing hyperinflation, and the costs that it entails, one group may consider a second option and accept a stabilization package. Because of symmetry, both groups decide to "cooperate" and accept a stabilization program where no subsidies are granted. Since both groups will accept the stabilization program, inflation will now go to zero. Next period, given that the costs of inflation are low due to remonetization, groups will demand subsidies again, and the cycle restarts.

The model also generates equilibria with constant low inflation. They obtain when the cost of operating in a financially adapted economy, τ, are large enough that it is preferable for individual agents to suffer the inflation tax rather than to operate with alternatives. A case of no inflation results whenever the costs of inflation are large enough; groups fear any resulting inflation and hence refrain from demanding subsidies.

It is easy to verify that welfare in the no-inflation region is greater than welfare with constant low inflation, which in turn is greater than welfare with high (cyclical) inflation. The main reason for this result is that (in any equilibria) the transfers received cancel out with the inflation tax, and only the deadweight losses of inflation and of financial adaptation remain.

7.4   Extensions

In the previous section we discussed the conditions under which a cyclical inflation pattern was feasible. In that specification high and low inflation alternate over time. However, a quick inspection of the inflation rates observed in figure 7.1 indicates that this path does not truly characterize the inflation dynamics observed in these two economies. Particularly, inflation appears to be increasing over several periods before a stabilization takes place. Additionally, though not explicit in Figure 1, many countries (Bolivia 1985, Israel 1985, Mexico 1987, Argentina 1991) do eventually implement successful stabilization. The question arises as to whether our model can accommodate this fact, or whether it forces countries to experience inflation forever. The purpose of this section is to develop two extensions which show that our previous specification can, with appropriate adjustments to the financial adaptation technology, accommodate these two additional properties of extreme inflation experiences. The results are contained in the following two propositions. As before, the proofs are in the appendix.

PROPOSITION 2   Inflation Escalation. Consider the economy described in section 7.2, but with $3J \leq e \leq 4J$. An equilibrium in which inflation follows $\{0, \pi, \Pi\}$, with $0 < \pi < \Pi$ exists for $S/(e - 2J) - K/(e - J) < \tau < S/2(e - 2J)$ and $\alpha < (e - 3J)$.

In our previous specification, the rigidity in money demand was low because the feasible cost-free adjustment in money demand was very large relative to the volume of transactions. In section 7.2, two periods of inflation were sufficient to induce complete substitution away from domestic currency. The threat of hyperinflation provided, then, the incentives to avoid requesting subsidies for two consecutive periods. In Proposition 2, the size (J) of the cost-free adjustment is reduced in comparison to the size (e) of the endowment. Thus, the risk of hyperinflation does not develop immediately, but only after several periods of rising inflation. The restrictions on τ are such that the expected disinflation (after stabilization) provides a sufficient incentive for remonetization.

PROPOSITION 3   Delayed (Permanent) Stabilizations. Consider the economy described in section 7.2, but with possible values for financial adaptation being $f_t \in \{0, J, 2J, \ldots, \max[f_i; i < t]\}$ and $f_t \leq e$. Let $T^* = \min\{\mathrm{int}[x | \alpha - xJ > 0]\}$. An equilibrium, in which inflation is increasing until time T^* and 0 afterwards, exists for $\alpha < (e - J)$ and $\tau < S/(e - J)$.

In this specification we assume full memory in the financial adaptation technology (i.e., it is costless to return to any level of financial adaptation previously attained). Once the economy learns how to deal with alternative means of payments it retains this capacity even when inflation is low and the economy has remonetized. Even though there is remonetization after stabilization, agents can automatically switch away from domestic currency up to the maximum substitution previously exercised. Hence, once stabilization has been achieved, there is never again an incentive to request subsidies, as this will automatically lead to a hyperinflation.

This specification induces delayed stabilization as in Alesina and Drazen (1991) where a spell of inflation is required to generate the consensus for a permanent stabilization. In their model, whoever first agrees to stabilize pays a higher fraction of the stabilization cost. Hence, groups engage in a war of attrition in an attempt to shift the burden of stabilization on their opponent. The Alesina–Drazen setup depends heavily on the assumption of imperfect information regarding the way in which inflation affects your opponent. We find that assumption implausible. Our specification provides the same dynamics in the absence of asymmetric information. In our model the consensus arises because money-demand dynamics lead to explosive rates of inflation which increases the cost of inflation to the point where stabilization becomes a dominant choice. Also, in Alesina–Drazen, the source of inflation is exogenous, while here it is derived as part of the equilibrium.

We believe that a case in-between the assumption in (2) (no memory) and that in Proposition 3 (full memory), would be the more realistic. Although we do not model that case explicitly (it gets much harder due to nonstationarity) we conjecture it has the potential to replicate closely the time series of inflation observed in figure 7.1, with cycles being bigger and faster each round. Eventually, when agents' expertise in dealing with alternative transaction technologies becomes large enough, permanent stabilizations take place, as suggested by Proposition 3.

7.5   Concluding Remarks

The chapter was motivated by the high and volatile inflation experiences of a number of developing countries, where inflation accelerates until stabilization programs are implemented. At stabilization points, the inflation rate is dramatically reduced, but it does not remain low for a long time. After a brief success, the programs are abandoned and inflation resumes. We explained those cycles in a simple political economy framework. We also showed that high inflation necessarily implies variable inflation, providing an alternative explanation for the correlation between inflation levels and variability (see Ball 1992 and references there).

The recurrent inflation–stabilization equilibrium entails high welfare losses for society, losses associated with the costs of inflation, its variability and the costs of operating in a financial system that it efficient as an inflation hedge but less so as a resource allocator. Societies like the ones described in this chapter will long for a stabilization program. However, when a program of fiscal restraint is assembled and offered to society, it will only be successful for a short time. While the lower inflation rate is welfare-enhancing, pressure groups will find it in their best interest to request transfers again, leading to a resumption of inflation.

Every time a stabilization plan falls apart—after some initial success—analysts argue that the necessary adjustments were not made. What those long-run adjustments are, is also a prediction of this model. In order to settle "distributional conflicts" in a permanent manner, structural reforms must either change the payoffs of the game or somehow induce more cooperative play: we believe that the key to a "durable" stabilization is a change in the rules of the game. These adjustments may sometimes include increasing the costs of inflation (i.e. de-indexation) or the costs of operation in currency substitutes. The last case is of particular interest since a large number of countries that suffer from inflation resort to financial repression (Giovannini and de Melo 1993, Roubini and Sala-i-Martin 1992). While repression is usually associated with a desire for an increased inflation tax base, we could interpret it as a move towards a more stable inflation rate. This relates to the observed difficulty of many economies that control high inflation to move to international levels of inflation. Many times, high inflation is followed by moderate inflation (Dornbusch and Fischer 1993). That feature is explained in our model by an increase in τ but not in α.

There are a number of possible extensions. If the pressure groups were of different size, the same pattern of equilibria would follow, but with high cyclical inflation obtaining for a smaller set of parameter values. In the limit, when only one group exists, the political economy game disappears and stable zero inflation is the only equilibrium. This exercise stresses the importance of "distributional conflict." Once the cost of transfers is perfectly internalized, inflation is no longer an equilibrium. On the other hand, if we increase the number of players, inflation will have to reach even higher values in order to induce the incentive to stabilize. (Similar results appear in Aizenman 1992 and Zarazaga 1993.)

While the game was worded in terms of demands for transfers, its logic could apply to the award of tax exemptions, trade policy, or any other policy intervention with distributional consequences and deadweight losses. To what extent recurrent policy cycles will appear in these situations is a question open to further research.

Appendix

Proof of Proposition 1   Throughout the proof, $\{x, y\}$ will denote a sequence $\{x, y, x, y, \ldots\}$. In particular, $\{x, x\}$ denotes the sequence $\{x, x, x, x, \ldots\}$.

Let $W^*(\pi_{t-1})$ be the (equilibrium) value function for an agent in an economy that experienced inflation rate π_{t-1} last period. Without loss of generality, we work with the function $V^*(\pi_{t-1}) = W^*(\pi_{t-1}) - e/(1-\delta)$.

(1a) To observe the high inflation cycle $\{0, \pi_3\}$, it is necessary that subsidy demands $\{s_t\}$ be $\{0, S\}$ and that aggregate financial adaptation $\{F_t\}$ be $\{J, 2J\}$.

First, we verify the conditions for the path of F to constitute a monetary equilibrium (i.e., $f_t = F_t$ for all t). Given an oscillatory path of inflation, it is clear that the optimal path for f is also oscillatory. The possible choices are $\{0, J\}$ and $\{J, 2J\}$.[10] The value of these paths (we use time averaging) is $v(\{0, J\}) = -\tau J + JS/(e - 2J)$ and $v(\{J, 2J\}) = -\tau J - \tau 2J + 2JS/(e - 2J)$. In order for $\{J, 2J\}$ to be the individually dominant strategy, we need $\tau < S/2(e - 2J)$, as stated.

Second, we verify the (MP) equilibrium to the game between groups. To observe cycles, the MP strategy has to be of the form of equation (5). The values of payoffs for the equilibrium path are

$$V^*(0) = -\tau 2J - \alpha\left(\frac{S}{e - 2J}\right) + \delta V^*(\pi)$$

and

$$V^*(\pi) = -\tau J + \delta V^*(0)$$

(notice that subsidies cancel with the inflation tax). Consider the case when $\pi_{t-1} = 0$. Strategy (5) requires $s = S$, giving payoff $V^*(0)$. Let $V^0(0)$ be the value of a group deviating to $s = 0$. Given $\tau < [S/2(e - 2J)]$, it is easy to verify that monetary equilibrium along the deviation implies $F = f = 2J$. Hence,

$$V^0(0) = -\frac{S}{2} - \tau 2J - \alpha\left(\frac{S/2}{e - 2J}\right) + \delta V^*(\pi).$$

For the deviation to be unprofitable we need $S/2 > [\alpha S/(e - 2J)] - [\alpha S/2(e - 2J)]$, or $\alpha < e - 2J$.

The alternative deviation is to demand subsidies during a "stabilization" period ($\pi_{t-1} = \pi_3$). Notice that, because the cost of transacting in an alternative currency is low and last period financial adaptation was at $2J$, individuals will move to $f = F = e$. This would lead to hyperinflation, making the deviation unprofitable for the group.

(1b) The proof for low-inflation cycles is similar to (1a) and it is omitted. We refer the reader to Theorem 3 of MST (1993), where we find conditions for the general $\phi(\pi)$ case. Those conditions simplify to $\tau > S/2(e - J)$ and $S/2 > \tau J + \alpha S[1/(e - J) - 1/2e]$ when $\phi(\pi) = \alpha \pi$.

(2) $\pi_t = \pi_1 \ \forall t$ implies $\{s_t\} = \{S, S\}$ and $\{F_t\} = \{0, 0\}$. $f = F = 0 \ \forall t$ requires $\tau > S/e$.

The value of the equilibrium strategy is $V^*(\pi) = -[\alpha S/e] + \delta V^*(\pi)$. The value of deviating to $s = 0$ is $V^0(\pi) = -[S/2] - [\alpha s/2e] + \delta V^*(\pi)$. (Notice that $f = F = 0$ also along the deviation, since π is even smaller.) The deviation is not profitable as long as $V^*(\pi) - V^0(\pi) > 0$, or $e > \alpha$.

(3) $\pi_t = 0$ for all t, requires $\{s_t\} = \{0, 0\}$ and $\{F_t\} = \{0, 0\}$. It is obvious that $f_t = F_t = 0$ for all t is the optimal choice of f. In order to evaluate the profitability of deviating to $s = S$, we have to specify off-equilibrium monetary behavior. For $\tau < S/2e$, the only consistent monetary behavior is $f = F = J$. For $\tau > S/2(e - J)$, the only consistent monetary behavior is $f = F = 0$. For intermediate values, both monetary equilibria are self-fulfilling. In that case, we consider $f = F = J$, since it induces no-inflation equilibrium for the larger set of parameter values. We proceed now to verify the conditions for profitable deviations for the two cases of τ smaller and greater than $S/2(e - J)$.

(a) When $\tau < S/2(e - J)$, an aggregate level of financial adaptation $F = J$ induces $f = F = J$, since $\tau < \pi = S/2(e - J)$. The value function of a deviation given that inflation was zero in last period and will be zero again next period is

$$V^S(0) = S - \pi(e - J) - \tau J - \alpha \pi + \delta V^*(0).$$

From (4) we have that $\pi = S/2(e - J)$ so that the above equation reduces to

$$V^S(0) = \frac{S}{2} - \tau J - \alpha \left(\frac{S/2}{e - J} \right).$$

Given that $V^*(0) = 0$, for a deviation to be profitable we require $V^S(0) > 0$ which results in

$$\frac{S}{2} > \tau J + \alpha \left(\frac{S/2}{e - J} \right),$$

so that zero-inflation will be an equilibrium (when τ is low) iff

$$\alpha > (e - J)[1 - 2J\tau/S].$$

(b) When $\tau > S/2(e - J)$, then $f = F = 0$. In that case, the gains from deviating from the postulated equilibrium are $V^S(0) = [S/2] - [\alpha S/2e]$. A deviation is unprofitable (when τ is high) as long as $\alpha > e$.

Proof of Proposition 2　We will show that there exists an oscillating equilibrium of phase 3, with demand for subsidies $\{S, S, 0\}$ and aggregate financial adaptation $\{2J, 3J, J\}$. The resulting inflation rates are $\{\pi, \Pi, 0\}$, where $\pi = S/(e - 2J)$ and $\Pi = S/(e - 3J)$.

The value of deviations from the monetary equilibrium is

$$v(J, 2J, 0) - v(2J, 3J, J) = 3J\tau - JS/(e - 2J) - JS/(e - 3J) < 0 \tag{i}$$

$$v(3J, e, 2J) - v(2J, 3J, J) = -2J\tau - (e - 3J)\tau - K + JS/(e - 2J) + S < 0. \tag{ii}$$

The first condition can be simplified to

$$\tau < \frac{1}{3}\left[\frac{S}{(e - 2J)} + \frac{S}{(e - 3J)}\right] \tag{A1}$$

and the second to

$$\frac{S}{e - 2J} - \frac{K}{e - J} < \tau. \tag{A2}$$

If both conditions are satisfied, all other deviations are not profitable.

The value functions for group behavior along the equilibrium path are

$$V^*(0) = -\alpha\frac{S}{e - 2J} - \tau 2J + \delta V^*(\pi)$$

$$V^*(\pi) = -\alpha\frac{S}{e - 3J} - \tau 3J + \delta V^*(\Pi)$$

$$V^*(\Pi) = -\tau J + \delta V^*(0).$$

When we analyze deviations from $V^*(0)$ we will require $\tau < S/2(e - 2J)$ (stricter than A1) in order for the monetary equilibrium to remain unchanged. When this is satisfied, the value of the deviation is

$$V^0(0) = -(S/2) - \alpha\frac{S}{2(e - 2J)} - \tau 2J + \delta V^*(\pi)$$

(since the monetary equilibrium remains unaltered, the state of the system next period will not change due to the deviation). The profitability condition is

$$V^*(0) - V^0(0) = (S/2) - \alpha\frac{S}{2(e - 2J)} > 0,$$

or $\alpha < (e - 2J)$.

A second local deviation is $s = 0$ when last period inflation was π (the intermediate level). The monetary equilibrium will remain the same if $\tau < [S/2(e - 3J)]$, which is true if $\tau < [S/2(e - 2J)]$. The value function is then

$$V^0(\pi) = -(S/2) - \alpha \frac{S/2}{e - 3J} - \tau 3J + \delta V^*(\Pi),$$

which gives a profitability condition

$$V^*(\pi) - V^0(\pi) = (S/2) - \alpha \frac{S/2}{e - 3J} > 0,$$

which implies $\alpha < (e - 3J)$. This is stronger than $\alpha < (e - 2J)$, thus this is the restriction imposed on α in the proposition.

Finally, we have to verify whether subsidies are demanded after periods of high inflation. But in this case hyperinflation results and this deviation is not profitable.

Proof of Proposition 3 This equilibrium requires a path of subsidies $\{S, S, \ldots, S, 0, 0, \ldots\}$. Value functions are now dated as the game becomes nonstationary. T^* is the period in which $V_t^S = -\infty$, so that the equilibrium strategy in that period is to stabilize. For previous periods, the value along the equilibrium path is

$$V_t^*(\pi_t) = -\tau t J - \alpha \left[\frac{S}{(e - t J)} \right] + \delta V_{t+1}^*(\pi_{t+1}).$$

The path of subsidies induces F to follow $\{J, 2J, \ldots, TJ, 0, 0, 0\}$ as long as $\tau < S/(e - J)$, which insures that financial adaptation takes place in the first period (and thus in all subsequent ones).

The incentive to deviate from the equilibrium path is given by

$$V_t^0 - V_t^* = \alpha \left[\frac{S}{(e - t J)} \right] - \alpha \left[\frac{S/2}{(e - t J)} \right] - S/2,$$

which reduces to $\alpha > (e - t J)$, monotonic in t. As long as $\alpha > (e - J)$, subsidies are demanded in the first period and keep being demanded until $t \geq (e - \alpha)/J$.

Finally, we should verify that deviations after the stabilization date are not profitable. But this follows from the fact that the set of feasible f's is now the same as at the stabilization date.

Notes

We are indebted to Alessandra Casella, George McCandless, Dani Rodrik, Andres Velasco, Yoram Weiss, Carlos Zarazaga, an anonymous referee, and seminar participants at Chicago, UCLA, I. DiTella, Georgetown, Maryland, USC, Irvine, NBER Economic Fluctuations Meeting, and the Latin American Meeting of the Econometric Society for valuable comments. This work was started while Sturzenegger and Tommasi were in the Department of Economics at UCLA, and we thank the support from the Academic Senate at UCLA. Tommasi also acknowledges financial support from the National Science Foundation through the Harvard/MIT RTG in Positive Political Economy.

1. Patinkin (1993) provides a view consistent with our formulation. He argues against the analysis of inflation as the outcome of a game the (monolithic and benevolent) government plays with the public. The type of accommodating behavior we assume can be justified by a variety of political micro foundations, i.e., maximization of survival chances (Ames 1987), minimization of a loss function whenever pressure groups have enough power to hurt the government, or the action of political entrepreneurs in the context of a decentralized decision making process. Aizenman (1992), Tabellini (1986), and Zarazaga (1993) have taken a similar approach to explain inflation.

2. The groups may represent capital-labor, agriculture-industry, Federal-State governments, workers-retirees, exporters-wage earners, state enterprises-private firms, different ministries within the government, or other dimensions of distributional conflict.

3. On this see Ball and Romer (1992), Heymann and Leijonhufvud (1995), Fischer (1986), Mankiw (1994, chap. 6), Patinkin (1993), and Tommasi (1994 and 1995).

4. In the working paper version, Mondino, Sturzenegger, and Tommasi (1993), hereafter MST (1993), we show that our main results hold as long as $\phi(y/x) - \phi(y/2x) > y/2$ as $x \to 0$. This condition will be satisfied for all convex, linear, and some concave functions.

5. In what follows, we drop the index i when no confusion arises. In equilibrium, it will be the case that $f_t(i) = f_t$ $\forall i$.

6. See Cagan (1956) for the classical hyperinflations and Vegh (1992) for the more recent high-inflation episodes. Vegh shows that there is strong re-monetization after each stabilization, and that even at extremely high inflation rates there is a floor below which domestic money demand will not fall. In appendix 2 of MST (1993) we discuss this evidence in more detail.

7. We analyze the case in which $e \in (2J, 3J)$, so that the financial technology reduces to $f \in \{0, J, 2J, e\}$. As we will see, this restricts the cycles (when they exist) to be two-period phased. Section 4 address extensions. In section 3.5 of MST (1993) we also discuss non-symmetric equilibria.

8. The sets A and B of parameter values for which none of the equilibria described in the Proposition exists, become empty with a more convex cost of inflation function ϕ.

9. The restriction that groups can only demand subsidies $s_t^j = \{0, S\}$ can be easily convexified to $s_t^j = [0, S]$. In the working paper version, Section 3.1, we show that there will exist an equilibrium with a sequence of subsidy demands $\{S, \Sigma, S, \Sigma, \ldots\}$ with $\Sigma < S$. Σ is the point where incremental subsidy demands trigger jumps in the inflation rate that turn this demand suboptimal. Also, the result of inflation cycles carries through to more general financial adaptation technologies. In MST (1993), Section 3.2, we allow individuals to choose

whether to adapt (from $f = 0$) upwards by J and pay a cost of βJ or to adapt up by $2J$ at a cost $2\beta J$. It is easy, though tedious, to find conditions on β, τ, and α such that inflation cycles exist.

10. We do not need to consider $\{2J, e\}$, from the assumption of large K.

References

Aizenman, J., "Competitive Externalities and the Optimal Seigniorage," *Journal of Money, Credit and Banking* 24 (1992), 61–71.

Alesina, A., and A. Drazen, "Why Are Stabilizations Delayed?" *American Economic Review* 81 (1991), 1170–1188.

Ames, B., *Political Survival. Politicians and Public Policy in Latin America* (Berkeley: University of California Press, 1987).

Ball, L., "Why Does High Inflation Raise Inflation Uncertainty?" *Journal of Monetary Economics* 29 (1992), 371–388.

Ball, L., and D. Romer, "Inflation and the Informativeness of Prices," Working Paper No. 4267, National Bureau of Economic Research, 1992.

Bentley, A., *The Process of Government* (Chicago: The University of Chicago Press, 1908).

Gagan, P., "The Monetary Dynamics of Hyperinflation," in M. Friedman, ed., *Studies in the Quantity Theory of Money* (Chicago: University of Chicago Press, 1956), 25–117.

Dornbusch, R. and S. Fischer, "Moderate Inflation," *World Bank Economic Review* 7 (1993), 1–44.

Fernandez, R., and D. Rodrik, "Resistance to Reform: Status Quo Bias in the Presence of Individual-Specific Uncertainty," *American Economic Review* 81 (1991), 1146–1155.

Fischer, S., *Indexing, Inflation and Economic Policy* (Cambridge: MIT Press, 1986).

Fudenberg, D. and J. Tirole, *Game Theory* (Cambridge: MIT Press, 1991).

Giovannini, A., and M. de Melo, "Government Revenue from Financial Repression," *American Economic Review* 83 (1993), 953–963.

Guidotti, P. and C. Vegh, "Losing Credibility: The Stabilization Blues," Mimeo, International Monetary Fund, 1992.

Havrilesky, T., "A Public Choice Perspective on the Cycle in Monetary Policy," *Cato Journal* 9 (1990), 709–718.

Heymann, D. and A. Leijonhufvud, *High Inflations* (Oxford: Oxford University Press, 1995).

Mankiw, N. G., *Macroeconomics*, 2nd ed. (New York: Worth Publishers, 1994).

Mondino, G., F. Sturzenegger, and M. Tommasi, "Recurrent High-Inflation and Stabilization. A Dynamic Game," Working Paper 678, Department of Economics, UCLA, January 1993.

Patinkin, D., "Israel's Stabilization Program of 1985, or Some Simple Truths of Monetary Theory," *Journal of Economic Perspectives* 7 (1993), 103–208.

Roubini, N., and X. Sala-i-Martin, "Financial Repression and Economic Growth," *Journal of Development Economics* 39 (1992), 5–30.

Tabellini, G., "Money, Debt and Deficits in a Dynamic Game," *Journal of Economic Dynamics and Control* 10 (1986), 427–442.

Tommasi, M., "The Welfare Effects of Inflation: Consequences of Price Instability on Search Markets," *American Economic Review* 84 (1994), 1385–1396.

———, "High Inflation: Resource Misallocations and Growth Effects," Mimeo, Harvard University, January 1995.

Vegh, C., "Stopping High Inflation," *IMF Staff Papers* 39 (1992), 626–695.

Zarazaga, C., "Hyperinflations and Moral Hazard in the Appropriation of Seigniorage," Working Paper 93-26, Federal Reserve Bank of Philadelphia, 1993.

8

The Common Property Approach to the Political Economy of Fiscal Policy

Andrés Velasco

8.1 Introduction

Three striking facts stand out regarding the recent fiscal policy of a number of countries. First, since 1973 there has been a pronounced and systematic increase in government spending and budget deficits (both measured as a percentage of GDP). This is true of both Organization for Economic Cooperation and Development (OECD) economies[1] and developing countries such as those in Latin America.[2] Second, in some cases fast debt accumulation as been allowed to continue unchecked for long periods of time, giving rise to a path that is inconsistent with intertemporal solvency. In some extreme cases, such as those of Mexico, Argentina, and Bolivia in the first half of the 1980s, drastic changes in spending and taxes were eventually required to restore solvency. In other serious but less dramatic cases—such as those of Belgium and Italy, where the public debt is above 100 percent of GNP and growing—fiscal stabilization is yet to occur. Third, countries often fix their exchange rates and then follow monetary and fiscal policies that are clearly incompatible with the maintenance of the peg. Examples include European countries such as Italy in the period leading to the ERM crisis of September 1992; African countries in the French Franc zone in the 1980s; and several South American countries—most notably Argentina and Brazil—which followed exchange-rate-based stabilization policies also in the 1980s. In all cases, fiscal and monetary profligacy lead to payments difficulties and either a maxi-devaluation or the outright abandonment of the fixed exchange rate policy.[3]

The worldwide increase in fiscal deficits and debt accumulation is not easy to reconcile with the neoclassical model (Barro 1979) that views debt accumulation as a way to spread over time the costs of distortionary taxation. While the neoclassical model fits the U.S. data reasonably well (Barro 1986), cyclical and intertemporal smoothing factors cannot fully account for the recent increase in peacetime deficits in OECD countries (Roubini and Sachs 1989).[4] Furthermore, the tax-smoothing model does not seem to fit the budget data from developing countries (Edwards and Tabellini 1991; Roubini 1991).

Even harder to justify as the result of rational government action are the debt bubbles (and sometimes the accompanying inflation) that occur when stabilization is delayed, as discussed by Alesina and Drazen (1991). If the need for an eventual fiscal correction can be foreseen, nothing can be gained by waiting. This is especially true if distortionary taxes, especially inflation, are used heavily during the transition.

Similarly puzzling is the phenomenon of fiscal profligacy under fixed exchange rates. After the collapse of the peg, inflation tax revenues must be increased by letting the currency float; in addition, fiscal spending may be cut, nonmonetary taxes raised, or both of these may be changed in some combination. Hence, a balance-of-payments crisis typically involves highly "nonsmooth" paths for government spending, taxes, inflation, and money holdings. This trajectory does not seem compatible with the actions of a government that tried to smooth the path of spending and the distortionary taxes.

In a pair of recent papers (Velasco 1993, 1998), I have attempted to develop a simple model that can throw light on some of these puzzling fiscal policies. To provide such an explanation, this chapter departs from the standard fiction of the fiscal authority as a single benevolent planner in two important respects. First, it allows for the possibility that those in control of the purse strings aim to maximize not just the utility of the average individual, but also the utility (prestige, clout, electoral popularity, chances for climbing up the political ladder) that they themselves get from fiscal spending. Second, it considers fiscal policy as the outcome of a political process in which spending power may be in the hands of several controllers—ministers, congressmen, state or local officials, managers of state enterprises, and so forth, depending on the precise institutional arrangement—who behave noncooperatively.

This approach is in the spirit of Patinkin (1993), who has recently written:

I cannot accept the view ... of government as a single, monolithic unit choosing policies to achieve an optimum for it. A democratic government—and frequently even a non-democratic one—is a coalition. Sometimes it is a formal coalition of several political parties (as in Israel, which indeed has never had a government which was not such a coalition); and sometimes an informal one (as in the United States, in which each of the different parties is in effect a coalition of different interests). And just as inflation is frequently explained as the result of the succumbing of the finance minister to the demands of different pressure groups in the economy (labor unions, different business interests and so on), so can it be explained as the result of the finance minister succumbing to the pressure of the ministers from the different parties that constitute the government: in fact, it is through these ministers that the aforementioned groups will generally be exerting their respective pressures on the government. (P. 115)

A key assumption in this approach is that the finance minister or budget director is weak, in that each spending agency within the government can simply set its own level of expenditures, while all such spending is to be financed with common resources (tax revenue, money creation, or public debt). That is way I refer to it as the "common property" approach to fiscal policymaking. This setup can be interpreted in one of three plausible ways. First, it may simply reflect dispersion of power inside the cabinet and an unstructured budget process, as suggested by Patinkin and explored in detail by Von Hagen (1992) for the case of European Union countries. Second, spending may be set by decentralized fiscal authorities representing particular geographical areas—witness countries with strong and deficit-prone regional governments such as Brazil, Argentina, Russia, or the former Yugoslavia. Third, transfers may be determined by money-losing state enterprises facing soft budget constraints, as in Mexico and Brazil in the 1970s or in Russia and some countries of Eastern Europe until recently. Section 8.2 below discusses each of these possibilities further and provides relevant empirical evidence.

The inefficiencies that arise when several groups or officials with redistributive aims have control over fiscal policy have recently been recognized in the literature. Weingast, Shepsle, and Johnsen (1981) and, more recently, Chari and Cole (1993) have characterized equilibria in which voting by representatives from different districts or constituencies leads to "pork barrel" spending. Aizenman (1992) and Zarazaga (1993) have stressed that if fiscal and/or monetary policy are decided upon in a decentralized manner, a "competitive externality" arises that gives the economy an inflationary bias. As Alesina and Perotti (1994) stress, however, these models are all essentially static, focusing on the level of expenditures rather than on the behavior of debt and deficits. The approach surveyed in this chapter, in contrast, focuses on the dynamic aspects of divided fiscal policymaking. Fiscal authorities are confronted with an explicit intertemporal trade-off: high deficits today mean lower spending or higher

taxes tomorrow. The key question is: does a divided government structure lead rational fiscal authorities to run debts and deficits that are "too
high" in some well-defined sense?

The canonical model outlined in section 8.3 below provides a yes
answer to this question. If government net assets (the present value of
future income streams minus outstanding debts) is the common property
of all fiscal authorities, then a problem arises that is logically quite similar
to the "tragedy of the commons" that occurs in marine fisheries or public
grazing lands (Levhari and Mirman 1980; Benhabib and Radner 1992).
Two distortions are present if N agents share the resource. First, each uses
the whole stock and not one Nth of it as the basis for consumption or
spending decisions. Second, the return on savings as perceived by one
agent is the technological rate of return (the rate of interest or the rate of
growth of natural resource stocks) minus what the other $N - 1$ agents
take out; hence, to the extent that savings depends positively on the rate
of return, each agent undersaves (overspends in the case of fiscal policy,
overexploits in the case of natural resources). In the context of fiscal
policy, this means that deficits are incurred and debts accumulated even in
contexts where there is no incentive for intertemporal smoothing, so that
a central planner guiding fiscal policy would run a balanced budget. Technically, these results arise as the Markov-Nash solution of a dynamic
game among the ministers that control fiscal policy.

This setup can be used to study a number of issues in the political
economy of fiscal policy. In section 8.4 below I discuss how the canonical
model can be extended to account for stabilizations—that is to say,
changes in fiscal policy that end the process of debt accumulation. To do
so I introduce the concept of reputational equilibria, in which ministers
coordinate on one possible path for spending and threaten to return to
the inefficient Markov-Nash path the period after a defection has been
detected. There is a second-best sustainable spending path that can be
supported by such behavior; how close it is to the first-best path of no
deficits and constant debt depends on parameter values. I also show that,
if an intratemporal distortion (such as a fixed cost of lobbying) is added to
the intertemporal distortion already described, the model can also give
rise to delayed stabilizations of the kind described by Alesina and Drazen
(1991). A fiscal stabilization may not be sustainable from low levels of
debt (high levels of government net assets), but may become sustainable
once debt reaches a sufficiently high level. Hence, countries with a low
initial level of debt may experience a delay until debt stocks became
stabilized.

Finally, a monetary version of the model (outlined in section 8.5 below) can be used to study the conduct of fiscal policy under fixed exchange rates. Countries often peg their currencies and then follow monetary and fiscal policies clearly incompatible with the maintenance of the peg. Examples included European countries such as Italy in the early 1990s; African countries in the French Franc zone in the 1980s; and several South American countries—most notably Argentina and Brazil—that also followed exchange-rate-based stabilization policies in the 1980s. In all cases, fiscal and monetary profligacy lead to payments difficulties and either a devaluation or the outright abandonment of the peg. Why governments should choose to follow such mutually inconsistent policies is an enduring puzzle for economists. Since a balance-of-payments crisis typically involves highly nonsmooth paths for government spending, taxes, inflation, and money holdings, this trajectory does not seem compatible with the actions of a maximizing government, which would normally attempt to smooth the path of spending and distortionary taxes. The divided government model provides some answers to this puzzle. As in the canonical model outlined above, common property over the Central Bank's reserves creates incentives for fiscal authorities to run down such reserves over time (this is simply accomplished by monetizing fiscal deficits under perfect capital mobility). Under some additional conditions, it may also provide incentives for reserves to be driven beyond a threshold where a speculative attack on the currency takes place. The Central Bank is then forced to let the exchange rate float, and the economy settles on a high-inflation steady state.

8.2 Suggestive Evidence

Where in the real world do we see fiscal policies conducted in a divided and noncooperative way? Three interpretations merit documenting and elaborating upon. Consider first the case in which political dynamics (both within the cabinet and between the cabinet and the parliament) render the finance minister weak and give substantial autonomy to spending ministers. While this phenomenon is probably present to some extent in many countries (as the discussion of Patinkin for the Israeli case suggests), only recently has evidence been compiled. In a detailed set of studies of the European Community in the 1970s and 1980s, Von Hagen (1992) and Von Hagen and Harden (1994) conclude that budgeting procedures that lend the finance minister "strategic dominance over spending ministers" and "limit the amendment powers of parliament" are strongly conducive to fiscal discipline. The opposite arrangement often leads to sizable deficits and debts. More specifically, Von Hagen (1992) constructs an index characterizing EU national budget processes on four grounds: (a) strength of the Prime Minister of Finance Minister in budget negotiations; (b) existence of overall budget targets fixed early on and limits on parliamentary powers of amendment; (c) transparency of the budget document; and (d) limited discretion in the implementation of the budget. The three countries with weakest budgetary procedures (those with the weakest finance minister, most parliamentary amendments, etc.) had deficits that averaged 11 percent of GDP in the 1980s, while the three countries with the strongest procedures had deficit ratios of 2 percent. The accumulated public debt stocks were also very different between these two sets of countries.[5]

Similar results are reported by Alesina et al. (1996) in their study of twenty Latin American and Caribbean countries. Using a methodology quite similar to that of Von Hagen, they find that the six countries with the strongest fiscal processes had, between 1980 and 1993, fiscal surpluses that averaged 1.8 percent of GDP; the seven countries with the weakest processes had deficit ratios of 2.2 percent over the same period.

The second context in which divided fiscal policymaking may arise is in countries with weak central governments and politically strong state or provincial governments. The cases of Argentina and Brazil—the former is studied in World Bank (1990a, b, c) and the latter in Shah (1990) and Bomfin and Shah (1991)—are instructive.[6] They are both federal countries in which over the last two decades many spending responsibilities have been transferred to the subfederal level. Lacking sufficient revenues of their own and facing unclear rules, subfederal governments have systematically run deficits that de facto have become the responsibility of the federal authorities. While details differ between the two countries and over time, there have generally been three mechanisms through which state and provincial entities could "pass on" their deficits: (a) borrowing from state development banks that in turn could rediscount their loans at the Central Bank—in effect monetizing the subfederal deficits; (b) obtaining discretionary lump sum transfers from the federal government, generally requested around election time and after large debts had been accumulated; and (c) accumulating arrears with suppliers and creditors, which (for either legal or political reasons) were eventually cleared up by the federal authorities. The implicit incentive structure is clear, and analogous to that in this chapter: understanding that at least part of the cost would be borne by others, subfederal governments have been tempted to overspend and overborrow. According to the World Bank (1990a), in Argentina "the lack of clear rules applying to the relationship between the different bodies of government is one of the main reasons for the repeated crises in public finances." The quantitative implications have indeed been important. In 1983–86, the first four years of restored democratic rule, the deficit of the provinces (before transfers from the center) averaged 4.5 percent of GDP. In 1986, the year after Argentina launched an ambitious monetary stabilization, that deficit reached 6.3 percent—and when combined with additional deficits run by state enterprises and the social security system, it amounted to a deficit for the total consolidated government of 4.6 percent of GDP, much of which had to be monetized. Unsurprisingly, the stabilization plan failed. Provincial finances deteriorated even further thereafter, as Argentina slid toward hyperinflation in the late 1980s.

The story of Brazil is similar. Four exchange-rate-based stabilization plans failed in the second half of the 1980s as a result of fiscal indiscipline, with much of the deficit coming from the state governments. And while the cases of Argentina and Brazil may be extreme, they are by no means unique. Similar troubles affected the former Yugoslavia. They are also becoming increasingly severe in Russia, as Wallich (1992) and Sachs (1994) argue.

Last, consider the case in which divided fiscal policymaking occurs as the result of the "soft budget constraints" faced by managers of state enterprises. As Kornai (1979, 1980)—who coined the phrase—emphasized, central authorities in planned economies have typically had great difficulty in forcing state firms to adhere to prespecified targets and budgets and behave in a financially disciplined way. Such firms have an incentive to pay excessive wages (thus simply reducing the profit stream that would go to the Treasury) and engage in large and risky investments (managers benefit from running larger firms but bear none of the investment risk). Bankruptcy is not a real threat, as government subsidies and bailouts from state banks often extend the life of distressed firms. Lipton and Sachs (1990), among others, have pointed out that this problem became increasingly acute with the decline of communism and the beginning of transition: "To the extent that state enterprises have been decontrolled, but without introducing real market competition at the same time, the result has been a worsening of financial indiscipline of the firm and, eventually, of the macroeconomy." The problem has indeed been large enough to threaten macroeconomic stability: Holzmann (1991) estimates that in Eastern Europe during the 1980s budgetary subsidies to state enterprises averaged almost 10 percent of GDP.

8.3   A Canonical Model

There are two symmetric groups, indexed by i, $i = 1$, 2.[7] Each is composed of a large number of identical individuals. The groups are represented by a political leader (a congressional leader or member of the cabinet, for example), whose job is to secure spending to benefit his or her constituency. The key assumption is that the central fiscal authority is weak, so minister i can determine spending g_i directly or through lobbying. This expenditure can be thought of as transfers to group i's members or spending on a local public good that only benefits group i.

The economy is small and open to international capital mobility; therefore, the real interest rate r is given parametrically. The government budget constraint is

$$f_t = (1 + r)f_{t-1} - g_{1t} - g_{2t}, \tag{1}$$

where f is public-sector wealth, defined as net financial assets plus the present discounted value of all revenues. Hence, f can fall, among other things, if governments borrow to finance fiscal deficits. I assume that the corresponding initial value f_0 is positive. Each minister's spending possibilities are constrained by (1), the standard no-Ponzi game (solvency) condition

$$\lim_{t \to \infty} f_t(1 + r)^{-t} \geq 0 \tag{2}$$

and the initial stock of wealth.

To ensure that the lack of coordination in ministers' actions does not lead to a violation of the solvency condition, it is necessary to impose a rule that prevents ministers' total desired net transfers from exceeding the maximum feasible amount. Suppose that after groups decide on their target expenditures g_{it}, these are satisfied by the central fiscal authority (the finance minister or the president) as long as

$$g_{it} \leq ((1 + r)/2)f_t \ \forall i \text{ and } \forall t. \tag{3}$$

Any minister whose desired net transfer violates (3) simply gets zero.[8] Application of this rule leads to $g_{1t} + g_{2t} \leq (1 + r)f_t$ for all t.[9]

Each minister controls g_i in order to maximize an objective function of the form[10]

$$V_{it} = \sum_{s=t}^{\infty} \log(g_{is})(1 + r)^{-(s-t)} \qquad i = 1, 2. \tag{4}$$

Notice that since the rate of discount is equal to the world rate of interest, there are no standard reasons for fiscal saving or dissaving. Hence, any fiscal deficit must be the result of the strategic interaction between the two ministers.

These constraints and the objective function provide the setting for a dynamic game between the two ministers. As is typical in this literature, I will characterize symmetric equilibria in Markov strategies, in which actions are a function of the state variable only.[11] A Markov strategy is a mapping from the state (in this case government wealth) to a particular spending policy. A pair of Markov strategies form a Markov-Nash equilibrium if they are best responses to each other at every level of the state.[12] In particular, assume each minister employs the policy rule $g_{it} = \phi f_{t-1}$, where ϕ is a policy parameter to be endogenously determined. Each minister takes into account that such a rule is being used by the other minister, but takes the actual structure of the rule as given. For any such rule that is expected to be followed by one player, we ensure that the other player's actions constitute a best response by solving the corresponding dynamic programming problem.

The value function corresponding to minister i's problem is

$$V_i(f_{t-1}) = \max\{\log(g_{it}) + (1+r)^{-1}V((1+r)f_{t-1} - \phi f_{t-1} - g_{it})\} \tag{5}$$

subject to (3).

The Euler equation is

$$\frac{g_{i(t+1)}}{g_{it}} = \left(\frac{1+r-\phi}{1+r}\right). \tag{6}$$

Also necessary for optimality is the transversality condition, which in this case can be written as

$$\lim_{t \to \infty} \left(\frac{1}{1+r}\right)^t \left(\frac{f_{t-1}}{g_t}\right) = 0. \tag{7}$$

Notice that, given the policy rule, and assuming symmetry, (1) becomes

$$f_t = f_{t-1}(1+r-2\phi). \tag{8}$$

Using the policy rule, (6) and (8), we can solve for ϕ:

$$\frac{r}{2} < \phi = \frac{r(1+r)}{1+2r} < \frac{1+r}{2}. \tag{9}$$

Hence, the Markov-Nash equilibrium consists of a pair of transfer policies, in which each minister transfers a portion $r(1+r)/(1+2r)$ of available net assets at all levels of the stock.[13] This pair of strategies is an equilibrium because, if one minister expects the other will use this policy, it is a best response to employ that same policy. This equilibrium is subgame perfect, because strategies are such that transfer levels are specified as a function of the state, not of time. Substituting this back into (8) we find that

$$\frac{f_t}{f_{t-1}} = \frac{1+r}{1+2r} < 1. \tag{10}$$

That is, there is an endogenously determined fiscal deficit, and net government assets go down over time.

Substituting (9) into (8) and then the result and the policy rule into (4), we find that the value associated with this noncooperative path, starting from any arbitrary level of wealth, is

$$V_i^{nc}(f_{t-1}) = \left(\frac{1+r}{r}\right)\left[\log\left(\left[\frac{r(1+r)}{1+2r}\right]f_{t-1}\right) + \frac{1}{r}\log\left(\frac{1+r}{1+2r}\right)\right], \tag{11}$$

where "nc" stands for "noncooperative."

By contrast, it is easy to show that a planner maximizing the joint welfare of the ministers would assign $g_{it} = (r/2)f_t$ $\forall t$. There would be no fiscal deficit and government assets would remain constant throughout. The utility that would be obtained from following such a first-best path is

$$V_i^{fb}(f_{t-1}) = \left(\frac{1+r}{r}\right)\log\left(\frac{rf_{t-1}}{2}\right), \tag{12}$$

where "fb" stands for "first-best."

Clearly, $V_i^{fb}(f_{t-1}) > V_i^{nc}(f_{t-1})$. The noncooperative equilibrium involves too high a propensity to consume out of government assets, and the reason is simple. Government net assets are the "common property" of both groups; and property rights are not defined over each group's share. As we know from the "tragedy of the commons" literature, this creates incentives for overconsumption and overborrowing.[14]

8.4   Fiscal Stabilization and Reform

Can the two groups, acting in a decentralized manner, ever coordinate on a better outcome? Can they ever coordinate on stabilization, with spending at levels such that the fiscal deficit is eliminated and government debt growth stopped? To answer these questions, I focus on trigger strategy equilibria, and characterize equilibrium paths along which groups receive

utilities that are at least as high as those that they could obtain by appro-
priating higher immediate spending and suffering retaliation later on. A
trigger strategy is an implicitly agreed-upon spending path for each
player i, $i = 1$, 2, plus the threat of a reversion to the stationary Markov-
Nash path after a defection takes place.[15] Suppose the agreed-upon
spending path involves spending λf_{t-1} per period. It is easy to check that
if both ministers adhere to this rule forever, each gets

$$V_i^\lambda(f_{t-1}) = \frac{1+r}{r} \left[\log(\lambda f_{t-1}) + \frac{1}{2} \log(1 + r - 2\lambda) \right]. \tag{13}$$

A group can always defect from the agreed-upon path at any time t. What
is consumption for each group after defection? The nondefecting group
continues to spend λf_{t-1} during the period of defection. The defecting party
picks g_t to maximize its value from deviating, which can be written as

$$V_i^d(f_{t-1}) = \log(g_t) + \frac{1}{2} \left[\log \left(\left[\frac{r(1+r)}{1+2r} \right] [(1+r)f_{t-1} - \lambda f_{t-1} - g_t] \right) \right.$$
$$\left. + \frac{1}{2} \log \left(\frac{1+r}{1+2r} \right) \right], \tag{14}$$

where "d" stands for "deviation," and which reflects the fact that after one
period both groups revert to the Markov-Nash path forever. Maximizing
this expression with respect to g_t readily yields $g_t = rf_{t-1}$, which is the
optimal deviation. Substituting this back into (14) we have

$$V_i^d(f_{t-1}) = \left(\frac{1+r}{r} \right) \left[\log(rf_{t-1}) + \frac{1}{r} \log \left(\frac{1+r}{1+2r} \right) + \frac{1}{1+r} \log(1 - \lambda) \right]. \tag{15}$$

Individual rationality dictates that, under trigger strategies, the agreed-
upon path will be followed if and only if $V^\lambda(f_{t-1}) \geq V^d(f_{t-1})$. Using (13)
and (15), one finds that this is equivalent to

$$\left(\frac{1}{1+r} \right) \log \left(\frac{\lambda}{r} \right) \geq \left(\frac{1+r}{r} \right) \log \left(\frac{1+r}{1+2r} \right) + \log \left(\frac{1-\lambda}{1+r-2\lambda} \right). \tag{16}$$

Recall the first-best (no-deficit, constant-debt) path requires $\lambda = (r/2)$
for each of the two ministers. If this solution satisfies inequality (16), then
the first-best path is sustainable through trigger strategies; if it is not, then
the best one can do is to choose the largest λ that satisfies (16). In contrast
to the first-best, such an outcome will involve a fiscal deficit and debt
accumulation, but less so than under the simple Markov-Nash equilibrium.

Notice that sustainability condition (16) is quite special in one respect: if does not involve the stock of net assets. This means that whether a given spending path is sustainable does not depend on how rich or poor the government is. The first-best, for instance, is either not sustainable at all or sustainable from all levels of the state. This clearly need not be a feature of this type of model. In the example considered, it depends to a large extent on the simplicity of the utility function, the linearity of the technology (the interest rate is independent of the level of assets), the absence of other types of costs associated with noncooperative behavior on the part of ministers, etc. Hence, by enriching the model in one of many directions, one may get the result that the ministers' ability to curtail debt accumulation depends on the level of debt itself. Consider next the simplest such example. Let the government budget constraint (1) become

$$f_{t+1} = (1 + r)f_t - z_t - g_{1t} - g_{2t}, \tag{17}$$

where the variable z_t represents a deadweight loss per period of time, which behaves according to

$$z_t = \begin{cases} 0 & \text{if } g_{it} = g_{2t} = \frac{1}{2}(rf_t - z_t) \\ z & \text{otherwise.} \end{cases} \tag{18}$$

Hence, if and only if both groups agree to stabilize, the deadweight loss disappears. This setup is justified by the presumption that there are static efficiency gains associated with stabilization. One possible interpretation is that government resources are no longer wasted in dealing with lobbyists or rent seekers, as in the work of Krueger (1974) or Bhagwati (1982). Alternatively, following Alesina and Drazen (1991), the net gain to government finances associated with stabilization could be interpreted as a switch to nondistortionary taxes or a lowering of tax collection costs, so that the government gets more revenue (net of costs) for each unit of output obtained from the private sector. Or, one could assume that stabilization produces a permanent increase in government income, perhaps in transfers from abroad intended to reward sound fiscal behavior. All that matters for the results below is that the gains from stabilizing extend beyond the dynamic benefits of curtailing spending and debt accumulation.

Consider now the corresponding incentives for good behavior under trigger strategies. For concreteness, focus on the stabilizing policies as the agreed-upon course of action, so that the value of continuation along the path is given by (12) (alternatively, (13) evaluated at $\lambda = (r/2)$). By contrast, if a minister deviates, he gets

$$V_i^d(f_{t-1}) = \left(\frac{1+r}{r}\right)\left[\log(rf_{t-1} - z) + \frac{1}{r}\log\left(\frac{1+r}{1+2r}\right) + \frac{1}{1+r}\log\left(1 - \frac{r}{2}\right)\right].$$
(19)

Comparing (12) and (19) it is clear that the difference $V^\lambda(f_{t-1}) - V^d(f_{t-1})$ is no longer independent of the asset stock. In particular, define f^* as the stock such that $V^\lambda(f^*) = V^d(f^*)$. It is easy to show that $V^\lambda(f_{t-1}) > V^d(f_{t-1})$ if $f_{t-1} < f^*$, and vice versa. Hence, the first-best stabilizing outcome can only be sustained once government assets are sufficiently low. The intuition is simple. For low levels of debt it pays to spend aggressively, for the deadweight losses are small relative to the benefits of high spending from a large asset stock. As a result, spending is high. But incentives change at higher levels of debt (lower net asset levels): because stabilization involves the elimination of the deadweight loss, the payoff associated with deviating falls more quickly than that associated with stabilization as debt rises. Put differently, the static gain associated with stabilizing becomes more desirable to groups as debt is accumulated and the government becomes poorer. Only when the stock of debt is so high that the payoff associated with deviation falls below that associated with stabilization does the latter become self-sustaining.

Hence, if at the start of the game net government assets are no larger than f^*, stabilization is effective immediately and no fiscal deficit is ever run. What happens if the economy begins at a higher net asset position (equivalently, at a lower public debt)? From the discussion so far it is not clear whether and how the economy will get to the point where stabilization is possible. In Velasco (1993) I characterize "switching equilibria" of the sort described by Benhabib and Radner (1992): groups follow Markov-Nash spending policies until the stock reaches a level such that it is individually rational to stabilize. At that point, a "switch" takes place and the fiscal deficit is eliminated. Equivalently, in the language of Alesina and Drazen (1991), stabilization is "delayed" until net assets reach their threshold point. The full characterization of such equilibria is complex, and I will not undertake it here. Heuristically, in this example it involves choosing an agreed-upon switching path, along which ministers spend more than one half of current income ($rf_{t-1} - z$) before reaching f^*, and exactly one half thereafter. A switching strategy consists of following such a path as long as no one deviates. If a deviation takes place, groups revert to Markov-Nash spending after one period. Hence, a switching strategy is nothing but a generalized trigger strategy. In turn, and as usual, a switching equilibrium is nothing but a pair of switching strategies, one for each player, such that neither group can improve its total payoff by a unilateral change in strategy at any point in the game. Along that equilibrium, therefore, government net assets fall continuously for a period of time. Eventually, a delayed fiscal stabilization takes place, and debt growth ceases.

8.5 Fiscal Deficits and Currency Crises

Paul Krugman's pioneering paper on currency crises (1979) elegantly showed how and when such crises occur. It left unanswered, however, the crucial question of why they are allowed to occur. In models of the Krugman type excessive money creation—caused by the need to finance a budget deficit—leads to reserve losses and the eventual collapse of a fixed exchange rate. After the collapse, inflation tax revenues must be increased by letting the currency float; in addition, fiscal spending may be cut, nonmonetary taxes raised, or both of these may be changed in some combination. Hence, a balance-of-payments crisis typically involves highly nonsmooth paths for government spending, taxes, inflation, and money holdings. This trajectory does not seem compatible with the actions of a maximizing government, which would normally attempt to smooth the path of spending and distortionary taxes. Since the need to finance large fiscal deficits with money is at the root of this process, any explanation of why balance-of-payments crises occur must rationalize the existence of these peculiar fiscal policies.

The common property approach to fiscal policy, with its built-in tendency toward fiscal deficits, provides a natural setting which to study this question. Consider a monetary version of the model in section 8.3. We must distinguish between the Fiscal Authority (FA), which is still composed of two ministers, and the Central Banks. From a fiscal point of view, the main change is that deficits can now also be financed by domestic credit from the CB. The FA's budget constraint is

$$a_t - a_{t-1} = r(k_{t-1} + a_{t-1}) + \frac{D_t - D_{t-1}}{E_t} - g_{1t} - g_{2t}, \tag{20}$$

where k_t is the gross stock of international reserves and a_t is the stock of FA assets, both of which earn the world interest rate.[16] The variable D_t is the nominal stock of CB credit extended to the FA. At initial time 0, central bank reserves are $k_{t=0} = k_0 > 0$ and gross FA assets $a_{t=0} = a_0$.

From the CB balance sheet, the rate of real domestic credit creation can be written as

$$\frac{D_t - D_{t-1}}{E_t} = m_t - m_{t-1} + \pi_t m_{t-1} - (k_t - k_{t-1}), \tag{21}$$

where $m_t \equiv M_t/E_t$ are real balances and $\pi_t \equiv (E_t - E_{t-1})/E_t$. Notice that (21) implies that reserves are not revalued as a result of nominal devaluations. Combining (20) and (21) we have

$$f_t - f_{t-1} - (m_t - m_{t-1}) = rf_{t-1} - g_{1t} - g_{2t} + \pi_t m_{t-1}, \tag{22}$$

where we have defined $f_t \equiv a_t + k_t$ as government net reserves. This is the budget constraint of the consolidated public sector.

Finally, let the private sector's money demand be given by

$$m_t = h(r + \pi_{t+1}), \qquad h'(\cdot) < 0.$$

Hence, the public's choices in what follows will be limited to setting its money demand contingent on its expectations of inflation. Notice that as long as the inflation rate is constant (as may be the case, for instance, under fixed exchange rates, in which case π_t is exogenously set by the Central Bank at a rate $\pi_t = 0$), money demand is constant as well and equal to $\bar{m} = h(r)$. Notice this means that under fixed exchange rates the budget constraint of the government becomes

$$f_t = (1 + r)f_{t-1} - g_{1t} - g_{2t}, \tag{23}$$

which is exactly what we had in the nonmonetary version of the model.

Each minister maximizes an objective function of the form

$$V_{it} = \sum_{s=t}^{\infty} [\alpha \log(g_{is}) + (1 - \alpha)u(\pi_{s+1})](1 + r)^{-(s-t)} \qquad i = 1, 2, \tag{24}$$

where α is a positive parameter. The idea behind such an objective function is that each minister, besides caring about his spending, also internalizes the utility of the public at large, which in turn derives utility from money balances and therefore dislikes inflation. As in the canonical model of section 8.3, these constraints and objective function provide the setting for a dynamic game between the ministers. Notice, first, that if the CB fixes the exchange rate as long as it has sufficient resources to intervene in the markets, the second term in objective function (24) is given from the ministers' point of view whenever the peg is in force. Hence, all that each minister i can do under fixed exchange rates is manipulate g_i, and the game between the ministers under fixed rates is very similar to that considered in section 8.3. In particular, when acting strategically the ministers have a tendency to overspend and drive down over time the stock of net government reserves.

But that is not the end of the story. If we assume (as did Krugman in his classic 1979 paper) that once reserves run out the CB floats the currency, then the actions of the ministers must reflect this possibility. The full equilibrium of this game is quite complex, and I shall not describe it in detail here. In essence, it first involves characterizing what happens once reserves run out—the ministers then fight over inflation tax revenues, and this determines the equilibrium rate of inflation under floating and the amount each minister can spend (both turn out to be constants), as well as the associated welfare level. The last ingredient is that the public does not sit idle; if it anticipates that reserves will be eventually exhausted, it runs the currency in a speculative attack whose size and timing are well defined along the lines characterized by Krugman. Understanding what is the payoff associated with exhausting reserves and ending the peg, and understanding what the public will do in such a case, ministers must decide on their optimal spending strategies.

In Velasco (1998), I show that this setting gives rise to Markov-Nash equilibria in which sustained fiscal deficits occur, causing reserves to decline over time. When the threshold is approached, expectations of an attack by speculators leads ministers to implement a spending policy that further depletes reserves; at the same time, the knowledge that ministers will engage in high spending triggers the speculative attack. As in Krugman, agents reduce their money holdings by buying up remaining reserves. A perfectly foreseen balance-of-payments crisis occurs and the economy settles on a high-inflation steady state.

In short, the bottom line of that paper is that—if there are political distortions that generate a bias toward excessive fiscal spending, and if Central Banks cannot be prevented from monetizing the resulting government deficits—fixed exchange rate regimes are extremely vulnerable.

8.6 Conclusions

Economists have spent much time and energy modeling the allocation of resources in those regions of the modern economy where the market system indeed allocates resources. But there is a very large portion of such economies—the government sector—within which there are no private property rights, and where the allocation of resources does not follow market forces. If we move beyond the view of government as a monolithic entity that behaves like a single individual, economics must provide an account of how economic decisions are made among government groups, and how politics both frames and partially determines those decisions. This chapter outlines one of the simplest possible models of a government with many controllers—one in which government net income is a "commons" from which interest groups can extract resources to finance their expenditures.

This setup has the striking macroeconomic implications that fiscal deficits emerge even when there are no reasons for intertemporal smoothing. Moreover, variations on the basic model can account for some observed and puzzling facts in actual fiscal policy. For instance, excessive fiscal deficits may be eliminated, but perhaps only after a delay during which government debt is built up. Countries that fix their exchange rate may follow fiscal policies that are incompatible with the maintenance of the peg, thus eventually causing a speculative attack on the currency and the end of the fixed-rate regime.

Notes

This chapter was written while I visited Harvard University under a fellowship from the Harvard/MIT Research and Teaching Group on Positive Political Economy, whose financial support and hospitality are gratefully acknowledged.

1. See Alesina and Perotti (1994).

2. The fiscal experience of a number of Latin American countries is also reported and analyzed in Tornell and Velasco (1995b) and references therein. See also the essays in Larrain and Selowsky (1991).

3. On Europe, see Buiter, Corsetti, and Roubini (1993), and Svensson (1993). The African case is discussed in detail in Tornell and Velasco (1995a) and references therein. The experience of Latin American countries is reported and analyzed in Tornell and Velasco (1994b) and references therein.

4. In a recent article, Bizer and Durlauf (1990) argue that U.S. tax rates do not seem to be a random walk, as implied by the theory. Rather, they find an eight-year cycle for tax changes, a feature suggestive of a political equilibrium.

5. More generally, Roubini and Sachs (1989, 1991) have shown that among OECD countries, those with proportional representation systems and fractionalized parties tend to display high deficits and debt.

6. Tornell and Velasco (1995a) discuss in detail the stabilization policies and fiscal troubles of Brazil and Argentina in the 1980s.

7. Everything that follows in this section holds if we allow for an arbitrary number of groups.

8. Notice that this rule is hardly restrictive, in that it prevents ministers from getting transfers equal to or larger than one half of the government's maximal wealth level, including both principal and current interest income on that wealth. Clearly, no transfer of that order of magnitude is imaginable in reality, short of a Czech/Slovak-style partition of the country.

9. Note that this rule simply prevents solvency from being violated as a result of the lack of coordination among ministers. Why the government as a whole (represented by the finance minister or president) chooses to remain solvent—or not to default—is a question beyond the scope of this chapter. I simply assume away the possibility of default, as does most of the literature on optimal fiscal policy.

10. Everything that follows in this section holds if we use a more general C.E.S. formulation for utility. The log form simply economizes on algebra.

11. For an analysis of such strategies in a similar game, see Tornell and Velasco (1992). Markovian equilibria are also characterized by Benhabib and Radner (1992) and Benhabib and Rustichini (1991).

12. Hence in this section, I assume away strategies such as trigger strategies, which depend on the history of the game.

13. Notice, incidentally that the transversality condition can be written as $\lim_{t \to \infty} \left[(1+r)^{-t} \frac{(1+2r)}{r(1+r)} \right] = 0$, which is always satisfied.

14. See Levhari and Mirman (1980) and Tornell and Velasco (1992) for examples.

15. For an example of such trigger strategies in a similar game, see Benhabib and Rustichini (1991).

16. Notice that, as is usual in the real world, the Central Bank transfers to the Treasury the income it earns on its reserves.

References

Aizenman, J. "Competitive Externalities and the Optimal Seigniorage Segmentation." *Journal of Money, Credit and Banking* 24 (February).

Alesina, A., and A. Drazen. 1991. "Why Are Stabilizations Delayed?" *American Economic Review* 81 (December).

Alesina, A., and R. Perotti. 1994. "The Political Economy of Budget Deficits." NBER Working Paper No. 4637, February.

Alesina, A., R. Hausmann, R. Hommes, and E. Stein. 1996. "Budget Institutions and Fiscal Performance in Latin America." NBER Working Paper No. 5586, May.

Barro, R. 1979. "On the Determination of the Public Debt." *Journal of Political Economy* 87.

————. 1986. "U.S. Deficits since World War I." *Scandinavian Journal of Economics* 88.

Benhabib, J., and R. Radner. 1992. "Joint Exploitation of a Productive Asset: A Game Theoretic Approach." *Economic Theory* 2(2).

Benhabib, J., and A. Rustichini. 1991. "Social Conflict, Growth and Inequality." New York University, C. V. Starr Center for Applied Economics, W.P. 91-46, September.

Bhagwati, J. 1982. "Directly Unproductive Profit-Seeking (DUP) Activities." *Journal of Political Economy* 90.

Bizer, D., and S. Durlauf. 1990. "Testing the Positive Theory of Government Finance." *Journal of Monetary Economics* 26.

Bomfin, A. N., and A. Shah. 1991. "Macroeconomic Management and the Division of Powers in Brazil: Perspectives for the 1990s." World Bank Working Paper No. 567, January.

Buiter, W., G. Corsetti, and N. Roubini. 1993. "Excessive Deficits: Sense and Non-Sense and the Treaty of Maastricht." *Economic Policy* 16, April.

Chari, V. V., and H. Cole. 1993. "A Contribution to the Theory of Pork Barrel Spending." Federal Reserve Bank of Minneapolis Staff Report 156.

Holzmann, R. 1991. "Budgetary Subsidies in Centrally Planned Economies in Transition." IMF Working Paper 91/11, April.

Kornai, J. 1979. "Demand versus Resource-Constrained Systems." *Econometrica* 47(4) (July).

———. 1980. *Economics of Shortage*. Amsterdam: North Holland.

Krueger, A. 1974. "The Political Economy of the Rent-Seeking Society." *American Economic Review* 64.

Krugman, P. 1979. "A Model of Balance of Payments Crises." *Journal of Money, Credit and Banking*.

Labán R. and F. Sturzenegger. 1994. "Distributional Conflict, Financial Adaptation and Delayed Stabilizations." *Economics and Politics* 6(3).

Larrain, F., and M. Selowsky. 1991. *The Public Sector and the Latin American Crisis*. San Francisco: ICS Press.

Levhari, D., and L. Mirman. 1980. "The Great Fish War: An Example Using the Cournot Nash Solution." *Bell Journal of Economics* 11.

Lipton, D., and J. Sachs. 1990. "Creating a Market Economy in Eastern Europe: The Case of Poland." *Brookings Papers on Economic Activity* 1.

Patinkin, D. 1993. "Israel's Stabilization Program of 1985" *Journal of Economic Perspectives* 7(2) (Spring).

Roubini, N., and J. Sachs. 1989. "Government Spending and Budget Deficits in the Industrial Countries." *Economic Policy*, April.

———. 1991. "Economic and Political Determinants of Budget Deficits in Developing Countries." *Journal of International Money and Finance* 10.

Sachs, J. 1994. "Russia's Struggle with Stabilization: Conceptual Issues and Evidence." Paper presented at the World Bank's Annual Conference on Development Economics, April.

Shah, A. 1990. "The New Federalism in Brazil." World Bank Working Paper No. 557 December.

Svensson, L. E. O. 1993. "Fixed Exchange Rates as a Means to Price Stability: What Have We Learned?" NBER Working Paper No. 4504, October.

Tornell, A., and A. Velasco. 1992. "The Tragedy of the Commons and Economic Growth: Why Does Capital Flow from Poor to Rich Countries? *Journal of Political Economy* 100, December.

————. 1995a. "Exchange Rate-Based and Money-Based Stabilization with Endogenous Fiscal Policy." NBER Working Paper No. 5300, October.

————. 1995b. Fixed versus Flexible Exchange Rates: Which Provides More Fiscal Discipline? NBER Working Paper No. 5108, May.

Velasco, A. 1993. "Are Balance of Payments Crises Rational?" Working paper, C. V. Starr Center for Applied Economics, New York University.

————. 1998. "A Model of Endogenous Fiscal Deficits and Delayed Fiscal Reforms" *Fiscal Institutions and Economic Performance*, ed. J. Poterba and J. Von Hagen. Chicago: University of Chicago Press for the NBER, forthcoming.

Von Hagen, J. 1992. "Budgeting Procedures and Fiscal Performance in the European Communities." Economic Papers No. 96, Commission of the European Communities, October.

Von Hagen, J., and I. Harden. 1994. "National Budget Processes and Fiscal Performance." *European Economy: Reports and Studies* 3.

Wallich, C. 1992. "Fiscal Decentralization: Intergovernmental Relations in Russia." Studies of Economies in Transformation, Paper No. 6, The World Bank.

Weingast, B., K. Shepsle, and C. Johnsen. 1981. "The Political Economy of Benefits and Costs: A Neoclassical Approach to Redistributive Politics." *Journal of Political Economy* 89, August.

World Bank. 1990a. "Argentina: Reforms for Price Stability and Growth." The World Bank.

————. 1990b. "Argentina: Provincial Government Finances." Washington, DC: The World Bank.

————. 1990c. "Tax Policy for Stabilization and Economic Recovery." Washington, DC: The World Bank.

Zarazaga, C. 1993. "Hyperinflations and Moral Hazard in the Appropriation of Seignorage." Working Paper 93-26, Federal Reserve Bank of Philadelphia, November.

9   Fiscal Discipline in a Union

Joshua Aizenman

9.1   Introduction and Summary

The purpose of this chapter is to investigate the need for fiscal discipline for an economy where the center has limited control over the spending patterns of the union members, and where the union members' behavior has repercussions for the future public debt. In practice, most unions are characterized by such a structure, differing in the degree to which the center has control of the fiscal behavior of its members, and the degree to which the union members have the ability to roll over part of their expenditure to the center. The weakness of the center is manifested frequently in the excessive spending of provincial governments, as has been the case in many developing countries.[1] Weak federal governments occasionally used both seigniorage and public debt to finance excessive spending of local governments, resulting in high inflation and a large public debt overhang.[2]

An interesting illustration of public debt dynamics in a weak federal system is found in a World Bank (1990) study of Argentina during the eighties, where the deficits of provincial governments was the key factor accounting for Argentina's fiscal deficit. For example, in 1986 the total fiscal deficit of the provinces was 6.2 percent of the GDP, much higher than the deficit of the public-sector enterprises and of social security combined.[3] Further insight can be gained from figure 9.1, plotting the public deficit as a percentage of the GDP for the twenty-two provincial governments in Argentina (figure 9.1a), and the average deficit of the provincial governments between 1981 and 1986 (figure 9.1b). Similar findings apply for Brazil, where states' overspending plays a key role in explaining the fiscal deficit.[4]

This chapter focuses on a generic model where there is an interaction between the center and the peripheries under conditions of limited mon-

Provincial   government   deficit

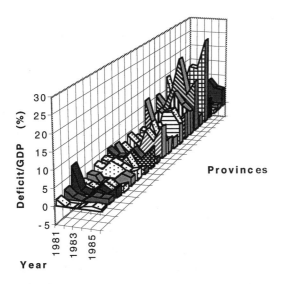

Average   Deficit/GDP
for   the   22   provinces

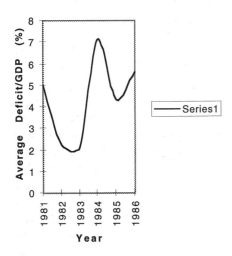

Figure 9.1
Deficit/GDP for the twenty-two provincial governments in Argentina

itoring. We refrain from modeling the institutional details that enable the opportunistic behavior of policymakers, as the reduced-form approach may encompass various economic structures. Consider an economy where the treasury is relatively weak, and where the fiscal decisions are the outcome of the behavior of several competing policymakers, called governors. We call the collective body, consisting of these policymakers, the administration. The governors represent various interest groups that compete for fiscal resources. These interest groups may be provincial governors in a country composed of several provinces, or states in a fiscal union, or any pressure groups seeking to promote their own agenda. The administration allocates the planned fiscal outlays among the governors. In the short run, governors may abuse their official budgets, entailing higher public debt. Over time, such opportunistic behavior is detected and punished by removing the governors and the administration. The public has preferences against higher public debt (as it reduces the future fiscal resources available for the provision of public goods or for public investment). It uses the public debt as an indicator regarding the competence of the administration to restrain the various governors, and it will oust high-debt administrations.[5]

Our model is non-Ricardian in several dimensions. First, the optimization problem solved by the administration and the governors does not necessary coincide with consumers' optimization. Hence, there is potentially an agency problem, and elections may be viewed as a mechanism designed to control the agent-principle separation. Second, the horizon of the administration is limited and endogenously determined. These non-Ricardian features may provide insight regarding the desirability to impose a constitutional ceiling on public debt/GNP ratio allowed.

The model supports the notion that the macroeconomic equilibrium is characterized by the existence of several regimes: cooperative, limited cooperation, and noncooperative regimes. A fully cooperative regime is supported if policies that maximize the expected utility of a representative governor lead to an outcome where none of the governors has the incentive to deviate. Otherwise, the administration will adjust the planned fiscal expenditure (and the resultant public debt) to the highest level that entails cooperation. We refer to the resultant outcome as limited cooperation. If the attainment of limited cooperation is not feasible, governors end up behaving opportunistically. This behavior entails maximizing their utility while ignoring the resultant negative externalities, leading to the noncooperative regime.

The public sector is characterized by negative externalities akin to the common pool problem.[6] The ability of local governors to shift some of their expenditure to the common pool of public debt encourages them to overspend, as they will share only part of the burden of future taxes, while sharing fully the present benefits. The ultimate outcome of the resultant externalities is that a noncooperative regime yields excessive current spending and shortens the effective planning horizon of the governors. The administration has a control variable (the planned public debt) that determines the planned fiscal allocation to the governors. The administration sets policies that maximize the expected utility of the representative governor, subject to the constraints imposed by their behavior. The existence of adverse externalities implies that the administration would set policies that induce the individual governors to prefer the cooperative outcome. The problem is akin to the organization of an intertemporal cartel, where the cartel manager chooses a price that is consistent with the lack of opportunistic behavior.

Adverse shocks are shown to induce a regime switch from a cooperative outcome to limited cooperation. A large enough unfavorable disturbance induces a switch to the noncooperative outcome. While a transitory adverse shock induces a higher public debt in the cooperative regime (in order to offset the transitory decline in income, thereby smoothing consumption), the switch toward limited cooperation entails a drop in the public debt (relative to the cooperative outcome). The adverse shock encourages the opportunistic behavior by increasing the marginal evaluation of the benefits of extra resources (due to the principle of diminishing marginal utility) and by shortening the planning horizon of governors. A drop in public debt is needed to "police" the union, preventing the tendency to overspend and to end up with the noncooperative outcome.

When we are in the limited cooperation regime, the binding constraint determining the pattern of public debt ant fiscal expenditure is the incentive constraint: preventing opportunistic behavior. This implies that with limited cooperation further drops in income will call for a *drop* in public debt, an outcome that does not occur in the cooperative regime. If the adverse shock is powerful enough, sustaining limited cooperation may become unfeasible. In these circumstances we end up in the noncooperative regime, where the behavior of the various governors shorten the effective horizon of all. Consequently, a regime switch resulting from adverse shocks may change the correlation among macroeconomic variables. In addition, it may yield nonlinearities, where the macroeconomic behavior is abruptly altered following the regime switch, which in turn will occur if the severity of adverse shocks reaches a certain threshold.

Our analysis reveals a fundamental difference between the cooperative regime and the other two regimes (the limited cooperation and non-cooperative one). As long as we are in the domain of the cooperative regime, stability is *assured*, and the public debt is used to cushion any shortfall in taxes. Once we reach limited cooperation or noncooperative outcomes, stability is *not assured*, and the economy is at the mercy of the relative strength of opportunistic forces.

Section 9.2 of the chapter introduces a model of a weak federal system where fiscal deficits are bond financed. In section 9.3 we characterize the possible regimes, the conditions yielding a regime switch, and the resultant patterns of the correlation among macroeconomic shocks. Section 9.4 closes the chapter with concluding remarks.

9.2   The Model

We review in this section the budget constraints, the political uncertainty, and the timing of events in the model.

9.2.1   The Planned Budget

The union is composed of n symmetric provinces (or states), each managed by a governor. The federal administration has access to fiscal revenue (T), which are equally divided among the states. The fiscal plan for period t is guided by a budget. It specifies a planned fiscal allocation of $\bar{G}_{t,i}$ to n governors $(i = 1, \ldots, n)$. The allocation divides equally the tax revenue (denoted by T), and finances the rest by issuing public debt, in the form of a one-period bond. We denote by b_t^p and b_t^a the planned and the actual sales of these bonds in period t. Thus,

$$\bar{G}_{t,i} = \frac{T_t + b_t^p - (1 + r)b_{t-1}^a}{n}, \tag{1}$$

where r is the real interest rate, assumed to be exogenously given. The tax rate is denoted by τ, the GNP by Y, so that $T = \tau Y$. To focus on the role of the public debt, we assume first that the tax rate and output are exogenously given, and that the only control variable available to the administration is the planned sales of bonds. b_t^p.

9.2.2   Budget Constraints and Political Uncertainty

The actual behavior of governors may diverge from the planned budget. Within each period there is limited monitoring of the actual activities of the governor. Each of them has a degree of flexibility in dictating the effective resources allocated to him from the center, so that the realized budget constraint facing a governor (assuming that he is not detected) is given by

$$G_{t,i} = \bar{G}_{t,i} + C^o_{t,i}, \tag{2}$$

where $C^o_{t,i}$ measures the opportunistic expenditure of governor i. The limited monitoring is manifested as a probability of detection: if the opportunistic expenditure of governor i exceeds a threshold C^o, he is detected and removed from office immediately, before implementing the opportunistic consumption. Otherwise, his actual fiscal behavior will be revealed at the end of period t with a probability of λ. This probability depends positively on the rate of the opportunistic consumption of governor i, and detection is certain after two periods. Detection occurs after the commitment of resources; hence, it does not impact the aggregate actual public debt.

We summarize the detection probability at the end of period t by[7]

$$\lambda_t = \begin{cases} \lambda(C^o_{t,i}) & \text{for } C^o_{t,i} \leq C^o \\ 1 & \text{for } C^o_{t,i} > C^o \text{ or if } C^o_{t-1,i} > 0. \end{cases} \tag{3}$$

Hence, in between period t and $t+1$ any remaining governors that abused their budget constraints in period $t-1$ are removed from office. Thus, opportunistic behavior pays (at most) for the duration of two periods. Detection and removal from office implies that the governor's utility at that period and after is normalized to zero.

The realized public debt is the outcome of the behavior of all the governors:

$$b^a_t = b^p_t + \sum_{i=1}^{n} C^o_{t,i}. \tag{4}$$

Its value is revealed at the end of period t, and the public uses it as an indicator regarding the competence of the administration. A higher value of the public debt implies that a greater portion of the tax revenue will be used to service the public debt, and hence less tax revenue will be available for fiscal activities (either for the provision of public goods or for public investment). Hence, a higher fiscal deficit is viewed as undesirable by the public, reducing the survival probability of the administration from period t to period $t+1$.

We denote by $\phi_{t,1}$ the survival probability of period t's administration to period $t+1$, and assume that $\phi_{t+1} = \phi(b^a_t)$, where $\phi'(0) = 0$, and $\phi' < 0$

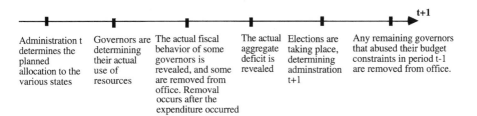

Figure 9.2
The timing of the game in period *t*

for $b_t^a > 0$.[8] The election of a new administration implies the removal of all the preceding governors.[9] We assume the absence of reputation effects, and thus ex ante all administrations and governors are alike. The representative governor (indexed by *i*) is maximizing his expected utility from his fiscal expenditure, given by

$$V_{t,i} = E_t \left\{ \sum_{k=t}^{\infty} \rho^{k-t} U(G_{k,i}) \right\} \qquad \rho \le 1,$$ (5)

and E_t denotes the expectation operator, based upon the information available at period *t*, and *U* is the periodic utility function, satisfying $U' > 0$ and $U'' < 0$, and $U = 0$ if the governor is out of office. The administration is setting policies in order to maximize the expected utility of the representative governor, taking into account the behavior of the atomistic governor as a feasibility constraint on the set of policies.

9.2.3 The Timing of Events

The timing of the game is summarized in figure 9.2. At the beginning of period *t* the administration determines the planned allocation to the various states, $\bar{G}_{t,i}$. This decision is equivalent to the determination of the planned public debt, b_t^p (note that the tax revenue *T* is exogenously given). Next, governors are determining their actual use of resources, $G_{t,i}$. If the opportunistic expenditure of governor *i* exceeds a threshold C^o, he is detected and removed from office immediately, before implementing the excessive expenditure. Otherwise, the actual fiscal behavior of governor *i* will be revealed at the end of the period with a probability of λ, after implementing the excessive expenditure. Governors that are detected abusing the planned allocation will be removed from office. At the end of the period the actual aggregate deficit b_t^a is revealed. Elections are taking place in between the two periods,

and the present administration is reelected with probability ϕ_{t+1}.[10]
The elected administration starts its tenure at the beginning of period
$t + 1$.

9.3 Equilibrium and Tacit Cooperation

We turn now to characterize the equilibrium in several steps. First, we
analyze the conditions determining the behavior of a governor. Next, we
analyze the incentive constraints imposed by the opportunistic governors
on the behavior of the administration. Finally, we apply these constraints
to characterize the factors determining the degree of cooperation achieved
via tacit cooperation.

Formally, our framework is a repeated game, in which a one-period
simultaneous move game is repeated each period.[11] Following the literature, we focus on the symmetric, efficient equilibrium from the players'
viewpoint. For a given planned deficit we derive the optimal behavior of
each governor. Sequential rationality and efficiency require the administration to choose the public debt that maximizes the utility of the representative governor subject to a feasibility constraint: The planned public
debt rate should be chosen so as to prevent the opportunistic behavior of
the atomistic governors. We start this section with a characterization of
the possible regimes, and continue with the derivation of the conditions
inducing the regime switch and the implications of the regime changes on
the pattern of public debt, ending with a discussion of possible extensions
of the model.

9.3.1 Classification of Possible Regimes

The equilibrium behavior of governors and the administration can be
traced with the help of a diagram that plots the expected utility of governors against the planned debt, under various degree of cooperation. We
proceed by studying the incentive of a representative governor (say governor i), focusing on the property of a symmetric equilibrium where all
other governors behave in the same manner. We adapt the following
notation: index c corresponds to the case where governor i cooperates,
index o corresponds to the case where he behaves opportunistically. Index
(c, o) corresponds to the cases where governor i cooperates, while all the
other governors behave opportunistically. Similarly, index (o, c) denotes
the case where governor i behaves opportunistically, while all the others
cooperate, etc. We turn first to evaluate the behavior of the opportunistic

governor in his first period in office. A governor who chooses to behave opportunistically at period t knows that he is out of office within not more than two periods. Applying (2), (3), and (5) we conclude that he sets $C_{t,i}^o$ in order to maximize expected utility at time t. If all the other governors cooperate, the resultant expected utility in an internal equilibrium (i.e., where $C_{t,i}^o < C^o$) is

$$V_t|_{o,c} = U(G_{t,i}^o) + \rho\phi_{t+1}|_{o,c}(1 - \lambda_t)U(\overline{G}_{t+1,i} + C^o), \tag{6}$$

where $\phi_{t+1}|_{o,c} = \phi(b_t^p + C_{t,i}^o)$.

The first-order condition determining opportunistic expenditure is[12]

$$\frac{\partial V_t|_{o,c}}{\partial C_{t,i}^o} = 0. \tag{7}$$

The optimal opportunistic expenditure equates the marginal benefit attributed to more resources obtained with the marginal cost generated by the higher probability of detection, plus the expected cost of servicing a fraction $1/n$ of the extra debt. If a corner solution applies, $G_{t,i} = \overline{G}_{t,i} + C^o$. Henceforth, we assume that the internal equilibrium characterizes the opportunistic expenditure.

If all the other governors behave opportunistically, the resultant expected utility is

$$V_t|_{o,o} = U(G_{t,i}^o) + \rho\phi_{t+1}|_{o,o}(1 - \lambda_t)U(\overline{G}_{t+1,i} + C^o) \qquad \text{where}$$

$$\phi_{t+1}|_{o,o} = \phi(b_t^p + (n - 1)C_{t,-1}^o + C_{t,i}^o). \tag{6'}$$

where $C_{t,-i}^o$ indicates that for $j \neq i$, $C_{t,j}^o = C_{t,-i}^o$. Thus, $V_t|_{o,c} > V_t|_{o,o}$.

We turn now to characterize the cooperative regime, where all governors cooperate. The expected utility attained with cooperation is denoted by $V|_{c,c}$, where

$$V_t|_{c,c} = U(\overline{G}_{t,i}) + \sum_{k=t+1}^{\infty} \rho^{k-t}\left[\prod_{j=t+1}^{k}\phi_j\right]U(\overline{G}_{k,i}). \tag{8}$$

Alternatively,

$$V_t|_{c,c} = U(\overline{G}_{t,i}) + \rho\phi_{t+1}|_{c,c}V_{t+1}|_{c,c}. \tag{8'}$$

If governor i cooperates, while all the others behave opportunistically, then governor i's utility is affected adversely by the opportunistic behavior of the other governors, as their expenditure shortens the horizon of all. Thus,

$$V_t|_{c,o} = U(\bar{G}_{t,i}) + \rho\phi_{t+1}|_{c,o}V_{t+1} \quad \text{where } \phi_{t+1}|_{c,o} = \phi_{t+1}(b_t^p + (n-1)C_{t,i}^o).$$
$$(8'')$$

Thus, opportunistic expenditure imposes a negative externality, short-ening the horizon of all policymakers. If this externality is large enough (i.e., if $\phi_{t+1}|_{c,o}$ is small), then $V_t|_{c,o} < V_t|_{o,o}$. An attempt by governor i to cooperate, while all the other governors behave opportunistically would imply that his expected utility would be below the expected utility of all the other governors, as they gain from the opportunistic expenditure at time t (and there is a high probability that all will be ousted from office at the end of the period).[13] In these circumstances, if $V_t|_{c,c} < V_t|_{o,c}$, then opportunistic behavior is the preferable strategy from the point of view of each governor. As all governors are facing the same problem, this will lead to an expected utility of $V_t|_{o,o}$.

Clearly, this situation may lead to an inefficient outcome, as the oppor-tunistic behavior shortens the horizon of all. This will happen if the op-portunistic expected utility ($V_t|_{o,o}$) is below the cooperative one, implying that the interaction among governors leads to an outcome that resembles the prisoner's dilemma. Note that the planned public debt set by the administration may affect the nature of the regime observed, and under certain circumstances may avoid the switch to the noncooperative regime. We turn now to illustrate this possibility.

Suppose that we start with a configuration of fiscal revenue and an out-standing past debt so that the cooperative regime is stable (as will be the case if $V_t|_{c,c} > V_t|_{o,c}$). Applying (8) it follows that

$$\frac{\partial V_t|_{c,c}}{\partial b_t^p} = \frac{MU_t|_c - \rho(1+r)\phi_{t+1}|_{c,c}MU_{t+1}|_c}{n} + \phi'_{t+1}|_{c,c}\rho V_{t+1}|_{c,c}. \quad (9)$$

Starting with zero public debt, the expected utility in the cooperative equilibrium will tend to rise with the public debt (recall that $\phi'(0) = 0$).[14] As we increase the public debt, the marginal benefit of the debt is eroded, while the cost (in terms of reducing the reelection probability) goes up. Hence, for a large enough public debt the expected utility in the coopera-tive regime will start declining with future increase in the public debt. The optimal public debt in a cooperative regime (denoted by $b_t^p|_c$) is deter-mined by the condition that $(\partial V_t|_{c,c})/(\partial b_t^p) = 0$: it balances the marginal value of resources achieved by higher public debt with the marginal cost resulting from the drop in the administration's probability of survival and the higher future repayment. Figure 9.3 summarizes the possible regimes. Curve CC describes the expected utility obtained by cooperation, drawn

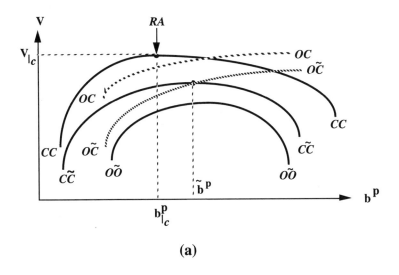

(a)

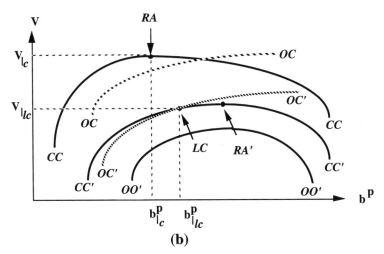

(b)

Figure 9.3
Planned debt and expected utility

against b_t^p. The bliss point achieved in the cooperative regime with the optimal public debt is denoted by RA.

We turn now to characterize the behavior of one opportunistic governor, while the others are cooperating. Applying (6), we infer that a higher planned public debt affects $V|_o$ by

$$\frac{\partial V_t|_{o,c}}{\partial b_t^p} = \frac{MU_t|_o - \rho(1+r)\phi_{t+1}|_{o,c}(1-\lambda_t)MU_{t+1}|_o}{n}$$

$$+ \phi'_{t+1}|_{o,c}\rho(1-\lambda_t)U(\bar{G}_{t+1,i} + C^o). \tag{10}$$

Similar to the cooperative regime, starting with zero public debt the expected utility of the opportunistic governor will tend to rise with the public debt (recall that $\phi'(0) = 0$). As we increase the public debt, the marginal benefit of the debt is eroded, while the cost (in terms of reducing the reelection probability) goes up. In comparison to the cooperative regime, however, a higher public debt induces smaller costs for the opportunistic governor, as (s)he attaches a lower weight to the future.[15] Hence, the presumption is that at the cooperative optimal public debt (point RA) a higher public debt is desirable for the opportunistic governor.[16] Curve OC describes the expected utility generated by the opportunistic behavior (assuming that all other governors cooperate), drawn against planned debt, b^p.

If the opportunistic expected utility, at the optimal cooperative public debt, is lower than the expected utility from cooperation, then we will observe cooperation. In terms of figure 9.3, this will happen if curve OC is below curve CC at the cooperative optimal public debt, leading to a cooperative equilibrium at point RA, where the public debt is at the level that maximizes the cooperative expected utility. We denote the corresponding public debt by $b_{|c}^p$. If the opportunistic utility is higher than the one achieved with cooperation at $b^p = b_{|c}^p$, cooperation is not self-sustained.

For example, suppose that the opportunistic and cooperative expected utility schedules are given by OC' and CC' (see figure 9.3b). Recall that curve OC' reports the expected utility of governor i who behaves opportunistically, while all the other governors cooperate. To infer the ultimate expected utility in the noncooperative regime, we add a plot of the expected utility if all governors behave opportunistically, denoted by OO' (see figure 9.3b).[17] Curves CC', OC', and OO' (figure 9.3b) depict a situation where the cooperative bliss point, RA' is not sustainable, because all governors will behave opportunistically. The resultant equilibrium yield an expected utility on curve OO'. In the example provided in figure

9.3b, the optimal sustainable equilibrium is characterized by the highest cooperative expected utility that does not lead to deviations (and thus $V|_{o,c} \leq V|_{c,c}$), at a point like LC, where curve OC' intersects with CC'. We denote the corresponding public debt by $b^p_{|lc'}$ and refer to it as the limited-cooperation public debt. This public debt is self-sustained as no benefits are obtained by the opportunistic behavior. The administration does not reduce the public debt below $b^p_{|lc'}$ as this will reduce expected utility; and it cannot push it above, due to the presence of opportunistic behavior.

9.3.2   Regime Switches and the Pattern of Public Debt

We turn now to evaluate the conditions that may induce an economy to switch from cooperation to an equilibrium where cooperation is limited. Suppose that the relevant curves in the initial equilibrium are CC and OC, and hence the equilibrium is at point RA, corresponding to the cooperative regime. Let us consider the impact of an adverse shock, like a transitory drop in taxes. For a given b^p_t, an adverse fiscal shock will shift curves OC and CC vertically by $[MU_t|_O](\Delta T)/n$ and $[MU_t|_C](\Delta T)/n$, respectively. Recall that $G|_{o,c} > G|_{c,c}$, and thus $MU_o < MU_c$. Consequently, for $\Delta T < 0$; $[MU_t|_C](\Delta T)/n < [MU_t|_O](\Delta T)/n < 0$. The drop is greater for the utility in the cooperative regime. This follows the fact that the pattern of consumption is front-loaded in the opportunistic regime, relative to the cooperative one. The principle of diminishing marginal utility implies that a drop in income equal in both regimes will induce a smaller drop in the expected utility associated with the opportunistic regime, since this regime is associated with a higher contemporaneous consumption. Consequently, if the adverse shock is large enough, the likelihood of cooperation diminishes and we may end up with limited cooperation, at a point like LC. Thus, we conclude that willingness to cooperate among governors is in short supply when times are bad.[18]

We turn now to evaluate the impact of transitory shocks on the optimal public debt. Suppose that there is a transitory drop in taxes. In the cooperative regime, it follows from (9) that[19]

$$-1 < \frac{d[b^p_t|_c]}{dT} < 0 \tag{11}$$

The public debt is used to smooth the governors' fiscal consumption throughout the business cycle, in line with the predictions of optimizing macroeconomic models (see Barro 1979). In the regime with limited cooperation, however, the behavior of the public debt is determined not by the "first-best" economic considerations described above. Instead, the dynamics of the public debt are determined by the binding incentive constraint—preventing opportunistic behavior dictates the pattern of debt. To verify this point, note first that in the vicinity of the limited cooperative equilibrium, curve CC' is flatter than curve OC' (otherwise everyone will be better off by increasing the public debt). Formally, defining D by $D = V|_o - V|_{c'}$ at $b_t^p = b_{t|lc}^p$, $D = 0$ and $\partial D / \partial b_t^p > 0$. Applying this information, we infer that

$$\frac{d[b_t^p|_{lc}]}{dT} = \frac{[MU_t|_c - MU_t|_o]/n}{\partial D / \partial b_t^p} > 0; \tag{12}$$

Further insight may be obtained by referring to figure 9.3a. Suppose that prior to the shock the relevant curves are CC and CO, and hence the equilibrium is at point RA, corresponding to the cooperative regime. The adverse shock shifts both curves down, but the shift of curve CC is larger. With a large enough adverse shock the economy reaches the threshold where opportunistic behavior becomes a viable option, threatening cooperation. This configuration is depicted by curves $\widetilde{CC}$ and $\widetilde{OC}$, figure 9.3a, where curve $\widetilde{OO}$ reports the expected utility if all policymakers behave opportunistically. At this threshold, if governor i behaves opportunistically while all the other governors cooperate, his expected payoff equals the cooperative payoff. The optimal planned public debt in this situation is depicted by $\tilde{b}^p$.[20] Note that if all policymakers behave opportunistically, the resultant expected utility must be lower than the one attainable with cooperation at the cooperative bliss point. Hence, curve $\widetilde{OO}$ must be below curve $\widetilde{CC}$ at $b = \tilde{b}^p$.[21]

A further drop in tax revenue (as will be the case if the adverse shock is greater than the one leading to $b = \tilde{b}^p$) will imply that we end up with OC' above CC' at the cooperative bliss point, as is shown in figure 9.3b. Now the cooperative outcome at point RA' is unattainable. At this point, the administration confronts the prisoner's dilemma. The representative governor (i) has the incentive to behave opportunistically, and the ultimate equilibrium yields an inferior outcome on curve OO'.[22] From the point of view of the administration, the constraints imposed by the opportunistic behavior imply that the optimal attainable allocation is point LC (figure 9.3b). The adjustment from the previous to the new equilibrium can be broken into two parts: moving from RA to RA', reflecting the adjustment within the cooperative regime, and the shift from RA' to LC, reflecting the regime switch. Note also that the regime switch is associated with a drop in the public debt, needed to avoid the opportunistic outcome (i.e., the public debt is lower at LC relative to RA'). Furthermore, when we operate in the regime associated with limited cooperation, further adverse shocks will force a drop in the public debt needed to sustain the limited cooperation, preventing the switch to a noncooperative outcome.[23]

If the shock is large enough, the drop in CC may be large enough that the new CC and OC do not share any points. In this case limited cooperation is not achievable—the noncooperative forces are powerful enough to prevent the attainment of limited cooperation. In terms of figure 9.3, this will imply that we end up on curve OO'. This is the case where the absence of cooperation releases powerful negative externalities: each governor ignores the adverse effect of opportunistic expenditure on the survival probability of all other governors, ending up with an inefficient outcome and shortening the political horizon of all governors. This is the stage where the resolution of the crisis may require fiscal reform, shifting more power to the center and tightening the monitoring of the various governors.

The regime switch may yield noncontinuities and nonmonotonicities, where the macroeconomic behavior is abruptly altered following the regime switch, which in turn will occur if the severity of adverse shocks reaches a certain threshold. In terms of equation (12), note that $\partial D/\partial b_t^p \to 0$ as we approach the switch from limited cooperation to the noncooperative regime. Consequently, the sensitivity of the macroeconomic variables (for instance, to public debt) to shocks increases sharply, and with regime switch we may observe discontinuity in the patterns of public debt. Figure 9.4 describes the dependency of public debt on the tax at time t, where

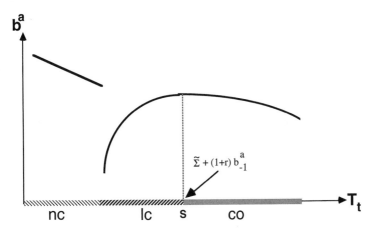

Figure 9.4
Taxes and public debt

regions co, lc, and nc correspond to the cooperative, limited cooperation, and the noncooperative regimes.[24]

Applying the above analysis, it follows that a large inherited public debt will tie the hands of the administration, preventing the use of debt finance to cushion adverse shocks. Let us denote by Σ the net resources available to the administration in the absence of new borrowing, $\Sigma_t = T_t - (1 + r)b^a_{t-1}$. Let $\tilde{\Sigma}$ stand for the lowest net resources under which cooperation is sustainable.[25] A cooperative equilibrium is sustainable as long as the realized tax revenue T exceeds $\tilde{\Sigma} + (1 + r)b^a_{-1}$. Hence, a higher outstanding public debt shifts the debt curve in figure 9.4 to the right, enlarging the range of the noncooperative regime and increasing the threshold level of taxes needed to sustain cooperation. The horizontal shift of the debt curve equals the change in outstanding debt, $\Delta[(1 + r)b^a_{-1}]$. Consequently, b^a_t can be rewritten as a function of the net resources Σ_t. The debt curve plotted in figure 9.4 can be conveniently summarized by

$$b^a_t = f[T_t - (1 + r)b^a_{t-1}], \tag{13}$$

where $f' = 0$ and $f'' < 0$ at $T = \tilde{\Sigma} - (1 + r)b^a_{-1}$.

9.3.3 Debt Dynamics

We turn now to investigate the evolution of debt over time. Further insight regarding debt dynamics is gained by redrawing figure 9.4, depicting the dependency of the actual public debt b^a against the past public debt b^a_{-1} (for a given tax revenue, T). Formally, let us define $b^a = g(b^a_{-1}; T_t)$ by

$$g[b^a_{t-1}; T_t] = f[T_t - (1 + r)b^a_{t-1}]. \tag{14}$$

Figure 9.5 plots the debt curve corresponding to g, holding T exogenously given.[26] If the debt curve is given by $AEBCD$, for debt levels below $\tilde{b}$ the public debt converges to point E, which is a stable cooperative long-run equilibrium. For debt levels above $\tilde{b}$ we observe convergence towards a stable, high-debt, noncooperative equilibrium at point F. The possibility of an explosive path in the noncooperative regime can not be ruled out, however. For example, if the debt curve is given be $AEBC'D'$, point F depicts an unstable equilibrium, and debt levels above $\tilde{b}$ are associated with explosive dynamics.

Figure 9.5 enables us to trace the evolution of the economy over time. The location of curve $AEBCD$ is determined by the tax revenue T, as is indicated by the position of point S'.[27] If the economy experiences a drop in tax collection, the debt curve in figure 9.5 shifts leftward, by $\Delta T/(1 + r)$.

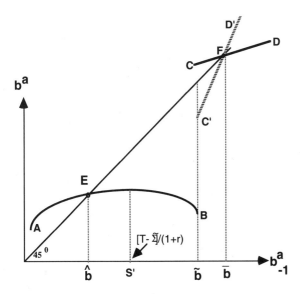

Figure 9.5
Debt dynamics

For example, suppose that we start in a long-run equilibrium at E, and taxes decline. If the drop in taxes is small, we stay in the domain of cooperation, converging towards a new long-run equilibrium with a gradual increase in the public debt. For intermediate values of adverse shocks, we enter the domain of limited cooperation. The adjustment in this case can be read in figure 9.6, panel (I), where the initial debt is $\hat{b}$, corresponding to the debt at the preceding long-run equilibrium.

In the example plotted, we observe an oscillatory convergence toward the new long-run equilibrium (point V). One can not rule out divergence, as will be the case if KL is steeper (i.e., if its slope is less than -1), leading the economy to a noncooperative regime.

If the drop in taxes is large (or if KL is steep), we end up with a noncooperative regime, where we observe the building up of debt, as is depicted in figure 9.6, panel (II). If the debt curve is CD, we observe a convergence path along the dotted curve, towards a new stable long-run equilibrium (point W). If the debt curve is $C'D'$, we observe divergence.

Figures 9.5 and 9.6 reveal a fundamental difference between the cooperative regime and the other two regimes (the limited cooperation and noncooperative one). As long as we are in the domain of the cooperative regime, stability is *assured*, and the public debt is used to cushion any shortfall in taxes. Once we reach limited cooperation or noncooperative

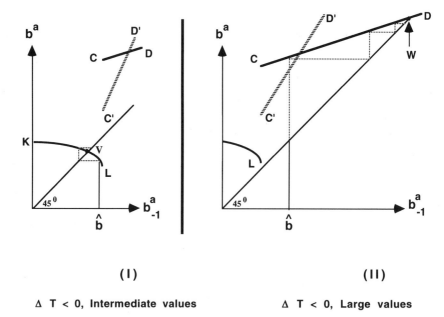

(I)   (II)

Δ T < 0, Intermediate values   Δ T < 0, Large values

Figure 9.6
Adjustment to adverse tax revenue shocks

outcomes, stability is *not assured*, and the economy is at the mercy of
the relative strength of opportunistic forces. In terms of our framework,
a sufficiently large public debt is a precondition for the regime switch
toward limited cooperation.

This suggests that constitutional limits on public debt may serve a useful
role. Suppose, for example, that tax T follows an autoregressive random
process. A larger public debt increases the threshold of tax revenue
needed to sustain cooperation. Alternatively, it increases the chances that
the economy will switch to a regime where cooperation is limited (or to
a noncooperative regime). In these circumstances public debt cannot be
used effectively to smooth public expenditure and public investment
throughout recessions, and stability is not assured.[28] Constitutional limits
on public debt can be viewed as an attempt to prevent the economy from
approaching a large debt buildup. When we approach the stage of limited
cooperation, constitutional limits may serve the role of a warning signal
that calls for fiscal restructuring. In the absence of such a restructuring, the
economy may switch to an explosive debt path, where the pressure for
fiscal restructuring may arrive much later, at a much higher, nonsustainable
level of public debt.

In reviewing the welfare implications of our model, we should keep in mind the non-Ricardian nature of our economy—the maximization carried out by the governors does not coincide with that of the public. Hence, the welfare of the public cannot be inferred without imposing further structure on the model. Nevertheless, potential instability associated with a noncooperative regime has negative welfare implications independent of the precise specification of public preferences, since the resultant instability leads to an explosive path of public debt. In order to infer further welfare implications, one should specify explicitly the utility of the public. The simplest way to do it is to consider the case where the public's periodic utility is (5), and the public horizon is unbounded. Thus, the main difference between the public and the governor is that the governor's horizon ends with his tenure, whereas the public's horizon does not.[29] In these circumstances the fiscal expenditure is front-loaded relative to one desired by the public, and the switch from a cooperative towards a noncooperative outcome is welfare worsening. The resultant adverse welfare effect would be further magnified if one adds public investment to the model—the shortening of the governor's horizon tends to bias its choice against public investment, in favor of fiscal consumption.

9.3.4   Monitoring and Noncooperative Traps

Our model can be modified to account for a more realistic environment, by changing the monitoring assumptions. For example, suppose that the monitoring ability of the center is adversely affected by the number of opportunistic governors. In these circumstances the number of opportunistic governors is an argument of the detection probability (λ_t), affecting it negatively.[30] While all our qualitative results continue to apply, the above modification increases the severity of noncooperative behavior, as the direct penalty associated with the noncooperative behavior diminishes with the number of offenders. Ultimately, it may introduce hysteresis that bites in bad times.

Suppose, for example, that at time t a new administration takes office, and an adverse transitory shock reduces output and taxes. The modified monitoring pattern does not affect the operation of the first two regimes (the cooperative and limited cooperation regimes), but affects considerably the pattern of behavior in the noncooperative regime. Once governors behave noncooperatively, detection of opportunistic behavior becomes harder, modifying the location of curve OO due to two conflicting forces. First, for a given planned public debt, the probability of detection in period t goes down, encouraging further the opportunistic spending at the present period, shifting the curve up. Second, the resultant greater actual public debt reduces the survival probability of the administration (ϕ), shifting the curve downward. While the net outcome regarding the location of the curve is uncertain, both effects work to increase the actual public debt and to shorten the horizon of the administration.

In terms of figure 9.6, it will shift the portion nc of the debt curve up, implying that the next administration starts with a potentially much greater public debt. Hence, in period $t + 1$ the economy starts with a larger debt overhang, which is equivalent to a new adverse shock, shifting curve CC further downward. In terms of figures 9.5 and 9.6, this pushes curve CD upward. Recalling that instability is associated with a debt curve CD above the 45 degree ray, we conclude that monitoring deficiency increases the likelihood for ending up with an unstable noncooperative system. Thus, monitoring efficacy that is adversely affected by the number of deviators increases the chance that a transitory adverse shock in period t will induce a noncooperative behavior in period $t + 1$ due to the greater buildup of debt. This implies that once we enter a noncooperative regime, it will become harder to reverse it, introducing an element of persistence that "bites" in bad times. If this effect is powerful enough, it may lead to noncooperative traps that behave as absorbing unstable states: once you find yourself in this trap, the way out may require a major overhaul of the system.

9.4   Concluding Remarks

Before closing the chapter, it is constructive to place it in its proper context within the existing literature. A contribution by Alesina and Drazen (1991) explained delays in stabilization in terms of a war of attrition between competing groups who behave noncooperatively. They focused on the timing of the switch from a noncooperative to a cooperative outcome. This chapter serves to illuminate the conditions inducing the opposite shift—switching the economy from a well-behaved regime where agents cooperate to a noncooperative outcome. It illustrates too that the menu of possible regimes is richer than the extremes of cooperative and noncooperative behavior, and that the regime switch has important implications for the continuity of and the correlation among macroeconomic variables, and for the dynamcic stability of public debt. This chapter provides an analytical framework that enables one to grasp the complex, two-way fiscal linkages between periphery and center, where limited cooperation may be sustainable for a significant duration.[31]

Notes

I would like to thank James Conklin, Mariano Tommasi, and the participants of the Texas monetary conference, April 1995, for useful comments. Any errors, however, are mine. The chapter is part of NBER's research in International Trade and Investment. Any opinions expressed are those of the author and not those of the NBER.

1. Some of the transmission generating the overexpenditure is accomplished via financial intermediation. For example, provincial governments may encourage (or overlook) the provision of credit by local banks to questionable local businesses against IOU notes. Upon the collapse of some of these businesses, there is political pressure on the central government to bail out the local banks (and perhaps the local businesses). If the financing of this rescue is done by increasing the public debt, the ultimate risk undertaking and expansionary policy of local provinces (or states) determines the volume of the questionable credit.

2. See World Bank (1990) for a case study documenting this pattern for Argentina, and Edwards and Tabellini (1990) for an empirical study of seigniorage and fiscal deficits in developing countries.

3. The study reports: "The provinces have been responsible for the largest and fastest growing portion of the public sector deficit. While provincial expenditures rose rapidly over the 1970–86 period, reaching over 11.2 percent of the GDP in 1986, total own-source provincial revenues actually dropped from a high of 5.6 percent of GDP to only 5 percent of GDP in 1986. The total fiscal deficit of the provinces in 1986 before transfers from the central government was 6.2 percent of the GDP, helping transform the national administration's before transfer surplus of 5.4 percent of GDP into a fiscal deficit of 4.6 percent of GDP after transfers" (World Bank 1990, 1).

4. For example, *The Economist* commented in its Latin American Survey (November 1993): "One would be to alter the formula that allocates revenues to states without giving them responsibilities to match. This exacerbates irresponsibility among state governments, which borrow recklessly from state-owned banks in the knowledge that they will if necessary be bailed out by the central bank. Overspending by the states—they owe about $50 billion— is a major cause of inflation."

5. Our model can be extended to allow part of the tax revenue to be spent on the provision of a public good. Our results continue to hold as long as the policymakers have the ability to use fiscal resources to expand their own consumption.

6. On the interplay of these externalities in a common currency area see, e.g., Canzoneri (1989), Casella (1991), and Aizenman (1992). On coordination problems in the macro context see, for example, Hamada (1976), Bryant (1985), Canzoneri and Gray (1985), Buiter and Marston (1985), Cooper and John (1988), Turnovsky, Basar, and D'orey (1989), Rogoff (1989), Alesina and Drazen (1991), Cukierman (1992), Tornell and Velasco (1992), and Mondino, Sturzenegger, and Tommasi (1994). For a survey of the literature on macroeconomic policies and politics, see Persson and Tabellini (1990).

7. The assumptions that detection is certain after two periods or if the opportunistic expenditure exceeds a threshold are done to simplify presentation. Our analysis can be readily extended to the case where there is no truncation of the horizon of the opportunistic governors. This will be the case where the detection probability at period $t + j$ is a function $\lambda(\ )$ of the net present value of all the opportunistic spending (discounted to period $t + j$).

8. We assume that the public uses the aggregate debt as an indicator of the competence of the administration. An alternative assumption is that the public attaches higher weight to the

new debt, and lower to past debt that was rolled over. Our analysis may be extended to cover this alternative specification.

9. Our analysis continues to apply for the cases where each governor i faces independent election, and his reelection probability is ϕ_i. If the repayment of the outstanding public debt is shared equally among the voters, the reelection probability of governor i will be adversely affected by the aggregate public debt, and positively related to the realized fiscal consumption in state (or province) i. Hence, in this case, $\phi_i = \phi_i(C_{t,i}^o, b_t^a)$, with $\partial \phi_i / \partial C_{t,i}^o > 0$ and $\partial \phi_i / \partial b_t^a < 0$. It can be verified that the key results of our chapter continue to apply in this modified structure.

10. Recall that we assume that detection is certain after two periods. Hence, in between period t and $t + 1$ any remaining governors that abused their budget constraints in period $t - 1$ are removed from office.

11. For a review of repeated games and tacit cooperation, see Tirole (1988).

12. The first-order condition is that $MU_t|_{o,c} = \lambda_t' \rho (1 + r) \phi_{t+1}|_{o,c} U(G_{t+1,i}) + \rho(1 - \lambda_t) \times \{((1 + r)\phi_{t+1} MU_{t+1}|_o/n) - \phi_{t+1}'|_{o,c} U(\bar{G}_{t+1,i} + G^o)\}$, where $MU_t|_o$ stands for the marginal utility at date t, evaluated at the opportunistic level of consumption. Notice that a governor who behaves opportunistically at time t is removed from office not later than the end of $t + 1$. Hence, if he remains in office for period $t + 1$, a corner solution characterizes his future expenditure: $G_{t+1,i} = \bar{G}_{t+1,i} + C^o$.

13. Note that $V_t|_{c,o} < V_t|_{o,o}$ if $\phi \to 0$.

14. A sufficient condition assuring that $\partial V_t|_{c,c}/\partial b_t^p > 0$ at $b_t^p = 0$ for the case where $\rho = 1/(1 + r)$ is that the inherited public debt b_{t-1}^a is positive, or that $\phi(0) < 1$ (i.e., the reelection probability is less than one).

15. The costs of higher public debt stem from the lower probability of reelection, and lower net resources in the next period (when repayment is due). The lower probability of survival of the opportunistic governor (relative to a governor who behaves cooperatively) implies that the expected cost of a higher public debt tends to be lower for him.

16. A sufficient condition for this is a large enough λ_t.

17. Curve OO' is defined by (6), for the case where $b_t^a = b_t^p + nC_{t,i}^o$.

18. Our analysis can be readily extended to account for the effects of permanent shocks, where the impact of a permanent drop in taxes is qualitatively similar, but stronger, than the impact of a transitory drop. In this case curves OC and CC drop vertically by $[MU_t|_O + \rho\phi_{t+1}(1 - \lambda_t)MU_{t+1}|_O](\Delta T)/n$ and $[MU_t|_C + \rho\phi_{t+1}MU_{t+1}|_C + \cdots](\Delta T)/n$, respectively.

19. It can be verified that

$$\frac{d[b_t^p|_c]}{dT} = -\frac{[MU_t'|_c]/(n^2)}{\partial^2 [V_t|_{c,c}]/\partial [b_t^p]^2} = -\frac{[MU_t'|_c]/(n^2)}{\dfrac{MU_t'|_c + \rho(1 + r)^2 \phi_{t+2|_{c,c}} MU_{t+1}'|_c}{n^2} + \phi_{t+2|_{c,c}}'' \rho V_{t+1}|_{c,c}} > -1.$$

20. Note that (11) implies that $\tilde{b}^p > b_{|c}^p$.

21. Let the optimal opportunistic consumption corresponding to $\tilde{b}^p$ be $G_{t,i}^o$, leading to expected utility of $V_t|_{o,o}$. Had the administration set the planned fiscal expenditure at the optimal opportunistic level, $\bar{G}_{t,i} = G_{t,i}^o$, the corresponding cooperative expected utility would have exceeded $V_t|_{o,o}$ (as it offers the same expenditure at time t, without the possible penalty associated with detecting the opportunistic behavior). Thus, $V_t|_{o,o}$ must be smaller than the expected utility attainable with cooperation at the cooperative bliss point.

22. We also assume that $V_t|_{c,o} < V_t|_{o,o'}$ as will be the case if the negative externality imposed by the opportunistic behavior is significant.

23. With limited cooperation the incentive constraint is binding: the public debt is set at the highest level that prevents noncooperative behavior. An adverse shock both increases the perceived marginal benefit of noncooperative behavior and cuts the marginal cost of deviating from the cooperative outcome, thereby increasing the temptation to behave opportunistically. The only way the center can curb this tendency is by increasing the effective horizon of governors, which requires lowering the debt.

24. Note that the switch to the noncooperative regime entails a change in the administration's operation. It will set the planned public debt at the level that maximizes the expected utility along curve OO.

25. The value of $\tilde{\Sigma}$ is defined in the following way. The reduced form of the expected utility of governor i depends on three factors: the net resources available to the administration, the planned public debt, and the degree of cooperation. Let $V|_k(b_t^p; \Sigma_t)$ denote the expected utility of a governor for a planned public debt b_t^p and net resources Σ_t in regime $k, k = (c, c)$ or (o, c). The cooperative equilibrium is sustainable only if $V|_{o,c}(b_t^p; \Sigma_t) \leq V|_{c,c}(b_t^p; \Sigma_t)$. We define $\tilde{\Sigma}$ as the lowest net resources under which cooperation is sustainable; $V|_{o,c}(b_t^p; \Sigma_t) = V|_{c,c}(b_t^p; \Sigma_t)$. In terms of figure 9.3a, at $\Sigma = \tilde{\Sigma}$ the corresponding curves are $\widetilde{CC}$ and $\widetilde{OC}$, intersecting at the cooperative bliss point (hence points RA and LC coincide). Thus, for $\Sigma_t < \tilde{\Sigma}_t$ cooperation is not sustainable, and we operate in the lc regime.

26. Note that $g'(b_{-1}^a) = -(1 + r)f'$, where f' is evaluated at $T_t - (1 + r)b_{t-1}^a$. Hence, if the real interest rate r is zero, then $g' = -f'$, and the shape of g can be easily inferred. Point S in figure 9.4 corresponds to point S' in figure 9.5. The graph in figure 9.5 is obtained by reflecting the graph of figure 9.4 on a two-sided mirror positioned vertically at point S. A similar procedure applies to the case where the interest rate differs from zero, using a "distorting mirror" to reflect the impact of the real interest rate.

27. Note that the location of the curve depends also on $\tilde{\Sigma}$, which in turn is determined by institutional arrangements. Throughout the analysis we assume these arrangements *held* constant.

28. This argument can be illustrated using figure 9.6. A higher outstanding public debt $((1 + r)b_{-1}^a)$ shifts the curve to the right, enlarging the range of the noncooperative regime, and increasing the threshold level of taxes needed to sustain cooperation.

29. Recall that we assumed that the utility of the governor is zero if (s)he is out of office. A more precise specification leading to similar results is obtained if we assume that the governor's preferences are similar to the group he represents, and that he or she gets extra utility from his status as a governor. For example, let the governor's i utility in period t be $(1 + g)U(G_{t,i}), g > 0$, and $U(G_{t,i})$ when the governor is ousted. Hence, the term g measures the utility gain from being the governor.

30. Alternatively, this occurs if more prevalent opportunistic behavior increases social tolerance toward it, making it an accepted norm rather than the exception. This is only one example of various reasons for a drop in the detection probability. The discussion in this subsection identifies the effects of an exogenous drop in the detection probability $(d\lambda < C)$, whatever is its source.

31. A possible recent example of limited cooperation is Brazil, where states are not ready (so far) to give up any resources to try to help a national stabilization plan (see *The Economist*, April 23, 1994). They recently voted down a proposal for the Treasury to withhold some monies aimed to generate a higher public-sector operational surplus), but they have not spent outrageously beyond their budget, averting (so far) hyperinflation.

References

Aizenman, J. 1992. "Competitive Externalities and the Optimal Seigniorage." *Journal of Money, Credit and Banking* 24: 61–71.

Alesina, A., and A. Drazen. 1991. "Why Are Stabilizations Delayed?" *American Economic Review* (December): 1170–1188.

Barro, R. 1979. "On the Determination of the Public Debt." *Journal of Political Economy* 87 (October): 940–971.

Bryant J. 1985. "Analyzing Deficit Finance in a Regime of Unbacked Government Paper. "*Economic Review*, 15: 17–27.

Buiter, W. H., and R. C. Marston, eds. 1985. *International Economic Policy Coordination*. New York: Cambridge University Press.

Canzoneri, B. M. 1989. "Adverse Incentives in the Taxation of Foreigners." *Journal of International Economics* 27: 283–297.

Canzoneri, B. M., and I. A. Gray. 1985. "Monetary Policy Games and the Consequences of Non-cooperative Behavior." *International Economic Review* 26: 547–564.

Casella A. 1991. "Participation in a Currency Union." *American Economic Review* 81: 847–863.

Cooper, Russell, and Andrew John. 1988. "Coordinating Coordination Failures in Keynesian Models." *Quarterly Journal of Economics* 103(3): 441–463.

Cukierman, A. 1992. *Central Bank Strategy, Credibility and Independence: Theory and Evidence*. Cambridge, MA: MIT Press.

Edwards, S. and G. Tabellini. 1990. "Explaining Fiscal Policies and Inflation in Developing Countries." NBER Working Paper 3493.

Hamada, K. 1976. "A Strategic Analysis of Monetary Interdependency." *Journal of Political Economy* 84: 677–700.

Mondino, G., F. Sturzenegger, and M. Tommasi. 1994. "Recurrent High Inflation and Stabilization: A Dynamic game." Manuscript, University of Chicago.

Persson, T., and G. Tabellini. 1990. "Macroeconomic Policy, Credibility and Politics." Chur, Switzerland: Harwood Academic Press.

Rogoff, K. S. 1989. "Reputation, Coordination and Monetary Policy." In *Modern Business Cycle Theory*, ed. R. J. Barro, 236–264. Cambridge, MA: Harvard Press.

Tirole, J. 1988. *The Theory of Industrial Organization*. Cambridge, MA: The MIT Press.

Tornell A., and A. Velasco. 1992. "The Tragedy of the Commons and Economic Growth: Why Does Capital Flow From Poor to Rich Countries?" *Journal of Political Economy* 100 (December): 1208–1231.

Turnovsky S. J., B. Tamer, and V. D'orey. 1989. "Dynamic Strategic Monetary policies and Coordination in Interdependent Economies." *American Economic Review* 78: 341–361.

World Bank. 1990. *Argentina: Provincial Government Finance*. Washington, DC: The World Bank.

10

The Rush to Free Trade in the Developing World: Why So Late? Why Now? Will It Last?

Dani Rodrik

A work on the political economy of trade liberalization in developing countries must address at least two puzzles. First, why has trade liberalization in these countries traditionally been so contentious? There is probably no area in economics where professional opinion is so united: the vast majority of economists see free trade, warts and all, as superior to protection. The attraction of free trade resides at one level in the theoretical elegance of the principle of comparative advantage—which, as Paul Samuelson once put it, is the only proposition in economics that is at once true and nontrivial.[1]

Even when the theory is complicated by second-best considerations under which trade restrictions can enhance efficiency, most economists remain in favor of free trade on practical grounds. Yet import-substitution policies relying on trade restrictions have been the orthodoxy among policymakers in developing countries for much of the postwar period. Until recently, policymakers usually resisted advice from academics and lending agencies to open up their economies to international competition (on the general subject of the political economy of policymaking in developing countries, see Bates 1988; Haggard and Webb 1993; Meier 1991; Rodrik 1992c; for earlier cases of liberalization, see Papageorgiou, Choksi, and Michaely 1990).

The second puzzle has to do with recent trends in developing countries. Since the early 1980s, developing countries have flocked to free trade as if it were the Holy Grail of economic development. Bolivia, Ghana, Mexico, Morocco, Turkey, and, more recently, scores of other countries in Africa, Asia, and Latin America have made considerable progress in dismantling their protectionist trade regimes, doing away with import licenses and quantitative restrictions. Argentina and Brazil have begun the

Originally published in *Voting for Reform: Democracy, Political Liberalization, and Economic Adjustment*, ed. Stephan Haggard and Steven B. Webb (New York: Oxford University Press, 1994), 61–88. Reprinted with permission.

same process in the past couple of years. Even India appears to have em-
barked on the road to trade liberalization after decades of heavy-handed
dirigisme. Table 10.1 provides capsule summaries of some of the more
significant reforms. Together with the historic transformation and opening of the Eastern European economies, these developments represent a
genuine revolution in policymaking. The puzzle is why is it occurring
now and why in so many countries all at once?

The key to these two puzzles might appear at first to be one and the
same. The reasons for the recent conversion to outward orientation must
be sought, at least initially, in the dissolution of the forces and motives
that led policymakers to resist reforms in the past. However, this line of
reasoning does not take us too far. The reasons for the free trade band-
wagon are more or less unique and derive from the intense, prolonged
macroeconomic crisis that surrounded developing countries during the
1980s. This crisis overshadowed the distributional considerations that had
blocked trade reform until the 1980s. A combination of special circumstances made governments eventually choose openness over further restrictions, the latter being the historical outcome during crises brought on
by unfavorable external circumstances.

The reasons that developing countries initially adopted import-
substitution policies and widespread trade restrictions are well known.
Early on, nationalist policymakers, as well as many development economists, perceived such restrictions as laying the basis for industrialization
and development. A temporary period of protection was required, it was
felt, for infant industries to grow and become competitive. Over time, the
problems with the infant-industry argument became increasingly evident.
The negative examples were the countless cases of infant industries that
refused to mature in old age and spawned inefficiencies throughout the
economy. The positive examples were the East Asian tigers (Hong Kong,
Republic of Korea, Singapore, and Taiwan [China]), where the early administration of outward-oriented policies was yielding spectacular results by
the 1970s. Yet despite the accumulating evidence, trade reform remained
sporadic and was often reversed.

To understand why requires understanding what trade policy does and
how it affects different groups in society. A large part of this chapter is
devoted to presenting a framework in which such an analysis can be
carried out, including discussion of the channels through which commercial and exchange rate policies work and their respective distributional
impacts. The main theme in this part of the chapter is that the central
political difficulty in undertaking trade reform is the exceedingly high

Table 10.1
Recent Trade Policy Reforms in Selected Developing Countries

Country	Reform
Argentina	Tariffs were reduced starting in October 1988; import licensing was abolished except for twenty-two items (vehicles and parts); in 1991, a three-level tariff structure was introduced (0, 11, and 22 percent)
Bolivia	Trade regime was overhauled in 1985, and quantitative restrictions were eliminated; as of April 1990, two basic tariff rates exist: 5 percent for capital goods and 10 percent for others
Brazil	Major trade reform was announced in March 1990 as part of the Collor stabilization package; almost all quantitative restrictions were to be phased out and replaced by tariffs; the average tariff was reduced to 25 percent in 1990 (from 37 percent); an average tariff rate of 14 percent was sought by 1994
Chile	Substantial reform occurred after 1973, with the elimination of quantitative restrictions and a uniform tariff rate of 10 percent (except for motor vehicles) achieved by 1979; the uniform tariff was raised to 35 percent briefly during the macroeconomic crisis of the early 1980s but was subsequently reduced to 15 percent
Ghana	Import licensing was substantially liberalized, and a uniform tariff was introduced for most imports
Indonesia	Trade has been continually reformed since 1986; by the end of 1988, only 20 percent of imports (by value) were subject to licensing
Jamaica	Quantitative restrictions were eliminated, and tariffs were lowered to 20 to 30 percent for most items
Mexico	Quantitative restrictions were substantially liberalized beginning in mid-1985; few import licensing requirements remain; tariffs were reduced to an average 11 percent by 1988; the maximum rate is 20 percent; Mexico acceded to GATT in 1986
Morocco	Protection was significantly reduced after 1983 through the elimination of some quantitative restrictions and the reduction of tariff rates; the maximum tariff was reduced from 400 to 45 percent
Nigeria	Trade liberalization was initiated in 1986; the import licensing system was reformed and substantial cuts undertaken in tariffs
Pakistan	In July 1988, a reform program was initiated to shift from nontariff measures to tariffs; import licensing was eliminated for a wide range of products; the maximum tariff was reduced to 125 percent (from 225)
Peru	The newly elected Fujimori government embarked on a stabilization package in August 1990, including substantial trade reform; all quantitative restrictions were eliminated, and the tariff system was simplified to include three rates (15, 25, and 50 percent) only; in March 1991, the top rate was reduced to 20 percent
Senegal	Most quantitative restrictions were removed during 1986–88; tariffs were selectively reduced
Tunisia	Licensing was removed from more than half of import items by mid-1990; the maximum tariff was reduced to 43 percent (from 220)

Table 10.1 (continued)

Country	Reform
Turkey	The general trend has been toward liberalization since 1980, including substantial liberalization of quantitative restrictions and licensing procedures
Venezuela	Comprehensive import liberalization was introduced in 1989; most import prohibitions were abolished, and tariffs were reduced to a maximum rate of 50 percent (from 80 percent); Venezuela acceded to GATT in 1990

Source: United Nations Conference on Trade and Development 1991; Whalley 1989; Williamson 1990; World Bank 1989; and national sources.

ratio of redistribution to aggregate gain that trade reform typically generates. The political cost-benefit ratio of trade reform, which will be defined more precisely, is generally very high. This is the source of the contentiousness of trade policy in normal times.

The second part of the chapter turns to the reforms of the 1980s, arguing that it is the pervasive crisis during those years that enabled these reforms. Desperate policymakers packaged reforms in the fiscal, monetary, and exchange rate areas—which were intimately linked to the crisis—which reforms in commercial policies—which were by and large only incidental. The depth of the crisis reduced distributional considerations to second-order importance and eliminated previous resistance. This raises the question of the sustainability of the reforms. If and when normal times and politics as usual return, will these reforms be undercut by the reemergence of the previous distributional coalitions? The last section of the chapter suggests some reasons to hope that they will not. The status-quo bias that helped entrench the previous policy regime is now likely to work in reverse. Provided macroeconomic stabilization proves successful and inflation and external balances are brought under control, backtracking from the reforms will not be easy.

Trade Reform, Distribution, and Economic Efficiency

We start by reviewing the standard partial-equilibrium analysis of trade liberalization. The general-equilibrium analysis—to which we must necessarily resort when reform involves more than a few items—is more complicated, but the wrinkles involved need not concern us for the moment. The next section extends the analysis in the general-equilibrium direction.

Figure 10.1 shows the domestic demand and supply (S) schedules for an import-competing commodity, say, steel. Let the import restriction take the form of a quota, with only a specified amount of imported steel allowed in the country. To simplify further, we assume that the home economy is small in the world market for steel (that is, the world price for steel is a given) and that domestically produced and imported steel are perfect substitutes for each other. The exchange rate is fixed at unity. The (fixed) world price is indicated in the diagram by p^*. Adding up horizontally the domestic supply with the import quota yields the supply curve faced by domestic consumers (S_q) inclusive of imports. The intersection of domestic demand with S_q (point C) gives the domestic price of steel in equilibrium, p_d. The gap between p_d and p^* is the protection provided to the domestic industry by the quota. It also represents the unit rent created by the quota. These rents accrue typically to holders of import licenses who get them through, depending on the context, political connections, bribery, or sheer luck.[2]

Now consider the consequences of eliminating the import quota. If domestic consumers can import as much steel as they want at price p^*, the new, free trade equilibrium is found at the intersection of the domestic demand schedule with the perfectly flat schedule for world supply (point D). The domestic price falls from p_d to p^*. Consequently, imports and domestic consumption increase, while domestic production decreases and quota rents vanish. The reform enhances the efficiency of resource allocation: previously, resources worth p_d were tied up in the domestic steel industry; releasing these resources and increasing imports at price p^*, achieves a net gain.

A detailed welfare analysis of the reform can be carried out to see who loses, who gains, and by how much. There are three groups of interest here: users of steel,[3] domestic producers of steel, and license holders. The lower panel of figure 10.1 shows the consequences for each of these groups. The gain to users of steel (or the economy in general) is captured by the area under the demand curve, ACDH. The loss to steel producers is the area under the domestic supply curve, ABGH. License holders, in turn, lose the quota rents amounting to the area BCEF. This leaves a net efficiency gain to the economy from removing the quota that amounts to the sum of two triangles, BFG and CDE.

At this point in the analysis the economics professor usually stops and rests his case, feeling smug after this unassailable demonstration of the superiority of free trade. Most students are probably left a bit uneasy the first time they are subjected to this logic. What is striking about the analysis is perhaps less the end product—the two triangles of efficiency gains—than the massive transfers of income from one group to another —the rectangles that appear or vanish—that are necessary to get there.

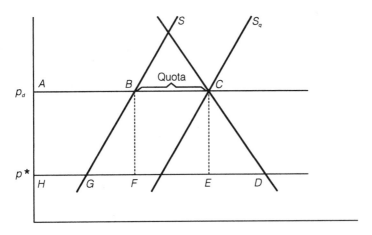

Figure 10.1
Trade reform and income distribution

License holders and steel producers lose out on chunks of income, while consumers (who may include downstream producers using steel as an input) gain by a magnitude that barely exceeds these losses. This leaves a net efficiency gain that amounts to two paltry triangles. In other words, the ratio of net gain to redistribution involved is quite small.

Economists have long been aware of the links between trade policy and income distribution. Some of the most fundamental theorems of trade theory concern precisely the distributional consequences of free trade (for example, the Stolper-Samuelson theorem; Stolper and Samuelson 1941). Development economists have spent much effort trying to ascertain whether these consequences are normatively desirable or not—that is, whether free trade improves equity. A good recent analysis is the study by Bourguignon and Morrisson (1989), which contains both cross-country regression analyses and case studies. Their main conclusion is that protection has a negative effect on income distribution.[4] More to the point, they find that the effect of trade policies on distribution is quantitatively very significant, even though their measure of trade policy is crude and subject to error. Everything else held constant, they find the income share of the richest 20 percent of the population to 4–5 percentage points higher in highly protectionist countries, where protectionist is defined by a mean effective rate of protection greater than 30 percent.

This suggests, then, that the prospect of too much redistribution may be the central political difficulty in trade reform. From the perspective of policymakers, the pure reshuffling of income must be counted as a political cost. In politics, rents and revenues that accrue on a regular basis create entitlements. Whether viewed as desirable or not, taking income away from one group is rarely easy for a politician to accomplish. And although most policy reforms undercut such entitlements, trade reform does so with a vengeance. Of course, the efficiency benefit of the reform is itself a source of political gain: it amounts to an increase in the size of the national pie, representing improvement in the well-being of at least some groups in society at no cost to others.

Such considerations can be formalized by devising an index of the political cost-benefit ratio (PCBR) of policy reform, defined as follows:

$$\text{PCBR} = \frac{1}{2}\left[\frac{(\sum_j |\Delta\text{income}_j| - \text{net gain})}{\text{net gain}}\right] \tag{1}$$

where net gain stands for the efficiency gain of the reform, j indexes groups (or individuals) in society, and Δ income, is the change in the income of group j. Note that net gain can also be expressed as $\sum_j(\Delta \text{ income}_j)$. The numerator is the sum of the absolute values of the income effects of the policy on different groups (net of the efficiency gain) and, therefore, is a measure of the total redistribution resulting from the policy. This is divided by two to get rid of the double-counting. In this way, the numerator becomes equivalent to the sum of losses suffered by the groups adversely affected by the reform. Hence, the numerator captures the political cost of the reform, while the denominator captures its benefit. The index is meant to quantify the notion that, for any amount of increase in the size of the national pie, as the amount of reshuffling of income required to achieve that increase grows, so does the cost of the change to policymakers. More specifically, the PCBR index answers the following question: how many dollars of income are shuffled from one group to another for every dollar of net efficiency gain?

Although the index is meant to be nothing more than a heuristic device, it can be given a solid theoretical foundation. Suppose, for example, that the policymaker wants to maximize a conventional social welfare function, subject to the constraint that no group of individuals is made worse off by the reform compared with the status quo. The policymaker has at his disposal only distortionary subsidies and taxes to undertake the requisite compensation. Then the cost-benefit calculus undertaken by the policymaker will bear a certain similarity to the index discussed above. In fact, the PCBR index can be viewed as representing a special case of the problem just stated. The appendix to this chapter provides a formal statement of this and more details.

This index has values that range between zero and infinity. When a policy is purely redistributive and achieves no net gain, the value of the index goes to infinity. When a policy increases some groups' incomes without taking income away from any other group (that is, when it is Pareto efficient), the index takes a value of zero. The latter case corresponds to the economist's proverbial "manna from heaven": it would be politically very desirable if it could be made a reality.

The preceding discussion already provided a hint that trade reform performs poorly when judged by this index. To see how poorly, we relate expression (1) to parameters of relevance to trade reform, distinguishing, once again, among consumers, import-competing producers, and rentiers. Let m denote import volume, q import-competing production, c total consumption of the importable, p the domestic price of the importable, p^* the world price, and t the (ad valorem) tariff-equivalent of the trade restriction initially. To a first-order approximation,[5] the income effects of trade reform can be summarized as follows:

Consumers $= -c\Delta p$

Producers $= q\Delta p$

Rentiers $= m\Delta p + tp^*\Delta m$

Net gain $= tp^*\Delta m$.

(Note the identity $m = c - q$.) Therefore, the index can be written as follows:

$$PCBR = \frac{-c\Delta p}{tp^*\Delta m} = \frac{1}{\mu\varepsilon t} \tag{2}$$

where μ is the share of imports (at border prices) in domestic consumption and ε is the absolute value of the import demand elasticity. The expression on the right-hand side relates the PCBR index to recognizable parameters. The index is increasing in t, μ, and ε.

Table 10.2 shows the range of values that the PCBR index can take under plausible combinations of these parameters. The import demand elasticity is fixed at 2 (which is relatively generous), and the other two parameters vary. In most reasonable circumstances, the PCBR lies above 5. In words, an index of 5 indicates that for each dollar of net income generated, five dollars of income are being reshuffled among different groups in the economy. This puts the analysis much closer to the pure redistribution case than to the Pareto-efficient case. Put bluntly, trade reform is politically inefficient.[6]

Table 10.2
Plausible Values of the PCBR Index under Trade Reform

	(t)		
μ	0.20	0.50	0.70
0.10	25.00	10.00	7.15
0.20	12.50	5.00	3.58
0.40	6.25	2.50	1.79

Note: $\varepsilon = 2$.

In fact, things are typically worse. By its very nature, trade liberalization creates a lot of winners whose identities cannot be discerned beforehand. That is because not all of the general-equilibrium ramifications of reform can be sorted out with perfect foresight. After reform, some entrepreneurs in import-substituting sectors will transform themselves into successful exporters; some new, unanticipated export opportunities will be created. Only after reform takes root does the full configuration of gainers and losers become evident. This kind of uncertainty leads to a systematic bias against policy reform: reforms that would receive adequate political support after the fact may fail to receive support before-hand when some of the gainers (or losers) from reform cannot yet be identified (Fernandez and Rodrik 1991). Hence, the uncertainty surrounding the distributional effects compounds the immediate difficulties raised by the distributional consequences themselves.

These arguments raise the question of why, if trade reform is politically so costly, it is ever undertaken. The maintained assumption behind the PCBR index is that altering the distribution of income is politically costly. This need not always apply. In particular, policymakers may want to reshape distribution—or be indifferent to it—following a transformation in political regime or a change in the underlying configuration of power. Indeed, historically sharp changes in trade policy have almost always been preceded (or accompanied) by changes in the political regime. This was true of the first significant move to free trade in modern history—the repeal of the Corn Laws in England in 1846—a move that reflected the growing political power of urban interests over landed interests. It was also true of the most significant case of reform in the developing world until the 1980s: the reforms that took place after Pinochet's coup in Chile in 1973. More evidence on this will be discussed later in this chapter. Not all political transformations result in trade reform, but sharp changes in trade policy are typically the result of such transformations.

What about the gradual, steady liberalization in the industrial world under the aegis of the General Agreement on Tariffs and Trade (GATT) during the postwar period? It is harder to credit changes in political regime for this process. The political acceptability of these reforms derived instead from the joint influence of two factors: (a) the gradualist nature of the reforms and (b) a favorable external environment in the form of unprecedented economic growth. The latter served to mask the distributive consequences of liberalization and allowed everyone to share in the benefits of recovery and, later on, increased prosperity. The gradual nature of the liberalization, meanwhile, ensured that these distributive effects would remain second order relative to the consequences of overall economic growth. The lesson is a simple, but valuable, one: the congruence of gradualism with increasing, all-around prosperity provides the most comfortable environment for trade reform.[7]

A Closer Look at the Distributive Consequences of Trade Reform

Since trade reform and distribution are so closely related, it is helpful to have a framework for analysis in which the links are laid out. As the reforms in question occur across the board, the framework should accommodate economy-wide (that is, general-equilibrium) repercussions. This section provides a sketch of such a framework.

Three sets of commodities and services must be distinguished: (a) importables, (b) exportables, and (c) nontradables. Each of these groups is associated with an "average" domestic price, denoted by p_m, p_x, and p_n, respectively. This classification is meant to be exhaustive; that is, all commodities and services produced in the economy should fit in one of these categories.[8] Table 10.3 shows the typical commodities classified under these headings; intermediate goods (such as chemicals) and capital goods, for example, are typically importables.

The table also shows how the domestic price of each aggregate relates to its world price. The domestic price (in pesos) of importables equals their world price (in dollars) multiplied by the exchange rate (defined as pesos per dollar) times 1 plus t_m, the tariff equivalent of all import restrictions. Not only duties and other taxes but also the ad valorem price equivalent of quota restrictions and other nontariff measures are included under t_m. In fact, t_m itself is usually not directly observable when trade restrictions, as so often, are primarily of a nontariff nature. It can be recovered, however, by comparing the price of domestic products with the price of close substitutes on world markets. The domestic price of exportables (for example,

Table 10.3
Matrix for Trade Policy Analysis

Commodity group	Domestic price	Relation to world price	Typical goods or services	Income group most directly affected
Importable	p_m	$ep_m^*(1 + t_m)$	Intermediate goods, capital goods, consumer durables	Import-substitution industrialists, holders of import licenses, organized labor
Exportable	p_x	$ep_x^*/(1 + t_x)$	Cash crops, light manufactures	Agricultural producers, export-oriented entre-preneurs
Nontradable	p_n	n.a.	Construction, labor services	Informal sector, unorganized labor

n.a. Not applicable.
Note: e, exchange rate (home currency per foreign currency); t_m, tariff equivalent of all import restrictions (including license premiums); t_n, tax equivalent of all export restrictions; prices with asterisks denote world prices (in foreign currency).

coffee or clothing) is related to the world price in a similar manner, where the export tax, t_x, captures the ad valorem price equivalent of all export restrictions. Note that an import tariff increases the domestic price of importables—the price paid by consumers and received by producers—while an export tax reduces the domestic price of the exportables.

Finally, note that prices of nontradables do not bear any systematic relationship (at least in the context of trade policy) to prices of similar goods on world markets. Since haircuts and cement are normally non-tradable (the first because of restrictions on labor mobility, the second because of transport costs), no arbitrage relationship exists that would pin down domestic prices in relation to foreign prices.[9] Hence, p_n is deter-mined exclusively by domestic demand and supply. The most important category of nontradables is labor services. The wage rate is consequently the most important nontradable price. When import-competing goods are protected by quantitative restrictions, they too become nontradables at the margin.

Table 10.3 also shows the identities of the income groups whose fortunes are most closely tied to each of these prices. Hence, the incomes of import-substituting industrialists, of import-license holders, and often of organized labor are determined in the first instance by p_m, the import-able price. The price of exportables, p_x, serves the same purpose for agri-cultural producers and export-oriented entrepreneurs. The nontradable price, p_n, determines income in the informal sector and unorganized labor.

Now, the well-being of each of these groups is determined not only by the price they receive for their production; other prices matter too, since these affect the costs of inputs and consumption. Real incomes are determined, therefore, by relative prices and not the absolute level of any single price. To draw the links between trade policy and distribution, it is important to know how specific relative are affected by trade policy.

But which relative prices? Since three prices exist in the economy, there are only two relative prices that are of independent interest, but there are many different ways of expressing them. For reasons that will be clear shortly, it is convenient to focus on (a) the relative price of importables to exportables and (b) the relative price of tradables to nontradables. These two relative prices are key to the resource allocation effects of trade policy, and any political-economy analysis must begin with them.

Using the definitions in table 10.3, the first of these can be expressed as follows:

$$\frac{p_m}{p_x} = \left(\frac{p_m^*}{p_x^*}\right)(1 + t_m)(1 + t_x).\tag{3}$$

The second relative price is obtained by lumping importables and exportables into a basket called tradables. Formally, the price of tradables, p_t, is a weighted average of p_m and p_x:

$$p_t = [ep_m^*(1 + t_m)]^\alpha \left[\frac{ep_x^*}{(1 + t_x)}\right]^{1-\alpha}$$

$$= e[p_m^*(1 + t_m)]^\alpha \left[\frac{p_x^*}{(1 + t_x)}\right]^{1-\alpha}\tag{4}$$

where α is the weight on importables. The second relative price is then given by the ratio of the price of tradables to nontradables:

$$\frac{p_t}{p_n} = \left\{\frac{e[p_m^*(1 + t_m)]^\alpha \left[\frac{p_x^*}{(1 + t_x)}\right]^{1-\alpha}}{p_n}\right\}\tag{5}$$

This ratio is also called the real exchange rate.

From an economic standpoint, the distinction between these two is useful because each has a distinct effect on resource allocation. On the one hand, changes in p_m/p_x are associated inversely with changes in an economy's openness: the higher this relative price is, the smaller the share of imports *and* exports is in national income (all else remaining equal) and the higher the level of import-substituting production. On the other hand, changes in p_t/p_n are typically associated with changes in the trade (or current account) balance: the higher this relative price is, the more positive the trade balance (again, all else remaining equal) is. These resource-allocation effects also define the criteria by which the success of commercial policy and of exchange rate policy should be measured: successful trade liberalization will increase the ratio of imports to gross national product (GNP) and of exports to GNP on a sustained basis; successful devaluation will reduce the trade deficit (or increase the surplus) without affecting domestic levels of inflation and unemployment. Finally, the two relative prices have distinct distributional consequences. The first relative price captures distributional conflict within tradables' sectors, whereas the second focuses on distribution across the tradables-nontradables cleavage.

Armed with these two relative prices, it is now possible to analyze the consequences of trade policy for the real incomes of different groups in society. For each policy in question, the analysis examines how these relative prices are affected and reads the implications for different groups with the help of the classification in table 10.3.

Commercial Policy

The term "commercial policy" captures the set of policies that have direct implications for the domestic prices of importables and exportables and thus affect the relative price p_m/p_x. As shown in equation (3), these are import and export taxes of various sorts, including quantitative restrictions, licensing, advance deposits on imports, prohibitions, and (often) commodity marketing boards. Note that the relative price of importables and exportables does not depend on the exchange rate, as e enters both the numerator and the denominator and cancels out; that is, exchange rate policy is distributionally neutral between import-competing and export-oriented interests. There are two notable exceptions, however. First, when some import-competing sectors are protected by quotas, rendering them nontradable at the margin, a real depreciation of the currency will hurt these sectors and benefit exporters (as well as remaining import-competing activities). Second, a devaluation under foreign currency rationing will act just like import liberalization. The latter case is discussed below.

Note the symmetry in the way that import and export taxes enter equation (3): import tariffs and export taxes have identical effects.[10] A 10 percent export tax has the same effect on p_m/p_x—and hence on the openness of the economy and on distribution within tradables—as a 10 percent import tariff and vice versa.[11] This demonstrates that import protection imposes a penalty on exporters that is identical to a direct export tax. Conversely, an export tax benefits import-competing interests. The logic works for subsidies also, as long as one keeps in mind that a subsidy is a negative tax. Hence, an export subsidy takes away some import protection and hurts import-competing interests as much as a direct reduction in protection.

Finally, commercial policy per se has no direct distributive consequence for groups that derive their income from nontradables, such as unorganized labor (or the informal sector). Equation (5) shows that a reduction in the import tariff would tend to increase the real incomes of labor (as p_t/p_n is reduced) but only as long as the nominal exchange rate (e) remains unchanged. If the import liberalization is packaged with a devaluation (see below), the effect on labor is ambiguous.

The situation may be quite different for organized labor in import-competing industries, where high profits may be shared with labor unions and be reflected in wage premia relative to the rest of the economy. The relaxation of import controls will bite into these labor "rents" and hurt these groups directly.

Exchange Rate Policy

Exchange rate policy affects a different relative price, that between all tradables and nontradables. This can be seen in expression (5) in which e enters the numerator. This is an important distinction between commercial policy and exchange rate policy and is often missed in general discussions of trade policy. At the risk of being repetitive, the distinction is summarized in table 10.4. A devaluation increases the domestic price of tradables and, all else remaining equal, raises p_t/p_m. Unlike commercial liberalization, a devaluation is likely to squeeze unorganized labor and

Table 10.4
Commercial Policy and Exchange Rate Policy

Policy	Relative price affected	Resource-allocation effect	Distributive effect
Commercial	p_m/p_n	Openness	Import-competing versus export-oriented interests
Exchange rate	p_t/p_n	Trade balance	All tradables versus nontradables; real wages

reduce real wages in terms of tradables (provided wages are determined predominantly by conditions in the nontradable sector). The reduction in real wages is the flip side of the increase in competitiveness brought about by devaluation. Also, a devaluation affects all tradable sectors symmetrically: both import-competing and export-oriented interests benefit from it, while commercial liberalization pits these two sectors against each other.

With respect to real wages, one point bears stressing. It is useful to distinguish between two concepts of the real wage: the product real wage and the consumption real wage. The product real wage is the nominal wage divided by the price of tradables, and it determines the competitiveness of domestic tradables. The consumption real wage is the nominal wage divided by an aggregate price index that includes the price of nontradables; it measures the purchasing power of wages and is the more appropriate index of workers' well-being. If nontradables are sufficiently important in workers' consumption basket and wages rise sufficiently more than the price of nontradables, consumption real wages could increase as a consequence of devaluation, while the product real wage falls.

Moreover, unlike commercial policy, which can be made effective by fiat, the economic success of exchange rate policy depends on the response of p_n (or wages). Equation (5) shows that the value of the real exchange rate p_t/p_n depends both on e and on p_n. For an increase in the nominal exchange rate to bring about an increase in the real exchange rate (that is, to achieve a real depreciation), p_n must not rise proportionately. As mentioned, p_n is determined by domestic supply and demand conditions. Making exchange rate policy effective, therefore, requires restrictive demand management policies that do not allow p_n (or wages) to rise along with e. This is the source of the oft-repeated admonishment to developing countries that exchange rate devaluation (expenditure switching) should be coupled with restrictive monetary and fiscal policies (expenditure reduction) to have an effect on the external balance. Economic effectiveness calls for income redistribution.

Devaluation When Foreign Exchange Is Rationed

A sharp distinction has been drawn here between the impacts of commercial and exchange rate policy on distribution and the allocation of resources. In some circumstances, however, the distinction disappears, and a devaluation becomes identical to commercial liberalization. This occurs when foreign exchange is rationed by the government and a black market exists for foreign exchange.

Pesos per dollar

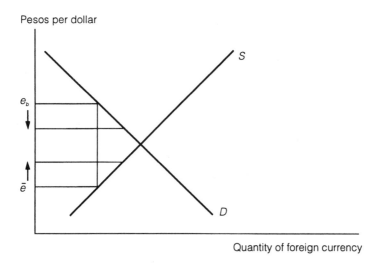

Quantity of foreign currency

Figure 10.2
Foreign currency rationing and multiple exchange rates

In the presence of a black market, there are at least two exchange rates: an official exchange rate, call it $\bar{e}$, at which only a limited number of transactions are carried out due to rationing by the central bank, and the black market rate, e_b, which represents the marginal cost of foreign exchange and to which importers must resort in order to satisfy their needs in excess of the official allocation (naturally, $e_b > \bar{e}$). This is shown in figure 10.2. Exporters must turn in their foreign exchange receipts at the lower price $\bar{e}$. Hence, domestic prices of importables and exportables are now given by $p_m = e_b p_m^*(1 + t_m)$ and $p_x = \bar{e} p_x^*/(1 + t_x)$. The relative price of importables to exportables becomes

$$\frac{p_m}{p_x} = \left(\frac{e_b}{\bar{e}}\right)\left(\frac{p_m^*}{p_x^*}\right)(1 + t_m)(1 + t_x) \tag{3'}$$

where the exchange rates have not canceled out (compare equation (3)). The gap between $\bar{e}$ and e_b represents rents that accrue to groups with access to dollars at the official rate (since these dollars are worth the black market price). Therefore, the rationing of foreign currency creates a situation that is entirely analogous to the imposition of a trade restriction. This can be seen from equation (3'): an increase in the exchange rate premium (that is, a larger gap between e_b and $\bar{e}$) works just like an increase in t_m or t_x.

Now consider a devaluation of the official rate (an increase in $\bar{e}$), which prompts an increase in the supply of foreign exchange as exporters respond by increasing their activity. As shown in figure 10.2, that leads, in turn, to a decrease in the black market exchange rate. The net effect is a fall in $e_b/\bar{e}$, which amounts to a fall in the price of importables relative to the price of exportables (see equation (3')). Now the devaluation works just like commercial liberalization and will have all the same consequences for resource allocation and distribution. In particular, the rents accruing to groups with access to official dollars will diminish. This is the case of a trade-liberalizing devaluation. By increasing the availability of foreign exchange, previously rationed, the devaluation allows more exports and more imports. Import-competing groups that would normally benefit from a devaluation are now hurt.

Compensated and Uncompensated Trade Liberalization

Consider a reduction in import barriers. In the medium to long run, there is no reason why the liberalization should have an adverse effect on the trade balance; even in the absence of adjustments in the exchange rate, endogenous changes in the price of nontradables will generally be enough to return the economy to external balance. In the shorter run, the situation may be a bit more complicated if p_n is not sufficiently flexible or, what amounts to the same thing in most contexts, if the operation of labor markets is plagued by rigidities. To make the point as starkly as possible, let us assume that p_n is fixed and does not adjust once import barriers are lifted.

Equation (5) on close inspection, shows that a reduction in t_m reduces the numerator of p_t/p_n and hence appreciates the real exchange rate. This makes domestic production less competitive and can be expected to deteriorate the external balance. Intuitively, cheaper imports replace domestic output. An endogenous reduction in p_n would insulate the external balance from the effect of the liberalization. In its absence, the government can achieve the same insulation by undertaking a devaluation. An increase in e raises the numerator in p_t/p_n and prevents the appreciation of the real exchange rate and the loss of competitiveness. With a compensating devaluation of this sort, the effects of liberalization are limited to those discussed above under commercial policy. The devaluation gives an added boost to exporters and alleviates some of the squeeze on import-competing groups.

The alternative is to do nothing with the exchange rate. This option was selected during the 1980s by many governments fighting triple-digit (and higher) inflation (such as Bolivia and Israel in 1985 and Mexico in

1988). The reason is that, in a high-inflation environment, stability in the nominal exchange rate may be needed as an anchor for the domestic price level. A devaluation may be perceived as too risky, lest it unleash inflationary expectations.

Clearly, the exchange rate cannot be targeted on the domestic price level and the external balance simultaneously. When it is targeted on the domestic price level, a compensating devaluation is ruled out. Consequently, the liberalization imposes a magnified squeeze on import-competing interests to the benefit of nontradable sectors. The ensuing deterioration in the current account balance can continue as long as there are capital inflows willing to sustain it. Living beyond one's means in this fashion can even create a sense of euphoria, but politically this can be dangerous. Powerful import-substituting interests are more likely to oppose vigorously an uncompensated liberalization than a compensated one. In Chile, for example, the early states of liberalization during 1975–78 took place in the context of a depreciating real exchange rate. Industrialists complained in earnest only after 1979, when the real exchange rate started to appreciate. Similarly, in Mexico liberalization during 1985–87 did not have detrimental effects on industry thanks to a depreciating exchange rate; starting in 1988, when the peso was stabilized and the trade reform speeded up, liberalization began to bite considerably more.

Distributive Consequences for the State

The discussion so far has left out a very important claimant on national income, the state (or the bureaucracy). The willingness of policymakers to undertake trade reform is often shaped as much by the perceived impact on the fiscal resources of the state or on the wealth of well-placed bureaucrats as by the pressure from below. The analysis of distribution closes by discussing briefly the main channels through which trade policy transfers resources to and from the state.

First and most directly, import and export taxes are a source of revenue for the public treasury. Trade taxes (including the profits of marketing boards) play a particularly important role in the poorest countries, where such revenues can make up between one-quarter and half of central government income. Under most circumstances, trade liberalization may be expected to reduce these revenues. But there are a couple of important exceptions to this rule. First, the initial stages of trade liberalization usually eliminate quantitative restrictions, often replacing them by tariffs. Such an imposition of tariffs should channel resources that previously ended up as quota rents toward public coffers. Second, when trade restrictions get too high and overvaluation of the exchange rate becomes extreme, trade taxes are typically dissipated in smuggling and other illicit activities. Correcting such problems can sharply increase government revenue despite the overall liberalization. A significant example of this took place in Ghana after 1983.

Exchange rate policy also has important implications for government finance, but the effects tend to be more subtle. Since exchange rate policy aims at changing the price of tradables relative to nontradables, the income effect on the public sector can be found by answering the following question: are nontraded goods and services a net source of income for the government or not? When they are, as when payroll taxes constitute an important component of government revenue and much of public spending goes to purchase tradables (military hardware, for example), a devaluation will leave the state sector poorer. When they are not, as is the case in oil-producing economies, the public sector benefits from a devaluation. Turkey and Venezuela are good examples of these cases, respectively. Sometimes the question is put differently: is the government a net seller or buyer of dollars in relation to the private sector? Useful as a first approximation, this question betrays a partial-equilibrium logic where a general-equilibrium one is needed.

As discussed above, much of trade policy is concerned with the creation and elimination of rents (Krueger 1974). These rents are often captured by individual bureaucrats. A government official who is entrusted with the disposition of scarce import licenses or foreign currency is endowed with a very valuable resource. Whether he cashes in on this resource by accepting bribes or simply basks in the self-importance created by his job, asking him to give up this resource willingly may be asking too much. This explains why restrictive trade regimes and foreign exchange crises often create within the government a powerful lobby in favor of their continuation and why successful implementation of reforms may require the replacement of middle echelons within the economic bureaucracy. Indonesia, which substituted a Swiss inspection firm for its customs bureaucracy, is a good case in point.

Why Has There Been So Much Trade Liberalization Lately?

It is time to address the second puzzle stated at the outset of this chapter: if trade reform is politically so difficult to undertake, why are so many countries doing it now? The mystery is heightened because the current wave of trade reform is taking place in an environment not conducive to its success: high inflation blunts the impact of relative-price changes achieved by trade reform, and recession makes the required reallocation of resources more costly.

Focusing on the distributional consequences of trade policy provides one potential key to the puzzle. Perhaps the powerful interests that benefited from protection and had successfully blocked reform were weakened by the debt crisis of the 1980s, which would explain the general move toward liberal policies. But the argument would require a demonstration that import-competing interests, the ones most severely hurt by reform, were weakened disproportionately. Such an argument would be difficult to construct. Of course, the debt crisis highlighted the urgency of earning foreign exchange and thus may have increased the political strength of exporters. By the same token, the need to conserve foreign exchange must have played into the hands of import-substituting groups. The crisis of 1982 and the ensuing macroeconomic mess were costly all around. It is not at all evident that import-competing groups bore the brunt of the effects or that they systematically lost out on the political front.

On the international scene, there were two clear winners: the World Bank and the International Monetary Fund (IMF). The crisis forced developing countries to line up at the gates of these Bretton Woods institutions, pleading for the imprimatur that would unlock debt rescheduling arrangements and new capital flows. The renewed importance of these institutions gave unprecedented salience to their orthodox arguments on economic management, that is, the need for trade liberalization, realistic exchange rates, and conservative monetary and fiscal policies. The bargaining was especially one-sided in Africa, where governments were poorly endowed with the technical expertise to evaluate and reshape standard prescriptions and lacked powerful patrons among rich countries, which would help moderate World Bank and IMF demands (for a recent study of the World Bank's relations with governments, see Mosley, Harrigan, and Toye 1991).

That the World Bank and the IMF became uncommonly powerful in their dealings with the governments of developing countries during the 1980s is indisputable. Yet it would be a mistake to picture the process of policy reform as one in which orthodox economic policies were externally imposed on unwilling policymakers. In some African cases, this characterization may have come close to being true—witness, for example, the cycle of reform and reversal in Zambia. But more often than not, reform has had a significant homegrown component, exceeding on occasion the

World Bank's or the IMF's expectations and stipulations. The Mexican liberalization since 1987, for example, has been more ambitious and has proceeded faster than some World Bank officials thought was prudent at the time. The recent Argentine, Brazilian, and Indian conversions cannot be credited to the Bretton Woods institutions either; these large countries have a long history of avoiding and evading World Bank conditionality on liberalization. External actors have played at best a modest role in initiating recent reforms.

The bulk of the credit must go instead to the dire economic circumstances in which most developing countries found themselves as a consequence of the prolonged macroeconomic crisis of the 1980s. The experience of high inflation and negative growth year after year eventually prepared the ground for embracing an entirely new set of policies. The continued deterioration in economic conditions shaped a general consensus that something had to be done. Put differently, the perceived overall gain from restoring the economy's health became, after a point, so large that it swamped distributional considerations.[12]

This point can be demonstrated using the PCBR index developed previously, which shows that the political cost-benefit ratio of trade reform declines dramatically when it is introduced in the context of stabilization policy. Consider a trade reform that is part of an overall economic stabilization package. The stabilization aims to reduce inflation and revive the economy by eliminating the foreign exchange stranglehold. The question of why trade reform is included in the package alongside the standard fiscal and monetary measures will be addressed later; suffice it to say that in practice trade reform arrived as part of an overall macroeconomic package of this sort. Now, stabilization differs from trade liberalization in one key respect: unlike trade liberalization, it holds the promise of generating benefits that will be shared by all. Few coherent interest groups can be identified as net gainers from triple-digit inflation and economic collapse, and hence most interest groups stand to benefit from an end to both.[13] Moreover, the deeper the crisis, the larger the overall net benefits from recovery.

The PCBR index for this reform can be calculated by tracking the effects of both the liberalization and the stabilization. The across-the-board benefit of stabilization is denoted by γ, the percentage increase in net income that accrues to all groups in the economy as a result of stabilization. γ is a proxy for the depth of the crisis (as well as for the likely success of the stabilization). Further, let θ denote the share of consumption of importables in GNP and ω the percent reduction in the price of

Table 10.5
The PCBR Index with Stabilization-cum-Trade Reform

γ	PCBR
0.00	5.00
0.10	0.69
0.25	0.30
0.50	0.16
1.00	0.08

Note: $t = 0.5$; $\mu = 0.2$; $\varepsilon = 0.2$; $\theta = 0.4$; $\omega = 0.2$.

importables relative to exportables as a consequence of the reform. The PCBR index for the stabilization-cum-liberalization package can now be expressed as:

$$PCBR = \frac{1}{\mu \varepsilon t + (\gamma/\omega\theta)}. \tag{6}$$

It is now a matter of simple algebra to demonstrate that when the all-around benefit of stabilization (γ) is large, it swamps the redistributive aspect of the trade reform. Table 10.5 shows how the PCBR index falls sharply with γ. When $\gamma = 0$, the PCBR index takes its usual high value—5.0 under the present parameter combinations. In the presence of a stabilization program that promises to make all groups better off by 10 percent ($\gamma = 0.1$), the index plummets to 0.69. With $\gamma = 0.25$, the index declines further to 0.30. Since relatively small increases in the growth rate of an economy can cause large jumps in the level of the present discounted value of income, an expectation that a successful stabilization will increase well-being 10 to 25 percent is not far off the mark.[14] Hence trade reform can suddenly start to look politically attractive if (a) it is perceived as an integral part of a stabilization package, and (b) the macroeconomy stands engulfed in a deep crisis.

The argument that economic crisis can promote reform is consistent with the evidence (scanty as it is) from earlier decades also. A recent World Bank research project analyzes liberalization episodes in nineteen developing countries during the period after World War II and before the debt crisis (Papageorgiou, Choksi, and Michaely 1990). Table 10.6, taken from this research, lists thirteen cases classified as episodes of "strong" and "fast" trade reform. The vast majority of these reforms—ten out of thirteen—took place in the context of either a change in political regime or a generalized perception of complete economic collapse, or both. The close association between economic collapse and reform was even more

Table 10.6
The Correlates of Trade Reform for Countries with Strong and Fast Reform Episodes

Country and year	Change in political regime	Perception of complete economic collapse
Argentina, 1976	×	×
Chile, 1956		×
1974	×	×
Greece, 1953		
Indonesia, 1966	×	×
Israel, 1952		×
Peru, 1979		×
Philippines, 1960	×	
Singapore, 1968	×	
Spain, 1977	×	
Sri Lanka, 1977	×	
Turkey, 1980		×
Yugoslavia, 1965		

Source: Papageorgiou, Choksi, and Michaely 1990.

evident in the 1980s, when each occurred again and again: no significant case of trade reform in a developing country in the 1980s took place outside the context of a serious economic crisis.

Two questions remain to be answered. First, why did the changes in trade policy take the form of liberalization rather than of closing up? After all, the logic of the argument is symmetric with respect to trade policy reforms in either direction. Second, why were trade reforms packaged with stabilization, if the relationship between trade policy and the debt crisis is incidental? (For an argument that the relationship is indeed incidental, see Rodrik 1992b). That is, why did policymakers perceive a need for commercial policy reforms on top of monetary, fiscal, and exchange rate reforms?

The answer to the first question is that the countries concerned for the most part initially did choose to protect rather than to liberalize. This reaction constituted the traditional response to foreign exchange crises: when dollars become scarce, policymakers in developing countries impose rationing and tighten quantitative restrictions. This is what happened in the early stages of the debt crisis. Turkey, which entered its debt crisis early in 1977, mucked around with halfway measures for two-and-a-half years until it decided to liberalize in 1980. Mexico started to liberalize in earnest in late 1987 (but some of the measures were announced in 1985–

still three years after the debt crisis hit). Peru was an extreme case of turning inward under García and until the Fujimori government took over. Argentina and Brazil took the better part of the decade before they decided to liberalize. Hence, liberalization was selected only after the alternative had been tried repeatedly and discredited. The crisis called for something new; import controls were not it.

The second issue—the packaging of stabilization with liberalization— is more mystifying. One factor was that the crisis had discredited the entire pattern of previous economic policymaking, including the commercial policy regime. To have credibility, policymakers had to make a clean break with the past, and this included doing away with the import-substitution regime. It may be too much to assume that the policymakers themselves were fully aware of the distinctions and of the full set of causal relations among the trade regime, the macroeconomic stance, and the economic crisis. Also, the World Bank must be given credit for having invented and successfully marketed the concept of "structural adjustment," a concept that packaged together microeconomic and macroeconomic reforms. Structural adjustment was sold as the process the countries needed to undergo in order to save their economies from the crisis. For governments that bought into the package, the distinction between sound macroeconomic policies that maintain external balance and stable prices, on the one hand, and policies that determine openness, on the other, was obfuscated.

Sustaining the Reforms

The argument made in the previous section is perhaps not very encouraging for the sustainability of trade liberalization into the 1990s. If the argument is correct, the reforms were enabled not by the dissolution of powerful import-competing coalitions, but by a deep economic crisis— necessarily of a temporary nature—that relegated distributional issues to second place behind the need to stabilize the macroeconomy. Once the crisis is over and politics as usual returns, will these coalitions not reassert themselves and demand a return to import protection? Possibly so. But there are reasons to think that it will not be easy for policymakers to turn their backs on the reforms.

The experience of Chile provides an instructive example. During the 1970s, a radical trade reform was imposed on Chilean business by a repressive dictatorial regime impervious to interest-group pressure. By the early 1980s, import-substitution policies had been replaced by a simple uniform tariff of 10 percent (motor vehicles being the sole exception). With the return of democracy at the end of the decade, a reasonable guess might have been that protectionist business interests would rise to the occasion and push for a return to some of the old policies under which they had prospered. Yet nothing of the sort happened. In fact, during the presidential election campaign in the fall of 1989, the trade regime never became an issue. All major groups, it would seem, were ready to live with free trade.

One reason that the open trade regime has not been challenged in Chile is the comparative success of its economy. While many of its neighbors were reeling under triple-digit inflation and negative growth, Chile managed to keep its inflation rate at or below 20 percent and grew at highly respectable rates. Why mess with success?

One lesson from the Chilean experience, then, is that when policies are demonstrated to work, they will gain legitimacy. When the economy starts to recover and inflation is firmly under control, some of the success— rightly or wrongly—will be attributed to the open trade policies. Indeed, probably the most important determinant of the sustainability of the liberalization will be the success of macroeconomic stabilization. In countries where inflation and external imbalances are brought under control, the reform package, including its commercial component, will have legitimacy and will be resistant to political attack, Bolivia provides an additional example: the memory of the successful 1985 stabilization after hyperinflation has created a political consensus on the desirability of liberal trade policies. Where stabilization fails, on the other hand, trade reform too will be prone to reversal.

A second lesson from the example of countries like Chile and Bolivia is that all policies create constituencies for their continuation. Outward-oriented policies generate new profit opportunities for entrepreneurs, some of whom may have been engaged only in import-substituting activities prior to reform. As new, previously unpredictable export activities appear, a new class of export-oriented businessmen is created. These entrepreneurs now have a stake in the new policy regime and will fight any attempt to reverse it. The distributional complications discussed in the first half of the chapter now operate in reverse: going back to protection will be difficult precisely because so much (re)redistribution will be involved.

Such status quo bias will help enlightened policymakers stick with open trade policies. But the policymakers themselves have also taken measures to avoid reversal. Governments in many countries have been imaginative in devising strategies for institutionalizing the reforms. Mexico, for example, first bound its tariff rates under the GATT and then began negotiations with the United States to enter a free trade agreement. By making reversal extremely costly, these actions have helped solidify the reforms. The appropriate strategies naturally depend on the context, but some helpful ones include adopting a uniform tariff to make individual tariff rates less susceptible to special-interest pleading from business; reorganizing the economic bureaucracy to reduce the power of officials who benefited directly from the previous licensing and rationing system;[15] and quickly establishing a credible export subsidy program to ensure that there is an interest group with a stake in outward orientation. These and other strategies are discussed at greater length elsewhere (see Panagariya and Rodrik 1991; Rodrik 1989a, 1989b, 1992a).

Creative policymakers will no doubt come up with more of these strategies. But institutional innovation notwithstanding, a point already made bears repeating: nothing will help sustain open trade policies more than a stable macroeconomic environment. The success of recent reforms, therefore, will ultimately depend less on their own direct effects than on the success of macroeconomic policy.

Appendix: The Political Cost-Benefit Ratio

A conventional utilitarian social welfare function is defined as follows:

$$V(\sigma_1, \ldots, \sigma_k; t) \equiv \sum_i U_i(\sigma_1, \ldots, \sigma_k; t)$$

where σi stands for various subsidies (and taxes) available to the policymaker for undertaking compensation, t is the generic trade policy instrument, and $U_i(\cdot)$ stands for group (or individual) i's utility function. Note that utility functions are reduced forms defined directly over the policy instruments. Since σ_i will generally be distortionary, $U_i(\cdot)$ and $V(\cdot)$ have the standard interpretation as in the literature on public finance.

The policymaker selects the tax or subsidy scheme to ensure that no group is made worse off subsequent to a trade reform than in the status quo. Denoting the status quo level of utility of group i by $\bar{U}_i$, this problem can be written as follows:

$$\text{Max}_{\{\sigma_i\}} V(\sigma_1, \ldots, \sigma_k; t) \; s.t. \; U_i(\sigma_1, \ldots, \sigma_k; t) \geq \bar{U}_1$$

$$U_n(\sigma_1, \ldots, \sigma_k; t) \geq \bar{U}_n. \tag{A.1}$$

The associated Lagrangean expression is given by:

$$\mathscr{L} = V(\sigma_1, \ldots, \sigma_k; t) + \sum_i \mu_i [U_i(\sigma_1, \ldots, \sigma_k; t) - \bar{U}i]$$

where μ_i are the Lagrange multipliers ($\mu \geq 0$). $V(\cdot)$ is assumed to be sufficiently well-behaved so that the second-order conditions for this problem are satisfied. Let $\{\sigma_i^*(t)\}$ represent the solution to this problem. We can then derive the maximum-value function $V^*(t)$:

$$V^*(t) = V[\sigma_1^*(t), \ldots, \sigma_k^*(t); t].$$

To the policymaker who must compensate the losers by using distortionary taxes and subsidies, the net benefit of trade reform is now given by $dV^*(t)/dt$. By the envelope theorem,

$$\frac{dV^*(t)}{dt} = \frac{\partial \mathscr{L}}{\partial t}$$

$$= \left[\frac{\partial V(\cdot)}{\partial t} \right] + \sum_i \mu_i \left[\frac{\partial U_i(\cdot)}{\partial t} \right].$$

Note that the constraints in equation 3A-1 will bind in the post-reform equilibrium only for groups that are made worse off; it will not bind for the winners. Hence, μ_i is equal to zero for beneficiary groups and greater than zero for losing groups. Consequently, $dV^*(t)/dt$ can be written as

$$\frac{dV^*(t)}{dt} = \left[\frac{\partial V(\cdot)}{\partial t} \right] + \sum_{\{losers\}} \mu_i \left[\frac{\partial U_i(\cdot)}{\partial t} \right]. \tag{A.2}$$

The first term here is simply the efficiency gain of the reform, and for a reduction in t, it will normally be positive. The second term represents the cost of compensating the losers: it is the weighted sum of utility losses suffered by groups adversely affected by the reform, with the weights being the Lagrange multipliers. Note that these multipliers summarize the (marginal) resource cost of compensation. For an efficiency-enhancing reform, the sign on the second term is always opposite to that on the first.

The PCBR discussed in the text can now be seen to represent a special case of the calculus expressed in equation (A.2), with gains and losses measured in income rather than utility. The denominator of the PCBR is the first term of equation (A2). The numerator, which equals the sum of losses, is the second term, with all μ_i that are positive set equal to unity.

Dixit and Norman (1986) have shown that under certain conditions (some curvature in the production-possibility frontier and the existence of a commodity for which all consumers are net buyers or sellers), a full set of commodity and factor taxes can ensure the Pareto-superiority of free trade over autarky (even in the absence of lump-sum taxes). In terms of the framework here, the Dixit-Norman result would imply that expression (A.2) is unambiguously negative and, therefore, that the PCBR is always less than unity. However, this need not be the case when the tax or subsidy scheme has administrative costs, when less than a full set of tax or subsidy instruments exists, or when there is a government revenue requirement.

Notes

The author is grateful to Stephan Haggard, Jim Leitzel, David Ellwood, Steven Webb, and seminar participants at Harvard University, Federal Reserve Bank of San Francisco, the World Bank, and University of California, Berkeley, for their comments. He also wishes to thank the Hoover Institution, where he was a National Fellow while writing this chapter.

1. Samuelson was challenged by a mathematician who disdained economics to come up with such a proposition; he confessed to being at a loss until he came up with the principle of comparative advantage. That it is true, Samuelson pointed out, need not be explained at great length to a mathematician. That it is nontrivial, he said, was evidenced by the long history of errors committed by individuals who had not understood it.

2. In rare cases, the government auctions import licenses to the highest bidders. In this instance, quota rents accrue to the government in the form of revenue from the auction.

3. Since steel is an intermediate product, these consumers are typically producers as well. The demand curve for steel reflects the derived demand for the commodity, taking into account all the links among industries up the processing chain, including consumers of final products that use steel (such as cars).

4. However, there is an alternative way of interpreting this evidence. Recent studies have shown that growth-damaging policies are more likely to be undertaken in countries where the distribution of income is skewed, at least where democratic regimes are concerned (see Alesina and Rodrik 1991, 1992; Persson and Tabellini 1991). Hence causality may well go in the other direction, such as from inegalitarian distribution to high levels of trade protection.

5. The approximation is based on calculus; that is, it ignores some interaction terms. It will be more accurate the smaller the trade reform.

6. To the extent that rent-seeking behavior dissipates some of the rents of trade protection, the efficiency gains of reform may be larger than those measured here. However, the rent-seeking literature generally exaggerates these gains. If individuals can waste resources competing for the rents generated by, say, quotas, they can also waste resources lobbying the government for the reimposition of quotas that have been taken away. Altering the incentives for rent-seeking behavior goes beyond simple changes in the level of trade protection.

7. Of course, the two may be related. Growth may be fostered by the ongoing liberalization, but given the lags and uncertainty involved, the relationship is unlikely to be exploitable for political purposes.

8. Some commodities can be simultaneously imported and exported, raising a difficulty as to whether they should be classified as importable or exportable. With sufficient disaggregation, this will rarely be a serious problem in the context of developing countries.

9. There are always exceptions: Venezuela exports cement to Florida as it is cheaper to transport cement via the ocean than to bring it overland by train or truck. In fact, in late 1991, cement producers in Florida were trying to bring antidumping action against Venezuelan exporters.

10. This result, known as the Lerner symmetry theorem, is surprisingly general. All that it requires is that the trade balance be insulated from the effect of the tariff or tax, as would occur when p_m is perfectly flexible or e is adjusted to maintain the trade balance unchanged. Often, however, and especially in the short run, macroeconomic equilibrium may fail to occur, and the symmetry may break down. The claims made in this paragraph lose their force when this is the case (see the discussion below on compensated and uncompensated trade liberalizations).

11. Sometimes this equivalence is stated in a different way: a 10 percent increase in tariffs is identical to a 10 percent increase in the export tax. As a moment's reflection will show, this does not follow from equation 10.3, unless t_m and t_x are initially zero.

12. Witness, for example, the following description of the Ghanaian experience: "Rent seekers who can control import licenses are usually a potent source of opposition to devaluation, but the crisis had become so bad in Ghana that the group benefiting from administrative allocation of foreign exchange was extremely limited. Indeed, by the early 1980s, the economy had deteriorated to such an extent that even senior government officials, who normally benefit from access to imported goods even in times of shortage, reported that they were going hungry and were concerned that they could not find food for their families" (Herbst 1991). For a formal model on the benefits of crisis for economic reform, which closely parallels the argument here, see also Drazen and Grilli (1990).

13. This does not mean that stabilization does not generate distributional conflict; Alesina and Drazen (1991) present a model based on such conflict. But in this model (and in reality), the conflict over stabilization is based not on who gains and who loses from stabilization, but on who gains more and who gains less. Therefore, the distributional conflict is on a lower order of magnitude than in the case of trade liberalization.

14. Let the stabilization increase the growth rate of the economy by only one percentage point, from 0 to 1 percent. Assume that individuals have a time discount rate of 8 percent. Then, this relatively small increase in the growth rate translates into a 14.3 percent increase in the level of individuals' wealth (present discounted value of income).

15. Onis (forthcoming) provides a good discussion of some of these institutional innovations in post-1983 Turkey: "The post-1983 governments aimed explicitly at weakening the role of the traditional bureaucratic elites ... Installing a managerial bureaucracy in the form of a select group of U.S. educated technocrats, recruited from outside the ranks of traditional bureaucracy, hence largely independent from both societal and intrabureaucratic pressures, has been perceived as a necessary condition for the consistent implementation of the economic program."

References

Alesina, Alberto, and Allan Drazen. 1991. "Why Are Stabilizations Delayed?" *American Economic Review* 81, pp. 1170–88.

Alesina, Alberto, and Dani Rodrik. 1991. "Distributive Politics and Economic Growth." NBER Working Paper 3668. Harvard University, National Bureau of Economic Research, Cambridge, Mass.

————. 1992. "Distribution, Political Conflict, and Economic Growth: A Simple Theory and Some Empirical Evidence." In Alex Cukierman and others, eds., *The Political Economy of Business Cycles and Growth.* Cambridge, Mass.: M.I.T. Press.

Bates, Robert H., ed. 1988. *Toward a Political Economy of Development: A Rational Choice Perspective.* Berkeley: University of California Press.

Bourguignon, François, and Christian Morrisson. 1989. *External Trade and Income Distribution.* Paris: Development Center of the Organization of Economic Cooperation and Development.

Dixit, Avinash, and Victor Norman. 1986. "Gains from Trade without Lump-Sum Compensation." *Journal of International Economics* 21, pp. 111–22.

Drazen, Allan, and Vittorio Grilli. 1990. "The Benefits of Crises for Economic Reforms." NBER Working Paper 3527. National Bureau of Economic Research, Cambridge, Mass.

Fernández, Raquel, and Dani Rodrik. 1991. "Resistance to Reform: Status Quo Bias in the Presence of Individual-Specific Uncertainty." *American Economic Review* 81 (December), pp. 1146–55.

Haggard, Stephan, and Steven Webb. 1993. "What Do We Know about the Political Economy of Economic Policy Reform?" *World Bank Research Observer* 8:2 (July), pp. 143–68.

Herbst, Jeffrey. 1991. "Exchange Rate Reform in Ghana: Strategy and Tactics." Robert S. McNamara Program Tenth Anniversary Publication. Economic Development Institute, World Bank, Washington, D.C.

Krueger, Anne. 1974. "The Political-Economy of the Rent-Seeking Society." *American Economic Review* 64:3, pp. 291–303.

Meier, Gerald M., ed. 1991. *Politics and Policy Making in Developing Countries.* San Francisco: ICS Press.

Mosley, Paul, Jane Harrigan, and John Toye, eds. 1991. *Aid and Power: The World Bank and Policy-Based Lending,* 2 vols. London: Routledge.

Onis, Ziya. Forthcoming. "Redemocratization and Economic Liberalization in Turkey: The Limits of State Autonomy." *Studies in Comparative International Development.*

Panagariya, Arvind, and Dani Rodrik. 1991. "Political Economy Arguments for a Uniform Tariff." NBER Working Paper 3661. National Bureau of Economic Research, Cambridge, Mass.

Papageorgiou, Demetris, Armeane Choksi, and Michael Michaely. 1990. *Liberalizing Foreign Trade: Lessons of Experience in the Developing World.* Cambridge, Mass.: Basil Blackwell.

Persson, Torsten, and Guido Tabellini. 1991. "Is Inequality Harmful to Growth?" NBER Working Paper. National Bureau of Economic Research Cambridge, Mass.

Rodrik, Dani. 1989a. "Credibility of Trade Reform: A Policy Maker's Guide." *World Economy* 12:1 (March), pp. 1–16.

————. 1989b. "Promises, Promises: Credible Policy Reform via Signalling." *Economic Journal* 99 (September), pp. 756–72.

————. 1992a. "Conceptual Issues in the Design of Trade Policy for Industrialization." *World Development* 20 (March), pp. 309–20.

————. 1992b. "The Limits of Trade Policy Reform in LDCS." *Journal of Economic Perspectives* 6 (winter), pp. 87–105.

————. 1992c. "Political Economy and Development Policy." *European Economic Review* 36 (January), pp. 329–36.

Stolper, Wolfgang, and Paul Samuelson. 1941. "Protection and Real Wages." *Review of Economic Studies* 9, pp. 58–73.

United Nations Conference on Trade and Development. 1991. *Trade and Development Report.* Geneva, Switzerland.

Whalley, John. 1989. "Recent Trade Liberalization in the Developing World: What Is Behind It, and Where Is It Headed?" NBER Working Paper 3057. National Bureau of Economic Research, Cambridge, Mass.

Williamson, John. 1990. *The Progress of Policy Reform in Latin America.* Policy Analyses in International Economics 28. Washington, D.C.: Institute for International Economics.

World Bank. 1989. *Strengthening Trade Policy Reform,* vol. 2. Washington, D.C.

II

How? (Strategies for Reformers)

11

The Design of Reform Packages under Uncertainty

Mathias Dewatripont and
Gérard Roland

The transition of former communist countries to market economies is one of the most important economic events of the second half of the century. Even though there exists no well-established economic theory of transition, rarely have economists been so assertive, emotional, and divided in their policy advice. Two camps have emerged in the debate: on the one hand, there are proponents of the "big-bang" approach, who argue for a quick and simultaneous introduction of all reforms. Works by authors generally acknowledged to belong to that category include David Lipton and Jeffrey Sachs (1990), Anders Aslund (1991), Andrew Berg and Sachs (1992), Maxim Boycko (1992), Roman Frydman and Andrzej Rapaczynski (1994), Kevin Murphy et al. (1992), Sachs (1993), Roman Frydman and Andrzej Rapaczynski (1994), and Wing Thye Woo (1994). On the other hand, there are those who favor a more "gradualist" approach and emphasize the sequencing of reforms. Works by authors in that category include Richard Portes (1990, 1991), Ronald McKinnon (1991), Roland (1991), Dewatripont and Roland (1992a, b), John McMillan and Barry Naughton (1992), Peter Murrell (1992), Xinghai Fang (1993), John Litwack and Yingyi Qian (1993), Philippe Aghion and Olivier Jean Blanchard (1993), and Shang-Jin Wei (1993).[1]

The defense of the big-bang strategy is often based on the complementarity of reform packages. Introducing partial reforms would eliminate their positive effects and disorganize the economy (Murphy et al., 1992; see also Susan Gates et al., 1993); therefore, all elements constitutive to the market economy should be introduced simultaneously in a comprehensive way (Lipton and Sachs, 1990). Political arguments are also often invoked in favor of a big-bang approach. Lipton and Sachs argue that new

Originally published in *American Economic Review* 85, no. 5 (1995): 1207–23. Reprinted with permission.

governments should use their *état de grâce* to implement painful reforms in one stroke.

In practice, it would seem that big-bang strategists have underestimated the political constraints of transition. In the course of going through the democratic process, all of the big-bang programs in Eastern Europe have undergone substantial modifications, rejections, or delays. Mass privatization in Poland and stabilization in Russia are two clear examples. Moreover, the political support for reform has not been very stable. Slovakia broke away from Czechoslovakia on the basis of a conservative platform. Elections in Russia have shown clear signs of popular backlash. Lithuania, Poland, and Hungary have seen the return of former communists to power; however the latter seem to accept the move toward capitalism, but at a more gradual pace than that advocated by radical reformers. One goal of this paper is to shed some light on the attractiveness of gradualist platforms.

China has always followed a more gradualist course, with spectacular growth performance (see McMillan and Naughton, 1992). In Eastern Europe, Hungary has also followed a relatively gradual transition. While it is too early to evaluate Hungary's overall success in comparison to its neighbors, it is interesting to note that the country managed to attract a large part of total foreign direct investment in Eastern Europe (6 billion out of 18 billion dollars in 1993).[2] A common characteristic of the reform process in China and Hungary is a specific sequencing: the small, private sector is developed prior to price liberalization, privatization, and restructuring.

We argue in this chapter that (i) gradualist reform packages have generally higher *ex ante* feasibility and can thus start earlier, and (ii) sequencing of reforms may create constituencies for continuing reforms and increase *ex post* irreversibility of enacted reforms. We present a model of transition that has uncertain outcomes of reforms and in which the government chooses the speed and sequencing of reforms. The model allows for two possible interpretations of government behavior. First, the government may be a social planner facing an optimal decision-making problem under uncertainty. Second, it may be a reform-minded government committed to reform for ideological or other reasons that faces constraints of political acceptability at each period in time.[3] We briefly outline our main arguments in the next paragraphs.

Large-scale reforms involve great aggregate and individual uncertainty.[4] In the case of Eastern Europe, it is not clear whether the outcome will be closer to the West German miracle or the Weimar Republic, not to speak of former Yugoslavia. Analysts of transition too often implicitly assume that the final outcome will necessarily be a version of the West German miracle, or that the worst-case scenario for reforms will always turn out to be better than the economic status quo.[5] In case of a negative aggregate outcome, the population may want a reversal of reforms. Even though a return to communism is now excluded, reversal of market reforms may be decided by populist and national conservative coalitions that include former communists. Boycko et al. (1991, 1992), for example, report that in Russia and the Ukraine, between 47 percent and 60 percent of respondents considered future renationalization of private businesses, with little or no compensation to owners, to be "quite likely" or "possible."

A big-bang strategy involves high reversal costs, which are often considered to be an advantage *ex post* since it reduces the reversibility of enacted reforms, which is a constant concern for reformers. From the *ex ante* point of view, however, high reversal costs in the case of a negative aggregate outcome may make a big-bang approach politically unfeasible. Gradualism makes reforms easier to start because it gives an additional option of early reversal at a lower cost after partial uncertainty resolution. It is indeed less costly for the population at large to experience a crackdown on the small private sector in an otherwise unreformed economy than it is to reinstate price controls, renationalize, etc. This quite general advantage of gradualism goes beyond the transition debate and may explain why politicians so often take a gradual approach to large-scale reforms even when there is strong complementarity of reforms.[6] Indeed, in the presence of aggregate uncertainty, gradualism allows a flexible approach to reforms with smaller costs of trial and error.

We show that strong complementarity does not necessarily weaken the case for gradualism but may, on the contrary, give it an additional advantage by building constituencies for further reform. If partial reforms are unstable, the choice at each stage of transition is between accepting the next reforms or reversing the previous ones. If the initial reforms have been a success, people are more willing to accept less popular reforms, so as to save on reversal costs and not lose the gains of the first reforms. Correct sequencing can thus create momentum by strengthening the support for reforms during the transition process. In contrast, incorrect sequencing (starting transition with the more painful reforms) undermines popular support and may unnecessarily lead to reform reversal. The case for gradualism thus crucially hinges on correct reform sequencing.

The additional option of early reversal under gradualism may, one could argue, deter investment compared with the big-bang approach, and early reversal may be the result of a lack of investment response. However, in the transition period, the option value of waiting to invest is quite high, and investment response tends to be small in any case. Under those circumstances, we show that gradualism may in fact generate more investment response before uncertainty resolution, thereby reducing *ex post* reversibility of enacted reforms.

It is useful to compare our results with related work. Dewatripont and Roland (1992a, b) also discuss the relative merits of a big-bang strategy versus gradualism from a political-economy point of view, but that analysis is based on informational asymmetries and does not involve aggregate uncertainty. *Ex ante* uncertainty plays a key role in the analysis of Raquel Fernandez and Dani Rodrik (1991), who address the issue of the *status quo bias* in large-scale reforms: a reform with an *ex ante* negative expected outcome that benefits a majority *ex post* is never voted in; whereas, status quo also prevails for reforms with positive *ex ante* outcomes but hurting a majority *ex post*, since they are expected to be reversed. Successful reforms must be both *ex ante* and *ex post* advantageous to a majority. In Fernandez and Rodrik's model however, there is no aggregate uncertainty and therefore also no option value of reversibility. In this paper, the analysis concentrates on the problem of *reform design* to overcome the status quo bias.

The plan of the paper is as follows. Section 11.1 presents the assumptions of the model. Section 11.2 makes the general case for gradualism. Sections 11.3 and 11.4 present results on the optimal sequencing of reforms, and section 11.5 analyzes investment under big bang and gradualism and its effect on reform outcomes. Section 11.6 contains concluding remarks.

11.1   Assumptions and Justifications

We consider a discrete-time, infinite-horizon framework, with discount factor $\delta < 1$. Two reforms are considered: $i = 1, 2$. Except in section 11.4, we assume all individuals to be identical so as to focus solely on *aggregate* uncertainty. Assume that the outcome generated by reform i depends on a partition of the set of possible states of nature having N_i elements, the kth element being denoted by $s_{ik} \in \{s_{i1}, s_{i2}, \ldots, s_{iN_i}\}$. We denote by $o(s_{1k}, s_{2m}, t)$ the outcome of both reforms t periods after they have been implemented and (s_{1k}, s_{2m}) have been realized. This is quite a general formulation, since the relevant partitions of states of nature may be characterized by various indicators such as the volume of investment started, the number of new private enterprises, and foreign trade results.

For simplicity, we assume that the outcome is time-invariant when both reforms have been implemented: $o(s_{1k}, s_{2m}, t) = o(s_{1k}, s_{2m})$ for all t, and, $O(s_{1k}, s_{2m}) = o(s_{1k}, s_{2m})/(1 - \delta)$. For simplicity, $O(s_{1k}, s_{2m})$ is assumed to be independent of sequencing: it remains the same, whether reform 1 or reform 2 is implemented first. There are thus, by assumption, no path-dependency effects associated with sequencing.

Realizations of states of nature for reform 1 are ranked (without loss of generality) in such a way that:

$$k > k' \Rightarrow E_m O(s_{1k}, s_{2m}) \geq E_m O(s'_{1k}, s_{2m}) \tag{1}$$

where $E_m O(s_{1k}, s_{2m})$ is the expected outcome of having both reforms implemented given that s_{1k} has been realized.

Let us now denote by $h(s_{ik}, t)$ the outcome t periods after only reform i has been implemented and s_{ik} is realized. A crucial assumption we make is that from $h(s_{ik}, t)$ one can recover s_{ik} and thus learn about the final payoff of reform.[7] Again for simplicity, let us assume $h(s_{ik}, t) = h(s_{ik})$ for all t, and define $H(s_{ik}) = h(s_{ik})/(1 - \delta)$. In reality, we could expect $h(s_{ik}, t)$ to decline with time. To take an example, if the first reform consists in encouraging the development of a small private sector, the outcome is likely to be positive in a first stage as the supply of goods and services to consumers is enhanced and as new wealth-and job-creating opportunities are available. At some stage of development, however, the private sector is likely to become increasingly dependent on the state sector for its inputs. As stressed by Murphy et al. (1992), the diversion of state-produced goods by the private sector may result in a loss of allocative efficiency. Without further reform in the state-owned sector, the development of the small private sector may thus become welfare-reducing over time. We assume here implicitly that such a low welfare outcome is reached immediately, which only makes partial reforms look worse.

Another feature of these reforms is their degree of *reversibility*: the *cost of reversal* of reform i when implemented alone is denoted by $-\xi_i$ (with $\xi_i < 0$). Similarly, the cost of reversing *both* reforms is denoted by $-\xi$ (with $\xi_1 + \xi_2 \leq \xi < \min\{\xi_1, \xi_2\} < 0$). Reversal costs are borne by the population. They are internalized by the government.[8]

We normalize the expected outcome to zero under "status quo." The status quo should not be interpreted too literally, since some changes take place even in the absence of reforms. Outcome $O(s_{1k}, s_{2m})$ is thus the *relative payoff* of pursuing market reform relative to taking a conservative platform. Similarly, "reversal" does not mean that one comes literally back to the status quo. Instead, ξ_i is the expected payoff of reversing reform i and returning to a conservative platform.

Let us finally come back to the objective function of the government. If the latter is a social planner having to choose between "big-bang" (both reforms being implemented at once) and "gradualist" policies (one reform being introduced before the other), it will choose the reform package that maximizes the *ex ante* expected outcome. If the government is instead composed of radical reformers facing constraints of political acceptability, it will choose its preferred solution subject to the constraint of majority vote (see section 11.4).

11.2   The Case for Gradualism

In order to compare a gradualist with a big-bang strategy in this simple framework, let us assume that, because of the required complementarity of reforms, $H(s_{ik}) < \xi_i < 0$ for all i and k. The real choice for society is thus between the status quo and implementation of *both* reforms.

"Big bang" implies trying both reforms at once, and undoing them both in the following period if it is worth the reversal cost. The expected payoff under a big-bang approach, denoted BB, is thus:

$$BB = (1 - \delta)E_{k,m}O(s_{1k}, s_{2m}) + \delta E_{k,m}\max\{\xi, O(s_{1k}, s_{2m})\} \tag{2}$$

where expectations are taken here *ex ante*, that is, before the realizations of either s_{1k} or s_{2m}.

We will compare BB with the maximum expected payoff under a gradualist strategy where reform i precedes reform j, denoted GR_{ij}. Calling reform 1 (or R_1) the first reform which is tried, obtaining GR_{12} implies: (i) trying reform 1 for one period; (ii) moving back to the status quo, *or* trying reform 2 (or R_2) for one period; (iii) in this last case, maintaining both reforms or undoing them both.[9]

Assume that, under R_1, s_{1k} has been realized. The decision to implement R_2 then yields the following expected payoff, denoted $R_2(s_{1k})$:

$$R_2(s_{1k}) = (1 - \delta)E_m O(s_{1k}, s_{2m}) + \delta E_m \max\{\xi, O(s_{1k}, s_{2m})\}. \tag{3}$$

Since k is ranked according to the expected payoff of implementing both reforms, we assume there exists $\tilde{k}$ between 1 and N such that:

$$R_2(s_{1k}) < \xi_1 \text{ if } k < \tilde{k}$$
$$R_2(s_{1k}) \geq \xi_1 \text{ if } k \geq \tilde{k}. \tag{4}$$

Consequently, noting $\Pr(k < \tilde{k})$ the probability of realization of a signal with index lower than $\tilde{k}$, the *ex ante* payoff under gradualism, GR_{12}, is:

$$GR_{12} = (1 - \delta)E_k H(s_{1k}) + \delta \Pr(k < \tilde{k})\xi_1 + \delta \Pr(k \geq \tilde{k})R_2(s_{1k}|k \geq \tilde{k}) \quad (5)$$

where $R_2(s_{1k}|k \geq \tilde{k})$ is the expected payoff of implementing R_2 if R_1 has been implemented, *conditional* upon $k \geq \tilde{k}$. Expression (5) is equivalent to:

$$GR_{12} = (1 - \delta)E_k H(s_{1k}) + \delta\,BB + \delta \Pr(k < \tilde{k})[\xi_1 - R_2(s_{1k}|k < \tilde{k})]. \quad (6)$$

This last condition shows the advantage and disadvantage of gradualism. Its advantage is to save on reversal costs by giving an option of early reversal when the prospects for further reform look disappointing.[10] The disadvantages are twofold. First, a period of partial reform must be suffered, which can be costly (for $H(s_{1k}) < 0$). Second, gradualism may unnecessarily delay the implementation of both reforms if BB is positive.

Still, gradualism dominates if the option value of early reversal is important enough. Intuitively, this is true if learning is not too costly ($H(\cdot)$ not too low), or if it is "fast enough," that is, if for given $O(\cdot, \cdot)$ and $H(\cdot)$, ξ is close enough to 1.

PROPOSITION 1   For $O(\cdot, \cdot)$ and $H(\cdot)$ given, if $\delta \to 1$, a necessary and sufficient condition for gradualism to dominate a big-bang strategy is that the early reversal option be exercised with positive probability: $GR_{12} > BB$ if and only if $0 < \Pr(k < \tilde{k}) < 1$. If instead $\delta < 1$, gradualism dominates if $0 < \Pr(k < \tilde{k}) < 1$ and $E_k H(s_{1k})$ is not too negative.

The proof is obvious, from (6).

Informativeness is the key necessary condition for gradualism to dominate the big-bang strategy in the sense that learning about the first reform tells whether to try the second reform or not, depending on the realization s_{1k}. If $\Pr(k < \tilde{k})$ were equal to zero, then the first reform would not be informative since one would always want to try the second reform. In that case, gradualism could still dominate big bang if $\delta < 1$; however, for $\delta \to 1$, informativeness of the first implemented reform becomes a necessary and sufficient condition for gradualism to dominate the big-bang strategy.[11] It is also a criterion for the choice of the sequencing of reforms, the topic of section 11.3.

Proposition 1 is quite general. In particular, it allows reforms to be complementary. Indeed, we have not introduced any restriction on the way in which $H(\cdot)$ or $O(\cdot, \cdot)$ depend on s_{1k} or s_{2m}.

In order to see more precisely the role of reform complementarity, let us now introduce as benchmark the case of *separable and independent reforms*: $O(s_{1k}, s_{2m}) \equiv H(s_{1k} + H(s_{2m})$, $H(s_{1k}) \equiv O_{1k}$ and $H(s_{2m}) \equiv O_{2m}$, and the distributions of outcomes O_{1k} and O_{2m} are independent. Assume moreover that $\xi = \xi_1 + \xi_2$.

By contrast, consider the following form of complementarity: $O(s_{1k}, s_{2m}) \equiv O_{1k} + O_{2m}$, but $H(s_{1k}) \equiv O_{1k}|\gamma$, with $\gamma < 0$ and $O_{1k} + \gamma < \min\{\xi_1, O_{1k} + E_m O_{2m}\}$ for all k. Under that assumption, partial reform is always dominated either by a return to the status quo or a move toward full reform. As above, we assume that $H(s_{1k})$ is a sufficient statistic for s_{1k}.

We now compare the case of separable reforms (no γ) and complementary reforms (with γ). Assume that at least one reform, reform 2, is unattractive *ex ante*:

$$(1 - \delta)E_m O_{2m} + \delta E_m \max\{\xi_2, O_{2m}\} < 0. \tag{7}$$

In the case of separable and independent reforms, when (7) holds, at most R_1 will be tried. In any case, gradualism is never optimal under separable and independent reforms. Indeed, one should try R_2 if and only if $(1 - \delta)E_m O_{2m} + \delta E_m \max\{\xi_2, O_{2m}\} > 0$, and doing so immediately is optimal because delay is then costly.[12] What happens when reforms are complementary? The answer is expressed in the following proposition.

PROPOSITION 2   When reforms are separable and independent, gradualism is never optimal; moreover R_2 is never implemented if it is unattractive *ex ante*. Under complementarity of reforms, gradualism may be optimal, even if outcomes are independent. Moreover, gradualism builds support for the whole reform package when R_2 is unattractive *ex ante*.

(See the appendix for the proof.)

Proposition 2 shows that, contrary to common belief, complementarity of reforms may be a necessary condition for the optimality of gradualism. Indeed, under separability and independence of reforms, each reform should either be implemented immediately or never. Instead, under complementarity, gradualism may still dominate a big-bang approach because of the option value of early reversal. Complementarity helps having the unattractive reform (R_2) accepted for two reasons: first, a refusal of the second reform implies incurring reversal costs of the first reform, because partial reform is always dominated. Second, if the first reform yields a "favorable" outcome (a high O_{1k}), it *builds support* for the entire package: not implementing the second one means losing O_{1k}.

The comparison between gradualism and a big-bang strategy could be extended along a spatial dimension. If there is one reform and two regions, gradualism would imply trying the reform in one region first. *Ex ante* feasibility is also increased, as the cost of reversal is smaller. Temporal and spatial gradualism share the same advantage of *lower experimentation costs* compared to a big-bang strategy. However, welfare aspects are different. Support for extending reform to another region can be built only if reform outcomes are correlated, not if they are independent, because a good outcome in one region is not shared with the other regions. Note that temporal and spatial gradualism combined (two reforms in two regions) will still lower reversal costs and increase *ex ante* feasibility. Chinese gradualism has followed both dimensions. Our analysis suggests that the Chinese way of experimentation with reforms may be viewed as a response to political-acceptability constraints.

Finally, note that the model can readily be extended to include a variable status quo payoff. If for example the status quo payoff declines over time, reforms may be initially unfeasible, but then, under the conditions of proposition 1, gradualism would be feasible before a big-bang strategy, which would become feasible only after further deterioration of the status quo. The logic of the model would predict that, with a declining status quo, big-bang packages are introduced in countries where crisis perceptions are greater. However, under the conditions of proposition 1, big-bang packages will only be introduced after the country has missed opportunities for gradualist packages, since the latter always become feasible earlier.

11.3 Optimal Sequencing of Reforms

After having established the conditions under which gradualism dominates a big-bang strategy, we now address the optimal *sequencing* of reforms. We assume complementarity of reforms as in proposition 2. In order to keep the discussion simple (without any real loss of generality), we assume that each reform i generates only one of two outcomes: O_{i1} and O_{i2}. O_{i1} is denoted by $G_i > 0$ and O_{i2} is denoted by $L_i < 0$, representing respectively "gain" and "loss." We define $E_i \equiv p_i G_i (1 - p_i) L_i$ where p_i is the probability of G_i. We maintain the assumption that final outcomes are not path-dependent. We compare the gradualist strategy where reform i is implemented first (yielding payoff GR_{ij}) with the strategy with the opposite sequencing (yielding GR_{ji}).

Note first that the informativeness condition of proposition 1 has an immediate implication for sequencing. Assume for example that $\xi_i = \xi_j = \xi/2$. Then, if $R_j(G_i) > \xi/2 > R_j(L_i)$ and $R_i(L_j) > \xi/2$, starting with reform i is informative, whereas starting with reform j is not, because one will always want to continue the reform process even after learning L_j. The reversal option therefore has no value under gradualism when reform j is implemented first but has value under the opposite sequencing. It is then straightforward to show that $GR_{ij} > GR_{ji}$.

To make the problem interesting, we will assume both reforms to be informative:

$$R_i(G_j) > \xi_i > R_i(L_j) \text{ and } R_j(G_i) > \xi_i > R_j(L_i). \tag{8}$$

Intuitively, it seems reasonable to start with a reform having a higher expected outcome, a sequencing we implicitly assumed in the previous section. To verify this conjecture, it is useful to rewrite the expression for GR_{ij} as follows:

$$GR_{ij} = (1 - \delta)(E_i + \gamma) + \delta p_i \max\{\xi_i, R_j(G_i)\} + \delta(1 - p_i) \max\{\xi_i, R_j(L_i)\} \tag{9}$$

where

$$R_j(G_i) = (1 - \delta)(G_i + E_j) + \delta p_j \max\{\xi_i, G_i + G_j\}$$
$$+ \delta(1 - p_j) \max\{\xi_i, G_i + L_j\}. \tag{10}$$

$R_j(L_i)$ is defined similarly. The following proposition is then easily established.

PROPOSITION 3   Assume that gradualism is optimal and that reforms i and j differ only in terms of their expected outcome: $\xi_i = \xi_j$, $p_i = p_j$, but $G_i = G_j + \Delta, L_i = L_j + \Delta$, and $\Delta > 0$. Then $GR_{ij} > GR_{ji}$ for $\delta < 1$ and $GR_{ij} = GR_{ji}$ for $\delta = 1$.

Proof   The assumptions imply $E_i > E_j$. Developing the expression for $GR_{ij} - GR_{ji}$, all terms cancel out except for $(1 - \delta)(E_i - E_j) > 0$.

In this case, the expected outcome for the second period is independent of sequencing, since reversal probabilities and costs are identical for both reforms. The only difference is thus the first-period expected outcome. It is then necessary to have positive discounting in order to take into account the higher first-period expected outcome of reform i compared to reform j. Despite its evident simplicity, the result of proposition 3 appears quite relevant since one very often observes politicians delaying less popular measures.

One might expect a similar result to hold for two reforms which differ only in the relative probability of good outcomes. Contrary to intuition, however, different effects come into play that may lead the policymaker, under some circumstances, to choose a reverse sequencing.

PROPOSITION 4   Assume that gradualism is optimal and that reforms i and j differ only in the probability of good and bad outcomes: $\xi_i = \xi_j$, $G_i = G_j$, $L_i = L_j$, but $p_i > P_j$. Then, $\mathrm{GR}_{ij} > \mathrm{GR}_{ji}$ if $\delta \max\{\xi, G_i + L_j\} > \xi_i$, $\forall \delta \leq 1$. However, $\mathrm{GR}_{ij} < \mathrm{GR}_{ji}$ if $\delta \to 1$ and $\delta \max\{\xi, G_i + L_j\} < \xi_i$.

(See the appendix for the proof.)

The intuition for this last result is based on the fact that, contrary to the conditions of proposition 3, the reversal probabilities are now changed as $p_i > p_j$. This brings two effects into play. On the one hand, starting with reform i increases the probability that both reforms will be achieved. If however G_i is realized in the first period and L_j in the second period, and if $G_i + L_j < 0$, the total reform outcome will be worse than under the status quo. In that case, a higher probability of G_i tends thus to decrease the expected outcome of reform, other things remaining equal. A second effect, corollary to the first one, is that when reform i is introduced first, the probability of having to incur the first-period reversal cost is also smaller. This increases the expected payoff of reform. For the latter positive effect to dominate, it is necessary to have $\delta \max\{\xi, G_i + L_j\} > \xi_i$. Of course, if $G_i + L_j > 0$, both effects are positive and it is always better to start with reform i.

We finally investigate sequencing along the dimension of risk. Other things remaining equal, is it better to start with a riskier reform or with a less risky one? We will first introduce some notation:

$$g_i \equiv G_i - E_i$$
$$\ell_i \equiv L_i - E_i. \tag{11}$$

Condition (11) implies that $p_i g_i + (1 - p_i)\ell_i = 0$. We now establish Proposition 5.

PROPOSITION 5   Assume that gradualism is optimal and that reforms i and j differ only in their riskiness: $\xi_i = \xi_j$, $p_i = p_j$, $E_i = E_j$, but $g_i > g_j$ and thus $\ell_i < \ell_j$. Then $\forall \delta \leq 1$, $\mathrm{GR}_{ij} \geq \mathrm{GR}_{ji}$, with strict inequality if $G_i + L_j > \xi$.

(See the appendix for the proof.)

It is optimal to start with the riskier reform because doing so increases the option value of reversibility, thereby increasing the expected outcome. This follows from the idea that increased volatility raises option values: whenever gains and losses of reform grow, the option value of reversibility grows, because the additional losses are avoided through earlier reversal.[13]

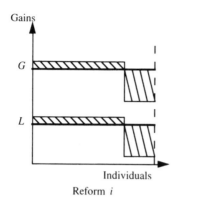 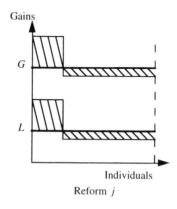

Reform i Reform j

Figure 11.1
Two reforms as mirror images
Notes: Reforms i and j have the same aggregate expected outcome, but reform i benefits a majority a bit and hurts a minority a lot; reform j hurts a majority a bit and benefits a minority a lot.

11.4   Sequencing of Reforms with Heterogeneous Agents

We now introduce *ex post* heterogeneity between agents and add idiosyncratic uncertainty to the aggregate uncertainty of reforms. Given two otherwise identical reforms, we ask whether it is better to start with a reform that provides a small gain to a majority or one that provides a big gain to a minority.

We start with two reforms, each generating outcome G with probability p and outcome $L < 0$ with probability $(1 - p)$. As we are concerned with sequencing, we assume that gradualism is optimal, a necessary condition for which is $G + L < \xi_i + \xi_j < 2G$.

We now add idiosyncratic uncertainty as follows. In each state of nature $S \in \{G, L\}$, for reform i, a proportion q_i of the population receives $S + g_i > S$, and a proportion $1 - q_i$ receives $S + \ell_i < S$, with $q_i g_i + (1 - q_i)\ell_i = 0$. This idiosyncracy leaves intact the expected payoff of each reform for the population. Let us moreover concentrate on the case in which the two reforms are "mirror images" of one another: $q_i = 1 - q_j > 0.5$, and $g_i + \ell_j = \ell_i + g_j = 0$. This special case, shown in figure 11.1, allows better isolation of the reason for which sequencing will matter with heterogeneous agents. The "mirror image" assumption means that reforms have identical expected payoff and riskiness but differ only in the skewness of the distribution of idiosyncratic shocks: reform i gives a small gain to a majority and a big loss to a minority, whereas reform j does exactly the opposite.

Note first that, given our assumptions, the introduction of hetero-geneity does *not* modify anything for the big-bang strategy. Assume majority rule at each stage of the decision process. *Ex post*, the median voter is one who has experienced net idiosyncratic gains, which are equal to $g_i + \ell_j = g_j + \ell_i = 0$. Heterogeneity is thus without consequence for reversibility and, from an *ex ante* perspective, the expected payoff under a big-bang approach remains unaffected.

The expected payoff is also unchanged if reform i, favored by a majority, is enacted first, even though the median voter after reform i experiences a net idiosyncratic gain g_i. He of course will want to continue the reform package if the aggregate outcome of reform i has been positive. Note also that his *ex post* stake in continuing will be higher the higher g_i. On the other hand, he will still prefer not to continue if the aggregate outcome has been negative, because he knows that reversal will take place anyway one period later.[14]

Things may however be different if reform j is enacted first. In the case of a favorable aggregate shock, the median voter experiencing ℓ_j may be reluctant to continue, because his net expected gain from doing so is

$$\{(1-\delta)(G + \ell_j + [pG + (1-p)L]) + \delta(1-p)(\xi_j + \xi_i)$$
$$+ \delta p(2G + \ell_j)\} - \xi_j. \tag{12}$$

The problem is thus that the median voter *learns* he is among the rela-tive losers of reform j, so that his stake in continuing the reform process is reduced. Starting with reform j could thus introduce an additional con-straint for the implementation of the reform package, as summarized in proposition 6.

PROPOSITION 6   Assume that gradualism is optimal and that reforms i and j only differ in the skewness of the distribution of idiosyncratic shocks: $\xi_i = \xi_j$, $G_i = G_j \equiv G$, $L_i = L_j \equiv L$, $p_i = p_j \equiv p$, $q_i g_i + (1 - q_i)\ell_i = q_j g_j + (1 - q_j)\ell_j = 0$, but $q_i = 1 - q_j$, $g_i = -\ell_j$ and $\ell_i = -g_j$. Then $GR_{ij} > GR_{ji}$ if (12) is negative, and $GR_{ij} = GR_{ij}$ otherwise.

The result of proposition 6 is in the same spirit as that of proposition 2. Appropriate sequencing makes it possible to build constituencies in favor of further reform. If a majority is better-off after the first reform, it has a stake in continuation, whereas the less well-off minority will not be able to influence the decision-making process. The main idea is that a gradu-alist package starting with reform i may be politically feasible, whereas the opposite sequencing may not be. Indeed, when starting with reform i, under a favorable aggregate shock a majority expects $R_j(G + g_i)$ after the first period whereas, when starting with reform j, a majority only expects $R_i(G + \ell_j)$. This sequencing may thus not be feasible because agents predict *ex ante* that reversal will take place after the first period because of insufficient support for reform continuation. The ability to build constituencies makes the difference between the two reform packages.[15]

Note finally that if *both* reform packages are feasible, they are *ex ante* identical, since in both cases a majority will reject reversal after the first period, provided no aggregate shock occurs. Because both reforms have the same expected outcome and riskiness, the absence of reversal then makes sequencing irrelevant.

While this simple example highlights the importance of "courting" the median voter along the path of reform, further work is clearly needed to analyze the impact of heterogeneity on reform design.

11.5   Gradualism and Investment

In previous sections, *ex post* reform outcomes were exogenous and not influenced by the design of reform packages. We now introduce endogeneity by asking how big-bang and gradualist reform packages compare in attracting welfare-enhancing foreign investment and thereby inducing *ex post* irreversibility.

The goal of this section is modest. It uses examples to investigate the claim that big-bang reform packages should necessarily be expected to trigger stronger responses from investors convinced by the irreversible nature of reforms. We show that this claim is unwarranted and that the investment response may be either higher or lower under gradualism. We leave for further research a more detailed analysis of irreversible investment behavior that would take advantage of recent advances on the subject (see, e.g., Avinash Dixit and Robert Pindyck, 1994).

We now add to the model of sections 11.1–11.3 irreversible investment, which is assumed to come from a foreign representative investor. We abstract from idiosyncratic uncertainty and assume that $O(s_{1k}, s_{2m}, I)$ increases with I, the aggregate foreign investment level. For simplicity, we assume again *binary outcomes*, that is, $s_{1k} \in \{G, B\}$ and $s_{2m} \in \{G, B\}$. We also assume symmetric reforms: $O(G, G, I) > O(G, B, I) = O(B, G, I) > O(B, B, I)$, with $\Pr(G, G) = p^2$, $\Pr(G, B) = \Pr(B, G) = p(1 - p)$, and $\Pr(B, B) = (1 - P)^2$.

An investment level I costs I by assumption, and its value to investors is lost under policy reversal. Otherwise, the discounted value of investment $V(\cdot)$ (assumed to be increasing and concave in I) is given by $V(G, G, I) >$

Table 11.1
Timing of Investment in the Model

Approach	Time	Event
Big bang	$t = 0$	• Initial investment (I_0) • Both reforms tried, (s_{1k}, s_{2m}) realized
	$t = 1$	• Additional investment (I_1) • Reversal or not
Gradualism	$t = 0$	• Initial investment (I'_0) • First reform tried, s_{1k} realized
	$t = 1$	• Additional investment (I'_1) • Reversal; otherwise second reform, s_{2m} realized
	$t = 2$	(If no reversal at $t = 1$) • Additional investment (I'_2) • Reversal or not

$V(G, B, I) = V(B, G, I) > V(B, B, I) > 0$ for $I > 0$. We assume that it takes one period for investment to become operational. This simplifying assumption means that, under gradualism, initial investment never becomes productive before both reforms are in place. More importantly, we do not have to make any assumptions about the productivity of investment under partial reform.

We make the following assumptions on the reversibility of reforms:

$$O(G, G, 0) > \xi$$

$$O(B, B, I) < \xi \qquad \forall I$$

$$O(G, B, I) \geq \xi \qquad \text{for } I \geq \bar{I} \qquad\qquad (13)$$

$$O(G, B, I) < \xi \qquad \text{for } I < \bar{I}.$$

Reform is thus irreversible in the presence of "good news," (G, G), whatever the investment response, and will be reversed under "bad news," (B, B), again whatever foreign investment has been realized. However, the level of investment matters for the reversibility of reform under "mixed news," (G, B) or (B, G).

The timing is as shown in table 11.1. We first concentrate on the case in which $\bar{I}$ is never reached (either under gradualism or a big-bang approach) under mixed news, so that foreign investors know they will enjoy the full benefit of their investment only under good news (G, G). clearly, I_1 and I'_2 will be positive only under (G, G). In this case, $I_0 + I_1 = I'_0 + I'_1 + I'_2 \equiv I_G$, where I_G is determined by $V'(G, G, I_G) = 1$ and $V'(\cdot)$ is the partial derivative of V with respect to investment. Moreover, I'_1 will be positive only if the first reform generates good news G. In this case, define $I'_{01} \equiv I'_0 + I'_1$.

I_G is reached later under gradualism, as the option value of waiting disappears only when (G, G) has been realized. This takes place at $t = 1$ under a big-bang approach, but only at $t = 2$ under gradualism. The following proposition shows that the option value of waiting to invest may be unambiguously smaller under gradualism.

PROPOSITION 7   Assume that $\bar{I}$ is too high to be chosen by foreign investors under either gradualism or a big-bang strategy: $I_G < \bar{I}$. Then, gradualism is characterized by a stronger investment response before uncertainty resolution: $I_G > I'_{01} > I'_0 > I_0$.

(See the appendix for the proof.)

For the simple case in which investment does not affect irreversibility, investment at $t = 1$ under gradualism after initial good news is thus higher than the initial investment response under a big-bang approach. If the first reform proves to be a success, the conditional probability of (G, G) is then higher, and therefore the value of waiting is lower. Interestingly, investment at $t = 0$ is also higher under gradualism because one learns less by waiting for one period: reversal occurs at $t = 1$ only with probability $1 - p$, and uncertainty resolution is only partial since the outcome of the second reform is not yet known.

Proposition 8 now considers the case where the investment response affects the reversibility of reforms. It states that gradualism may imply more or less irreversibility than a big-bang strategy.

PROPOSITION 8   (a) Assume $I_G > \bar{I} > I'_{01}$. Then, for $p \leq 1/2$, the incentive under gradualism to choose I instead of I'_0 at $t = 1$ is higher than the incentive under a big-bang approach to choose $\bar{I}$ instead of I_0. (b) If, however, under the same assumptions, $\bar{I}$ is chosen at $t = 0$ under big-bang strategy, gradualism implies less irreversibility than the big-bang strategy and a lower immediate investment response.

(See the appendix for the proof.)

The intuition of part (a) of proposition 8 is as follows. After the success of the first reform, foreign investors may feel it profitable to invest up to $\bar{I}$, thereby avoiding reversal in case the second reform is unsuccessful. Gradualism encourages them to do this for two reasons: first, because they are already more optimistic about the final outcome, their investment will be profitable with a higher probability, the conditional probability of (G, G) being p, compared to p^2 under the big-bang approach. Second, investing $\bar{I}$ creates (profitable) irreversibility with a conditional probability of $1 - p$, compared with $2p(1 - p)$ under a big-bang approach. This favors investment under gradualism provided $p \leq 1/2$ In case $\bar{I}$ is triggered by gradualism at $t = 1$ after the success of the first reform, full reform will then go through with probability p, instead of p^2 under big bang. Gradualism may thus create more *ex post* irreversibility.

Part (b) of Proposition 8 says that the opposite may also be true. Specifically, assume that the big-bang strategy triggers $\bar{I}$ at $t = 0$, so that reversal occurs only with probability $(1 - p)^2$. Gradualism then implies less irreversibility, since reversal occurs with a higher probability $(1 - p)$, after bad news concerning the first reform. Moreover, the initial investment response is lower than $\bar{I}$, since there is less of an urge to prevent reversal.

11.6 Conclusion

We have shown in this chapter how, in the presence of large-scale reforms, as with transition in postcommunist countries, gradualism increases the political acceptability of reforms. Moreover it allows constituencies to be built favoring further reform: correct sequencing of reforms uses the "sweet pill" of promising results in early reforms to gain acceptance of the "bitter pill" of later reforms, taking strategic advantage of the complementarity of reforms to push entire reform packages through the political process.

Propositions 3, 4, and 6 on optimal sequencing are suggestive in the current context of transition. A few illustrative examples follows.[16]

First, consider the development of the small private sector in China and Hungary prior to more comprehensive reforms. In China, the non-state sector's share of industrial output increased from 22 percent in 1978 to 47 percent in 1991 and the private sector from zero to more than 12 percent over the same period (Qian and Xu, 1993). In Hungary, the small private sector was already producing about 10 percent of industrial output by 1990 (Hare and Revesz, 1992). Liberalizing the small private sector is a popular measure that provides a supply response in emerging markets and may enhance political sustainability of reforms.

Second, in most economies in transition, the best firms tend to be privatized first. Not only have some governments explicitly received advice to privatize the most profitable firms first (Irena Grosfeld, 1990), but it has also generally been the case in practice (see Konstantine Gatsios [1992] on Hungary, Wendy Carlin and Colin Mayer [1992] on Eastern Germany, and Roman Frydman et al. [1993] for all countries in transition).

Third, the phase of restructuring and closing of unprofitable (loss-making) enterprises is generally delayed. Macroeconomic figures show that employment falls initially less than output, and thus that the decline in employment is delayed (European Community Commission, 1992;

Michael Burda, 1993). Only in Eastern Germany have there been significant measures to close loss-making enterprises. There are good economic reasons to delay restructuring (see, e.g., Aghion and Blanchard, 1993) but political constraints also play a role. Restructuring involves the loss of substantial rents for well-organized groups of the population, and it requires countervailing political momentum.

While the above experiences are consistent with our results, they can also shed light on potential policy mistakes. For example, one can wonder whether the adverse domestic reaction to price liberalization in Russia might have been avoided if government policy had first favored the emergence of a small private industrial and service sector as in Hungary. Second, it might have been a grave sequencing mistake for Boris Yeltsin not to have taken advantage of the August 1991 putsch to push immediately for further political reform (new congressional elections and a new constitution), prior to further economic reform.

Our model is a first step in the analysis of reform design under aggregate uncertainty. As noted in section 11.3, the model could be extended to include a declining status quo over time. Such an extension would probably reinforce some of our results on the advantages of gradualism. Indeed, with increasing net expected stochastic payoffs, gradualist reform packages can be initiated earlier than big-bang packages because of the option value of reversal. Moreover, the incentive to adopt further reforms after promising earlier results will be reinforced because of declining reversal payoffs. In the area of transition, natural extensions would be to add more structure to the model, in order to compare competing plans with similar timings (for example, to privatize, or to liberalize the economy). Our framework could also be applied to other large-scale reform problems, such as European unification, which is also following a (very) gradualist course.

Appendix

Proof of Proposition 2 The first part of the proposition is clear from the discussion in the main text. Therefore, we will concentrate on the complementarity case. From proposition 1, we know that it is possible to have $GR_{12} > BB$. What remains to be proved is that $GR_{12} > 0$ can happen despite condition (7). Under separability and independence, R^2 is chosen if and only if

$$(1 - \delta)E_m O_{2m} + \delta E_m \max\{\xi_2, O_{2m}\} > 0$$

which we have assumed is not true. Instead, under complementarity and independence, R^2 is chosen after R_1 has been implemented and O_{1k} has been realized if

$$R_2(O_{1k}) - \xi_1 = (1-\delta)(O_{1k} + E_m O_{2m}) + \delta E_m \max\{\xi, O_{1k} + O_{2m}\} - \xi_1$$

$$= (1-\delta)(O_{1k} - \xi_1 + E_m O_{2m})$$

$$+ \delta E_m \max\{\xi_2, O_{1k} + O_{2m} - \xi_1\}$$

$$> 0. \tag{A1}$$

This can be satisfied even if (7) is violated, because $\xi_1 < 0$ and because O_{1k} may be positive.

Proof of Proposition 4   Using (8) and (9), we have

$$GR_{ij} = (1-\delta)(E_i + \gamma) + \delta(1-p_i)\xi_1 + \delta p_i(1-\delta)(G_i + E_j) + \delta^2 p_i$$

$$\times \{p_i(G_i + G_j) + (1-p_j)\max\{\xi, G_i + L_j\}\}$$

and a similar equation for GR_{ji}. Under the conditions of proposition 4, we have

$$GR_{ij} - GR_{ji} = \delta(1-\delta)[(1+p_j)G_i - (1-p_j)L_j](p_i - p_j) + \delta(p_i - p_j)$$

$$\times [\delta \max\{\xi, G_i + L_j\} - \xi_i]. \tag{A2}$$

When $\delta \max\{\xi, G_i + L_j\} > \xi_i$, both expressions on the right-hand side of (A2) are positive. Therefore, $GR_{ij} > GR_{ji}$. If however $\delta \max\{\xi, G_i + L_j\} < \xi_i$, then the second expression on the right-hand side is negative. When δ tends to 1, the first expression tends toward 0, and we are thus left with a negative expression. Therefore, $GR_{ij} < GR_{ji}$.

Proof of Proposition 5   Recall from section 11.3 that $GR_{ij} = (1-\delta) \times (E_i + \gamma) + \delta BB + \delta(1-p_i)[\xi_i - R_j(L_i)]$. $GR_{ij} - GR_{ji}$ is then equal to $\delta(1-p_i)[(\xi_i - R_j(L_i)) - (\xi_j - R_i(L_j))]$. This expression is positive because $R_i(L_j) - R_j(L_i) = \delta p_i[\max\{\xi, L_j + G_i\} - \max\{\xi, L_i + G_j\}] \geq 0$, with strict inequality if $G_i + L_j > \xi$.

Proof of Proposition 7   Under the big-bang approach, increasing investment by dI at $t = 0$ generates a net benefit of

$$p^2 dV(G, G, I) - dI.$$

The above expression takes into account that, at $t = 1$, reversal will take place whenever (G, G) is not realized. If instead, investment is raised by dI at $t = 1$ after learning (G, G), then the net benefit at time 0 is

$$\delta p^2(dV(G, G, I) - dI)$$

since investment is delayed by one period and (G, G) is realized only with probability p^2. The net gain of investing at $t = 0$ instead of $t = 1$ is thus

$$(1 - \delta)p^2 \, dV(G, G, I) - (1 - \delta p^2) \, dI. \tag{A3}$$

Following (A3), I_0 is determined by

$$V'(G, G, I_0) = \frac{1 - \delta p^2}{(1 - \delta)p^2}. \tag{A4}$$

What about gradualism? Let us start with I'_m. Increasing investment by dI at $t = 1$ when the first reform was a success generates

$$pdV(G, G, I) - dI$$

since, at $t = 2$, reform will be maintained only under (G, G). Instead, raising investment by dI at $t = 2$ under (G, G) generates, as of time 1:

$$\delta p[dV(G, G, I) - dI].$$

I'_m is thus determined by

$$V'(G, G, I'_m) = \frac{1 - \delta p}{(1 - \delta)p}. \tag{A5}$$

Since p is bigger than p^2, and since $V'(\cdot)$ is decreasing in I, we have $I'_m > I_n$.

What about I'_0? Investing dI at $t = 0$ generates

$$p[(1 - p)(1 - \delta) \, dV(G, B, I) + pdV(G, G, I)] - dI.$$

Indeed, investment becomes productive after the first reform has been implemented. If it is a success, the second reform is tried. If it is a failure, reversal takes place after the first period during which the investor has enjoyed $(1 - \delta)V(G, B, I)$. If it is a success, the investor enjoys the full value of $V(G, G, I)$.

Instead, investing dI at $t = 1$ if the first reform is a success will generate

$$\delta p[pdV(G, G, I) - dI]$$

as of time 0. The net gain of investing at $t = 0$ instead of $t = 1$ is

$$(1 - \delta)p^2 \, dV(G, G, I) + (1 - \delta)p(1 - p) \, dV(G, B, I) - (1 - \delta p) \, dI. \tag{A6}$$

Following (A6), I'_0 is determined by:

$$pV'(G, G, I'_0) + (1 - p)V'(G, B, I'_0) = \frac{1 - \delta p}{(1 - \delta)p}. \tag{A7}$$

Because of concavity of $V(\cdot)$ and because $V(G, B, I) < V(G, G, I)$ we have $0 < V'(G, B, I) < V'(G, G, I)$. The comparison between (A5) and (A7) implies $I'_0 < I'_{01}$. On the other hand, comparing (A4) and (A7) implies $I_0 < I'_0$. Finally, since I_G is determined by $V'(G, G, I_G) = 1$, we clearly have $I_G > I'_{01}$.

Proof of Proposition 8 Under the big-bang approach, increasing investment from I_0 to I at $t = 0$ yields a net gain of

$$(1 - \delta)p^2[V(G, G, \bar{I}) - V(G, G, I_0)] - (1 - \delta p^2)(\bar{I} - I_0)$$

$$+ 2p(1 - p)V(G, B, \bar{I}). \tag{A8}$$

Indeed, under (G, G), $(\bar{I} - I_0)$ is simply undertaken one period earlier, and $V(G, G, \bar{I}) - V(G, G, I_0)$ is enjoyed one period earlier. In the other states of nature, investment is zero after the first period, and investment totaling $\bar{I} - I_0$ will induce irreversibility except under (B, B).

Instead, under gradualism, increasing investment from I'_{01} to I at $t = 1$ yields a net gain of

$$(1 - \delta)p[V(G, G, \bar{I}) - V(G, G, I'_{01})] - (1 - \delta p)(\bar{I} - I'_{01})$$

$$+ (1 - p)V(G, B, \bar{I}). \tag{A9}$$

Once again, under (G, G), $(\bar{I} - I'_{01})$ is undertaken one period earlier, while irreversibility results from such investment.

Expression (25) can be rewritten as

$$(1 - \delta)p^2[V(G, G, \bar{I}) - V(G, G, I'_{01})]$$

$$- (1 - \delta p^2)(\bar{I} - I'_{01}) + 2p(1 - p)V(G, B, \bar{I})$$

$$+ (1 - \delta)p^2[V(G, G, I'_{01}) - V(G, G, I_0)] - (1 - \delta p^2)(I'_{01} - I_0). \tag{A10}$$

Since $(1 - \delta)p^2 V'(G, G, I_0) = (1 - \delta p^2)$, the sum of the last two terms of expression (A10) is negative. Moreover, for $2p \leq 1$, the rest of expression (A10) is smaller than expression (A9), which proves part (a).

For part (b), assume that expression (A8) is positive [which means that expression (A9) is also positive]. A big-bang strategy thus yields irreversibility with probability $1 - (1 - p)^2$. What about gradualism? At $t = 0$, foreign investors expect $\bar{I}$ to be reached at $t = 1$ if the first reform is a success. However, if it is a failure, reversal takes place without waiting for the result of the second reform, thus with probability $1 - p$. Irreversibility is thus less probable than under the big-bang approach. The incentive to invest at $t = 0$ under gradualism is

$$p[pdV(G, G, I) + (1 - p)\, dV(G, B, I)] - dI$$

since irreversibility is expected to occur with probability p. Instead, investing at $t = 1$ if the first reform is a success generates

$$\delta p[pdV(G, G, I) + (1 - p)\, dV(G, B, I) - dI]$$

as of time 0. Therefore, investment at $t = 0$ under gradualism is the same as I_0' defined in (A7) in the proof of proposition 7. It is thus less than I_{01}' and less than $\bar{I}$.

Notes

We thank Alberto Alesina, Olivier Blanchard, Patrick Bolton, Alex Cukierman, Brigitte Granville, Claus Kastberg, Pat Kehoe, John Litwack, Paul Milgrom, Torsten Persson, Gilles Saint-Paul, Guido Tabellini, Thierry Verdier, Ernst-Ludwig von Thadden, participants in the ESF Workshop on Political Economy in Sesimbra (Portugal) in June 1992, seminar participants at DELTA (Paris), Leuven, Brussels, the London School of Economics, Queen Mary College, IGIER (Milan), Stanford, Berkeley, and Harvard, and two anonymous referees for their comments and suggestions.

1. This rough classification into two camps should not hide the fact that transition involves multiple dimensions and that disagreements over the speed of reforms varies across reforms. For example, there is widespread agreement that macroeconomic stabilization should not be gradual. There is much less agreement on the speed of liberalization, privatization, and restructuring. Authors like Blanchard et al. (1991), Stanley Fischer and Alan Gelb (1991), and Janos Kornai (1990) emphasize the need for big-bang strategies along certain dimensions and the need for gradualism along other dimensions.

2. See, for example, Paul Hare and Tamas Revesz (1992) on Hungary and Qian and Chenggang Xu (1993) on China. Qian and Xu propose an interesting explanation of China's success compared to Eastern Europe.

3. As will become clearer in what follows, we rule out the case of a government less interested in reforms than in remaining in power.

4. In the political-science literature, Adam Przeworski (1991) distinguishes between the aggregate and distributional effects of transition, but with less emphasis on uncertainty.

5. For an exception, see Murrell (1992) who makes an evolutionary argument for gradualism based on the political philosophy of Edmund Burke, Karl Popper, and Michael Oakeshott. In particular, Murrell's argumentation on reversal costs is close to the one modeled in this chapter.

6. European unification is an example of such a gradualist approach.

7. Under a big-bang approach, s_{1k} and s_{2m} cannot necessarily be recovered from $O(s_{1k}, s_{2m})$, but this involves no real loss of relevant information.

8. Reversal costs may be different for the incumbent government and for the population. This could be an interesting topic for further research.

9. "Cycling" (going back and forth with the same reform) is wasteful in terms of reversal costs. Similarly, trying R_2 after having reversed R_1 is worse then trying R_2 *directly after* R_1: reforms should be tried only in the perspective of implementing them both, and reversing R_1 before trying R_2 means incurring ξ_1 unnecessarily.

10. In the absence of reversal costs, the desire to experiment with reform may accelerate its process, as stressed in a recent paper by Graziella Bertorchi and Michael Spagat (1993).

11. For example, if the second reform has a bad expected outcome and if H is nonnegative, then gradualism improves the expected outcome simply by delaying the second reform.

12. Of course, gradualism may be optimal if the distribution of O_{2m} depends on the realization of O_{1k}. Indeed, after realization of O_{1k}, R_2 will be implemented in period 2 only if
$$(1 - \delta)E_m(O_{2m}|O_{1k}) + \delta E \max\{\xi_2, (O_{2m}|O_{1k})\} \geq 0.$$

13. Note that politicians whose main motive is to remain in power may not want to pursue this strategy.

14. Still, for this it is necessary to have $\xi_i > (1 - \delta)[L + g_i + (pG + (1 - p)L)] + \delta(\xi_i + \xi_j)$, which is verified for δ close enough to 1 or for g_i not too high.

15. Under alternative institutional assumptions, one may have to target a powerful lobbing minority having veto power, and optimal sequencing may lead to a different order of reforms than in the case of majority rule.

16. See Roland (1991) for a ranking of specific transition measures in the spirit of propositions 3, 4, and 6, and Roland (1993) for an analysis of *perestroika* along these lines.

References

Aghion, Philippe and Blanchard, Olivier Jean. "On the Speed of Transition in Eastern Europe." Mimeo, Massachusetts Institute of Technology, 1993.

Aslund, Anders, "Principles of Privatization," in Laszlo Csaba, ed., *Systemic change and stabilization in Eastern Europe*. Dartmouth, U.K.: Aldershot, 1991, pp. 17−31.

Berg, Andrew and Sachs, Jeffrey, "Structural Adjustment and International Trade in Eastern Europe: The Case of Poland." *Economic Policy*, April 1992, (14), pp. 117−73.

Bertorchi, Graziella and Spagat, Michael. "Structural Uncertainty and Subsidy Removal for Economies in Transition." Mimeo, Brown University, 1993.

Blanchard, Olivier Jean; Dornbusch, Rudiger; Krugman, Paul; Layard, Richard and Summers, Lawrence. *Reform in Eastern Europe*. Cambridge, MA: MIT Press, 1991.

Boycko, Maxim. "When Higher Incomes Reduce Welfare: Queues, Labor Supply, and Macro Equilibrium in Socialist Economies." *Quarterly Journal of Economics*, August 1992, *107*(3), pp. 907−20.

Boycko, Maxim; Shiller, Robert and Korobov, Andrei. "Popular Attitudes Towards Free Markets: The Soviet Union and the United States Compared." *American Economic Review*, June 1991, *81*(3), p. 385−400.

―――. "Hunting for Homo Sovieticus: Situational versus Attitudinal Factors in Economic Behavior." *Brookings Papers on Economic Activity*, 1992, (1), pp. 127−81.

Burda, Michael. "Unemployment, Labour Markets and Structural Change in Eastern Europe." *Economic Policy*, April 1993, *8*(16), pp. 101–38.

Carlin, Wendy and Mayer, Colin. "Restructuring Enterprises in Eastern Europe." *Economic Policy*, October 1992, (15), pp. 311–52.

Dewatripont, Mathias and Roland, Gérard. "Economic Reform and Dynamic Political Constraints." *Review of Economic Studies*, October 1992a, *59*(4), pp. 703–30.

———. "The Virtues of Gradualism and Legitimacy in the Transition to a Market Economy." *Economic Journal*, March 1992b, *102*(411), pp. 291–300.

Dixit, Avinash and Pindyck, Robert. *Investment under uncertainty*. Princeton, NJ: Princeton University Press, 1994.

European Community Commission. "Employment Developments in Central and Eastern Europe." *Employment observatory: Central and Eastern Europe*, 1992, (1), pp. 1–14.

Fang, Xinghai. "Essays on the Processes of Economic Transition." Ph.D. dissertation, Stanford University, 1993.

Fernandez, Raquel and Rodrik, Dani. "Resistance to Reform: Status Quo Bias in the Presence of Individual-Specific Uncertainty." *American Economic Review*, December 1991, *81*(5), pp. 1146–55.

Fischer, Stanley and Gelb, Alan. "The Process of Socialist Economic Transformation." *Journal of Economic Perspectives*, Fall 1991, *5*(4), pp. 91–106.

Frydman, Roman and Rapaczynski, Andrzej. *Privatization in Eastern Europe: Is the state withering away?* London: Central European University Press, 1994.

Frydman, Roman; Rapaczynski, Andrzej and Earle, John S. *The privatization process in Central Europe*. London: Central European University Press, 1993.

Gates, Susan, Milgrom, Paul and Roberts, John. "Complementarities in the Transition from Socialism: A Firm-Level Analysis." Mimeo, Stanford University, 1993.

Gatsios, Konstantine. "Privatization in Hungary: Past, Present, and Future." Centre for Economic Policy Research (London) Discussion Paper No. 642, 1992.

Grosfled, Irena. "Prospects for Privatization in Poland." *European Economy*, March 1990, (43), pp. 149–59.

Hare, Paul and Revesz, Tamas. "Hungary's Transition to a Market Economy: The Case Against a 'Big-Bang.'" *Economic Policy*, April 1992, (14), pp. 227–64.

Kornai, Janos. *The road to a free economy*. New York: Norton, 1990.

Lipton, David and Sachs, Jeffrey. "Creating a Market Economy in Eastern Europe: The Case of Poland." *Brookings Papers on Economic Activity*, 1990, (1), pp. 75–133.

Litwack, John and Qian, Yingyi. "Economic Transition Strategies: Imperfect Fiscal Commitment Can Favor Unbalanced Investment." Mimeo, Stanford University, 1993.

McKinnon, Ronald. *The order of economic liberalization*. Baltimore, MD: Johns Hopkins University Press, 1991.

McMillan, John and Naughton, Barry. "How to Reform a Planned Economy: Lessons from China." *Oxford Review of Economic Policy*, Spring 1992, *8*(1), pp. 130–43.

Murrell, Peter. "Conservative Political Philosophy and the Strategy of Economic Transition." *East European Politics and Society*, Winter 1992, *6*(1), pp. 3–16.

Murphy, Kevin; Shleifer, Andrei and Vishny, Robert. "The Transition to a Market Economy: Pitfalls of Partial Reform." *Quarterly Journal of Economics*, August 1992, *107*(3), pp. 889–906.

Portes, Richard. "Introduction to Economic Transformation of Hungary and Poland." *European Economy*, March 1990, (43), pp. 11–18.

————. "The Path of Reform in Central and Eastern Europe: An Introduction." *European Economy*, 1991, Special Issue No. 2, pp. 3–15.

Przeworski, Adam. *Democracy and the market: Political and economic reforms in Eastern Europe and Latin America*. Cambridge: Cambridge University Press, 1991.

Qian, Yingyi and Xu, Chenggang. "Why China's Economic Reforms Differ: The M-Form Hierarchy and Entry/Expansion of the Non-State Sector." *Economics of Transition*, June 1993, *1*(2), pp. 135–70.

Roland, Gérard. "Political Economy of Sequencing Tactics in the Transition Period," in Laszlo Csaba, ed., *Systemic change and stabilization in Eastern Europe*. Dartmouth, U.K.: Aldershot, 1991, pp. 47–64.

————. "The Political Economy of Transition in the Soviet Union." *European Economy*, March 1993, (49), pp. 197–216.

Sachs, Jeffrey. *Poland's jump to the market economy*. Cambridge, MA: MIT Press, 1993.

Wei, Shang-Jin. "Gradualism versus Big Bang: Speed and Sustainability of Reforms." Mimeo, Harvard University, 1993.

Woo, Wing Thye. "The Art of Reforming Centrally Planned Economies: Comparing China, Poland and Russia." *Journal of Comparative Economics*, June 1994, *18*(3), pp. 276–308.

12

Gradualism versus Big Bang: Speed and Sustainability of Reforms

Shang-Jin Wei

"Yu su ze bu da" (More haste, less result).
—Lunyu, *The Analects of Confucius* (chapter on Zhi Lu)

12.1 Introduction

There is little debate on the need for centrally planned economies to be transformed into market-oriented ones. In contrast, countless debates have not resolved the issues of an optimal speed and sequence to bring about such changes. A big bang or shock therapy approach implements various reforms (on monetary policy, privatization, trade and exchange rates, and so on) quickly, in a concentrated time frame, whereas a gradualist approach spreads various reforms over an extended period.

At one level, the case for big bang is quite strong. Reforms in transition economies typically are widely perceived to be beneficial to the majority of the populace. This is demonstrated by the popular zeal in overthrowing old authoritarian regimes. If an opinion survey were conducted in those countries on whether they would like to turn their economies overnight into a Western European or North American style, an overwhelming majority would presumably express affirmation. On the other hand, actual reform programs are often delayed or derailed because of popular discontent with the programs. Theoretically speaking, it may not be surprising that a reform with few winners and many losers can be politically difficult to implement.[1] But the economic reform programs in formerly planned economies are presumed to benefit a majority. It may seem puzzling that

Originally published in *The Canadian Journal of Economics* 30, no. (4B) (1997): 1234–47. Reprinted with permission.

reforms with *many winners* and *few losers* are politically so difficult.[2] This chapter demonstrates that the political difficulty may partly be related to the speed with which a reform is implemented.

Several arguments have been proposed in support of a big bang approach to various types of reform. First, in the context of privatization, a big bang approach provides a critical scale of privatized sector in the economy so that the privatized firms will be efficient (Roland and Verdier 1994). Second, a big bang may increase the credibility of a reform (Lipton and Sachs 1990a,b). Third, the gradualist alternative gives time to reform opponents to organize themselves and thus invites a more formidable resistance (Krueger 1993). Fourth, in the context of price reforms, a gradual reform is undesirable because it may induce an intertemporal speculation (goods hoarding) (van Wijnbergen 1992). Fifth, if any reform program needs consensus approval, sequential plans may not work due to time inconsistency (Martinelli and Tommasi 1995). Finally, a big bang approach brings the benefits more quickly (World Bank 1991).

On the other hand, there are also supportive arguments for a gradualist approach to reform.[3] First, a gradualist approach may avoid excessive cost, especially for the government budget (Dewatripont and Roland 1992a,b; Nielsen 1993). Second, it avoids an excessive reduction in living standards at the start of a reform (Wang 1992). Third, it allows trial and error and midcourse adjustment (World Bank 1991). Fourth, it helps a government gain incremental credibility (Fang 1992).[4]

This chapter investigates the political economy of the choice of reform strategies. It points out another possibility that could make gradualism politically preferred to the big bang.[5] When the outcomes of reforms are uncertain to individuals, a gradual or sequential approach splits the resistance force, and can thus increase the programs' chance of surviving attacks by special interests groups.[6]

Let me make clear that I am not proposing gradualism to be the better approach in all circumstances. Rather, I simply point out one important implication of the different reform speeds that has to be taken into account in deliberating alternative reform strategies.

It is important to clarify the meaning of a gradualist approach since different people may well have different definitions in mind. I will define a gradualist approach to reform as a sequential implementation of minimum bangs.[7] A minimum bang is a simultaneous implementation of a minimum set of reforms that can be implemented independent of other reforms without failure. Conceptually, we can distinguish a gradualist from a piecemeal approach. The latter simply implements different parts of a reform package in many steps without regard to the possible "strong interdependence" among them.[8] In contrast, a gradualist approach assigns different parts of a reform program into groups. Within each group, there is strong interdependence. Across groups, there is no strong interdependence. Reforms within the same group are better implemented simultaneously. For the type of massive and fundamental changes that have to take place in the former centrally planned economies, there are likely many blocks of reforms. Within each block, there is "strong interdependence" so that a minimum bang is the best strategy. The appropriate context in which to place this chapter is that it is about the optimality of different strategies in implementing a set of blocks or minimum bangs.

It is also important to note at the outset that, even across a set of minimum bangs, a gradualist approach may not always be better than a big bang. In fact, as I will elaborate later, as long as a big bang is politically preferred to no reform, it is preferred to gradualism both in terms of political support as well as in terms of economic efficiency.

The basic message of the chapter is demonstrated in a model pioneered by Fernandez and Rodrik (1991) for a different purpose. They show that a reform that would benefit a majority ex post, can be blocked by another majority ex ante. The key to their result is that individuals do not know before a reform whether they will be winners or losers. Utilizing their framework, this chapter focuses on comparing different degrees of political difficulty for two implementation strategies of a given reform.

The next section offers an intuitive overview of the argument. Section 11.3 presents a formal model. Finally, section 11.4 concludes the chapter.

12.2   An Intuitive Argument

The central message of the chapter is that a "good" reform program may not be able to overcome political resistance if it is implemented by a big bang, but may become political viable if it is implemented by a gradualist approach.

Consider a small open economy with three sectors. There are altogether ten people in the economy, with four in an export sector x, three in an import-competing sector y, and the remaining three in another import-competing sector z. Both sectors y and z receive government tariff protection, so that their domestic prices are higher than the world market levels.

Suppose the objective of a reform program is to remove tariffs in the two import-competing sectors. I will make assumptions to ensure that the reform is "good" in the sense that it will benefit a majority of the population. Once the tariffs are gone, assume one person in each import-competing sector can successfully switch to sector x (after paying a small switching cost). The reform program will benefit unambiguously all four persons originally in the x sector, since the prices for goods y and z become lower. So they all approve the reform. The two persons who have switched from y and z sectors also benefit from the reform, so they approve the reform too. In all, there will be six people approving the reform. Therefore, as long as the reform gets implemented, it would not be overturned by a majority vote ex post.

We are interested in comparing two possible strategies to implement the reform. A *big bang* approach would remove the two tariffs at the same time. A *gradualist* approach would remove the two tariffs in two steps.

To simplify the story, suppose that everyone is identical ex ante. That is, no one knows whether he or she will gain or lose from the reform. Furthermore, for any individual, the gain from a successful transition to the x sector and the loss from staying in the import-competing sector after the tariff removal are close in magnitude.

Big-Bang Approach

The two tariffs are lifted at the same time.

Ex ante, everyone in the y and z sectors has a one in three chance to be a winner, but a two in three chance to be a loser. Therefore, all these people may (rationally) expect to be a loser. Consequently, they choose to vote against the reform. Thus, an excellent reform program, one that will benefit a majority (six persons) ex post, could be blocked by another majority (six persons) ex ante.[9]

Of course, if there exists a mechanism for the winners to compensate the losers after the reform, then any reform that enlarges the size of a pie will always be supported regardless of approaches. Typically, such compensation mechanism is not available and is thus ruled out here.[10]

A Gradual Approach

The reform is carried out in two stages. In the first stage, only the tariff on good z is lifted. In the second stage, the tariff on good y is lifted. Further-

more, the second reform will be put on the ballot in period two even if
the first reform fails politically.

The First Stage (removal of tariff on good z)
The prices of goods x and y are unchanged (tied down by the world
market), but the price of good z is lowered. Everyone in sectors x and y
benefits and thus supports this stage of the reform. Since people in these
two sectors already constitute a majority $(4 + 3 = 7$, or 70 percent of the
population), this stage of reform would be voted in regardless of the
opinion of the people in sector z. (Once the first part of the reform is implemented, the x sector will employ five workers, while the z sector will
employ two persons.)

The Second Stage Reform (removal of tariff on good y)
Now, everyone in sectors x and z benefits from a lower price on good y.
Since they constitute a majority of the population $(5 + 2 = 7)$, this stage
of reform will also be carried out regardless of the opinion of the people
in sector y. Hence, the gradualist approach helps the reform program to
proceed successfully.

The discussion is not complete if we do not ask the following question:
why do the people in sectors y and z not act collectively in period one to
block the entire reform program? In order for them to cooperate, people
in sector z in period one have to promise and convince people in sector y
that they will protect the interest of people y in the next period. But any
such promise is not time-consistent, and in the absence of a commitment
mechanism will not be easily trusted. Therefore, people in sectors y and z
are not likely to collude. Toward the end of the next section, three other
difficulties of cooperation will be discussed.

12.3   A Simple Model

Consider a three-sector perfectly competitive small open economy in
which each sector produces a distinct good, x, y, and z. The x sector is an
export sector whose output price is tied down by the world market and set
to be one. The y and z sectors are import-competing sectors that receive
separate government tariff protection. The tariff-inclusive prices are P_y
and P_z, respectively.

All the three sectors use labor as the only factor of production and have
constant-returns-to-scale technology. Thus, using M_j to denote output in

sector j,

$$M_j = \frac{L_j}{a_j}$$

and, using L to denote the size of the total labor force,

$$L_x + L_y + L_z = L,$$

where $a_j > 0$, $j = x, y, z$. For notational simplicity, we set $a_x = 1$.

Labor's initial distribution among the sectors, (L_x^0, L_y^0, L_z^0), is given by history. Perfect competition in the labor market ensures that

$$w_j = \frac{P_j}{a_j} \qquad j = x, y, z.$$

Assume that the tariffs are such that the initial prices of the goods are $P_y^0 = a_y$, and $P_z^0 = a_z$. Therefore, the initial wages in the three sectors are $w_x^0 = w_y^0 = w_z^0 = 1$.

It is costly to relocate labor between the sectors. Let c_{jki} denote the individual-specific cost for person i to switch from j-sector to k-sector, where j, $k = x$, y, z. The individual-specific cost c_{jki} is revealed when and only when the reform starts.[11] However, the probability density function, $f_{jk}(c)$, for c_{jki} is known to everyone before the reform. For simplicity, we assume $c_{jki} = c_i$. That is, for a given individual i, the cost is the same regardless of the origin and destination of a switch.

The ultimate objective of the reform program in this economy is to remove the tariffs in the two import-competing sectors. After the reform, the wages in the y and z sectors fall necessarily as the prices of goods y and z fall. The reform program (reduction of the two tariffs) can be implemented in two ways: either by a big bang or by gradualism. To meaningfully compare the two approaches, we use the minimalist setup: a two-period framework. A big bang approach removes simultaneously the two tariffs in period one, while a gradualist approach removes them in two steps (removing the tariff on good z in period one, and then the tariff on good y in period two).

Suppose the initial labor allocation is such that the sum of workers in any two sectors is greater than in the third one, that is,

$$L_j^0 < \frac{1}{2} L \equiv \frac{1}{2}(L_x^0 + L_y^0 + L_z^0),$$

where $j = x, y, z$. These can be satisfied if, for example, each sector employs one-third of the population.

Suppose individuals' preferences (indirect utility functions) are identical, risk-neutral, and given by

$$U(P_1, I_1) + \beta U(P_2, I_2),$$

where

$$U(P, I) = V(P_y, P_z)I = \frac{I}{P_y^\delta P_z^\tau}.$$

I is the individual's income level, β is her subjective discount factor, $0 < \delta$, $\tau < 1$, and $\delta + \tau < 1$.

Ex Post Situation

For simplicity, we assume that, immediately after the reform, the values of the individual-specific sector-switching cost are revealed, regardless of whether they switch in the first or second period.[12] An individual i will not regret the reform if one of the three conditions are met:

$$(1 + \beta)V(P_y'', P_z'')w_y'' > (1 + \beta)V(P_y^0, P_z^0)w_y^0$$

or

$$V(P_y'', P_z'')[w_y'' + \beta w_x'' - c_i] > (1 + \beta)V(P_y^0, P_z^0)w_y^0$$

or

$$V(P_y'', P_z'')[(1 + \beta)w_x'' - c_i] > (1 + \beta)V(P_y^0, P_z^0)w_y^0. \tag{1}$$

The right-hand side of all three inequalities is the lifetime utility for an individual in sector y without the reform. The left-hand side of the first inequality is the postreform lifetime utility by staying in sector y. The first inequality corresponds to the case in which everyone in sector y unambiguously gains from the reform because of the lower prices. In this case, the reform will be carried out regardless of the implementation strategy. To make the discussions more interesting, from now on we will focus on cases when this is not true.

The left-hand sides of the second and the third inequalities are the postreform utility when individual i switches to sector x at $t = 2$ and $t = 1$, respectively. Comparing the two strategies of switching, it is clear that she will never switch at $t = 2$, since that is dominated by the strategy of switching at $t = 1$. To summarize, an individual i in sector y will approve the reform if and only if the inequality 1 is satisfied.

An analogous inequality describes the condition for an individual j in sector z to support the reform ex post.

Big Bang Reform

With a big bang approach to the reform, everyone knows that the price vector will be (P_y'', P_z'') in both periods. Consider individual i in sector y. This individual can stay in sector y or switch to another sector. She has eight ways of switching sectors including (a) switching to sector z at $t = 1$ and staying there at $t = 2$, (b) staying in sector y at $t = 1$ and switching to sector z at $t = 2$, (c) switching to sector x at $t = 1$ and staying there at $t = 2$, (d) staying in sector y at $t = 1$ and switching to sector x at $t = 2$, and (e) various detours at $t = 1$ before switching to sectors x, y, and z at $t = 2$.

We note first, that if the individual ever switches, she would only switch to sector x, since P_x'' is strictly greater than both P_y'' and P_z'', and the switching costs are the same across the sectors. Second, for the same reason, if she ever switches, she would switch at $t = 1$ without delay. Therefore, her options now narrow down to two: either staying in sector y for both periods, or incurring a cost c_i, switching to sector x at $t = 1$, and staying there at $t = 2$.

She would take the second option if and only if her utility of doing so is greater than that under the first option. That is, she switches to sector x if

$$(1 + \beta)W_x'' - c_i > (1 + \beta)w_y''$$

or

$$c_i < c_{y^*} \equiv (1 + \beta)(w_x'' - w_y'').$$

Similarly, an individual j in sector z will switch to sector x if and only if her switching cost $c_j < c_z^*$, with c_z^* analogously defined.

Ex ante, people in sector y would vote against the big bang reform, if the expected utility after the reform is lower than the utility under the status quo. That is, the reform is not supported if

$$V(P_y'', P_z'')\left\{ F(c_{y^*})\left[w_x'' - \int_{c_L}^{c_{y^*}} \frac{cf(c)}{F(c_{y^*})}dc \right] + [1 - F(c_{y^*})]w_y'' \right\}$$

$$+ \beta V(P_y'', P_z'')\{F(c_{y^*})w_x'' + [1 - F(c_{y^*})]w_y''\} < (1 + \beta)V(P_y^0, P_z^0)w_y^0, \qquad (2)$$

where $F(\cdot)$ is the (unconditional) cumulative distribution function for the sector-switching cost.

We now want to demonstrate that there exist cases in which a reform that would be supported by a majority ex post will be blocked by another majority ex ante, if it is implemented by the big bang approach. That is, we will find cases in which both inequalities (1) and (2) are satisfied simultaneously.

By the definition of c_y^*,

$$w_y'' = w_x'' - \frac{c_{y^*}}{1 + \beta}.$$

Hence,

$$P_y'' = a_y \left(w_x'' - \frac{c_{y^*}}{1 + \beta} \right) = P_y^0 \left(1 - \frac{c_{y^*}}{1 + \beta} \right).$$

Similarly,

$$P_z'' = a_z \left(w_x'' - \frac{c_{z^*}}{1 + \beta} \right) = P_z^0 \left(1 - \frac{c_{z^*}}{1 + \beta} \right)$$

Inequality (1) (ex post approval by a majority) becomes

$$c_i < (1 + \beta) - (1 + \beta) \left(1 - \frac{c_{y^*}}{1 + \beta} \right)^\delta \left(1 - \frac{c_{z^*}}{1 + \beta} \right)^\tau,$$

and inequality (2) (ex ante opposition to the big bang by a majority) becomes

$$(1 + \beta)\{F(c_{y^*}) + [1 - F(c_{y^*})]w_y''\} - \int_{c_L}^{c_{y^*}} cf(c)\, dc$$

$$< (1 + \beta) \left(1 - \frac{c_{y^*}}{1 + \beta} \right)^\delta \left(1 - \frac{c_{z^*}}{1 + \beta} \right)^\tau.$$

As an example, let us assume, following an example in Fernandez and Rodrik (1991), that c_i follows a uniform distribution on $[0, c^u]$. Hence, the density function $f(c) = 1/c^u$, and $F(c^*) = c^*/c^u$. There are many sets of parameter values such that both inequalities (1) and (2) are satisfied simultaneously. $\beta = 0.9$, $\delta = \tau = 0.3$, $a_y = a_z = c^u = 1$, and $P_y''/P_y^0 = P_z''/P_z^0 = 0.8$ is one such example.

Gradualist Approach to Reform

We first make explicit one assumption in our following discussion. The government will put the second reform on the ballot regardless of whether the first one passes the ballot. With a gradualist approach, the price vector will be (P_y^0, P_z'') for $t = 1$ and (P_y'', P_z'') for $t = 2$, respectively. As before, whenever individual i in sector y wants to switch sectors, she would only want to switch to sector x and to do so at $t = 1$. Therefore, she would switch to sector x if and only if

$$V(P_y^0, P_z'')(w_x'' - c_i) + \beta V(P_y'', P_z'')w_x'' > V(P_y^0, P_z'')w_y^0 + \beta V(P_y'', P_z'')w_y''$$

or

$$c_i < c^{**} \equiv \beta(w_x'' - w_y'')\frac{V(P_y'', P_z'')}{V(P_y^0, P_z'')}.$$

A subscript y is omitted in c^{**} since the discussion here is focused on individuals in sector y only. For a later discussion, we will also need to know individual i's decision rule on sector switching when the tariff on good y is lifted in the second period but the tariff on good z is never removed. That is, the price vector evolves as (P_y^0, P_z^0) at $t = 1$ and (P_y'', P_z^0) at $t = 2$. Again, individual i would only switch to sector x at $t = 1$ if she ever wants to switch at all. She would switch to sector x if and only if

$$V(P_y^0, P_z^0)(w_x'' - c_i) + \beta V(P_y'', P_z^0)w_x'' > V(P_y^0, P_z^0)w_y^0 + \beta V(P_y'', P_z^0)w_y''$$

or

$$c_i < c^{\#} \equiv \beta(w_x'' - w_y'')\frac{V(P_y'', P_z^0)}{V(P_y^0, P_z^0)}.$$

Since

$$\frac{V(P_y'', P_z'')}{V(P_y^0, P_z'')} = \left(\frac{P_y^0}{P_y''}\right)^{\delta} = \frac{V(P_y'', P_z^0)}{V(P_y^0, P_z^0)},$$

we have

$$c^{\#} = c^{**}.$$

To see how the gradualist approach works, let us start from $t = 2$. At the beginning of this period, people will be asked about their opinion on the elimination of a tariff on good y. As before, everyone in sector x will be in favor of the tariff reform. It is important to note that people in sector z will also be in favor of it, since a lower price on good y unambiguously increases the utility of people in sector z.

Can people in sectors y and z act collectively to oppose the tariff reform on either goods y or z? The answer is negative for an important reason.

Even if sector-z people promise to oppose a removal of tariff on good y in the second period in exchange for sector-y people's similar action in the first period, such a promise is not time-consistent. In other words, regardless of what people in sector y have done at $t = 1$, it is always ex post optimal for people in sector z to support the removal of tariff on good y in the second period. Furthermore, each sector in a real economy is likely to have a large number of people, so that any such promise will be difficult to enforce. Consequently, any such promise by people in sector z will not be believed by people in sector y.

Now let us consider $t = 1$ when people are asked about their opinions on removing the tariff on good z. For an individual i in sector y, her lifetime utility when the tariff on z is removed, would be

$$V(P_y^0, P_z'') \left\{ F(c^{**}) \left[w_x'' - \int_{c_L}^{c^{**}} \frac{cf(c)}{F(c^{**})} dc \right] + [1 - F(c^{**})] w_y'' \right\}$$

$$+ \beta V(P_y'', P_z'') \{ F(c^{**}) w_x'' + [1 - F(c^{**})] w_y'' \}.$$

Her utility when the tariff on good z is not removed will be

$$V(P_y^0, P_z^0) \left\{ F(c^{\#}) \left[w_x'' - \int_{c_L}^{c^{\#}} \frac{cf(c)}{F(c^{\#})} dc \right] + [1 - F(c^{\#})] w_y'' \right\}$$

$$+ \beta V(P_y'', P_z^0) \{ F(c^{\#}) w_x'' + [1 - F(c^{\#})] w_y'' \}.$$

The last two expressions have taken into account the fact the price of good y will be P_y'' at $t = 2$. Since $V(P_y^0, P_z'') > V(P_y^0, P_z^0)$, $V(P_y'', P_z'') > V(P_y'', P_z^0)$, and $c^{\#} = c^{**}$, everyone in sector y will always prefer to remove the tariff on good z at $t = 1$.

Therefore, the two-stage reform will always have majority support in each stage.

Robustness to the Two-Period Assumption

Does the result depend on the two-period framework? Technically, the two-period assumption is important only because it permits us to do backward inductions. The same type of backward inductions can be carried out in a multiple-period model with known terminal date. Such an extension will one change the result.

In principle, in an infinite horizon environment (or a finite model with uncertain terminal date), there exists the possibility of collusion by people in sectors y and z to block collectively the reform. However, three reasons may make the collusion more difficult. First, most governments probably do not offer the same set of programs time and again in the future. Second, a real economy is not that of ten people, as in our example in the previous section, but that of one million people or more. Consequently, the numbers of people in the real-life equivalent of sectors y and z are large. Collusion involving a huge number of people is difficult.[13]

Third, we could introduce uncertainty about the government stability, either because the same government may change its mind or a different government may be in power in future. If people place a positive probability on the event that the next-stage reform may not be carried out, then it works the same way as lowering people's subjective discount factor. This will also make collusion more difficult since a high discount factor is required for collusion to occur in an infinite horizon model.

The Virtues of a Big Bang Approach

For a completion of our argument, we now point out that, even in the context of this model, a big bang approach, or simultaneous implementation of many minimum bangs, can be preferred to a gradualist approach under a range of circumstances.

First, whenever both big bang and gradualism are politically feasible (i.e., either in the absence of a status quo bias in a democratic setting or in a benevolent dictator setting), the big bang is economically more efficient, because it brings the benefits more quickly.[14]

Second, whenever status quo bias can be overcome (i.e, big bang is preferred to no reform), the big bang is in fact politically preferred to alternative reform strategies. By being "politically preferred," I mean that if the big bang is compared in a pairwise way with any of the following, it will win majority support: (a) gradualism A (reforming y at $t = 1$ and reforming z at $t = 2$); (b) gradualism B (reforming z at $t = 1$ and reforming y at $t = 2$); (c) partial reform A (reforming sector y only); (d) partial reform B (reforming sector z only).

To see why the big bang is preferred to the alternatives, we note first that the most preferred reform by everyone in sector x is the big bang. In comparing gradualism A (reforming y first and z next) with the big bang, people in sector y also prefer a big bang to delaying the benefit of removing a tariff on z. Therefore, a majority (people in sectors x plus y) would support the big bang. Similar reasoning applies to other pairwise comparisons.

12.4   Concluding Remarks

One important feature of reforms is that, ex ante, people are not sure whether they are necessarily gainers or losers. This chapter argues that, in the presence of this uncertainty, a gradualist approach may be politically more sustainable than a big bang strategy, because it splits the resistance force and allows an uninterrupted political support for the reform.

On the other hand, if the popular support for the reform program is strong at the start, then a big bang approach is better both because it brings the benefits faster, and because it is politically preferred to various schemes of partial or gradual reforms.

One important question that this chapter does not address is: when gradualism is the better strategy (relative to a big bang), what determines an optimal sequencing? There are serious works on the subject,[15] but how political constraints might alter the optimal sequence has not been explicitly considered. Such will be an important extension to this chapter.

Notes

I would like to thank Michael Barnes, Barry Eichengreen, Raquel Fernandez, Jeff Frankel, Roger Gordon, Joe Kalt, Peng Lian, Yingyi Qian, Bruce Reynolds, Dani Rodrik, Ken Rogoff, Gerald Roland, Mariano Tommasi, seminar participants at NBER, Harvard, UC Santa Cruz, and CES-ASSA joint session, and especially Claus Nielsen, Guofu Tan and three anonymous referees for helpful comments, Greg Dorchak and Esther Drill for able editorial assistance and Harvard University's William F. Milton Fund for financial support.

1. See, for example, Buchanan and Tullock (1962).

2. Fernandez and Rodrik (1991) provided an argument upon which this chapter builds.

3. The earliest statement that I can find in favor of a gradualist approach is what Confucius said about twenty-five centuries ago in *Lunyu*, which is cited at the beginning of the chapter.

4. The experience of Chinese reform during the 1980s is often interpreted as evidence supporting the superiority of a gradualist approach. For studies of Chinese reform, see Harrold (1992), Jefferson, Chen, and Singh (1992), Lin (1992), McMillan and Naughton (1992), Perkins (1992), Yusuf (1993), and Zou (1992). For a dissenting view on the implication of Chinese experience, see Sachs and Woo (1994).

5. Dewatripont and Roland (1992a,b) also argue that, under the political constraint that a program needs a majority or unanimous support, a gradualist approach imposes less pressure on resource/government budget than a big bang. They do not discuss, however, whether one approach may be politically more sustainable than the other, which is the central focus of this chapter. In terms of the structure of the models, they assume asymmetric information between the government and workers with respect to workers' ability. In contrast, this chapter assumes individual uncertainty on transition costs, but the government and workers have the same ex ante information. Wyplosz (1993) points out that there is a distinction between economic efficiency and political acceptability. See Tommasi and Velasco (1996) for an updated survey of relevant papers including this chapter.

6. In a descriptive article, Rodrik (1990) emphasizes the importance of a sustainable policy environment for an eventual success of structural adjustment programs. In a separate review article, Rodrik (1993) forcefully concludes that an explicit understanding of political economy forces in a reform process is as important as the content of the reform package itself for its success.

7. This terminology is from Williamson (1991).

8. For an exposition of some pitfalls of a piecemeal approach (partial reform), see Murphy, Shleifer, and Vishny (1992).

9. This is the insight of Fernandez and Rodrik (1991). As they point out in that article, it is just as easy to construct examples in which a bad program, one that will be opposed by a majority ex post, will be approved by a majority ex ante. Such program will be reversed once the uncertainty is resolved.

10. One reason that a compensation mechanism is not available is because it is not time-consistent. That is, the realized winners of a reform will not want to compensate the losers after the reform. If winners constitute a majority, as is presumed for an economic transition program, an ex ante promise would not be credible.

11. This is a simplification from the setup of Fernandez and Rodrik (1991) in which individuals have to take a general investment before learning their sector-switching cost.

12. The possibility of delaying the sector-switching cost by switching in period two would bring in more cases to discuss without altering the basic message of the chapter.

13. In a matured democracy, the existence of well-organized lobby groups partially solves the problem, since coordination among a small number of lobby groups, political parties, or parliament members is easier than among numerous individuals. In a transition economy where composition of a parliament, political parties, or organized interest groups are all in infancy and typically unstable, coordination is likely to be harder.

14. As a counterexample, Lian and Wei (1997) constructed a multisector model in which a big bang reform can sometimes be dominated by a gradual one even on the efficiency ground.

15. See Edwards (1990) and McKinnon (1991).

References

Buchanan, James M., and Gordon Tullock. 1962. *The Calculus of Consent: Logical Foundations of Constitutional Democracy*. Ann Arbor: University of Michigan Press.

Coricelli, Fabrizio, and Gian Maria Milesi-Ferretti. 1993. "On the Credibility of Big Bang Programs: A Note on Wage Claims and Soft Budget Constraints in Economies in Transition." *European Economic Review* 37(2–3): 387–395.

Dewatripont, M., and G. Roland. 1992a. "The Virtues of Gradualism and Legitimacy in the Transition to a Market Economy." *The Economic Journal* 102: 291–300.

———. 1992b. "Economic Reform and Dynamic Political Constraints." Working paper, April. Forthcoming in *Review of Economic Studies*.

Edwards, Sebastian. 1990. "The Sequencing of Economic Reform: Analytical Issues and Lessons from Latin American Experience." *The World Economy* 13: 1–14.

Falvey, Rod, and Cha Dong Kim. 1992. "Timing and Sequencing Issues in Trade Liberalization." *The Economic Journal* 102: 908–924.

Fang, Xinghai. 1992. "Economic Transition: Government Commitment and Gradualism." Working paper, Stanford University.

Fernandez, Raquel, and Dani Rodrik. 1991. "Resistance to Reform: Status Quo Bias in the Presence of Individual-Specific Uncertainty." *American Economic Review* 85(5) (December): 1146–1155.

Harrold, Peter, 1992. "China's Reform Experience to Date." World Bank Discussion Papers, China and Mongolia Department, No. 180.

Havrylyshyn, Oleh, and John Williamson. 1991. *From Soviet disUnion to Eastern Economic Community?* Policy Analysis in International Economics 35. Washington, DC: Institute for International Economics, October.

Jefferson, Gary H., Kang Chen, and I. J. Singh. 1992. "Lessons from China's Economic Reform." *Journal of Comparative Economics* 16(2): 201–225.

Krueger, Anne O. 1993. *Political Economy of Policy Reform in Developing Countries*. Cambridge: MIT Press.

Lian, Peng, and Shang-Jin Wei. 1997. "To Shock or Not to Shock? Economics and Political Economy of Large-Scale Reforms." Forthcoming in *Economics and Politics*.

Lin, Justin Yifu. 1992. "Rural Reforms and Agricultural Growth in China." *American Economic Review* 82(1): 34–51.

Lipton, D., and J. Sachs. 1990a. "Creating a Market Economy in Eastern Europe: The Case of Poland." *Brookings Papers on Economic Activity* 1: 75–147.

———. 1990b. "Privatization in Eastern Europe: The Case of Poland." *Brookings Papers on Economic Activity* 2: 293–341.

Martinelli, Cesar, and Mariano Tommasi. 1995. "Economic Reforms and Political Constraints: On the Time Inconsistency of Gradual Sequencing." Unpublished manuscript, Universidad Carlos III de Madrid and UCLA.

McKinnon, Ronald I. 1991. *The Order of Economic Liberalization: Financial Control in the Transition to a Market Economy*. Baltimore: The Johns Hopkins University Press.

McMillan, John, and Barry Naughton. 1992. "How to Reform a Planned Economy: Lessons From China." *Oxford Review of Economic Policy* 8(1): 130–143.

Murphy, Kevin M., Andrei Shleifer, and R. W. Vishny. 1992. "The Transition to a Market Economy: Pitfalls of Partial Reforms." *Quarterly Journal of Economics* 57(3): 889–906.

Nielsen, Claus K. 1993. "Multi-stage versus Single-stage Reform: Normative Strategies for Reducing Status-quo Bias in Trade Reform." Working paper, Aarhus University.

Perkins, Dwight H. 1992. "China's 'Gradual' Approach to Market Reforms." Working paper, Harvard Institute for International Development.

Rodrik, Dani. 1990. "How Should Structural Adjustment Programs Be Designed?" *World Development* 18(7): 933–947.

———. 1993. "The Positive Economics of Policy Reform." *American Economic Review* 83(2): 356–361.

Roland, Gérard, and Thierry Verdier. 1994. "Privatization in Eastern Europe: Irreversibility and Critical Mass Effects." *Journal of Public Economics* 54(2): 161–183.

Sachs, J., and Wing Woo. 1994. "Structural Factors in the Economic Reforms of China, Eastern Europe and the Israel Soviet Union." *Economic Policy* (April): 102–145.

Tommasi, Mariano, and Andres Velasco. 1996. "Where Are We in the Political Economy of Reform?" *Journal of Policy Reform* 1: 187–238.

van Wijnbergen, S. 1992. "Intertemporal Speculation, Shortages and the Political Economy of Price Reform." *Economic Journal* 102(415): 1395–1406.

Wang, Yijiang. 1992 "East European Puzzle and Chinese Enigma: Institutional Change as a Resource Allocation Problem." Working Paper, University of Minnesota. Paper presented at a CES-ASSA joint session in Anaheim, CA, January, 1993.

Williamson, John. 1991. Chap. in *International Financial Policy: Essays in Honor of J. J. Polak*, ed. Jacob A. Frenkel and Morris Goldstein. Washington, DC: International Monetary Fund.

World Bank. 1991. *World Development Report 1991: The Challenge of Development*. New York: Oxford University Press.

————. 1992. *Russian Economic Reform: Crossing the Threshold of Structural Change*. New York: World Bank.

Wyplosz, Charles. 1993. "After the Honeymoon: On the Economics and the Politics of Economic Transformation." *European Economic Review* 37(2–3): 379–386.

Yusuf, Shahid. 1993. "The Rise of China's Nonstate Sector." Working paper, The World Bank.

Zou, Gang. 1992. "Enterprise Behavior Under the Two-Tier Plan/Market System." Working paper, University of Southern California.

13

Sequencing of Economic Reforms in the Presence of Political Constraints

César Martinelli and
Mariano Tommasi

13.1 Introduction

Several economists[1] have argued for sequencing market-oriented reforms, such as macroeconomic stabilization and trade liberalization, in a particular order. Several countries, mostly in Latin America, have apparently ignored this advice and implemented all types of reform simultaneously. As a result, these countries have endured high unemployment as well as balance-of-payment problems.[2]

An explanation for the apparent failure to follow the prevailing economic advice could be that policymakers doubted its accuracy and therefore felt little obligation to follow it. In this chapter we explore an alternative explanation: policymakers may have faced political constraints that made big bang reforms the best (and in some cases the only) *feasible* strategy.[3]

The argument is based on the distributive consequences of reform. By widening the scope of efficiency-improving reforms, the government is more likely to gain the support of larger segments of the population if the losers of each particular measure benefit from other measures. If the government needs to pass a threshold of popular support at each step, a gradual process risks being stopped at each stage by the group being hurt at that point. Hence, the government may need to implement all reforms simultaneously even if this entails some aggregate costs. That is, the gradual introduction of reforms in some specific order can be time-inconsistent even if it is optimal from an economic point of view. Notice that we assume that there is an economic case for gradual sequencing. This is far from obvious, although it has been part of the conventional wisdom in policy circles in Latin America for some time. The reader who is skeptical about the economic case for gradualism should read our

Originally published in *Economics and Politics* 9, no. 2 (1997): 115–131. Reprinted with permission.

chapter as a further argument for comprehensiveness of reform, on top of economic ones like those in Mussa (1982).

Our chapter provides a counterpoint to recent contributions that have argued for sequencing reforms on the basis of other assumed payoff structures and rules of the political game. Moreover, our chapter also undermines some of the economic arguments for gradualism that rely on lack of credibility, which in turn must be a consequence of political infeasibility (see, e.g., Calvo 1989). In other words, if the political constraints are overcome by means of big bang reform, a part of the economic case for gradualism may disappear as well. We discuss this literature in section 13.2.

We develop the argument in section 13.3, using a simple game-theoretic model. The model portrays a country in a political deadlock about reform proposals that hurt strongly organized interest groups. The government is represented as an agenda setter interested in carrying out economic reforms. Under democratic conditions, and without precommitment, only far-reaching reforms, even if quite costly, have hope for success. The more general message is that, once we incorporate political sustainability restrictions into the analysis, the optimal course of action for a government interested in reform may be different from the one we would infer from an unconstrained economic perspective.

In section 13.4 we illustrate the argument with an economic example, which has the following characteristics. Public-sector restructuring results in a large number of workers looking for new jobs. Simultaneous trade liberalization calls for further reallocation of resources, thus leading to more unemployment. The resulting rate of unemployment is excessively high due to congestion externalities in labor markets. This suggests a gradual sequencing of economic reforms. We identify political-economic constraints that preclude an agenda-setting government from following such a path, rendering a big bang as the best feasible strategy. Section 13.5 offers concluding remarks.

13.2   An Overview of Related Literature

13.2.1   Economic Literature on Sequencing of Reforms

It is instructive to review briefly the arguments in favor of gradualism given by economists advising reforming countries. The early literature on timing and sequencing of economic reforms was spurred by the experience of the Southern Cone of Latin America in the late 1970s and early 1980s. The attempted liberalizations under military rule in Chile, Argentina, and

Uruguay led to a series of bank panics and financial collapses. These difficulties were soon interpreted as due to mistakes in the order of liberalization (Díaz Alejandro 1985; Corbo and De Melo 1985; Edwards and Cox-Edwards 1991.) the need to balance the central government finances before undertaking other reforms was commonly emphasized. The debate centered on the order of liberalization of the trade and capital accounts, with the majority of authors favoring the opening of the former before the liberalization of the latter in order to avoid undesirable capital flows (see, e.g., McKinnon 1991). Most of the early literature was informal; the emphasis was in giving policy advice to avoid the difficulties that plagued efforts at economic reform in Latin America. Edwards (1992b) summarizes these views.

Subsequent research has been more precise in making statements about welfare gains or losses associated with different sequences. It is important to make the distinction between economic reform and economic restructuring. In economies that have been highly distorted, economic restructuring is bound to take a long time, even if economic reform (a collection of policy decisions) occurs all of a sudden. The question here is whether transition costs are minimized by a particular policy sequence. Clearly, under frictionless competitive equilibrium assumptions, welfare maximization is obtained by removing all distortions simultaneously. As long as the perceived private costs and benefits correspond to the true social costs and benefits, private economic agents will choose the socially correct pace of adjustment following a full-scale liberalization. "Radical reform" is the first-best reform strategy, argued Mussa (1982) early on in the debate. Hence, arguments for gradualism must rely on the presence of distortions during the adjustment process.

One possibility is the presence of preexisting distortions in one or several markets that cannot be removed at the time the reform plan is announced. Potential candidates are labor-market interventions, domestic capital-market imperfections, and limits to foreign indebtedness that are not perceived as binding by individual agents (see, for instance, Edwards and van Wijnberger 1986, Edwards 1992a,b). In all of these cases, one can imagine circumstances in which the second-best reform strategy will involve some degree of gradualism for instance in the sequencing of trade and capital account opening.

A related argument by Calvo (1989) emphasizes the equivalence of imperfect credibility to an intertemporal distorsion. If the public wrongly believes that a trade liberalization will be reverted in the future, quantitative control of the capital account may be called for. The problem with this type of argument is that it assumes the credibility problem arises because the government "knows better" than the public what is going to happen in the future. A closer look at the source of the credibility problem is necessary to assess the right policy response. For instance, if imperfect credibility arises because the public is unsure about the "true preferences" of the government, overshooting can act as a signaling device (Rodrik 1989). Or, as argued in the next section, if credibility problems are related to political sustainability of the reforms, a big bang can be the only way of cutting through the Gordian knot of implicit rents generated by government interventions.

Other authors such as Murrell (1992) argue in favor of gradualism on the basis of an evolutionary approach: rapid reforms that disrupt existing relationships also destroy existing information stocks. Murrell also emphasizes the benefits of flexibility when undertaking policy measures under imperfect information. (A similar argument is presented in Dewatripont and Roland (1995), which we discuss below.)

More recently, Gavin (1993) has focused on inefficiences inherent to the adjustment process itself. The private-sector response to reform may be suboptimal (too fast) if there is a congestion externality due to limited capacity of absorption in the labor market. A related problem is the lack of an adequate safety net to buffer the effects of massive labor displacement during the process of economic transformation. Latin American and Eastern European countries have had fragmentary and rudimentary systems for income maintenance and welfare delivery (Przeworski 1991). Our example in section 13.4 introduces a congestion externality of this type to make gradualism optimal from the point of view of economic efficiency.

13.2.2   The Political-Economic Literature

It is instructive to compare our results with other papers in the literature, which have argued for sequencing of reforms on the basis of other assumed payoff structures and rules of the game.

Dewatripont and Roland (1992a,b) discuss the merits of gradualism versus fast reform in the context of a model of industrial restructuring in which a reform-minded government faces a sector requiring massive layoffs. In the case they present, fast reform may be too costly because it entails paying the same exit bonuses to all laid-off workers, even though they have different (privately known) outside opportunities. As a solution, the government may be able to use agenda-setting powers to pass a gradual series of measures that, if proposed as a package, would be rejected by workers because it would give them a negative expected payoff.

Wei (1993) advances a related argument in favor of the gradual sequencing of reforms, based on an insight originally posited by Fernandez and Rodrik (1991). Wei explains that, due to individual uncertainty about the distribution of gains and losses from the reform, an economically efficient reform may not obtain the approval of the majority ex ante even if it could do so ex post. If this is the case with the full set of economic reforms, then the reforms can be achieved if one designs a sequence of specific measures, each of which enjoys a majority of support ex ante.

Dewatripont and Roland (1995) offer a different argument in favor of sequencing reforms based on aggregate uncertainty about the outcomes of reforms. If reversing the reform process is costly, the authors note, gradualism makes reforms easier to initiate because it keeps open the possibility of early reversal. Furthermore, strong economic complementarity can help ingrain the (gradual) reform process once it has begun. If initial reforms prove successful, but cannot be sustained without some others that are less popular, in the next stage people will be confronted with a choice between costly reversal or acceptance of further reforms. Correct sequencing thus can strengthen popular support for reform.

In terms of the underlying *payoff structure*, we deviate from these contributions by assuming that (1) the reform package as a whole has a positive net outcome for the relevant political players, although some specific reforms have a negative effect on some of these politically organized groups, and (2) this is known to the actors. On the one hand, it is hard to believe that market-oriented economic reform as a whole could have a negative expected outcome. On the other, individual and aggregate uncertainties about the outcomes of reform are probably more problematic in transitions from former communist to market economies than in economic reforms in developing countries that have had a long experience with the market. Both Wei (1993) and Dewatripont and Roland (1995) focus on the process of transition to the market, while we focus on the process of reform in developing economies.[4] Also, one could add uncertainty to our model, without necessarily altering the main conclusions.

Another major difference between the approach of Dewatripont and Roland (1995) and ours is that we assume that economic complementarity of reforms is not strong enough to deter interest groups from attempting to halt the process midway. Strong complementarities are more plausible when the basis of a market economy are completely absent, which is the case for former communist economies but not for developing economies.

For instance, the assets of firms to be privatized cannot be properly valued if prices are not freed. On the other hand, it is likely that macroeconomic stabilization or public sector reform can be carried out successfully even in the absence of trade liberalization.[5]

In terms of the *political game*, while previous contributions assume majority rule, we assume that policy decisions are subject to the veto power of politically organized groups.[6] The choice of veto power over majority rule is motivated by the structure of political decision making in many developing countries, particularly in Latin America, where a broad consensus is needed for any reform involving substantial gains and losses for different groups (see, e.g., the conclusions of Burgess and Stern (1993)). In many of these countries dissatisfaction among certain groups is enough to bring down the government (Ames 1987). Our results are consistent with majority rule if the benefits of each particular reform are concentrated and the costs are diffuse. However, we believe that in many cases reform is precisely about *suppressing* distortions that benefit a minority at the expense of the majority.

Under our assumptions, simultaneous introduction of reforms permits the government to overcome potential veto threats because losses due to one specific measure are compensated by other reforms such that all politically organized groups are net beneficiaries of the package. In contrast, if the government were to attempt a gradual sequencing of reforms, and approval had to be obtained at each step of the process, some groups could benefit from derailing the process at some point.

If the government and the interest groups were able to make credible commitments to implement the complete optimal sequence, that would be the recommended course of action. In other words, "constitutional" agreements such as social pacts, or agreements with international institutions with very high costs of reneging, might enable the implementation of reforms with lower transition costs.

While we do not think that there is a right set of assumptions about the payoff structure and the political game valid for all reform episodes, we believe that the assumptions necessary for our argument have been satisfied in a number of cases, particularly in Latin America. We turn now to a formal presentation of the argument.

13.3   The Political Economy Case for Radical Reform

In this section, we use a simple game in extensive form to show the logic of the following argument: by widening the scope of efficiency-improving reforms initiated simultaneously, a government can gain the support of larger segments of the population. For many agents, losses from one reform can be more than compensated by gains from the others. Hence, linking the fate of the reforms can be a way of weakening the opposition to them. If the government is not able to commit to a certain course of action, it may need to implement all reforms simultaneously, even if economic reasoning would call for a gradual sequencing of reforms.[7]

Consider a government trying to implement reforms F and T. We could think of them as a fiscal reform and a trade reform. There are two interest groups, f and t. Reform F, if carried out alone, will hurt group f and will benefit group t. The opposite is true for reform T. It is assumed that, on optimality grounds, reform T should be carried out after F is in place. This could be the case because, for instance, fiscal reform provides macroeconomic stability needed to minimize transition costs associated with trade reform.

If the optimal sequencing of reforms is pursued—that is, if T is undertaken after F is completed—both f and t end up being better off than in the initial situation. However, group t would prefer that the reform process be truncated after reform F is accomplished.

Alternatively, the government can start both reforms simultaneously. The payoffs of following this approach are higher for f and t than those from the initial situation, but lower than those obtained after the optimal sequence of reforms.

The government is modeled as an agenda setter who holds the initiative to propose reforms at several points in time. We assume that the government is interested in maximizing the sum of the utilities of the groups. The same results can be obtained from a number of specifications of the government's objective. For example, a predator government that takes a percentage of the total pie and a government that is a perfect agent for one group are also consistent with the payoff specification. We also assume that pressure groups can veto any reform plan. In deciding a sequence of proposals, the government must take into account not only economic considerations (the payoffs associated with the final result) but also the possibility of successfully installing the entire reform package. Neither the government nor the different interest groups have the capacity to commit to their actions.

Figure 13.1 shows schematically the extended form of this game.[8]

Payoffs have been chosen for illustration purposes and reflect the following assumptions: (1) there is a need for reform (low payoff of status quo); (2) if feasible, a gradual sequencing of reforms is preferable to a

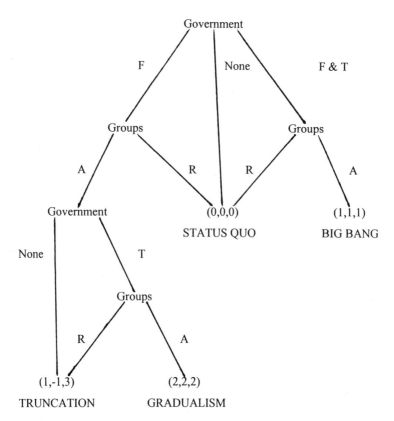

Figure 13.1
Payoffs: (Government, Group *f*, Group *t*)

simultaneous introduction of all reforms; and (3) a partial or truncated implementation of reforms will favor one group and hurt the other.

The government has three choices at the initial node: propose a gradual sequence of reforms (starting by reforming sector *F*), do nothing, or propose a comprehensive attempt at reform. If the government makes a proposal, the groups can accept it or reject it. The opposition of any group is enough to paralyze the government's proposal.

It is easy to see that comprehensive reform is the unique subgame-perfect equilibrium of the game (a subgame-perfect equilibrium requires rational choice by every decision maker at every possible node of the game, whether or not it is reached in equilibrium.) Suppose the government attempts to follow a gradual reform and proposes *F*. Group *f* will veto this proposal because, if *T* is proposed at the next stage, group *t* will veto it, and group f will end up being worse off than in the status quo. Hence, even though a gradual sequence is preferred to comprehensive reform by the interest groups and the government, it is not going to be proposed.

Notice that if group t could commit to accepting the government proposal in the second stage, both interest groups and the government would be better off. In this sense, there is a time-consistency problem similar to the well-known time-consistency problem in games between the government and the general public. The absence of any commitment device in the case of sequenced reforms is crucial for the results.

Our results are also consistent with some alternative assumptions about the payoff structure and the political game. For instance, the payoff corresponding to the status quo could be -2 for both interest groups and the government. The interpretation would be that F is beneficial for both interest groups so that nobody stands to lose from truncated reform. In that case, truncated reform would be feasible. However, a big bang would still be the best reform path from the point of view of the government. That is, we do not require that *each* reform hurts somebody, only that some reforms along the optimal gradual sequence hurt enough people to risk that the process of reforms be halted. In terms of the political game, we do not require that *everybody* in the economy have veto power nor that the government cares about he utility of *everybody* in the economy. What is required is that a blocking coalition be able to stop the optimal gradual sequence at some point, and that all potential blocking coalitions expect to be better off after the comprehensive introduction of reforms.

Finally, our results are not inconsistent with majority voting. To see this, suppose there is a third group that suffers losses from each reform. Payoffs to the government would not change if the third group's losses are relatively minor. If each of the three groups represents a third of the population, bunching the two reforms together would still be the only way to gather enough political support to install all of the reforms successfully. Note, however, that this majority voting scenario relies on the benefits of each reform being concentrated and its costs diffuse, which we consider contradictory to actual reform experiences in the Third World. The reality of concentrated costs and diffuse benefits in recent reform processes, therefore, fuels our preference for the veto power assumption over that of majority voting. Concentrated costs have prevailed because various sectors of society have had to renounce their apportionment of special privileges.

13.4   A General Equilibrium Model with Transitional Unemployment

This section is intended to demonstrate that payoffs that are strategically equivalent to those in figure 13.1 can be obtained from a fully specified economic model.

13.4.1   The Economy

Consider an economy with two sectors, one producing exports (X) and the other producing importables (Y). Both sectors use labor (L) as a factor of production. There are three different types of agents in this economy: workers (who supply all the labor), owners of the export firms, and owners of the firms that produce importables. Agents in this economy only consume importables. The exchange rate and the international prices of exports and importables are equal to one. In the initial situation, there is a tariff, τ, on imports and a fraction of the labor force, L_b, is absorbed by a useless bureaucracy. This extreme assumption captures the reality of overemployment and low productivity in the public sector. Agents live for three periods. Time is indexed by $t = 0, 1, 2$. There is no discounting.

The technology for producing exports and the technology for producing importables are given by

$$X_t = L_{x,t}^{1/2}$$
$$Y_t = L_{y,t}^{1/2}, \tag{1}$$

where X_t and Y_t are, respectively, the production of exports and the production of importables at time t, and $L_{x,t}$ and $L_{y,t}$ are, respectively, employment in the export and importable sectors at time t. It will be assumed that firms are restricted in their decisions to increase their use of labor, in such a way that

$$L_{j,t} \in [0, L_{j,t-1} + K_{j,t}]; \qquad j = X, Y, \tag{2}$$

where $K_{j,t}$ is the capacity of labor absorption of sector j in period t.[9]

Time 0 is taken to be the preexisting (distorted) situation, with salaries being identical across sectors, $w_{x,0} = w_{y,0} = w_{b,0}$, and no unemployment. The action transpires over periods 1 and 2. At the beginning of each period, each worker has to decide whether to stay at his current job or to quit and search for employment elsewhere. It is not possible to look for employment in more than one sector, and once a worker quits, (s)he cannot work in the same firm in that period. Public employment (L_b) is treated as a policy variable. Let $S_{j,t}$ be the number of workers looking for a job in sector j at the beginning of period t. If the number of workers searching for employment in sector j exceeds the capacity of absorption of that sector ($S_{j,t} > K_{j,t}$), then some of those workers will remain unemployed. The probability of finding a job in sector j at time t equals $\min\{K_{j,t}/S_{j,t}, 1\}$.

Production takes place after (some of) the searching workers and firms are matched. Firms are assumed to pay wages equal to the value of the marginal product of labor in the sector. That is,

$$w_{x,t} = \tfrac{1}{2} L_{x,t}^{-1/2}$$
$$w_{y,t} = (1 + \tau_t) \tfrac{1}{2} L_{y,t}^{-1/2}, \tag{3}$$

where τ_t is the level of tariffs at time t.

Labor is supplied inelastically by employed workers. The quantity of labor available in the economy is normalized to one. At the beginning of each period we have

$$\bar{L}_{x,t} + \bar{L}_{y,t} + L_{b,t} + S_{x,t} + S_{y,t} = 1, \tag{4}$$

where $\bar{L}_{x,t}$ and $\bar{L}_{y,t}$ are workers who remain employed in each sector from the previous period, $L_{b,t}$ are workers who remain employed in the bureaucracy, and $S_{x,t}$ and $S_{y,t}$ are workers searching for a job in each of the two productive sectors. After matching takes place, workers will either be employed in one of the two productive sectors, employed in the bureaucracy, or unemployed, such that

$$L_{x,t} + L_{y,t} + L_{b,t} + U_t = 1. \tag{5}$$

We now proceed to specify the value functions on the basis of which workers will make their search choices. At $t = 2$ (the final period), the value of searching for a job in sector j, $V_{j,2}$, will be given by the probability of getting a job in sector j multiplied by the wage expected in that sector (since the value of being unemployed during the final period is equal to zero):

$$V_{x,2} = \min\left\{\frac{K_{x,2}}{S_{x,2}}, 1\right\} w_{x,2}$$
$$V_{y,2} = \min\left\{\frac{K_{y,2}}{S_{y,2}}, 1\right\} w_{y,2}. \tag{6}$$

Notice that the wage that will result each period is supposed to be correctly anticipated, even though the decision to look for a job in a given sector is made at the beginning of the period.

The values of search at $t = 1$ are

$$V_{x,1} = \min\left\{\frac{K_{x,1}}{S_{x,1}}, 1\right\}(w_{x,1} + \max\{w_{x,2}, V_{y,2}\})$$

$$+ \left(1 - \min\left\{\frac{K_{x,1}}{S_{x,1}}, 1\right\}\right)\max\{V_{x,2}, V_{y,2}\}$$

$$V_{y,1} = \min\left\{\frac{K_{y,1}}{S_{y,1}}, 1\right\}(w_{y,1} + \max\{w_{y,2}, V_{x,2}\})$$

$$+ \left(1 - \min\left\{\frac{K_{y,1}}{S_{y,1}}, 1\right\}\right)\max\{V_{x,2}, V_{y,2}\}. \tag{7}$$

They include the probability of finding a job multiplied by the value of the job (wage at $t = 1$ plus value of optimal choice at $t = 2$ for an employed worker), plus the probability of unemployment multiplied by the value of unemployment (the value of the optimal choice at $t = 2$ for an unemployed worker).

In equilibrium,

$$V_{x,2} = V_{y,2}$$
$$V_{x,1} = V_{y,1}. \tag{8}$$

Given a set of policy parameters (τ_1, $L_{b,1}$, τ_2, and $L_{b,2}$), we can obtain equilibrium search decisions, wages, employment, production, and profits in each sector in each period, as well as expected payoffs for the different types of agents. We now proceed to provide one example in which a sequential reform (paring the bureaucracy first and lowering tariffs later) is the most desirable policy from the point of view of the government, but in which the political environment makes that sequence infeasible, leaving comprehensive reform as the best feasible option.

13.4.2 The Political Environment

Suppose that a reformist government intends to pass trade reform and fiscal reforms, which would take tariffs and the level of superfluous employment in the public sector to zero. In the initial situation, distortions in the economy are given by $\tau_0 = 0.30$ and $L_{b,0} = 0.20$, and there is no unemployment. The initial capacity of absorption of new labor in the export sector, $K_{x,1}$, is set at 0.07. As we will see, this implies that gradualism does not lead to unemployment, but big bang reform does. There are no other constraints to the capacity of absorption of new labor (that is, $K_{x,2} = K_{y,1} = K_{y,2} = \infty$).

The following are the institutional rules:

1. the government is the agenda setter. During period 1, it can propose contemporaneous changes in τ_1 and $L_{b,1}$. During period 2, it can propose contemporaneous changes in τ_2 and $L_{b,2}$. We assume that $\tau_t \in \{0, 0.30\}$ and $L_{b,t} \in \{0, 0.20\}$ to concentrate on the question of sequencing, ignoring issues of speed.

2. Each group of agents (workers, producers of importables, and exporters) has the power to veto any policy initiative. In case of veto, the resulting outcome is the status quo. As political agents, producers of importables and exporters seek to maximize profits in their respective sectors, and workers seek to maximize aggregate payments to labor.

3. The budget is balanced via proportional income taxes or subsidies.

4. The objective of the government is to maximize aggregate income.

5. There are no side payments.

13.4.3   Solution to the Game

Aggregate real income of workers (I_l), of exporters (I_x), and of owners of the importable firms (I_y) are given, respectively, by the total payroll, profits in the exports sector, and profits in the importables sector, deflated by the price of importables $(1 + \tau)$:

$$I_{l,t} = \frac{w_{x,t}L_{x,t} + w_{y,t}L_{y,t} + w_{b,t}L_{b,t}}{1 + \tau_t}$$

$$I_{x,t} = \frac{X_t - w_{x,t}L_{x,t}}{1 + \tau_t}$$

$$I_{y,t} = \frac{(1 + \tau_t)Y_t - w_{y,t}L_{y,t}}{1 + \tau_t}. \tag{9}$$

Equations above represent pretax income. Let T represent taxes needed to close the budget. T is equal to payments to public-sector employees minus tariff revenues. We ignore intertemporal balance of payment issues and assume that imports equal exports in every period. Hence,

$$T_t = \frac{w_{b,t}L_{b,t}}{1 + \tau_t} - \frac{\tau_t}{1 + \tau_t}X_t. \tag{10}$$

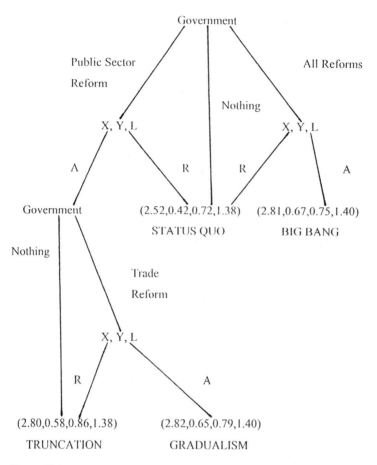

Figure 13.2
Payoffs: (Government, X, Y, L)

It is easily verified that

$$I_{l,t} + I_{x,t} + I_{y,t} - T_t = X_t + Y_t. \tag{11}$$

Let $I_t \equiv I_{l,t} + I_{x,t} + I_{y,t} - T_t$ represent the total consumption of import-ables by the economy (equal to total production evaluated at international prices). Stage payoffs (payoffs per period) to workers, owners of X, owners of Y, and the government are, respectively, $(1 - t)I_l$, $(1 - t)I_x$, $(1 - t)I_y$, and I, where $t = T/(I + T)$ is the tax rate. Given that there is no dis-counting, each group tries to maximize the sum of payoffs over periods 1 and 2. The extensive form of the game is depicted in figure 13.2. The appendix shows how to compute payoffs.

There are two possible paths from the initial situation to an undistorted economy. One possibility is to eliminate in the first period the distortion caused by bureaucratic employment and in the second period the distortion created by the tariff. That is, $L_{b,1} = 0$, $\tau_1 = 0.3$, and $L_{b,2} = \tau_2 = 0$. We call this path gradualism. The other possibility is to remove all distortions in period 1. That is, $L_{b,1} = \tau_1 = L_{b,2} = \tau_2 = 0$. We call this other path big bang.[10]

As we show in the appendix, unemployment under a big bang is larger than under gradualism. Gradualism is preferable to a big bang not only from an efficiency perspective, but also from the point of view of income distribution, since unemployed workers are the least favored social group in the model. The feasibility problem with gradualism is the following: Suppose that everybody agrees with the prescribed decisions in period 1. When period 2 arrives, producers of importable goods will not find it convenient to support a move toward free trade. Therefore, gradualism is not a credible path to free trade because it is not politically sustainable.

A big bang entails a lower aggregate payoff than gradualism during period 1, and it implies that some workers will be unemployed (more generally, it implies more unemployment than is strictly necessary). However, unlike gradualism, it is a politically sustainable path to an undistorted economy.

13.5 Final Remarks

An understanding of the conditions under which political considerations induce biases toward radical reform is important both to evaluate recent experiences in developing countries and to help in the design of new reform programs.

In this chapter, we offer a possible explanation for why a number of Latin American countries, some of which failed to complete gradual reforms in the early 1980s, have undertaken comprehensive reform programs in recent years. These attempts were somewhat surprising to outside economic analysts given their increased economic and administrative costs in relation to gradual reform processes. A key motivation seems to have been that a more extensive package of reform permitted a wider accumulation of political support. Thus, reform has usually been accompanied by political realignment. Since to sector of society wants to be first in renouncing its apportionment of special privileges, reformist governments felt it was necessary to cut through the Gordian knot of government-created rents.

From a normative point of view, our main insight is that political considerations can make reforms "complementary," even in circumstances in which economic reasoning would indicate that reforms should be made sequentially. Policymakers may need to be well aware of those considerations in implementing reform programs. Our result stands in contrast to Rodrik's (1989) recommendation of undertaking deep reforms with a narrow scope. As a former finance minister of New Zealand put it, "Large packages provide the flexibility to ensure that losses suffered by any one group are offset by gains by the same group in other areas" (Douglas 1990). Our result also highlights the need for international agencies to assess the political restrictions while assisting countries undertaking liberalization processes. Ideally, these institutions, as well as international treaties, might play a role as commitment devices to allow for the implementation of reforms with lower transition costs.

Appendix: Computing Payoffs for Figure 13.2

Table 13.A shows *stage* payoffs (that is, payoffs per period) to the different groups under different scenarios.

The initial situation is represented by column I. Since there is no initial unemployment, $L_{x,0} + L_{y,0} = 0.8$. From (3) and $w_{x,0} = w_{y,0}$ we obtain $L_{y,0} = (1.3)^2 L_{x,0}$. This implies $L_{x,0} = 0.3$, $L_{y,0} = 0.5$, and $w_0 = 0.91$. From there we can obtain $I_0 = X_0 + Y_0 = 1.26$. Using equations (9) and (10) we obtain the other elements of column I.

Column IV shows a steady state in which all distortions have been removed and there is no unemployment. Again, wages are equalized. the derivation is identical to that of column I. That column shows the maximum possible value of the level of aggregate income.

Table 13.A
Stage Payoffs

	I	II	III	IV
τ	0.3	0.3	0.0	0.0
L_b	0.2	0.0	0.0	0.0
NI_x	0.21	0.29	0.31	0.36
NI_y	0.36	0.43	0.39	0.36
NI_l	0.69	0.69	0.69	0.71
I	1.26	1.40	1.39	1.42

We consider two possible paths from I to IV. The first one is a gradualist process given by setting $L_{b,1} = 0$, $\tau_1 = 0.3$, and $L_{b,2} = \tau_2 = 0$. Column II represents transition during a gradualist process. No unemployment arises during a gradualist process: If we let $L_{x,1} + L_{y,1} = 1$, using (3) we obtain $L_{x,1} = .37$ (which is consistent with $L_{x,0} = 0.3$ and $K_{x,0} = 0.07$). From there we can obtain $I_1 = X_1 + Y_1 = 1.40$. Using equations (3), (9), and (10) we obtain the other elements of column II.

The other path from I to IV is a big bang given by setting $L_{b,1} = \tau_1 = L_{b,2} = \tau_2 = 0$. Column III represents transition during a big bang. In this case, the constraint on labor absorption by sector X is binding in the first period. Hence, $L_{x,1} = L_{x,0} + K_{x,1} = 0.37$. There is no unemployment in the final period, so that equations (7) and (8) imply $(K_{x,1})/(S_{x,1})w_{x,1} = w_{y,1}$. Using equation (3) and $S_{x,1} = 1 - L_{x,0} - L_{y,1}$ we obtain $(0.7)/(S_{x,1}) \times 0.82 = \frac{1}{2}(0.7 - S_{x,1})^{-1/2}$. From the last expression we obtain $S_{x,1} = 0.09$ and then $L_{y,1} = 0.61$. From there we can obtain $I_1 = X_1 + Y_1 = 1.39$. Using equations (3), (9), and (10) we obtain the other elements of column III.

The status quo payoffs in figure 13.2 correspond to twice the payoffs of column I. The truncated reform payoffs correspond to twice the payoffs in column II. The gradualist reform payoffs correspond to the payoffs in column II plus the payoffs in column IV. Finally, the radical reform payoffs correspond to the payoffs of column III plus the payoffs of column IV.

Notes

We thank Christopher Clague, Anne Krueger, Gian Maria Milesi-Ferretti, Martin McGuire, Dani Rodrik, Seongwan Oh, Mancur Olson, Adam Shapiro, Rich Sicotte, Peter Rosendorff, Gordon Tullock, Michael Wallerstein, an anonymous referee, and seminar participants at UCLA, Georgetown, Maryland, MFI, Columbia, Chicago, MIT, and the WEA meetings for helpful comments. This chapter was written while the first author was a student and the second author a faculty member at UCLA, and revised while the second author was a fellow at the Harvard/MIT RTG in Positive Political Economy. We thank the financial support of the UCLA Academic Senate, of the Project on "Institutional Reform and the Informal Sector" (IRIS) at the University of Maryland under Cooperative Agreement DHR-0015-A-00-0031-00 with the Center of Economic Growth of the US Agency for International Development, and of the Spanish CICYT (grant SEC 93-0839).

1. E.g., Calvo (1989), Corbo and De Melo (1985), Corbo and Fischer (1990), Edwards (1992a, b), Fischer (1986), Frenkel (1982), Harberger (1986), Krueger (1981), McKinnon (1984, 1991).

2. These countries include Bolivia, Ghana, Mexico, and Poland (World Bank 1991, 117), Argentina (Dornbusch 1992), and Peru (Paredes 1991). For comprehensive analysis of reform episodes, we refer the reader to the volumes edited by Bates and Krueger (1993) and Haggard and Kaufman (1992).

3. This chapter is concerned with the introduction of measures in different fronts (such as macroeconomic stabilization or trade liberalization), not with the speed of reform in each particular front. We (and many previous authors) are guilty of using *speed* terminology ("gradual," "radical," "big-bang") to talk about *sequencing* issues. See Tommasi and Velasco (1996) for a more detailed discussion of this distinction.

4. It is interesting to note the contrast between the assumptions in Dewatripont and Roland (1992a,b) and those in Fernandez and Rodrik (1991) and Wei (1993). Workers know their chances of getting a job in the growing sectors all too well in Dewatripont-Roland, while they have no clue in Fernandez-Rodrik-Wei.

5. Also, Martinelli and Tommasi (1995) show that even under the conditions necessary for gradualism to have lower experimentation costs (in Dewatripont and Roland 1995), the distributional implications of the different reforms can lead to the gradual path being time-inconsistent in a political game.

6. Veto power by interest groups is a common assumption in the literature on the *delay* of reforms (Alesina and Drazen 1991; Drazen and Grilli 1993). The assumption of veto players is also implicit in Dewatripont and Roland (1992a,b). In their model of industrial restructuring, they assume that the government cannot fire workers from the inefficient sectors, but has to bribe them to exit.

7. A similar idea underlies the discussion about economic reform in Buchanan (1991). In a similar vein, Rodrik (1994) argues that a government may be able to sneak in a reform with distributive consequences alongside one with across-the-board benefits by packaging the two together.

8. In order to simplify figures 13.1 and 13.2, we have used single nodes to represent the simultaneous moves of groups. *A* means acceptance by *all* groups, while *R* means rejection by *any* group.

9. The sector-level behavior we describe can be obtained by having n firms with technology $q_{i,t} = (l_{i,t}/n)^{1/2}$, with $l_{i,t} \in [0, l_{i,t-1} + K_{i,t}/n]$. This stark but simple way of capturing convex costs of training new workers is inspired by Gavin (1993).

10. Another path, which we are ignoring, would consist of lowering tariffs in period 1 and reducing the bureacracy in period 2. We could call this path "gradualism with the wrong sequence" because it would entail suppressing the most important distortion in the second period. We ignore this path because it would lead to lower payoffs for the government than any of the other two.

References

Alesina, Alberto, and Allan Drazen. 1991. "Why are Stabilizations Delayed?" *American Economic Review* 81: 1170–1188.

Ames, Barry. 1987. *Political Survival: Politicians and Public Policy in Latin America*. Berkeley: University of California Press.

Bates, Robert, and Anne Krueger. 1993. *Political and Economic Interactions in Economic Policy Reform: Evidence from Eight Countries*. Cambridge: Basil Blackwell.

Buchanan, James. 1991. "Achieving Economic Reform." Chap. 9 in *The Economics and the Ethics of Constitutional Order*. Michigan. Ann Arbor: University of Michigan Press.

Burgess, Robin, and Nicholas Stern. 1993. "Taxation and Development." *Journal of Economic Literature* 31: 762–830.

Calvo, Guillermo. 1989. "Incredible Reforms," In J. Braga deMacedo, G. Calvo, P. Kouri, and R. Findlay, 217–34. *Debt, Stabilization and Development: Essays in Memory of Carlos Diaz Alejandro*, ed. Basil Blackwell.

Corbo, Vittorio, and Jaime De Melo. 1985. "Liberalization with Stabilization in the Southern Cone of Latin America: Overview and Summary." *World Development*, 13 (*August*): 5–15.

Corbo, Vittorio, and Stanley Fischer. 1990. "Adjustment Programs and Bank Support: Rationale and Main Results." In *Adjustment Lending Revisited: Policies to Restore Growth*, ed. V. Corbo, S. Fischer, and S. Webb. Washington, DC: The World Bank.

Dewatripont, Mathias, and Gérard Roland. 1992a. "Economic Reform and Dynamic Political Constraints." *Review of Economic Studies* 59: 703–730.

———. "The Virtues of Gradualism and Legitimacy in the Transition to a Market Economy." *Economic Journal* 102: 291–300.

Dewatripont, Mathias, and Gérard Roland. 1995. "The Design of Reform Packages under Uncertainty." *American Economic Review* 85: 1207–1223.

Díaz Alejandro, Carlos. 1985. "Good Bye Financial Repression, Hello Financial Crash." *Journal of Development Economics* 19: 1–24.

Dornbusch, Rudiger. 1992. "Progress Report on Argentina." Working paper. December.

Douglas, Roger. 1990. "The Politics of Successful Structural Reform." *The Wall Street Journal*, January 17.

Drazen, Allan, and Vittorio Grilli. 1993. "The Benefits of Crises for Economic Reforms." *American Economic Review* 83: 598–607.

Edwards, Sebastian. 1992a. "Sequencing and Welfare: Labor Markets and Agriculture." NBER Working Paper No. 4095.

———. 1992b. "The Sequencing of Structural Adjustment and Stabilization." ICEG Occasional Paper No. 34.

Edwards, Sebastian, and Alejandra Cox-Edwards. 1991. *Monetarism and Liberalization: The Chilean Experiment*. Chicago: University of Chicago Press.

Edwards, Sebastian, and Sweder van Wijnbergen. 1986. "Welfare Effects of Trade and Capital Market Liberalization: Consequences of Different Sequencing Scenarios." *International Economic Review* 27 (February): 141–148.

Fernandez, Raquel, and Dani Rodrik. 1991. "Resistance to Reform: Status Quo Bias in the Presence of Individual-Specific Uncertainty." *American Economic Review* 81: 1146–1155.

Fischer, Stanley. 1986. "Issues in Medium-Term Macroeconomic Adjustment." *The World Bank Research Observer* 1: 163–182.

Frenkel, Jacob. 1982. "The Order of Economic Liberalization: A Comment." In *Economic Policy in a World of Change*, ed. K. Brunner and A. Meltzer. North Holland.

Gavin, Michael. 1993. "Unemployment and the Economics of Gradualist Reform." Mimeo, Columbia University.

Haggard, Stephan, and Robert Kaufman. 1992. *The Politics of Economic Adjustment*. Princeton: Princeton University Press.

Harberger, Arnold. 1986. "Welfare Consequences of Capital Inflows." In *Economic Liberalization in Developing Countries* ed. N. Choksi and G. Papageorgiou. Oxford: Basil Blackwell.

Krueger, Anne. 1981. "Interactions between Inflation and Trade-Regime Objectives in Stabilization Programs," in *Economic Stabilization in Developing Countries*, ed. W. Cline and S. Weintraub. Washington, DC: Brookings Institution.

Martinelli, Cesar, and Mariano Tommasi 1995. "Economic Reforms and Political Constraints: On the Time-Inconsistency of Gradual Sequencing." Universidad Carlos III, Madrid. Mimeo.

McKinnon, Ronald. 1984. "The International Capital Market and Economic Liberalization in LDC's." *The Developing Economies* 22 (December): 476–81.

McKinnon, Ronald. 1991. *The Order of Economic Liberalization: Financial Control in the Transition to a Market Economy*. Baltimore: Johns Hopkins University Press.

Murrell, Peter. 1992. "Evolutionary and Radical Approaches to Economic Reform." IRIS Working Paper No 5. University of Maryland. Forthcoming in *The Economics of Planning*.

Mussa, Michael. 1982. "Government Policy and the Adjustment Process." In *Import Competition and Response*, ed. J. Bhagwati. Chicago: University of Chicago Press.

Paredes, Carlos. 1991. "Epilogue: In the Aftermath of Hyperinflation." In *Peru's Path to Recovery: A Plan for Economic Stabilization and Growth*, ed. C. Paredes and J. Sachs. Washington, DC: Brookings Institution.

Przeworski, Adam. 1991. *Democracy and the Market. Political and Economic Reforms in Eastern Europe and Latin America*. Cambridge and New York: Cambridge University Press.

Rodrik, Dani. 1989. "Credibility of Trade Reform: A Policymaker's Guide." *The World Economy* 12: 1–16.

Rodrik, Dani. 1994. "The Rush to Free Trade in the Developing World: Why So Late? Why Now? Will it Last?" In *Voting for Reform: Democracy, Political Liberalization and Economic Adjustment*, ed. S. Haggard and S. Webb. Oxford University Press.

Tommasi, Mariano, and Andrés Velasco. 1996. "Where Are We in the Political Economy of Reform?" *Journal of Policy Reform* 1: 187–238.

Wei, Shang-Jin. 1993. "Gradualism versus Big Bang: Speed and Sustainability of Reforms." Mimeo, Harvard University.

World Bank. 1991. *World Development Report: The Challenge of Development*. Oxford: Oxford University Press.

III

Who? (The Identity of Reformers)

14

Promises, Promises:
Credible Policy Reform via
Signalling

Dani Rodrik

A government initiates a series of important reforms, including trade and financial liberalisation and disinflation policies. But the private sector (and possibly foreign creditors) do not fully believe that the reforms will persist. Should the government attempt to enhance its credibility? How can it do so? What are the consequences for the economy and the reforms if it is unable to?

Experience and theory both suggest that lack of credibility can be very costly indeed. For an important example, consider orthodox policies of disinflation that rely on sharp reductions in monetary growth. Unless the private sector becomes convinced that the monetary contraction will continue, the result may well be wages and prices set at too high a level relative to the future stock of monetary aggregates. The consequent reduction in real liquidity may then exert strong recessionary forces. A conceptually similar outcome obtains in the case of trade-liberalising reforms lacking credibility. When a future reversal of the liberalisation is anticipated, the private sector will tend to over-borrow from abroad, running "too large" a deficit on the current account (Calvo, 1986; see also van Wijnbergen, 1985). Both types of problems do indeed occur. The first is frequently suggested as a major reason why reductions in inflation are typically associated with large output costs; and the second has been observed in Chile and Argentina in the late 1970s, and in Mexico in 1988. In both cases, the adverse consequences of the lack of credibility could be serious enough to force even the best-intentioned government to abort the reform process, thereby validating the suspicions of the private sector.

More generally, as Calvo (1986) has pointed out, lack of credibility is functionally equivalent to a distortion in the structure of intertemporal relative prices: economic agents base their actions on prices which differ

Originally published in *The Economic Journal* 99 (1989): 756–72. Reprinted with permission.

from those that will materialise if the reform is carried out to fruition. The presence of this distortion in turn creates a second-best environment, with all the usual second-best complications. Hence the reform, while beneficial on its own, may lead to losses in overall welfare if perceived as lacking sufficient credibility. Similarly, there may be a second-best role for introducing additional distortions in the economy to the extent that these either offset the distortions associated with the problem or enhance the government's credibility.

Determining the appropriate policy stance in such a context requires knowledge of the sources of the credibility gap. The question is: why would the public fear that the policy reforms will be reversed *despite* the government's assurances to the contrary? Answers to this question based on rational behaviour fall under three broad categories.

First, the government's reforms may be inconsistent with other policies being pursued simultaneously, and be recognised as such by the public. Examples of such situations abound. Trade reform in the presence of pegged exchange rates (with prices sticky downwards) will not be viable, as the Chilean case has demonstrated. Similarly, disinflationary policies which do not concurrently tackle the public-sector budget deficit will lack credibility, irrespective of whether orthodox or heterodox measures are utilised. The establishment of "target zones" for major currencies will not be a solution to exchange-rate volatility unless the governments concerned undertake the requisite monetary-fiscal policy combinations to maintain their exchange rates within the appropriate bands. In all these cases, policy reform does not pass the credibility test because the public understands that it violates budget constraints or accounting identities.

Secondly, there might be a genuine time-inconsistency problem for the government: its optimal ex-post strategy may differ from its optimal ex-ante strategy. For example, once the private sector sets wages and prices, the authorities may find it tempting to disinflate less than they had promised in order to get some output gains (Barro and Gordon, 1983). Similar temptations to "surprise" the private sector may exist with trade policy as well (see Staiger and Tabellini, 1987). In circumstances where the authorities have an ex-post incentive to renege on their promises, it is of course perfectly rational for private agents to discount announcements of future policy reforms—or assurances of the continuation of present reforms. Potential solutions to the time-inconsistency problem can be found in commitments and reputation-building, neither of which, however, will do the job costlessly. Commitments have the disadvantage of tying the government's hands against unforeseen contingencies in which freedom of action would have been desirable ex ante (see Rodrik and Zeckhauser, 1988). Reputations can be built only by using up valuable time. The final source of credibility problems is incomplete or asymmetric information: private sector decision-makers may not be able to tell how serious the government really is about the reform process. In other words, they may be in the dark about the true objectives of the government in power, or may "confuse" it with an alternative government whose objectives differ. Imperfect information of this sort is likely to be particularly prevalent in countries where governments (and finance ministers) rotate rapidly, and in developing countries in particular. Notice that this is radically different from the time-inconsistency case above wherein the private sector understands the government's motivations only too well.[1] The resolution of the credibility problem in such instances will require the government to "signal" its true type. Whether this is good policy or not will in turn depend on the cost of investing in the appropriate signal.

This chapter is concerned with this last type of credibility problem. The framework I will consider is one in which the private sector is unable to distinguish between a government intent on trade reform and one which simply feigns interest in reform because this is a precondition for direly needed foreign aid.[2] The general message that will come across is that the rate at which the reform is introduced may serve to convey the government's *future* intentions, and hence act as a signal of its "type." More specifically, credible policy reform will require going overboard: the government will have to go much further than it would have chosen to in the absence of the credibility problem. In the case considered here, the reform-minded government will buy credibility by not only eliminating protection, but actually *subsidising* imports (exports). This provides a solution to the credibility problem in that the reformist government's nemesis would never find it advantageous to go as far. Signalling in this fashion is of course costly, and its ultimate desirability will depend on a number of factors. But, and this is the key point, achieving credibility will always require a *larger* policy reform than would have been dictated in the absence of the credibility problem.[3]

The model to be analysed below contrasts the behaviour of a "liberalising" government with that of a "redistributive" government. The former values trade reform because of the usual allocative efficiency gains to be derived therefrom, and intends to stick with the liberalisation. The latter uses tariff revenues to redistribute income to favoured groups in society, and, due to the absence of alternative policies, prefers some protection to none. I assume, as is usually the case, that trade liberalisation is supported by foreign assistance from multilateral institutions, with the aid conditional on the launching of the reform. This is a crucial part of the story. Since foreign assistance may well provide a motive for the "redistributive" government to mimic the "liberaliser" for a while, the public cannot be entirely sure in the initial stages of the reform as to which sort of government it faces. Consequently, governmental assurances that the reform will not be reversed in the future are taken with a reasonable grain of salt. Notice that foreign aid results in a hidden cost: by skewing the incentives of the "redistributive" government, it makes it more difficult for the "liberalising" government to reveal its true type.

The outline of the chapter is as follows. Section 14.1 lays out the basic model and discusses the costs engendered by the lack of credibility. In our case, the costs are reflected in sub-optimal levels of investment, as private savings fall in anticipation of higher prices for imported goods in the future. In section 14.2, the sources of the credibility problem are examined by introducing a "redistributive" government with an objective function that differs from that of the "liberaliser." Section 14.3 analyses the circumstances under which separating and pooling equilibria will occur, and discusses the likely benefits (and cost) of achieving credibility for the "liberalising" government via signalling that leads to separation. Concluding observations are offered in section 14.4.

14.1 The Costs of Lack of Credibility

We start with a stylised model of an economy that allows a relatively straightforward analysis of credibility issues. To focus on the new issues, we will abstract from many real-world aspects. In particular, the assumption will be that the domestic economy produces a single good which is not consumed at home, and that all consumption and investment goods are imported. To incorporate the dynamic considerations raised above, we will look at a two-period model. Since trade reform will typically take place under conditions of either capital-account restrictions or credit rationing abroad, capital flows will be assumed to be non-existent save for the possibility of foreign aid. The domestic economy is taken to be small in world markets, and all world prices will be fixed at unity by an appropriate choice of units.

Let $f(k, l)$ and $F(k + i, l)$ be the production functions for domestic output in the first and second period, respectively, and i be first-period investment. (Given the two-period horizon, there will be no investment in the second period.) The economy's fixed and fully-employed initial endowments of capital and labour are denoted by k and l. The level of investment in the economy is determined by maximising the present discounted value of net benefits of investment:

$$\max_i[\delta F(k + i, l) - i],$$

where δ is the domestic discount factor (one over one plus the nominal interest rate). I will assume throughout that imports of investment goods are not subject to tariffs, so that the domestic and world prices of investment goods are identical and fixed at unity. Notice that since all producer prices are fixed (and independent of tariffs), changes in δ will correspond directly to changes in the *real* interest rate relevant to investment decisions. Solving the above maximisation problem yields

$$\delta F_1(k + i, l) - 1 = 0, \tag{1}$$

where the numbered subscript denotes a partial derivative with respect to the relevant variable. This defines an implicit investment function of the form $i = i(\delta)$, with

$$di/d\delta \equiv i'(\cdot) = -F_1/(\delta F_{11}) > 0,$$

since the production function is concave in k. Desired investment rises as the discount factor increases (or the interest rate falls) since future gains in output become more valued relative to present consumption.

Consumers are represented by a two-period expenditure function $E[(1 + t\delta(1 + T), W]$, where W denotes welfare, and t and T denote first- and second-period tariffs, respectively. This function gives the present discounted value of expenditures required to achieve welfare level W when first- and second-period prices are $1 + t$ and $1 + T$. Notice that the second-period price is discounted by δ, and that the *real* discount factor for consumers is given by

$$q \equiv \delta(1 + T)/(1 + t).$$

The consumption rate of interest is in turn a negative function of q, and can be expressed as $(1/q) - 1$. This intertemporal relative price will play a crucial role throughout the analysis, as it is the chief determinant of savings behaviour.

The levels of consumption in the two periods can be derived by taking the appropriate partial derivatives of the expenditure function:

$$c = E_1(\cdot) \quad \text{(first-period consumption)}, \tag{2}$$

$$C = E_2(\cdot) \quad \text{(second-period consumption)}. \tag{3}$$

Since all consumption goods are imported, a tariff is here equivalent to an economy-wide consumption tax. And since tariff revenue will be redistributed in lump-sum fashion back to the private sector, tariffs will not give rise to their usual *static* efficiency costs in the present framework. As the costs of protection are well known, little harm is done in abstracting from them in order to concentrate on intertemporal sources of welfare losses arising purely from credibility problems. Of course, in the absence of static efficiency costs, the "liberalising" government would have formally no reason to remove protection. Keeping such costs in the background, we will assume that it will want to pursue trade reform nonetheless.

Equilibrium in the economy requires intertemporal equality between aggregate income (net of investment spending) and consumption expenditures:

$$E(\cdot) = Y, \tag{4}$$

where Y represents the present discounted value of net income:

$$Y = f(k, l) - i + tc + B + \delta[F(k + i, l) + TC]. \tag{5}$$

First-period income consists of production revenues net of investment expenditures plus tariff revenue *plus* a foreign transfer of amount B which is contingent on first-period trade reform. Notice that foreign assistance is taken to come in the form of a grant rather than a loan (i.e., it is not paid back); this is to simplify the algebra only and will not affect the qualitative results. Second-period income in turn consists of second-period production and tariff revenues.

Since foreign borrowing/lending is ruled out, equilibrium also requires equality between income and expenditure in each period separately. Given (4), one of these two conditions is redundant, and we choose to express the first-period constraint only:

$$(1 + t)c = f(k, l) - i + tc + B. \tag{6}$$

This equates first-period domestic savings to investment expenditures. Equations (4) and (6) together will determine the welfare level W and the discount factor δ (or the interest rate).

Now consider a trade reform. The government reduces t to zero and promises that in the second period T will be zero as well. This clears the way for foreign aid. But suppose that the public does not believe that the reform will be maintained. The underlying determinants of this lack of credibility will be discussed later. For the moment, assume that consumers are risk-neutral, and that they act in the certainty that the future level of tariffs will be given by $\tilde{T} > 0$. (In other words, $\tilde{T}$ is the certainty-equivalent level of the second-period tariff.) We will first treat $\tilde{T}$ parametrically, and then endogenise it in the sections to come.

What are the consequences of the lack of credibility? The anticipation that tariffs will increase in the future reduces the real consumption rate of interest (raises the real consumption factor), and hence depresses first-period savings. In response, investment has to fall, and welfare is reduced due to a sub-optimal level of investment.

To see these effects at work, we analyse the comparative statics of the model (with $t = 0$). Differentiating (4) and (6) and making the appropriate substitutions, we first express the response of the real discount factor (q) to changes in $\tilde{T}$:

$$0 < dq/d\tilde{T} = [\delta/(1 + \phi)] < \delta, \tag{7}$$

where

$$\phi \equiv [(1 + \tilde{T})/i'](-\delta E_{22}\{1 + \tilde{T}[\delta E_{2W}/(E_{1W} + \delta E_{2W})]\}) > 0.$$

The various cross-derivatives of the expenditure function are signed as follows: E_{22} is non-positive due to the negative semi-definiteness of the substitution matrix, and E_{1W} and E_{2W} are positive under the assumption that present and future goods are both "normal" with positive income elasticities of demand. Notice that q increases with $\tilde{T}$, but that the effect is dampened due to a reduction in δ. (In the absence of changes in δ, $dq/d\tilde{T}$ would have equalled δ.) That is, $\delta = \delta(\tilde{T})$ with $d\delta/d\tilde{T} < 0$. The welfare level, in turn, is directly related to the consumption rate of interest:

$$dW = (1/\theta)\delta\tilde{T}E_{22}\,dq, \tag{8}$$

where $\theta \equiv (E_W - \delta\tilde{T}E_{2W}) > 0$ (see Dixit and Norman, 1980, p. 187). Hence

$$dW/d\tilde{T} = [\delta^2/\theta(1 + \phi)]\tilde{T}E_{22} \le 0. \tag{9}$$

This expression is unambiguously negative whenever evaluated at an initially positive level of $\tilde{T}$. But when the credibility problem is "small," the associated welfare losses are of second order of importance. An explicit expression for the welfare losses associated with the lack of credibility can be found via a first-order Taylor approximation. Letting $\Delta W \equiv W(\tilde{T}) - W(0)$ represent the difference between the welfare levels resulting under imperfect and full credibility, respectively:

$$\Delta W \cong [\delta^2/\theta(1 + \phi)]E_{22}\tilde{T}^2 < 0. \tag{10}$$

Notice that the cost is proportional to the square of the anticipated tariff, and is larger the stronger is intertemporal substitutability in consumption (represented by E_{22}).

The welfare costs of imperfect credibility arise from the intertemporal distortion introduced by anticipations of future tariffs. The consumption rate of interest is reduced artificially, resulting in sub-optimal levels of saving and investment in the economy. In the present framework, consumers and producers make *all* of their decisions in the first period; the second period's consumption level is entirely determined by previous investment and saving decisions. Consequently, no changes in consumption or investment behaviour are possible when the government's true intentions are revealed in the second period. The economy suffers from an anticipated *but unrealised* reversal in the trade reform in exactly the same way that it would from an actual reversal.[4] Lack of credibility is functionally equivalent to unsuccessful reform.

Notice in addition that no time-inconsistency problems arise for the "liberalising" government. Once the second period comes around, the government's best strategy remains to follow its original promise of zero tariffs, irrespective of the anticipations harboured by the public.

For later reference, it will also be useful to perform the comparative statics of the system with respect to changes in the foreign transfer, B. Differentiating (4) and (6) once again (with $t = 0$), we are left with

$$\begin{bmatrix} \theta & -\delta\tilde{T}E_{22} \\ E_{1W} & (E_{12} + di/d\delta) \end{bmatrix} \begin{bmatrix} dW \\ d\delta \end{bmatrix} = \begin{bmatrix} dB \\ dB \end{bmatrix}.$$

The determinant (det) can be shown to be positive, so we have (after simplifying by using the homogeneity properties of $E(\cdot)$):

$$dW/dB = (1/\text{det})[(di/d\delta) - \delta E_{22}] > 0,$$

and

$$d\delta/dB = (1/\text{det})\delta E_{2W} > 0.$$

Notice that an increase in the transfer raises the discount factor and therefore stimulates investment. The effect comes about as the increase in first-period income leads to a less than equal increase in desired first-period consumption.

14.2   The "Redistributive" Government

The discussion above has taken for granted the existence of a credibility problem for the government (as in van Wijnbergen, 1985, Calvo, 1986, and Froot, 1988).[5] In order to endogenise credibility partially it is convenient to conceptualise the problem as arising from an inability on the part of the public to distinguish the "type" of the government in power. The private sector maximises its expected utility given its prior beliefs regarding the likelihood that it faces the "bad" type and that the reform will be aborted. Let T^R denote the value of the tariff that will obtain if the reform is reversed, and π be the prior probability attached to the reform being maintained. The expected value of the second-period tariff, denoted $\exp(T)$, can be written as follows:

$$\exp(T) = \pi 0 + (1 - \pi)T^R.$$

When the public is unable to tell the "type" of the government in place, π will be generally indeterminate and will depend on history and other characteristics of society; I will therefore treat it as exogenously given. In a "separating" equilibrium, on the other hand, π will be known to be either zero or unity. In this sense, π is a direct measure of the credibility of reform.

We define the "certainty-equivalent" level of the second-period tariff as that level which, if known with certainty, would make consumers behave in exactly the same fashion as in the expected utility maximisation described above. Denoting the certainty-equivalent level of the second-period tariff by $\tilde{T}$, we can show that $\tilde{T}$ and $\exp(T)$ are related in the following manner:

$$\tilde{T} = \exp(T) + \delta\xi\pi(1 - \pi)(T^R)^2, \tag{11}$$

where ξ is a composite term involving first- and second-order derivatives of the indirect utility function, and has an indeterminate sign (this is shown in an appendix available to the interested reader on request). Since the second term involves the square of the second-period tariff, it is of second-order importance compared to the first term.[6] In what follows, I will generally ignore it. Notice that, as expected, $\tilde{T}$ is linked positively to T^R and negatively to π.

Completing the model now requires description of the behaviour of an alternative government that would find it profitable to abort the reform process. I confine myself to a case which is fairly general in its applicability. Consider a government whose objectives are primarily distributional: to resdistribute income to a favoured group in society from a less-favoured group.[7] Suppose further that tariffs are the sole means of raising revenue for this purpose. Then, this "redistributive" government will attempt to achieve its distributional aim at least cost to overall efficiency. Letting superscripts denote the two groups in society, we could visualise its objective function as being the following:

$$\max_{t,T} W^1 \quad \text{s.t.} \quad W^2 \geq \overline{W},$$

where

$$W^1 = V(1+t, \quad \delta(1+T), \quad Y^1 + Q],$$

$$W^2 = V(1+t, \quad \delta(1+T), \quad Y^2 - Q],$$

$$Y^i = \gamma^i Y, \quad i = 1, 2, \quad \gamma^1 + \gamma^2 = 1,$$

$$Q = tc^2 + \delta TC^2.$$

$V(\cdot)$ denotes an indirect utility function, and γ^i is the share of each of the two groups in total income *before* redistribution. We will treat individuals in the two groups as being identical in all respects but their label, and will assume that intertemporal demand functions are homothetic. This way, aggregate behaviour—aggregate levels of consumption and the discount rate—will be independent of income distribution.

The "redistributive" government strives to maximise the welfare of the first group subject to a minimum welfare level for group 2. It does so by redistributing *all* tariff revenue to the former group; hence group 1 receives in lump-sum fashion the tariff payments made by group 2 (Q) to supplement its income. The higher the level of tariff revenues, the more redistribution this government can undertake. The tariffs that solve the above problem will be denoted by t^R and T^R. Notice that as long as the constraint $W^2 \geq \overline{W}$ continues to bind, no time-inconsistency problems arise, since once t is chosen the only way of guaranteeing $\overline{W}$ to the second group is by selecting the level of T which is optimal ex ante. But when the constraint does not bind, the pre-commitment and time-consistent policy paths may diverge (see the next section).[8]

Consider first the case where foreign assistance is non-existent ($B = 0$). Then provided that the constraint $W^2 \geq \overline{W}$ is not binding at $t = T = 0$, the "redistributive" government will choose to have positive levels of protection so as to benefit group 1. What will be the optimal levels of the tariffs? Given its objective function, the "redistributive" government has the incentive to transfer income from one group to the other at least cost in terms of efficiency. This can be achieved by setting the tariff rates in the two periods equal to each other, i.e., $t^R = T^R$. This allows the economy to remain intertemporally efficient. Denote the common level of the tariff as $\bar{t}$. Since $\bar{t}$ keeps group 2 just at $\overline{W}$, it must be the case that

$$E[1 + \bar{t}, \delta^*(1 + \bar{t}), \overline{W}] = (1 + \bar{t})E(1, \delta^*, \overline{W})$$

$$= \gamma^2[f(\cdot) - i^* + \delta^* F(k + i^*, .)],$$

where the starred variables are fixed at the levels that obtain in the absence of intertemporal distortions (i.e., when $t = T$). This allows us to derive an explicit expression for the "optimal" tariff:

$$\bar{t} = \{\gamma^2[f(\cdot) - i^* + \delta^* F(k + i^*, .)]/E(1, \delta^*, \overline{W})\} - 1. \tag{12}$$

We could think of this as the pre-existing level of the tariff before the reform government takes over.

So far, the "redistributive" government and the "liberaliser" would necessarily reveal themselves by their choice of trade policies in the initial period: the first settles on $t = \bar{t}$, the second on $t = 0$. In practice, there will occasionally be reasons for the "redistributive" government to act out of character. In the context of developing countries, this will be typically the case when balance-of-payments difficulties force the government to seek the "green light" from multilateral organisations such as the IMF or the World Bank. Obtaining the requisite foreign assistance will then require a number of reforms which the government will undertake to appease its foreign creditors, but will not particularly feel committed to maintaining. Indeed, once the foreign-exchange constraint is alleviated, back-tracking will be the natural temptation.[9]

In the present framework, the foreign transfer B serves to highlight the problem. I assume that the transfer is contingent on trade reform being carried out in the first period, with tariffs lowered to zero. In the second period, no additional transfers are made, and the government can freely choose its policies. Will the "redistributive" government reduce tariffs in the first period? If B is large enough, it clearly will. Setting $t = 0$ has the cost of preventing income redistribution in the first period. But this cost can be more than offset by the relaxation of the overall budget constraint as a consequence of the foreign transfer. In fact, the transfer may also allow the "redistributive" government to impose a higher tariff in the *second* period than it would otherwise have been able to. The latter follows from the fact that the relaxation of the overall budget constraint allows the second group to be squeezed to a greater extent than before. The next section provides more detail on these issues.

14.3   Pooling and Separating Equilibria

I will first consider the characteristics of pooling and separating equilibria, and then use these to discuss how the government can successfully signal its type and distinguish itself from the "redistributive" government.

Pooling equilibrium. Consider a pooling equilibrium wherein the two types of government both set first-period tariffs equal to zero, and hence become indistinguishable. For this to be an equilibrium, the "redistributive" government has to find it preferable to forsake redistributive policies in the first period. Let the maximum-value function associated with this government's optimisation problem be written as $W^1(t^R, T^R)$. In the absence of pooling, t^R will be non-zero, and foreign assistance will not be forthcoming. Then $t^R = T^R = \bar{t}$ as discussed above. In a pooling equilibrium, by contrast, the "redistributive" government is constrained to set $t^R = 0$, but can choose T^R otherwise optimally. As will be shown below, this optimal level of T^R will depend, among others, on B and π; let it be written as $T^R = T^R(B, \pi)$. Pooling will be a possible equilibrium when the following inequality holds:

$$W^1[0, T^R(B, \pi); B > 0] \geq W^1(\bar{t}, \bar{t}; B = 0). \tag{13}$$

It ought to be clear that $W^1[0, T^R(B, \pi)]$ is an increasing function of B: as the amount of foreign aid increases, the intertemporal budget constraint is relaxed, and potential welfare of both groups in society rises. Hence the larger is B, the greater the likelihood that a pooling equilibrium will result. The borderline level of B, denoted by B^{min}, is defined implicitly by the relation $W^1[0, T^R(B^{min}, \pi); B = B^{min}] = W^1(\bar{t}, \bar{t}; B = 0)$.

Let us suppose that the level of B indeed exceeds B^{min}, and that the economy is stuck in a pooling equilibrium. We can now characterise this equilibrium more fully. We already know that $t = 0$, and that $\tilde{T}$ is linked to T^R via expression (11). To determine T^R in turn, we have to bear in mind that the ex-ante and ex-post levels of second-period consumption (and hence of welfare) will differ for each group. That is because first-period decisions are based on $\bar{T}$, whereas the actual outturn will be either 0 or T^R. This affects the *actual* redistribution to take place in the second period, and drives a wedge between the ex-ante and ex-post levels of welfare for each group.

Consider the situation from the perspective of the second group. Let $\delta(\tilde{T}, B)$ be the function linking the discount factor to the (certainty-equivalent) second-period tariff rate and the foreign transfer (see section

14.1). Distinguishing anticipated from actual outcomes by using "~" with the former, and letting superscripts distinguish the two groups, we first have:

$$E(1, \delta(\cdot)(1 + \tilde{T}), \tilde{W}^2] = \gamma^2(f(\cdot) - i[\delta(\cdot)] + B + \delta(\cdot)F\{k + i[\delta(\cdot), .]\}). \quad (14)$$

This ensures that planned expenditures are consistent with the present discounted value of resources available to the second group. However, if in the second period the government in power reveals itself as the redistributive type, T is set at $T^R > \tilde{T}$, and this group's real income and consumption fall. To represent the situation, define a restricted expenditure function $\bar{E}(\cdot)$ which yields the minimum expenditure level required to reach a given level of welfare when first-period consumption (c^2) is *pre-determined*:

$$\bar{E}(1 + T^R, W^2; c^2) = \min_{c^2} [(1 + T^R)C^2 \text{ s.t. } U(c^2, C^2) \geq W^2], \quad (15)$$

where:

$$c^2 = E_1[1, \delta(\cdot)(1 + \tilde{T}), \tilde{W}^2]. \quad (16)$$

Then, second-period equilibrium requires

$$\bar{E}(1 + T^R, W^2; c^2) = \gamma^2 F\{k + i[\delta(\cdot)], . \}, \quad (17)$$

i.e., consumption expenditures must be in line with the higher-than-anticipated second-period tariff. Given T^R, equations (14), (16), and (17) jointly determine first-period consumption (c^2), ex-ante welfare $(\tilde{W}^2)$, and ex-post welfare (W^2) for the second group. An analogous set of equations can be written also for the first group.

Notice that a time consistent path of policy would require that the constraint $W^2 \geq \bar{W}$ be binding for the "redistributive" government in equilibrium. This is because the second group can always be squeezed to the limit in the second period—once all savings and investment decisions have been made—without incurring any efficiency costs. Hence, the equations above can be used to solve for the optimal choice of T^R. To do so, we fix W^2 at $\bar{W}$, and let the three equations determine T^R, c^2, and $\tilde{W}^2$. This defines an implicit function $T^R = T^R(B, \pi)$.

Of particular interest is the nature of the linkage between B and T^R in such a pooling equilibrium. While the algebra here gets messy, the basic story is clear. An increase in B raises real income in the economy both through its direct effect and through the induced increase in investment (the latter being at a suboptimal level given $T^R > 0$). That in turn stimulates first-period consumption, and makes room for a greater squeeze of the less-favoured group through a larger tariff in the second period. Hence a larger amount of foreign aid will result in a greater intertemporal distortion.

Foreign assistance therefore has two important hidden costs in terms of the credibility of the reform process. First and foremost, it makes a pooling equilibrium more likely, and increases the probability that a genuinely reform-minded government will be confused with one whose motives are different. Secondly, by relaxing the economy-wide budget constraint, it permits a larger redistributive role for a government so inclined, and a more generous application of distorting policies to that end.

Notice, however, that the "redistributive" government pictured here also cares about efficiency. This sets a natural limit to how far it would like to pursue an intertemporal wedge. In particular, it is possible that for sufficiently high levels of T^R, further increases in B will be welfare-*reducing* for this government, as the added costs of the intertemporal distortion (since T^R is increasing in B) may be severe enough. In such a case, it would prefer to allow the constraint on W^2 not to bind. But this would require an ability to precommit to a level of the second-period tariff which is lower than that required by time consistency. Short of such pre-commitments, the redistributive government will always be tempted to tax the second group to the maximum extent, as there are no efficiency costs of doing so once the second period starts.

Separating equilibrium. Let us now turn to *separating* equilibria. In such equilibria the "liberalising" government will not face a credibility problem. It is clear from the above discussion that this will be the case whenever $B < B^{min}$, i.e., whenever foreign inflows are not sufficiently large to persuade the "redistributive" government to undertake trade reform in the first period. The more interesting questions arise when $B \geq B^{min}$, yet the "liberalising" government can successfully signal its type in order to achieve separation. How can it do so, and will it want to?

In general, governments will have a multitude of signals available to them. But the better signals are the ones that can communicate the desired message most directly. In the present framework, the most direct signal of the government's future intentions is the first-period tariff itself. The appropriate signal can be communicated by implementing a *negative* tariff, or an import subsidy. (A positive tariff would clearly not do the job since it makes the "redistributive" government only keener to imitate.) Such a signal conveys important information to the public since an import subsidy increases the cost to the "redistributive" government of mimicking the "liberaliser." And the "liberalising" government can profitably send such a signal, even though the subsidy policy is going to be costly to it too.

To see these points, it is useful to determine first the costs of an import subsidy to the "redistributive" government. Based on this, we can then argue that with a sufficiently large first-period subsidy, pooling will no longer remain an equilibrium. Finally, we can check to see whether this signalling strategy is a profitable one for the "liberalising" government.

To start with, consider the effect of a first-period subsidy on the "redistributive" government's welfare. The subsidy has both distributional and efficiency costs for the "redistributive" government. It distorts the relative price of second-period consumption even more, i.e., it reduces the consumption rate of interest further. In addition, with the subsidy in place, the resources available to the government for redistributive purposes will be lower: some of the second-period tariff revenue now goes to subsidise the first-period consumption of the less-favoured group, and cannot be used to transfer income to the favoured group. To offset this, the government may want to raise T^R further, but at the margin the cost of doing this has increased as well: the subsidy exacerbates the intertemporal distortion, and on this account makes a *lower* T^R preferable. Hence the "redistributive" government is caught in a bind, which will be reflected in a lower level of welfare for the favoured group. Effectively, the subsidy worsens the trade-off between efficiency and distribution for this government. Its value as a signal of the reformist government's intentions resides precisely in this fact.[10]

Since the first-period subsidy increases the cost to the "redistributive" government of imitating the "liberaliser," pooling will no longer remain a possible equilibrium for a sufficiently high level of s. Denote by s^* the minimum level of the subsidy needed to achieve separation. The optimal second-period tariff of the redistributive government is now written as $T^R(s^*, B, \pi)$. The level of s^* is then implicitly defined by the following equality:

$$W^1[-s^*, T^R(s^*, B, \pi); B > 0] = W^1(\bar{t}, \bar{t}; B = 0), \tag{18}$$

where $W^1(\cdot)$ is once again the maximum-value function for the "redistributive" government. Past a certain level s^*, this government will prefer to give up the foreign aid B and will revert to its separating strategy of imposing a uniform tariff $\bar{t}$ in both periods.

When will the "liberalising" government signal? The question now becomes whether the "liberalising" government will find it in its interest to separate via signalling in this fashion. The answer has to be ambiguous in general since signalling is costly: it imposes efficiency costs on this govenment as well. In the present framework, such costs could be avoided in principle by subsidising imports in the second period also. This way, the inter-temporal distortions induced by the first-period subsidy could be elemi-nated (or, more generally, reduced). But the problem with this strategy is that it is time-inconsistent. Once the second period comes around, the "liberalising" government will no longer have the incentive to imple-ment the subsidy, as it generally prefers to avoid trade distortions, and the private sector will have already irrevocably allocated its consumption intertemporally. This in turn implies that the "promise" of a second-period subsidy will not be credible, and hence will not yield the desired pattern of intertemporal substitution.

Given that the "liberaliser" cannot avoid the cost of signalling, how far will it be able to go? Notice that the marginal efficiency cost of the first-period subsidy is *lower* for this government than it is for the redistributive government, provided separation is achieved. The reason is simple. Once the signal is communicated, the expected second-period tariff falls to zero, and the welfare cost of the first-period subsidy is therefore lowered. In effect, a "small" enough subsidy, which is successful in separating the two governments, will lead to only second-order welfare losses to the reformist government. Since the reduction in the intertemporal distortion achieved by credibility is a source of first-order welfare gain, the balance will be in favour of signalling whenever s^* is small enough. In other words, credible reform will have a bias towards overshooting its target.

More can be said. To the reformist government, the cost incurred by lack of credibility is proportional to the distortion in the consumption rate of interest caused by it (see section 14.1). Now, a credible signal via the subsidy creates a distortion in the consumption rate of interest which is *equivalent* to that created by the lack of credibility: in both cases future goods are rendered more expensive relative to present goods. Therefore, the government will pursue the signalling strategy (provided it does in-duce separation) up to the point where the intertemporal price distortion is equal to that it would otherwise suffer under pooling. Denote by s^{max} the rate of the subsidy that causes a level of distortion *identical* to any given $\tilde{T}(B, \pi)$, where $\tilde{T}(B, \pi)$ stands (as before) for the intertemporal price distortion under pooling and no subsidy. The level of s^{max} is defined implicitly by

$$\delta/(1 - s^{max}) = \delta[1 + \tilde{T}(B, \pi)]. \tag{19}$$

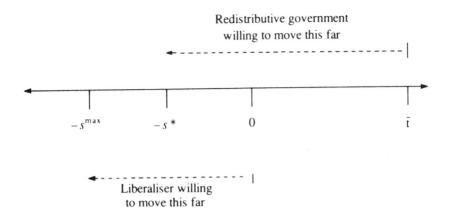

Figure 14.1
Signalling equilibrium

This expression equates the consumption rate of interest resulting from a first-period subsidy (and no credibility problem) with that emerging in a pooling equilibrium (with no subsidy). Or:

$$s^{max} = \tilde{T}(\cdot)/[1 + \tilde{T}(\cdot)]. \tag{20}$$

This tells us the maximum rate of subsidisation the "liberalising" government is willing to undertake, provided separation is thereby achieved. (Notice that the subsidy has been defined throughout in specific rather than ad-valorem terms. In the latter case, s^{max} would be defined simply by $s^{max} = \tilde{T}$.)

Whether the signal will be employed and a separating equilibrium will result can now be easily determined. The answer depends on the relationship between s^* and s^{max} (see figure 14.1). As long as $s^{max} > s^*$, it will pay to signal, and the reformist government will select $s = s^*$.[11] When $s^{max} < s^*$, effective signalling will be too costly, and the government will resign itself to living with the credibility problem and choose $s = 0$.[12] In the unlikely case that $s^{max} = s^*$, the government will be indifferent between the two strategies.

Finally, consider whether the "liberalising" government would be willing to ask its foreign creditors to *curtail* their assistance so as to reduce the incentive of the "redistributive" government to mimic. Provided s^* is small enough, this will not be a profitable strategy since the income losses due to reductions in B will be first-order and large relative to the costs of increasing s. But with large s^* (i.e., costly signalling) there will exist a tradeoff at the margin between B and s.

14.4   Concluding Remarks

The purpose of this paper was to make precise an intuition that is commonly shared: the credibility of policy reform is intimately linked to the magnitude of the reform, and, by implication, the pace at which it is carried out. The argument offered here is that policy overshooting may have the consequence of distinguishing a genuinely reform-minded government from its more equivocal counterparts. That in turn has the effect of rendering the reform process more credible than it would otherwise have been, alleviating many problems introduced by the credibility gap. To be sure, the size of reform is not the only signal that will generally be available to policy-makers.[13] But such a signal has the advantage that its message is carried within the policy itself, and hence is relatively easily decoded by its recipients. Other, less direct signals will often require that the public disentangle complicated general-equilibrium relationships.

While many of the conclusions drawn in the preceding sections are specific to the model analysed, the basic argument is a robust one. At the outset of any reform, the public will typically be unable to fathom the true motivations of the government undertaking the reform. Since the distorting policies in question have been put in place by those in power to begin with, what reason is there to believe that the authorities now "see the light"? The confusion becomes worse when, as is often the case, the policy freedom of the government is temporarily restricted as a consequence of a crisis whose resolution requires the cooperation of actors in favour of reform. In the present model, such a situation was created by the availability of foreign assistance contingent on trade reform. But clearly such instances are more general. For lack of alternatives, a temporary crisis will frequently require incoherent and ill-intentioned policy-makers to act (temporarily) just like coherent and well-intentioned ones. Signalling via policy-overshooting can then help reduce the confusion.

With respect to trade reform proper, the conclusions of the present paper run against much conventional wisdom regarding the advantages of gradualism. While I have not considered any of the usual justifications for gradualism, the credibility argument made here serves to qualify the usual arguments made in that context. In practice, the nature of the tradeoff between these possibly conflicting considerations will depend on the importance of the credibility gap. The more severe are the credibility problem and its consequences, the more likely it is that a sharp break with the past will be viewed as attractive.

Notes

I have benefited from the comments of Avinash Dixit, Sweder van Wijnbergen, two anonymous referees, and participants at seminars at Princeton, University of Michigan, and the Board of Governors of the Federal Reserve System. The usual caveat applies.

1. Imperfect information regarding the government's objective function can in fact alleviate time-inconsistency problems, where such problems exist. For an example in the macroeconomic context, see Backus and Driffill (1985).

2. Such circumstances are common in developing countries, as can be seen from the following excerpt regarding trade reform in the Philippines during the early 1980s: "There was little to support the view that President Marcos who initiated the reforms strongly believed in the desirability of free trade ... [T]he crucial factor for free trade may have been the foreign credit received in exchange for it. To the Marcos government, a balance-of-payments crisis was far more costly than dealing with a domestic lobby for protection" (Clarete, 1988, p. 102).

3. This conclusion is consistent with the apparent empirical regularity that trade reforms are more likely to be successful when they are undertaken wholesale and in such a way as to create a major break with the past. A recent review of 37 liberalisation episodes in 19 countries concludes that "the likelihood of survival of a liberalization attempt is substantially higher where the initial policy measures undertaken are major and significant: halting or hesitating policy actions leading to a very gradual liberalization are much more likely to cause a collapse. This is particularly true in instances of countries (characteristic of most of Latin America) in which the history restrictions on trade is long and pervasive" (Papageorgiou et al., 1986). The authors conjecture that this might be partly due to reasons having to do with credibility.

4. In a richer model, the private sector would normally have the ability to adjust some of its behaviour once the expectations upon which it acted is proved wrong. This would then drive a wedge between the ex-ante and ex-post levels of welfare. For an interesting analysis of such issues in a different context see Persson and Svensson (1983). See also below.

5. For other models that endogenise credibility see Engel and Kletzer (1987) and Rodrik (1989).

6. The certainty-equivalent tariff is close, but not identical, to the expected value of the second-period tariff, even though consumers are assumed to be risk-averse in income. This follows from the fact that the indirect utility function is not linear in prices.

7. This is somewhat reminiscent of the framework considered by Alesina (1987) in which the existence of two political parties with different trade-offs between inflation and unemployment is shown to generate a business cycle that accompanies the political cycle.

8. In this case, the maximisation problem of the redistributive government has to be stated differently involving a two-stage decision: first maximise over T, given t; secondly, choose t given second-period decision rule linking T to t.

9. Witness the recent case of Zambia, which is described in the colourful prose of *The Economist* as follows: "Now Mr Kaunda has told the IMF to get lost. He wants to service no debts, get no new loans and have no new policies. Instead he is imposing on his people a new, tighter version of the bad old policies that led to the trouble in the first place, and whose only—bogus—merit is that they are not imposed by foreign bankers" (May 9, 1987, p. 13).

326   Dani Rodrik

10. An appendix, available on request, provides more detail on these issues.

11. As is well known, the uniqueness of separating equilibria cannot be established without some restrictions on updating rules for out-of-equilibrium events (see Cho and Kreps, 1987). With reasonable restrictions, the uniqueness of the $s = s^*$ equilibrium can be established easily. This is shown in an appendix available to the interested reader on request.

12. In this case, the intertemporal distortion could be severe enough for the government to be willing to forsake B and set $t > 0$.

13. In a recent paper, for example, Persson and van Wijnbergen (1987) examine the possibility that wage-price controls may act as a signal of a disinflationary government's intentions.

References

Alesina, A. (1987). "Macroeconomic policy in a two-party system as a repeated game." *Quarterly Journal of Economics*, vol. 102, pp. 651–78.

Backus, D., and Driffill, J. (1985). "Inflation and reputation." *American Economic Review*, vol. 75, pp. 530–8.

Barro, R. J., and Gordon, D. B. (1983). "A positive theory of monetary policy in a natural rate model." *Journal of Political Economy*, vol. 91, pp. 589–610.

Calvo, G. (1986). "Incredible reforms." Unpublished paper, University of Pennsylvania.

Cho, I.-K., and Kreps, D. M. (1987). "Signaling games and stable equilibria." *Quarterly Journal of Economics*, vol. 102, pp. 179–221.

Clarete, R. (1988). "The recent Philippine trade liberalization: Can the multilateral trade system sustain it?" In *The Small Among the Big*, vol. II (ed. John Whalley). London, Ontario: Centre for the Study of International Economic Relations, The University of Western Ontario.

Dixit, A. K. and Norman, V. (1980). *Theory of International Trade*. Digswell Place, Welwyn, Herts: James Nisbet and Company Limited and the Cambridge University Press.

Engel, C. and Kletzer, K. (1987). "Trade policy under endogenous credibility." NBER Working Paper No. 2449.

Froot, K. (1988). "Credibility, real interest rates, and the optimal speed of trade liberalization." *Journal of International Economics*, vol. 25, pp. 71–93.

Papageorgiou, D., Michaely, M. and Choksi, A. (1986). "The phasing of a trade liberalization policy: Preliminary evidence." World Bank: CPD Discussion Paper No. 1986–42.

Persson, T. and Svensson, L. E. O. (1983). "Is optimism good in a Keynesian economy?" *Economica*, vol. 50, pp. 291–300.

Persson, T. and Svensson, L. E. O. and van Wijnbergen, S. (1987). "Signaling, wage controls and monetary disinflation policy." Unpublished paper.

Rodrik, D. (1989). "Liberalization, sustainability, and the design of structural adjustment programs." World Bank: Unpublished paper.

Rodrik, D. and Zeckhauser, R. (1988). "The dilemma of government responsiveness." *Journal of Policy Analysis and Management* vol. 7, Fall.

Staiger, R. and Tabellini, G. (1987). "Discretionary trade policy and excessive protection." *American Economic Review*, vol. 77, pp. 823–37.

van Wijnbergen, S. (1985). "Trade reform, aggregate investment and capital flight: On credibility and the value of information." *Economics Letters*, vol. 19, pp. 369–72.

15

Credibility of Policymakers and of Economic Reforms

Alex Cukierman and
Mariano Tommasi

15.1 Introduction

The process of market-oriented economic reforms that swept a large part of the developing world is a great source of questions for students of political economy. Why did these countries undertake such drastic and in many cases surprising measures? What explains the similarities and differences across cases? Why did some countries advance much faster and more successfully than others? Even within countries, why did some policymakers have more success than others in their reform attempts? The literature on such heady topics, already quite abundant, is reviewed in Rodrik (1996) and in Tommasi and Velasco (1996).

In this chapter, we concentrate on the identity of the policymakers who undertook reforms. As Rodrik (1993, 1996) notes, one of the paradoxes of this process is the fact that many market-oriented reform efforts, which included such measures as trade liberalization, fiscal adjustment, and deregulation, were implemented by a formerly populist president that often belonged to a historically interventionist party. Examples include Argentina under Peronist President Menem, Peru under President Fujimori, Bolivia under populist President Paz Estenssoro, and Brazil under President Cardoso.

Peronist President Carlos Menem implemented an extensive and quite successful transformation of Argentina into a market-friendly economy. This was particularly surprising since "Peronism has been virtually synonymous with populism and protectionism" (Rodrik 1993, 356). As our model will explain, Menem brought a comparative advantage to the reform process in that he could credibly claim that such reforms were necessary and good for most Argentines. Moreover, "Menem used Peronist language even as he conveyed new proposals. The public, far from considering this to be contradictory, understood it quite well. The public knew that Peronism had changed, was speaking of privatization, of producing, of integrating Argentina in the world, of foreign investment, and that none of if meant it was any less Peronista. When he announced his program and began implementing it, when he opened up to entrepreneurs..., Menem did not lose any of his electoral support" (Mora y Araujo 1991, English quote from Packenham 1992).[1] As a matter of fact, Menem was reelected in 1995 in the midst of a recession induced by the "Tequila shock."

President Fujimori was first elected in Peru by being to the left of the opposing candidate Vargas Llosa, with the electoral support of populist APRA and of the left. Like Menem, he was the "president like you" candidate, which distinguished him from an opponent that appeared to middle and lower class voters as "oligarchic" and "IMF-oriented." Nonetheless, Fujimori implemented tough market-oriented reforms. Inflation was reduced from 7,650 percent in 1990 to 57 percent in 1992. Fujimori mounted an aggressive campaign to privatize some of the largest state-owned enterprises and restored the country's credit worthiness. Despite his closure of Congress, he was considered by Peruvians a success (his approval rate following the closure was 80 percent). Fujimori was also reelected after changing the constitution to allow for reelection.

The orthodox 1985 stabilization in Bolivia was successfully implemented by Víctor Paz Estenssoro—one of the leaders of the MNR (a revolutionary movement with socialist orientation)—who had pursued inflationary spending policies in his previous presidency. He, like Menem, was able to overcome trade union opposition, since he could claim to be a representative of the working class.

Fernando Collor de Melo was elected President of Brazil in 1989 as the right-center candidate over the left-center candidate Lula. He later pledged to liberalize the Brazilian economy, with very limited success. There were other elements, but analysts believe that his structural situation was a big obstacle (Packenham 1992). It took Fernando Enrique Cardoso, one of the authors of the influential dependence theory manifesto *Dependence and Development in Latin America*, to push forward the reforms.

There are also episodes outside Latin America which seem to follow this pattern, such as the economic reforms under the Solidarity government in Poland and under the socialist government of Felipe Gonzalez in Spain.

All these cases run counter the analysts' first intuition, which is to expect market-oriented swings to be creatures of right-wing govern-

Table 15.1
Instances of Market-Oriented Reforms

Government		Successful	Not successful
Left		Australia 1983	
		New Zealand 1989	
		Spain 1982	
Center		Colombia 1989	
		Poland 1990	Brazil 1987*
		Portugal 1985	Perú 1980
		Indonesia 1982	
		Mexico 1987	
Right	Democratic	Turkey 1980**	
	Military	Chile 1983	
		Korea 1979	

Source: From the tables of Williamson and Haggard (1994, 563).
Notes: *Unsuccessful "because" government not from the Left (according to Packenham 1992). ** Center-Right

ments.[2] Indeed, John Williamson asked the contributors to his (1994) edited volume on economic policy reform to look into such conventional wisdom. Table 15.1 is obtained from those thirteen cases summarized in Williamson and Haggard (1994). They found little support for the association of market reforms with right-wing administrations. As a matter of fact, in only three out of their thirteen cases was market-oriented reform implemented by what they classify as right-wing governments. Interestingly, these three cases included the two military dictatorships in their sample (Chile and Korea). This tendency would suggest that under fairly democratic conditions, market-oriented reforms are more likely to be implemented by governments coming from the left, or center-left, of the political spectrum. More generally, large shifts in policy are likely to involve "reversals" of a party's traditional policy position.

This phenomenon is reminiscent of some well-known foreign policy episodes. These events include the mutual concessions made by hawkish-Prime Minister Begin and hawkish President Sadat in their historical accord at Camp David, as well as the overture to Mao Tse-tung's China made by President Nixon, a figure with impeccable anti-Communist credentials.[3]

In this chapter, we develop a model that explains why, and in particular under what conditions, market-oriented reforms are more likely to be implemented by parties from the left. The crucial element in our story is the existence of an asymmetry of information between the government (the policymaker or party in power) and the general public (represented by the median voter). In particular, we postulate that policymakers are better informed than the general public about the way in which policies map into outcomes. Such an asymmetry has been recognized at least since Downs's pioneering work (Downs 1957) and has been recently utilized in related work by Alesina and Cukierman (1990), Harrington (1993), Roemer (1994), Coate and Morris (1995), Lupia and McCubbins (1995), Schultz (1996), and others.[4]

The model identifies as condition for "policy reversals" (i.e., a policy implemented by a party that traditionally opposes such policies) that the policy changes under analysis should be large and should occur infrequently. These two conditions seem to hold in the economic reform and foreign policy examples above. Also, the effects of policy should be uncertain, and only materialize far into the future over time. (In terms of the model, it is necessary that the true outcome is not observed until after some key political filter is passed.)

The specific model we use here is a referendum game, in which policies need the approval of a majority of voters or key players before their implementation. As argued below, the veto power implicit in a referendum is meant to represent a large class of possible actions by key political players that might block the implementation of policies.

In a companion paper (Cukierman and Tommasi 1996), we illustrate similar ideas with a different institutional structure: a representative democracy in which the incumbent party commits to a policy platform. If reelected, the party implements the proposed policies. The two works also differ in that in Cukierman and Tommasi (1996) we treat the action space as continuous while here it is discrete. The stark formulation we use here enables us to develop specific implications for the credibility of policies and of policymakers in terms of voters' posterior beliefs about the variable that is the private information of the policymaker. In the other paper, we obtain smoother implications for the likelihood of implementation of policies by alternative parties; in particular, *moderate* right-wing policies are more likely to be implemented by right-wing parties (and similarly for the left), but *extreme* right-wing policies are more likely to be implemented by left-wing parties (and vice versa). The broad conditions of (i) asymmetric information, (ii) only large and infrequent policy changes, and (iii) delayed outcomes apply in both our direct *and* representative democracy models.

15.2   The Model

We present a referendum game between a policymaker and the voting public, similar to the one in Lupia (1992, 1993). The wording is intentionally general, since we believe the ideas from the model apply to a broad set of government policies, not just economic reforms.[5] Notice that this structure is more general than the specific institution of referendum. In many countries (especially LDCs) approval of key interest groups is a prerequisite for the successful implementation of any policy (Bates 1990). The ways in which disapproval is converted into effective actions are varied, ranging from binding referenda to assassinations.

The structure is kept to the bare minimum necessary for identifying conditions that are conducive to policy "reversals." The formal analysis focuses on the case in which the policymaker in power is of the "left" type. The symmetric case of a right-wing policymaker is not analyzed explicitly, but it is in the background. The main results come from comparing the differential ability of right-wing (R) and left-wing (L) policymakers to implement certain policies.

Preferences of player j—L, R, or voters—are given by

$$U_j = -|z - (c_j + \gamma)|, \tag{1}$$

where z is the policy implemented, c_j is a constant for each player, and γ is a stochastic variable. The ideal policy of any player depends on the type-specific "taste" parameter c_j, as well as on the realization of the exogenous state of nature parameter γ. γ induces unidirectional shifts in the preferred policies of everyone, capturing the effect of external circumstances. To simplify the exposition we assume, without loss of generality, that $c_L = -c$, $c_R = c > 0$, and $c_m = 0$, where c_m is the bliss point of the median voter. Hence $U_L = -|z - (\gamma - c)|$ and $U_m = -|z - \gamma|$

The timing of events (summarized in figure 15.1) is as follows. First, L observes the realization of the random variable γ that affects everybody's payoffs. Then he chooses between doing nothing (in which case the status quo policy, which we normalize to 0, prevails) or proposing a policy $x_L \in \{-x, x\}$, where $x > 0$. We interpret $-x$ as a left-wing policy (to the left of the status quo), and x as a right-wing policy.[6] After a policy x_L is proposed, voters choose $v \in \{0, 1\}$, where 0 is a vote against and 1 a vote for the proposed policy. Voters have single-peaked symmetric preferences; hence, the outcome is decided by the median voter, with bliss point $c_m (= 0)$.

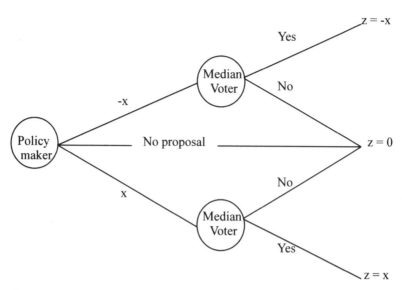

Figure 15.1

Variable z denotes the final policy. $z = 0$ if the policymaker choose not to propose an alternative or if the proposed alternative is voted against. $z = x_L$ if the proposed alternative is accepted by voters.

The prior distribution of γ, which is common knowledge, is

$$\gamma = \begin{cases} -a & \text{with probability } p \\ 0 & \text{with probability } (1 - 2p) \\ a & \text{with probability } p, \end{cases} \tag{2}$$

where $a > 0$. If $\gamma = a$, right-wing policies become relatively more desirable for everyone. As explained in section 15.1, the underlying idea is that policies map into outcomes in an uncertain way. Even though people have well-defined stable preferences over outcomes, the uncertainty over the mapping from policy to outcomes induces reduced-form preferences over polices that have a "stochastic" component. The key assumption of the model is that the policymaker is better informed than the median voter about that mapping. In particular, he or she observes the realization of γ while the voters do not. Voters will infer something about γ from the policy proposals and the identity of the policymaker making them. In section 15.3 we provide specific examples from economic and foreign policymaking.

Let $S_L : \{-a, 0, a\} \rightarrow \{-x, 0, x\}$ be the (left-wing) policymaker strategy, and $S_m : \{-x, x\} \rightarrow \{0, 1\}$ be the strategy of the voter. We will use $\pi(\gamma|x_L)$ to denote the posterior probability that the voter assigns to that particular value of γ given that the government proposed policy x_L. Let $B = \{\pi(-a|-x), \pi(0|-x), \pi(a|-x); \pi(-a|x), \pi(0|x), \pi(a|x)\}$ be the voter's posterior belief system about γ after observing the choice of x_L.[7]

15.2.1 Equilibrium

The game is a sequential game of incomplete information; a natural solution concept is Perfect Bayesian Equilibrium (PBE). A PBE of this game consists of a strategy for the policymaker, a strategy for the median voter, and beliefs (over γ) for the voter, which satisfy three properties. First, the voter's beliefs are consistent with L's strategy and the priors; that is, they are generated by Bayesian updating whenever possible. Second, the voter's strategy is optimal given these beliefs and L's strategy. Finally, L's strategy is optimal given the voter's strategy and beliefs.

We now introduce three conditions that will generate an equilibrium with the feature that it takes a left-wing party to implement a right-wing policy.

$$a - c > x/2 \tag{A1}$$

$$c > x/2 \tag{A2}$$

$$p < 1/3. \tag{A3}$$

Notice that A1–A3 characterize a nonempty set of parameter values. We discuss the role and interpretation of each condition below.

Let $x(\gamma)$ be the action chosen by L as a function of his observation of γ, and let $v(x)$ be the vote chosen after observing proposal x.

Consider the strategies S_L^* and S_m^* such that

$$S_L^* : x(-a) = x(0) = -x, x(a) = x;$$

$$S_m^* : v(-x) = 0, v(x) = 1;$$

and the belief system B^*:

$$\pi(-a| - x) = p/(1 - p) \qquad \pi(-a|x) = 0;$$

$$\pi(0| - x) = (1 - 2p)/(1 - p) \qquad \pi(0|x) = 0;$$

$$\pi(a| - x) = 0 \qquad \pi(a|x) = 1.$$

Define the equilibrium E^* as $\{S_L^*, S_m^*, B^*\}$.

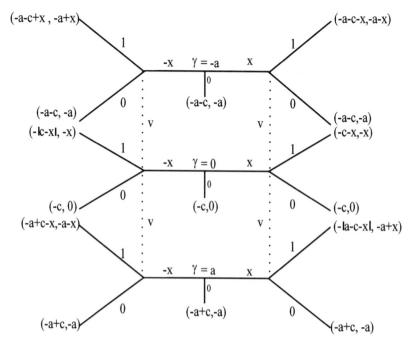

Figure 15.2

PROPOSITION 1   If A1–A3 are satisfied, then:

1. (Existence) E^* is a PBE.

2. (Uniqueness) E^* is the only equilibrium that survives iterated elimination of weakly dominated strategies.

Proof Note that this is a signaling game. First L learns his "type" $\gamma \in \{-a, 0, a\}$. Then he sends a message $m \in \{-x, 0, x\}$. Then the voter chooses an action $v \in \{0, 1\}$. (If L chooses $m = 0$, then the voter's action is irrelevant.) The resulting game is depicted in figure 15.2.

(1) To prove that E^* is a PBE, consider first the left-wing policymaker *with type* (i.e., *who has observed*) $-a$. He is supposed to choose $-x$, which will be rejected. Deviating to action 0 does not change his payoff. Deviating to x will lead to acceptance and a payoff of $-a - c - x$ rather than his equilibrium payoff $-a - c$. This deviation is unprofitable for $x > 0$. Now take the left-wing policymaker with type 0. He is also supposed to chose $-x$. Deviating to action 0 does not change his payoff. Deviating to action x decreases his payoff to $-c - x$ from $-c$. Finally, take L with type a. He is supposed to choose action x, which will be accepted, resulting in

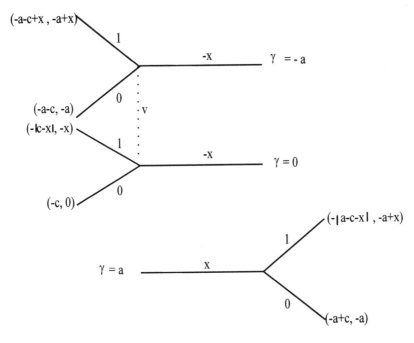

Figure 15.3

payoff $-|a - c - x|$. Deviating results in a payoff $-a + c$. If $a - c - x > 0$, this is unprofitable for $x > 0$. If $a - c - x < 0$, this is unprofitable for $a - c > x/2$. Both conditions are satisfied, so there is no profitable deviation for the policymaker.

Now turn to the voter. If he sees message x, he assumes the policymaker is of type a. His best response is $v = 1$, since $-a + x > -a$. On the other hand, if he sees $-x$, he assumes L is of type $-a$ with probability $p/(1 - p)$ and of type 0 with complementary probability, using Bayes's rule. Voting $v = 0$ is optimal if $p < 1/3$, as assumed in (A3). Therefore, the voter does not want to deviate from the proposed equilibrium.

(2) To show uniqueness, we begin by noting (from figure 15.2) that for L with type $-a$, $-x$ weakly dominates 0 and x, because $-a - c + x > -a - c > -a - c - x$; therefore, we can prune these two strategies. Next, for L of type a, x weakly dominates 0 and x, because $-|a - c - x| > -a + c > -a + c - x$; therefore, we can prune these two strategies. Finally, note that for L of type 0, $-x$ weakly dominates 0 and x because $-|c - x| > -c > -c - x$, so we can prune these strategies. This results in the much-simplified game depicted in figure 15.3.

In the reduced game, the voter is better off voting yes to proposal (message) x. On the other hand, when he sees the message $-x$, he uses Bayes's rule to update his beliefs, and given $p < 1/3$, he rejects the proposal. Hence, only E^* survives iterated elimination of weakly dominated strategies. Q.E.D.

15.2.2 Intuition

In equilibrium, the left-wing policymaker proposes left-wing policies for $\gamma = -a$ and $\gamma = 0$, while he proposes right-wing policies for $\gamma = a$. The median voter will accept the right-wing policies and reject the left-wing ones from L.

Remember that $\gamma \in \{-a, 0, a\}$ is a parameter that affects everybody in the same direction. In economic applications, we would call it an "efficiency" effect. (A1) requires a to be large enough to induce L to choose x when $\gamma = a$, that is, large enough to overcome his leftist "preference." If this were not the case, L would always prefer policy $-x$, and policy proposals would convey no information.

Condition (A2) requires the "ideological" preference effect to be large enough to induce a tendency toward $-x$ for $\gamma = 0$ (when there is no efficiency effect, he indulges in his leftist tendencies). Notice that this tendency is the source of L's credibility problem when $\gamma = -a$, that is, when left-wing policies are indeed efficient. This is commonly referred to as a "cry wolf" situation. This finding is consistent with that of Schultz (1996) who shows that polarization (a large c in our model) is likely to generate inefficient policies—policies that do not maximize the median voter's welfare given the true state of nature (γ in our model). Notice that if c were even larger, (A1) would be violated and the left-wing policymaker might always choose $-x$, which would lead to a situation even more inefficient than that of E^*.

Condition (A3) states that the probability of $\gamma = -a$ has to be small enough compared to the probability of $\gamma = 0$ so that the median voter votes against $-x$. (If the probability of $-a$ is high, then it might be beneficial to accept $-x$ from any party). Parties propose policies that are "ideologically" motivated often enough—with likelihood $(1 - 2p) >$ $1/3$—so that they have a credibility problem. If, when voters observed $x_L = -x$, they assigned a high probability to the truth being $-a$, then they would tend to accept it. In that case, anyone could implement any policy and we wouldn't have the "*only* Nixon could go to China" effect.

In order to completely characterize the situation, an analogous analysis for the case where the incumbent is R leads to an equilibrium with:

$S_R^* : x(a) = x(0) = x, x(-a) = -x;$

$S_m^* : v(-x) = 1, v(x) = 0;$

and the belief system B^*:

$\pi(-a| - x) = 1 \qquad \pi(-a|x) = 0;$

$\pi(0| - x) = 0, \qquad \pi(0|x) = (1 - 2p)/(1 - p);$

$\pi(a| - x) = 0, \qquad \pi(a|x)$

15.2.3 Implications for Credibility and Information Transmission

Politicians usually justify their policy proposals by claiming that the state of the world is the one that (if believed) would elicit maximum public support for their proposed policies. In the context of our model, the statement that would elicit maximum support (if believed) for policy $-x$ (for policy x) is "$\gamma = -a$" ("$\gamma = a$").[8] One measure of the credibility of policy proposals is, therefore, the posterior probability assigned by the public to the event $\gamma = -a$ (or a) when policy $-x$ (or x) is proposed.[9] For this definition of credibility we obtain:

RESULT 1 (CREDIBILITY OF A GIVEN POLICYMAKER ACROSS POLICIES)

$$\pi(a|x_L = x) = 1 > \pi(-a|x_L = -x) = p/(1 - p) \qquad \text{(i)}$$

A left-wing policymaker has more credibility when he proposes right-wing policies than when he proposes left-wing policies.

$$\pi(-a|x_R = -x) = 1 > \pi(a|x_R = x) = p/(1 - p) \qquad \text{(ii)}$$

A right-wing policymaker has more credibility when he proposes left-wing policies than when he proposes right-wing policies.

That is, credibility increases as politicians move away from their "ideological" positions. Note that credibility depends on the policy-policymaker *pair*.

RESULT 2 (CREDIBILITY ACROSS POLICYMAKERS FOR A GIVEN PROPOSAL)

$$\pi(a|x_L = x) = 1 > \pi(a|x_R = x) = p/(1 - p) \qquad \text{(i)}$$

A left-wing policymaker is more credible than a right-wing policymaker when announcing a right-wing policy.

$$\pi(-a|x_R = -x) = 1 > \pi(-a|x_L = -x) = p/(1 - p) \qquad \text{(ii)}$$

A right-wing policymaker is more credible than a left-wing policymaker when announcing a left-wing policy.

Our analysis has implications also for the transmission of information embedded in policy announcements, which relates to work on strategic models of talk in political decision making—Austen-Smith (1992), Gilligan (1993), and Gilligan and Krehbiel (1989)—and in the choice of monetary policy—Cukierman and Meltzer (1986), Stein (1989), and Cukierman and Liviatan (1991). We could measure the degree of information that voters have at the end of the game, by the posterior probability that they assign to the true value of γ, $\pi(\gamma|\gamma)$. This leads to:

RESULT 3 (INFORMATION TRANSMISSION)   When L is in office:

$$\pi(-a|-a) = p/(1-p) < \pi(0|0) = (1-2p)/(1-p) < \pi(a|a) = 1;$$

and the converse is true when R is in office.

Hence, voters obtain better information the further away is the required policy from the ideological position of the party in office.

As was the case for credibility, the quality of information transmission depends both on the policy and on the policymaker's type. Crawford and Sobel (1982) find that equilibrium signaling is more informative when agent's preferences are more similar. Here we find that equilibrium signaling is more informative, the further away the action (signal) from the exante preferences of the sender. In a wider sense, this result is consistent with that of Crawford and Sobel since (when L is in office) the information transmission is maximal when $\gamma = a$, that is, when the *relative* divergence between the objectives of L and of the median voter is the smallest.

Information acquisition is passive in our model. Calvert (1985) analyzes the (active) choices of a political actor seeking costly advice. He shows that in some cases it is best to seek biased sources of information that are very unlikely to give advice contrary to the actor's priors. In the event that the unexpected recommendation is given, it contains a lot of information (very similar to our result.) In Calvert (1985) the bias is just assumed, while here it is derived as an equilibrium action of the informed agent, given his preferences.

15.3 Applications

The purpose of this section is to provide some applications of the framework of section 15.2 to specific policy issues; namely, to reinterpret the objective function (1) as a reduced form from a more structured situation of collective choice. We provide an economic application (to market-oriented reforms) and a foreign-policy application.

15.3.1 ECONOMIC: A Simple Model of Market-Oriented Reforms

There are three groups in society: rich (R), middle class (M), and poor (P). Rich and poor can be reinterpreted as any other distributive cleavage, with the government having some power for (and some interest in) redistribution. We can think of group P as trade unions, urban dwellers, import-competing sectors, and so forth; and of R as export sectors, nontradable sectors, and so forth. The income of each group is given by

$$y_M = kY$$
$$y_P = d(1-k)Y \qquad\qquad\qquad (3)$$
$$y_R = (1-d)(1-k)Y,$$

where Y is aggregate income, $k \in [0, 1]$ is an exogenous parameter, and $d \in \{\underline{d}, d_s, \bar{d}\}$ is a policy parameter. Variable d_s is the status quo, $\underline{d}$ is a right-wing policy with less redistribution towards the poor, and $\bar{d}$ is a left-wing policy. Let $d_s = \frac{1}{2}(\bar{d} + \underline{d})$. We will interpret a movement from d_s to $\underline{d}$ as a market-oriented shift. (It is worth repeating here that we are agnostics, so that R and P should not be taken to literally mean rich and poor.) Assume that party L's objective is a weighted average of y_M and y_P, while party R's objective is a weighted average of y_M and y_R.

Aggregate income, which realizes after policy implementation, equals

$$Y = Y_0 + \gamma(d_s - d). \qquad\qquad\qquad (4)$$

Equation (3) captures the *distributive* effect of policy d, equivalently to the role played by the heterogeneity implicit in $c > 0$ in section 15.2, while (4) captures the (stochastic) *efficiency* effect of policy d.

Equation (2) in section 15.2 characterizes the prior beliefs over γ, which has the same interpretation as before—"the correct model of the world," or "the way the economy really works" (Roemer 1994). We interpret $p < 1/3$ as the probability that the policymaker becomes convinced (by facts, readings, advice) that the true model of the world is $\gamma = a$ (or $-a$). Variable γ is private information to policymakers, and the crux of the problem is the differential ability of right-and of left-wing policymakers to communicate credibly different values of γ.

The information structure and decision sequence is the same as that in section 15.2. Assume, for simplicity, that the median voter equals group M. Normalize policy as $(d_s - d)$, so that $x = (d_s - \underline{d})$, $x_s = 0$, and $-x = (d_s - \bar{d})$. Policy x represents a decrease in redistribution from R to P (or an increase in redistribution from P to R.) Policy $-x$ represents an increase in redistribution toward P.

If the "efficiency" effect is such that $\gamma = a$, everybody shifts to the right, in the sense that x becomes relatively more desirable. This shift might be enough to induce group M to prefer less redistribution, but not enough for P to prefer it. Imagine a policymaker observing $\gamma = a$, stating that "tough adjustments are needed" and proposing $x = (d_s - \underline{d})$. Who has the credibility to do so? As our analysis of the previous section suggests:

RESULT 4 (COMPARATIVE ADVANTAGES IN POLICY IMPLEMENTATION) A left-wing policymaker will be able to implement a market-oriented swing, not feasible for a right-wing government.

Symmetrically, if a major move to the left were necessary, a right-wing policymaker is more likely to succeed.

So far, we have interpreted successful implementation of market reforms by a left-wing policymaker as a case in which he convinces group M that these measures are efficiency enhancing. We could also build a case in which the approval of P is necessary for the reforms and the efficiency effect is so strong that even P benefits from $x = (d_s - \underline{d})$. In that case, if L proposes x, R's benefit no matter what, so they approve. P's approve since it is their representative (L) who is proposing, while they would reject if the policy had been proposed by a right-wing policymaker.[10]

15.3.2 POLITICAL (Foreign Policy): Land for Peace

Imagine a country involved in important territorial disputes, with frequent armed confrontations. We can think of "lank" (x) and "peace" (P) as two arguments in the utility function, with different people having different preferences (marginal rates of substitution.) For instance, a "dove" (left-wing) will have very flat indifference curves in the $x - P$ space, and a "hawk" (right-wing) will have very steep ones—it requires a large gain in peace to compensate for a small loss of territory.

There is also a transformation curve that shows feasible combinations of land and peace, which depend among other things on the domestic situation and foreign policy of the "enemy." Normalizing the current territory (land) to 0, territorial concessions $-x$ presumably map into increases in peace (decreases in the likelihood of armed confrontation.) Territorial expansion x maps into decreases in P. The exact marginal rate of transformation is not known with certainty. It is reasonable to argue that policymakers are better informed than the average citizen about the domestic situation and foreign strategy of the enemy.[11] Imagine that the policymaker observes $y = -a$; that is, territorial concessions would map into a large increase in the chances for peace. If this were public information, doves as well as "intermediates" will be in favor of making those concessions, while extreme hawks might still oppose.

The question is, what type of policymaker will have more credibility (and hence will be able to influence the voting decision of nonextremists) when proposing $-x$: one with a hawkish or one with a doveish past? The answer seems to be the former. Examples are Menachem Begin (and more recently Yitzhak Rabin), Annuar-el-Sadat, and, stretching the application, Richard Nixon.

15.4   Concluding Remarks

The developing world has been swept by a wave of market-oriented economic reforms. Despite common elements of this process, important variations across cases have occurred (for instance, the differences in timing and speed between Argentina and Brazil.) In this chapter we argue, as does Packenham (1992), that one of the factors that facilitates the implementation of (badly needed) reforms is the identity of the party in office, in particular the partisan relationship of the elected president to the historical legacy of statism. Parties coming from the left have extra credibility stemming from their structural situation, and thus can call upon sacrifices from the populace in order to shift to (what they claim will be) a more efficient and hence wealthier economy in the future.

We formalized this notion in the context of a game of asymmetric information in which the policymaker knows more than the public about the possible future outcomes of the measures under consideration. This formalization links naturally with the literature on policymaking under incomplete information, which has interesting implications in terms of the efficiency of public policy as a function of political and institutional variables. In particular, it relates to work on political competition when the public is uncertain about the way the economy works (as in Harrington 1993, and in Roemer 1994), the effects of political polarization on the efficiency of policy (as in Schultz 1996), and the efficiency of redistributive policies (as in Coate and Morris 1995).[12]

On the theoretical side, the next step would be to incorporate explicitly into consideration political competition (with and without commitment). On the empirical side, table 15.1 provides some suggestive evidence, but more precise testing of the model's predictions must await further work.

Notes

Tel-Aviv University and Center for Economic Research (Tilburg University) and Universidad de San Andrés respectively. We acknowledge the financial support of CIBER at UCLA, the Ammon Ben Nathan Chair in Economics at Tel-Aviv University and the Harvard/MIT RTG in Positive Political Economy. We are indebted to Marcelo Clerici, Gregory Hess, Eric Rasmusen, Adam Shapiro, Robert Shimer, Lones Smith and seminar participants at Boston College, Brown, Chicago, Dartmouth, Geneva, IGIER, MIT, Tel-Aviv, UCLA, CEMA and Universidad de San Andrés for helpful comments.

1. Packenham also discusses the previous administration: President Alfonsin (1983–1989) represented the Union Civica Radical, a historically middle-class, centrist party. He also attempted privatization and stabilization with little success. Some of the fiercest obstacles were the (Peronist-related) trade unions.

2. This perception owes much to the fact that right-wing military governments in the Southern Cone and East Asia were among the earliest reformers in the developing world, and that domestic and foreign business interests are often at the forefront in pressing for policy reform.

3. We are not the first to make this connection. See, for instance, Rodrik (1994) and Packenham (1992).

4. Krehbiel (1991) and the literature referenced there emphasize the assymetry of information within legislatures between the committes and the floor.

5. An early theoretical discussion and evidence on policy choices in referenda, in the context of school budgets, appears in Romer and Rosenthal (1979). Banks (1990) extends the analysis to an asymmetric information environment, in a spirit similar to that of this chapter. A recent summary and extension of work on the setter model is provided by Rosenthal (1990).

6. Our decision to model policy choices as discrete is not difficult to justify. On the one hand, the results do not depend on this assumption, as suggested by the companion paper Cukierman and Tommasi (1996). But also, the cases we have in mind seem to involve a somewhat discrete choice set. Policy choices in the Arab-Israeli conflict are not over squared centimeters of land to be relinquished, but over entire regions, like the Sinai or Gaza Strip. Economic policymaking, broadly defined, also seems to have elements of discreteness, as stressed by Harrington (1993). In the case of economic reforms in the developing world, the issue is whether to have extensive or minimal government intervention in the economy. Perktold (1994) identifies conditions under which equilibrium choices of the *degree* of government intervention will be discrete.

7. A belief system is a probability measure for each history of play (Osborne and Rubinstein 1994, 223). For brevity, we do not discuss beliefs after $x_L = 0$, since those beliefs are irrelevant. The public takes no action if there is no proposal to change the status quo.

8. In Roemer (1994) political parties make announcements about "the way the economy works" (γ in our model), and then propose policies. In his model, there is complete con-

vergence of policies (median voter theorem) but different parties announce different γ's to try to influence people's reduced-form preferences. Roemer does not model the formation of beliefs explicitly, he just postulates a mapping from announcements to beliefs. Here, we deduce the belief-formation process from the rational (Bayesian) behavior of voters.

9. The notion of credibility in the text is by no means the only one possible. Alternative notions of credibility are discussed in Cukierman (1992, chap. 11).

10. On a related issue, Martinelli and Tommasi (1994) argue that the implementation of reform packages might suffer from time-consistency problems. Groups that benefit from early reforms but suffer from later reforms may block the later stages, making some reform paths time-inconsistent. An implication of the logic of this section is that policymakers may, then, start a reform sequence by implementing the measures that hurt their own constituencies.

11. Intelligence services report to the head of the executive (and sometimes to a few ministries) but not to the general public.

12. It also relates to work on strategic models of talk and of information acquistion in political decision making—as in Austen-Smith (1990, 1992, 1993), Gilligan and Krehbiel (1989), Gilligan (1993), Banks (1990), and Calvert (1985).

References

Alesina, Alberto, and Alex Cukierman. 1990. "The Politics of Ambiguity." *Quarterly Journal of Economics* (November): 829–850.

Austen-Smith, David. 1990. "Information Transmission in Debate." *American Journal of Political Science* 34: 124–152.

Austen-Smith, David. 1992. "Strategic Models of Talk in Political Decision Making." *International Political Science Review* 13: 45–58.

Austen-Smith, David. 1993. "Information Acquisition and Orthogonal Argument." In *Political Economy: Institutions, Competition and Representation.* ed. W. Barnett, M. Hinich and N. Schofield, 407–436. Cambridge University Press.

Banks, Jeffrey. 1990. "Monopoly Agenda Control and Asymmetric Information." *Quarterly Journal of Economics* (May): 445–464.

Bates, Robert. 1990. "Towards a Macropolitical Economy in the Field of Development." In *Perspectives on Positive Polical Economy* ed. J. Alt and K. Shepsle, 31–54. Cambridge: Cambridge University Press.

Calvert, Randall. 1985. "The Value of Biased Information: A Rational Choice Model of Political Advice." *Journal of Politics* 47: 530–555.

Coate, Stephen, and Stephen Morris. 1995. "On the Form of Transfers to Special Interests." *Journal of Political Economy* 103(6): 1210–1235.

Crawford, Vincent, and Joel Sobel. 1982. "Strategic Information Transmission." *Econometrica* 50: 1431–1451.

Cukierman, Alex. 1992. *Central Bank Strategy, Credibility, and Independence: Theory and Evidence.* Cambridge, MA: The MIT Press.

Cukierman, Alex, and Nissan Liviatan. 1991. "Optimal Accommodation by Stong Policy-makers under incomplete Information." *Journal of Monetary Economics* 27: 99–127.

Cukierman, Alex, and Allan Meltzer. 1986. "The Credibility of Monetary Announce-ments." In *Moneary Policy and Uncertainty*, ed. M. Neumann, 39–68. Baden-Baden: Nomos Verlagsgesellschaft.

Cukierman, Alex, and Mariano Tommasi. 1996. "When Does it Take a Nixon to Go to China?" Universidad de San Andrés, August. Mimeo.

Gilligan, Thomas. 1993. "Information and the Allocation of Legislative Authority." *Journal of Institutional and Theoretical Economics* 149(1): 321–341.

Gilligan, Thomas, and Keith Krehbiel. 1989. "Asymmetric Information and Legislative Rules with a Heterogeneous Committee." *American Journal of Political Science* 33: 459–490.

Harrington, Joseph. 1993. "Economic Policy, Economic Performance, and Elections." *American Economic Review* 83: 27–42.

Krehbiel, Keith. 1991. *Information and Legislative Organization*. Michigan Studies in Political Analysis. Ann Arbor: University of Michigan Press.

Lupia, Arthur. 1992. "Busy Voters, Agenda Control and the Power of Information." *American Political Science Review* 86: 390–403.

Lupia, Arthur. 1993. "Credibility and the Responsiveness of Direct Legislation." In *Political Economy: Institutions, Competition and Representation*, ed. W. Barnett, M. Hinich and N. Schofield 379–404. Cambridge: Cambridge University Press.

Lupia, Arthur, and Mathew McCubbins. 1995. Can Democracy Work? Persuasion, Enlight-enment, and Democratic Institutions." Unpublished manuscript, Program on Political Econ-omy, Harvard University.

Martinelli, Cesar, and Mariano Tommasi. 1994. "Sequencing of Economic Reforms in the Presence of Political Constraints." IRIS Working Paper No. 100, University of Maryland, February. Forthcoming in *Economics & Politics*.

Mora y Araujo, Manuel. 1991. *Ensayo y Error: La Nueva Clase Politica que Exige el Ciudadano Argentino*. Buenos Aires: Editorial Planeta.

Osborne, Martin and Ariel Rubinstein. 1994. *A Course in Game Theory*. Gambridge, MA: The MIT Press.

Packenham, Robert. 1992. "The Politics of Economic Liberalization: Argentina and Brazil in Comparative Perspective." Paper presented at the 1992 Meeting of the American Political Science Association.

Perktold, Josef. 1994. "Interaction of Market and Government Failures in an Intervention Game." UCLA, November. Mimeo.

Rodrik, Dani. 1993. "The Positive Economics of Policy Reform." *American Economic Review* 83: 356–361.

Rodrik, Dani. 1994. "Comment" to chapter 4, "The European Periphery." In *The Political Economy of Policy Reform*, ed. J. Williamson, 212–215. Washington: Institute for International Economics, pp. 212–215.

Rodrik, Dani. 1996. "Understanding Economic Policy Reform." *Journal of Economic Literature* 34 (March): 9–41.

Roemer, John. 1994. "The Strategic Role of Party Ideology When Voters Are Uncertain about How the Economy Works." *American Political Science Review* 88(2) (June).

Romer, Thomas and Howard Rosenthal. 1979. "Bureaucrats Versus Voters: On the Political Economy of Resource Allocation by Direct Democracy." *Quarterly Journal of Economics* (November): 563–587.

Rosenthal, Howard. 1990. "The Setter Model." In *Advances in the Spatial Theory of Voting*, ed. J. Enelow and M. Hinich, 199–234. Cambridge: Cambridge University Press.

Schultz, Christian. 1996. "Polarization and Inefficient Policies." *Review of Economic Studies* 63: 331–343.

Stein, Jeremy. 1989. "Cheap Talk and the Fed: A Theory of Imprecise Policy Announcements." *American Economic Review* 79: 32–42.

Tommasi, Mariano, and Andrés Velasco. 1996. "Where Are We in the Political Economy of Reform?" *Journal of Policy Reform* 1: 187–238.

Williamson, John. 1994. *The Political Economy of Policy Reform*. Washington: Institute for International Economics.

Williamson, John, and Stephan Haggard. 1994. "The Political Conditions for Economic Reform." In *The Political Economy of Policy Reform*, ed. J. Williamson, 527–596. Washington: Institute for International Economics.

16

The Feasibility of Low Inflation: Theory with an Application to the Argentine Case

Ricardo López Murphy and
Federico Sturzenegger

When will the government learn that it cannot make money with money?
—Unidentified Buenos Aires Cab Driver

16.1 Introduction

During the late 1980s Argentina experienced two hyperinflations in the short span of a year. These were not isolated events but rather the natural conclusion of decades of high government deficits and chronic inflation dating back to the early 1950s. To illustrate the consequences of these policies, table 16.1 shows Argentina's GDP as a percentage of that of other countries for 1950, 1965, and 1989. These values are computed by comparing the PPP adjusted GDPs and show a persistent decline in relative positions against both OECD and developing countries.

Table 16.2 shows similar statistics for the inflation rate for 1950–60, 1960–70, 1970–82, and 1982–89. The inflation rates of Argentina are uniformly above those of developed and middle-income countries, and mirror the decline in relative GDP. Interestingly, the comparison with Chile and Brazil shows that while inflation performance did not differ substantially, as in the period up to 1970, there was only a moderate decline in relative GDP. However, during the last two decades, as Argentina's inflation rates soared to even higher levels, the country lost positions against even these high inflation economies.

The above evidence does not pretend to be conclusive. It does suggest however that inflation played an important role in Argentina's poor economic performance. What this paper asks is why, when the process of runaway inflation is so predictable and its implications so far-reaching,

Originally published in *Policy Reform* 1 (1996): 47–73. Reprinted with permission.

Table 16.1
Argentina GDP Performance

	1950	1965	1989
Germany	111	60	39
Australia	57	51	37
Japan	236	87	43
USA	44	40	27
France	89	64	40
Italy	156	95	42
Spain	277	130	65
Korea	656	498	93
Chile	152	147	113
Brazil	295	264	115
Mexico	366	300	116

Source: F. de la Balze (1993).

Table 16.2
Argentina Inflation Performance

	1950–60	1960–70	1970–82	1982–1989
High Income	2.3	4.3	9.0	4.2
Middle-High Income	5.9	3.0	16.4	30.9
Chile	30.7	33.0	144.3	20.5
Brazil	15.2	46.1	42.1	284.3
Argentina	20.9	21.4	136	395.2

Source: Own computation from FIEL database.

was it so difficult for Argentina to achieve price stability on a permanent basis. We also ask what allowed fiscal and monetary reform to take place by early 1991 and whether or not these reforms may be expected to last.

In order to deal with this question we first briefly review the literature on delayed stabilization. Next, we present a new hypothesis on why reform was not possible until very late in the inflation process. In our story we analyze the mechanism by which policy makers' actions transmit information about the state of the economy. This allows for the construction of a story tailored to the Argentine experience which helps in understanding many apparent puzzling developments, such as why the Peronists strongly opposed any attempt at structural reform during the period 1986–1989—while they were in opposition—when they themselves implemented a strong program of economic reform when in power

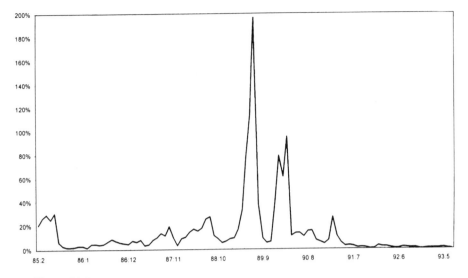

Figure 16.1
Monthly inflation rate

after 1989. Interestingly, voters supported them both times. We conclude the analysis by discussing conclusions for formerly centrally planned economies (FCPE's)

The chapter is organized as follows. Section 16.2 reviews the fact regarding Argentine hyperinflation and stabilization. Because these facts have been reviewed elsewhere, we are extremely brief, concentrating on new evidence only.[1] Section 16.3 reviews the literature on delays and presents our model on voting behavior. Section 16.4 discusses how exogenous and endogenous factors were conducive to stabilization towards the early 1990s. Section 16.5 concludes by summarizing policy implications for FCPE's.

16.2   The Facts

16.2.1   The Inflation Process

After a long period of megainflation, hyperinflation began in February 1989 triggered by the floating of the exchange rate under conditions of wide fiscal and quasi-fiscal disequilibrium, with inflation peaking over 200 percent in July of 1989. A second round of hyperinflation began in December of 1989 reaching 100 percent in March 1990. Figure 16.1 shows the evolution of monthly inflation rates since 1985.

Table 16.3
Fiscal Accounts

	Primary deficit	Global deficit	Total deficit
1985	−1.57	2.84	4.93
1986	−1.19	2.01	3.20
1987	0.69	4.15	4.82
1988-I	1.55	4.30	6.41
II	−1.02	2.50	5.60
III	0.47	2.26	5.03
IV	1.71	4.24	6.68
1989-I	3.43	5.51	10.39
II	−2.37	5.62	29.16
III	0.17	3.94	7.35
IV	−1.44	4.01	7.87
1990-I	−1.65	1.37	2.12
II	−2.79	2.11	2.80
III	−1.10	1.71	2.38
IV	−0.86	0.94	1.61
1991-I	0.14	1.41	1.99
II	−1.23	0.46	0.92
III	−2.18	−0.59	−0.33
IV	−3.82	−1.92	−1.68

Source: Datafiel.
Note: All values in percentage of GDP.

Table 16.3 shows the fiscal accounts for the same period demonstrating that the inflation process had its roots in a persistent fiscal imbalance. The table distinguishes the primary deficit from the global deficit, which includes interest payments, and the total deficit, which includes the quasi-fiscal component. The quasi-fiscal deficit measures spending which originates in the Central Bank. There are many measurement problems, particularly when trying to assess the magnitude of the quasi-fiscal component, because Central Bank debts are difficult to measure and track. Thus, the numbers shown should be taken with caution, especially during the first two quarters of 1989.[2] However, while the numbers clearly show that there was never any serious control of fiscal accounts until late 1991, this was much less clear at the time.

Figure 16.2 shows the evolution of real M1 during the same time period. Notice that there appears to be a floor to money demand and that money demand is extremely variable close to this lower bound. In fact, between January 1989 and March 1990, money demand first decreased

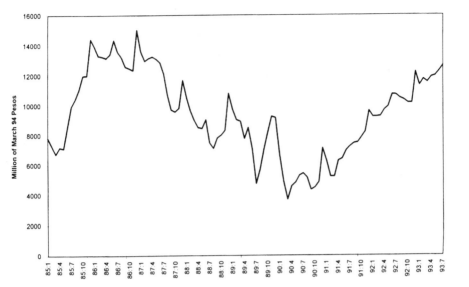

Figure 16.2
Real money

from about 10 billion March 1994 pesos to only 5 billion in June, re-
bounded to 9 billion in November before falling to 3.7 billion by March.
Thus, the dynamics of money demand must have also played an important role in explaining inflation during this period.

Finally, it is argued that the announcements of the opposition candidate,
Carlos Menem, before the elections of May 1989, suggesting the need of
wage increases and expansionary fiscal policies, induced a flight out of
money and thus fueled the inflation process. Figure 16.3 bears on this
point by showing the residuals to money demand for the period between
June 1988 and April 1989. We have used the Kiguel and Neumeyer
(1994) specification which we believe is the most careful estimation available for this period.[3] The residuals were mostly negative since June 1988,
indicating indeed a flight out of money. Thus, there is some evidence that
Menem's announcements contributed to the hyperinflation of the winter
of 1989. In fact, Sturzenegger (1994) estimates a bubble term for both
hyperinflations which measures the component of inflation which is driven
not by fundamentals but by self-fulfilling expectations. He shows that in
both cases about 80 percent (per month) of inflation, at the peak, can be
accounted for by this expectational term. For the second hyperinflation,
when fiscal accounts where improving, this almost fully explains the inflation rate. For the first hyperinflation, the deficit also played a critical role.

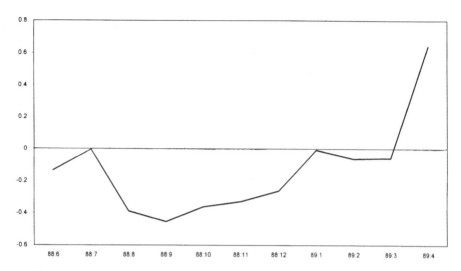

Figure 16.3
Menemshocks (K-N-S)

Figure 16.4 shows the evolution of Argentina's country risk since January 1989. This risk premia is computed as the excess return over Libor for the Bonex 82 (a dollar denominated government bond). An interesting feature of the data is that this risk premia increased substantially in the first five months of 1989. We associate this increase to uncertainty about the policies of the future government and as to how the economy would cope during the transition period (there was a seven month interval between elections and the transfer of power). The risk premia reached its maximum on May 10, four days before the presidential elections and well before hyper-inflation developed.[4] In fact, once the new government took over in July, even in the face of social chaos, risk premia indicators were falling rather than increasing. Yet, the increase in risk premia in 1989 is dwarfed in comparison with the effects of the Bonex Plan of January 1990 which forced a monetary contraction by converting deposits into long term government bounds.[5] However, while it is true that the risk premia increased substantially, it also fell very quickly. By May it was already below the 1989 peak, and by the end of the year it had fallen to pre-hyperinflationary levels. Thus, the credibility effects of the Bonex plan appear to have dwindled away very quickly while at the same time allowing an increase in the maturity of public debt which improved the fiscal accounts in the long run.

We identify two stylized facts from this discussion. First, that an important source of uncertainty are policy responses. The risk premium

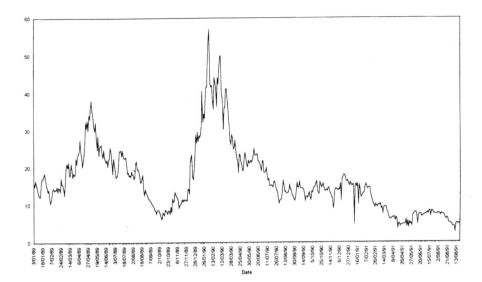

Figure 16.4
Risk premia

peaked before the election and during the Bonex Plan when future government policies were highly unpredictable. Thus, we believe that a good
model of inflation has to address directly the uncertainty introduced
by government policies. Second, that the underlying causes of inflation
explosions are extremely unclear. While the persistence of inflation is easily
explained by the fiscal numbers, money dynamics induced by crazy announcements, or bubbles induced by expectational effects, are important
components of an explanation of inflation explosions. This leaves agents
confused and uncertain as to the extent of fiscal reform which is necessary
for stabilization. These two stylized facts will be the main elements of our
voting model discussed below.

16.2.2 The Political Process

We now make a brief summary of some political developments which
were taking place alongside the inflation process described above. The
Radicals were in office since December 1983. The Radicals have a long
political tradition and have consistently represented Argentina's middle
class. The Peronism (the other major political force) is much less defined,
historically encompassing groups which spread from the far left to the
far right. It was clear, though, that the Peronists were "to the left" of
the Radicals. In late 1988 Carlos Menem, a popular politician from the

northwest famous for running huge budget deficits and increasing public employment in his home state, won the Peronist nomination for the May 1989 presidential election and began campaigning on a vague platform which emphasized notions such as "productive revolution" and "salariazo" (*wage-spurt*). His contender, from the Radical party, defined very clearly his future policies stressing the need for fiscal austerity, privatizations and market oriented reforms. Menem achieved a clear victory in the May elections and inflation, which had already accelerated substantially, became quickly out of control. The previous administration, scheduled to leave office in December, had to step down in July of 1989 in the midst of hyperinflation, lootings and social revolt. Soon after being sworn in, Menem announced he was going to implement a sweeping program of structural reform and fiscal austerity. What was puzzling to many was the complete change in policy orientation from what had been hinted during the election campaign. Menem's program moved him way to the right of the political spectrum. Also puzzling is that in doing so, he kept most of his constituency intact and retained very high approval rates.

This brief review indicates some of the facts of the political process which we believe our model should be able to capture. Among these: why a left wing candidate was able to implement fiscal reform, and why reneging from campaign promises can carry substantial popular support.

16.3   Why the Reform Took So Long

16.3.1   Previous Literature

A first set of hypotheses as to why suboptimal action is taken (in our case excessive inflation financing) is that it arises from ignorance, or, in other words, because policy makers *did not know* better. Though unappealing as an explanation,—irrationality or ignorance may justify any type of behavior—many policy makers repeatedly argue that they do in fact make mistakes. DiTella (1991) states:

> However, if not irrationality, at least ignorance of basic economic criteria is a necessary ingredient of any valid explanation [for the pervasiveness of populist policies]...it is obvious...an extraordinary degree of ignorance and naïveté about the ways in which these problems had to be tackled. Inevitably, we have to go back to the view that ignorance is one of the more deeply seated roots of this very counterproductive course.
>
> We have learned the hard way, and we know the appropriate means,...But new knowledge and new attitudes mean that the future...will fortunately not be the same.

The basic problem with this hypothesis is that it cannot explain the pervasiveness of the inflation phenomenon or the fact that no learning takes place even when similar policies are tried over and over again. In the presence of repeated inflation cycles as documented by Kiguel and Liviatan (1991), how can we believe that policy makers are not aware that they are engaged in a non-sustainable path?[6]

An alternative strand of literature suggests that, rather than out of ignorance, stabilizations may have been delayed because they were not optimal, that is, because policy makers *didn't want* to implement them. Stories along these lines can easily be constructed by justifying some sort of cost to stabilization. For example, in high inflation economies inflation is usually taken into account by a tax system with very high ex-ante tax rates but which are low ex-posts. Stabilization thus requires a reduction in tax rates in order to avoid an increase in tax burdens. The uncertainty as to whether this would be done, or about how it would be done, increases the uncertainty associated with stabilization and for risk averse agents (or policy-makers) may induce a delay in the implementation of the reform package.[7]

An alternative approach to explaining the persistence of inflation concentrates on the interaction of interest groups in a subsidy (or redistributive) game to appropriate government resources. In this case stabilization is delayed because policy makers *cannot* implement it. It may be the case that there are sectors which are favored by inflation. For example, borrowers from the public sector were strongly subsidized by the inflation rate and labor unions could justify important nominal wage increases. If this pro-inflation coalition is strong enough, reform will not be feasible.[8] Alesina and Drazen (1991) construct a model in which agents dislike inflation and there is asymmetric information as to how much inflation affects each group. In a war-of-attrition setup this leads to stabilization delays. As long as inflation persists, each agent updates his/her belief on the endurance of the other group to inflation. Eventually the weaker groups concede to stabilization and pay a higher share of its costs. Others have suggested that the subsidy game has the characteristics of a prisoner's dilemma situation and may thus lead to excessive inflation.[9] If agents try to appropriate resources from a common pool (the inflation tax resources) it is not surprising that this will lead to excessive use of inflation. However, once agents perceive that they are stuck in a suboptimal equilibrium and that persistence of the status quo leads to a further deterioration of the situation with increasing costs, reform is implemented.

16.3.2   A Voting Model

In this chapter we propose an alternative story for delays which concentrates on analyzing the behavior of voters in a context of uncertainty.[10]
Our model has two periods (0 and 1) and three players, two political
parties called L and R and a median voter. We assume preferences of
voters are unimodal so that it is proper to concentrate on the median
voter. The voter decides at the beginning of each period which political
party, either L or R, holds office. The politician sworn into office (the
incumbent) chooses a policy action to be implemented during the period
from a given set $A = \{a_1, a_2\}$. The opposition party may choose to
"acquiesce," in which case the policy chosen is implemented, or may
choose to "challenge," in which case the action chosen by the party in
power is implemented with probability $\alpha > 1/2$, i.e., there is an advantage
to hold office.

An underlying random variable, denoted θ^t, indicates the preferred
policy for the median voter in period t. Politicians observe θ after an election and before choosing actions. Voters observe only policy actions. The
variable θ exhibits persistence over time, i.e., the expectation for θ at the
beginning of period $t + 1$ equals the value believed to have prevailed in
the previous period. All agents start period 0 with a flat prior over θ, with
$E_0 \theta^0 = 0$ (where the subscript indicates the time when the equation is
computed). The timing of the game is depicted in figure 16.5.

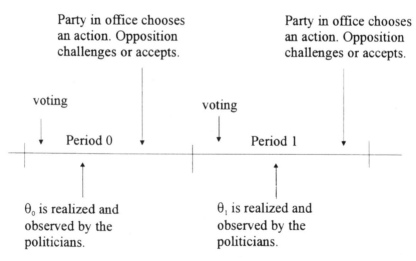

Figure 16.5
Timing of the game

It may seem puzzling that voters cannot observe what is preferred by them while politicians can. However, the correct interpretation for θ is that it represents "what should be done." What we tried to convey in our empirical discussion is that it is never clear what appropriate policies are. Politicians who take office can, however, observe economic reality first hand and therefore are in a much better position to figure out the appropriate response to the specific conditions prevailing in each period. In fact, this response will depend on information which sometimes is available only once in office: the state of public accounts, the capacity of the public employees to implement new directives, the extent of corruption, the availability of foreign aid, etc. Only when actually implementing policies can these uncertainties by resolved. The assumption that the party which is not in office can also observe θ derives from the fact that it actively participates in policy decisions, for example, in Congress.

It may also be argued that, in the fact of a hyperinflation, policy recommendations should be clear so that there could not have been much uncertainty or disagreement as to what should have been done. However our empirical discussion suggested a number of explanations for inflation explosions. While there may have been little doubt that some adjustment was necessary, much less consensus existed on the size of such adjustment. The restrictions imposed on what is known by each player in the model attempt to capture the fact that information is, in high inflation economies, not only scant but also difficult to analyze. Only those actors with potential access to power have the possibility of bringing together a sufficient number of analysts which can find out how to deal with the situation. Political parties, both in power and in opposition, have therefore access to information and analyses not available to voters.

Each political party is "ideological" à la Alesina (see Alesina 1989); that is, each party i has an observable preferred outcome which will be denoted a_i^*. For simplicity it will be assumed that a_L^* and a_R^*, satisfy $a_L^* < 0 < a_R^*$ and that $a_R^* = -a_L^*$. However, they also care about the median voter.[11] Politicians, when deciding what action to implement, will attempt to minimize the loss function:

$$L_i(a_i^0, a_i^1) = [d_i(a_i^0 - a_i^*)^2 + c_i(a_i^0 - \theta^0)^2] + \delta[d_i(a_i^1 - a_i^*)^2 + c_i(a_i^1 - \theta^1)^2],$$
(1)

where a_i^t denotes the action chosen in period t, by party i and δ denotes the discount factor. The coefficients d_i and c_i indicate how willing she is to sacrifice her preferences for the well being of the median voter. If the ratio d_i/c_i is very high then the politician is very "ideological" and she mostly cares about her preferred outcome. If, on the contrary, this ratio is very low, the politician is very "pragmatic" and will tend to implement the socially preferred outcome.

The median voter himself has loss function equal to[12]

$$L_m(a_i^0, a_i^1) = |a_i^0 - E_0\theta^0| + \delta|a_i^1 - E_1\theta^1|. \tag{2}$$

Because there is uncertainty as to the state of nature, an equilibrium will be characterized by a voting rule and a set of policy responses to that voting rule which conform a Perfect Bayesian Nash equilibrium.[13] That is, voters' choice of policy maker must be optimal given the information which is feasible to derive from the politician's actions, and these must be an optimal response to such a voting rule. In the next subsection, we will consider a simplified version of the problem described above in which politicians of party L and R fully discount the future. This simplified version would not be interesting if it could not be shown that the results extend to the case in which politicians care about actions in both periods as specified in (1). The appendix shows that, in fact, this is the case. We have chosen to present in the text a case which is simpler, but yet delivers the same set of results.

The thrust of our model is given by the fact that actions undertaken by politicians reveal information about the state of nature and may therefore aid voters in assessing which is the optimal policy. By restricting the set of actions to a two point set, $A = \{a_R = a_R^* = a_L = a_L^*\}$, this transmission of information is not perfect. Furthermore, by giving politicians different characteristics there will be asymmetry in the response to both parties' actions, this, in turn, will lead to interesting voting dynamics.

16.3.2.1 The Solution

Given the setup, voting behavior in period 0 is trivial. Because $E_0\theta^0 = 0$, and $|a_R| = |a_L|$, the voter is indifferent between political parties. We assume that he chooses party R. In the second election, he will choose that politician which is more likely to implement his preferred policy choice. That is, if the believes $\theta > 0$ he will prefer a_R, and if he believes $\theta < 0$, he will prefer a_L.

The problem for politician R is to choose an action which minimizes her loss given the state of nature θ. If she chooses action a_R her loss is

$$L_R(a_R) = c_R(a_R - \theta)^2. \tag{3}$$

If she chooses action a_L her loss is

$$L_R(a_L) = d_R(a_L - a_R)^2 + c_R(a_L - \theta)^2. \tag{4}$$

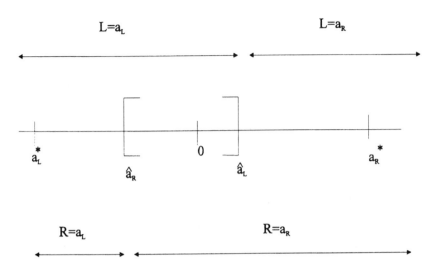

Figure 16.6
Reaction functions

(And similarly for politician L.) Simple algebra will show politician R will choose action a_R as long as

$$\theta > \frac{1}{2}\frac{d_R}{c_R}(a_L - a_R) = \hat{a}_R, \tag{5}$$

where θ is the state of nature revealed after the election. Notice from (5) that the cutoff point for politician R is negative (his preferred action is positive) so that she will be willing to sacrifice social welfare for political interest. To what extent she will be willing to do this will depend, as mentioned before, on the ratio d_R/c_R. When this ratio is very high she will always stick to her preferred choice independently of the state of nature; if the ratio is very low it is more likely she will implement the socially optimal policy. A similar exercise can be done for politician L. Figure 16.6 shows the reaction function of both policy makers to different underlying states of nature.

In what follows we will assume that $d_L/c_L < d_R/c_R$ (party L is less ideo-logical). An equilibrium is characterized by a voting rule and a reaction function for both parties. The voting rule postulated states that L should be chosen if the voter observes $\{a_R, a_L\}$ or $\{a_L, a_L\}$, R if he observes $\{a_R, a_R\}$, and that a coin with equal probabilities should be tossed if he observes $\{a_L, a_R\}$, where $\{a_i, a_j\}$ indicates the policy chosen by party R and party L respectively. The reaction function for party R implements a_R

if $\theta > \hat{a}_R$, and a_L otherwise. Finally, party L implements a_L if $\theta < \hat{a}_L$ and a_R otherwise.

If these are the strategies played by the political parties then voters' beliefs should be obtained from Bayes's updating of his prior according to the strategies played in equilibrium. If the voter observes $\{a_R, a_R\}$ then he should conclude that the shock is to the right of $\hat{a}_L$. Similarly, if the voter observes $\{a_L, a_L\}$ being played, the median voter will know that the shock is to the left of $\hat{a}_R$. The voting rule then ensures that the optimal policies are implemented in period two, though this is irrelevant because, in these two cases, there is consensus among both parties about economic policy.

If the shock is in between $\hat{a}_L$ and $\hat{a}_R$, i.e., if the policy of the incumbent is challenged, the median voter also updates his beliefs about θ using Bayes's rule. It is clear that depending on the ratios of d_i/c_i this update may carry relevant information for his voting decision in period 1. In fact, the expectation for θ in period 1 will equal

$$E_1 \theta^1 = \frac{1}{4}\left[\frac{d_L}{c_L} - \frac{d_R}{c_R}\right](a_R - a_L),\tag{6}$$

so that depending on the degree of ideologization of both parties, the median voter will re-assess the optimal policy. Because $(a_R - a_L) > 0$, equation (6) indicates that $E_1 \theta^1 < 0$, or that the expectation of the voter will move in favor of the less ideologized political party (party L in our setup). Then, a challenge of the incumbent's policy will lead the median voter to change her assessment about the state of the economy in such a way that favors the opposition. Given these beliefs, voter choice as determined by his voting strategy is rational.

We now check whether politicians have an incentive to deviate. Given the simple specification of the model, this will not be the case. Politician R will gain nothing by playing a_L for values of θ larger than $\hat{a}_R$, nor will she gain anything by playing a_R for values of θ smaller than $\hat{a}_R$. Similarly for party L. Thus, the previous equilibrium describes a Perfect Bayesian Equilibrium for this game.

The area $X = [\hat{a}_R, \hat{a}_L]$ indicates that in which reforms are challenged. In this area, the policy of the party in power is implemented with probability α, with $1/2 < \alpha < 1$. Area X also indicates the states of nature for which policies implemented may not correspond to the preference of the median voter. For instance, in the area $[\hat{a}_R, 0]$ the median voter will prefer to have a_L implemented but this will happen only with probability $(1 - \alpha)$. Conversely, if θ is in the interval $[0, \hat{a}_L]$ the median voter wants a_R but this policy will be challenged and implemented only with probability α. We consider the size of this area to provide a measure of the inefficiency of the political system and thus, to indicate the likelihood of generating extreme inflation.

Let us begin by discussing some simple results generated by the model.

SIMPLE RESULT #1   If both political parties are pragmatic and care only about the median voter, the area of reform blocking disappears, i.e., $X = \varnothing$.

Proof Pragmatic policy makers have $d_i/c_i = 0$, so that $\hat{a}_R = \hat{a}_L = 0$ from (5). This implies $X = \varnothing$. $\square$

In the traditional specification of Downs (1957), the above preferences correspond to what are called "office-motivated" politicians. In economies with "office-motivated" politicians there is consensus and the policies implemented coincide with the preference of the median voter. Thus, the political system is efficient, and because there is no policy blocking, the probability of very inefficient outcomes, such as extreme inflation, is very low.

SIMPLE RESULT #2   If both political parties are completely ideological, actions reveal no information.

Proof Ideological political parties have $d_i/c_i = \infty$, so that $\hat{a}_L = +\infty$ and $\hat{a}_R = -\infty$, from (5), so that actions are independent of the state of the world. $\square$

In this case, all policies are automatically blocked and the political system is at maximum inefficiency.

SIMPLE RESULT #3   (Cukierman, Edwards, and Tabellini 1992) Political polarization increases the probability of blocking of reforms.

Proof If $|a_R - a_L|$ increases, $\hat{a}_R$ falls and $\hat{a}_L$ increases for given d_i/c_i from (5). $\square$

Given a certain amount of "ideologization" an increase in polarization will reduce the area where consensus is achieved. Thus, polarized political systems will be less efficient and blocking of reforms becomes more likely. This result is tested empirically in Cukierman, Edwards and Tabellini (1992).

We consider now the situation depicted in figure 16.7 which has been constructed to describe several features that we believe characterized the political and economic situation in Argentina in the late 1980s and which

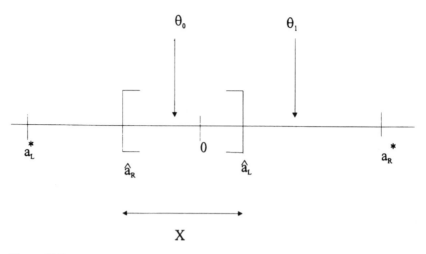

Figure 16.7
Argentina in the late 1980s

we described above. The initial shock (revealed after the first election) is θ_0. The second shock (revealed after the second election) equals θ_1. Furthermore, as before, we assume that $0 < d_L/c_L < d_R/c_R < \infty$ and that the median voter initially voted for party R.[14] After being sworn into office, party R implements action a_R which party L challenges. Observing these actions the median voter updates his beliefs on the true state of the world and computes, using (6), a new $E_1(\theta^1 | \theta^0 \in X) < 0$. The median voter then prefers a_L rather than the previously chosen a_R.[15] This leads us to our first result.

NEW RESULT #1   Even when both the political parties stick to their pre-electoral promises the median voter may change its desired policy preference and block the policies it has just voted.

In the case of Argentina, this may explain why voters in a context of increasing inflation voted in the elections of 1987 and 1989 for candidates which were blocking all possibility of fiscal reform. Machinea (1991) claims that

although authorities bore some of the responsibility for that failure [that of the stabilization attempts of 87–89], the main obstacle was the total opposition of the Peronists to any government initiative (the Peronists controlled the Senate, most provinces, and to some extent the General Confederation of Labor)... some initiatives did come through, but they sometimes lacked the required depth and strength, or were blocked by the opposition parties.

In the model, the blocking of reforms was providing information that the fiscal situation was not as bad as suggested by the party in office. This shifted the median voter in favor of the opposition party.

We believe that the blocking of reforms during the last two years of the Radical government also contributed substantially to the deterioration of the economic situation inducing a right-ward shift in the state of nature. However, once the new administration from party L takes office and observes θ_1 to the right of $\hat{a}_L$, it finds convenient to implement a_R. This leads to our second new result.

NEW RESULT #2   Switching completely from the policies announced in the campaign may carry substantial popular support.

When policy maker L announces the implementation of a_R she reveals, in a way which is not feasible for the more ideological party, that the states of nature are such that a_R should be implemented. In the case of Argentina this is illustrated by the following excerpts from the press in the months after the implementation of a far-reaching reform program:

> In the name of Peronism, the *nebulous* populist and statist ideology that has stifled Argentina for nearly a half-century, he has created its very opposite. The President explains his lurch toward the free market as being simply a matter of recognizing that state socialism ... was headed for a dead end.
>
> Yet somehow Menem has managed to retain the loyalty of most of the Peronist rank and file ... A March (1992) survey by a Buenos Aires polling firm found that 63% of those questioned felt optimistic about the future. (*Time*, July 13, 1992; italics added)

Notice that while in our setup party L will never undertake a reform which would not be also implemented by party R, it is in a better situation to convince the voters of the need of such a reform. In this sense, the implementation of policies by the most unlikely candidate carries stronger information about the benefits of such a policy and makes it more feasible from a political viewpoint.[16]

The model also sheds some light on the campaign strategies. During the presidential race of 1989, the Radicals tried to convey the message that the state of nature had moved substantially to the right in figure 16.7 and that strict fiscal adjustment was required. In our model, announcements carry no credibility, only actions are relevant. We can nevertheless use the model to understand why the Radicals chose to be clear about their future policies, while Menem tried to transmit information about himself rather than about what he planned to do in office. In fact, the leitmotif of the Menem campaign, *"follow me,"* can be understood as an attempt to transmit the message that he was a policy maker who was going to implement the socially preferred outcome, without specifying what this meant. That is, he tried to convey the message that he was a "pragmatic" rather than an "ideological" policy maker. In our model, the degree of ideologization is given and not a policy choice. Then, the Peronists, who had an advantage in this dimension, tried to make this point clear. The Radicals who were at a disadvantage, could only hope to win the elections by convincing voters that their view of the world was the correct one.

16.3.2.2 Strategic Behavior

Consider a modified version of the previous game. Both parties have the same characteristics as before with the difference that now they also derive utility from being in office (these are the ego rents in Rogoff and Sibert (1988)). We assume these rents are additive in the utility function and equal in value to h. The process describing the state of nature is as before, i.e. it satisfies that $E_{t+1}\theta^{t+1} = \theta^t$. Again, we are interested in a Perfect Bayesian Equilibrium.

The equilibrium is given by the same voting strategy as before; that is, to vote R if $\{a_R, a_R\}$ is observed, to vote L if $\{a_R, a_L\}$ or $\{a_L, a_L\}$ is observed, and to toss a coin with probability $(1/2, 1/2)$ if $\{a_L, a_R\}$ is observed. The strategy for party R is to play a_R if $\theta > \hat{a}_R$ and a_L otherwise. For party L, the optimal strategy is to play a_R if $\theta > \hat{a}_L^*$ and a_L otherwise. The appendix shows that $\hat{a}_L < \hat{a}_L^*$. The intuition for this result should be clear: party L may be willing to challenge a policy even if it prefers the current policy choice in order to shift voters' perceptions in its favor. As long as h is not large enough, in particular as long as $|\hat{a}_L^*| < |\hat{a}_R|$, it will still be the case that the voter should vote for party L after observing a contesting of policy a_R. The appendix also shows the set of beliefs which supports the equilibrium. What is important for our purposes is a new proposition which results from the fact that $\hat{a}_L < \hat{a}_L^*$.

NEW RESULT #3   A candidate may block a reform which she expects to implement if in power.

In our setup, this happens if the shock $\theta \in [\hat{a}_L, \hat{a}_L^*]$. In this case, the politician blocks a reform to convince voters to put her in office, in spite of knowing that she would implement exactly the same policy she is challenging if elected. The purpose of her move is that by blocking the reform process she transmits the information that states of nature are not as bad as suggested by the party in power and shifts the median voter in her favor. Notice that this result depends critically on the asymmetry imposed on the game. By deviating from its preferred choice, party L profits from the imperfect information induced by the different degrees of ideologization. If $d_L/c_L = d_R/c_R$, there cannot be any strategic move, as in that case, it would no longer be rational for the voter to vote for party L after observing actions $\{a_R, a_L\}$.[17]

An interesting observation is that within the set of values of h which support the equilibrium described, a higher value attached to being in office generates a higher incentive to resign economic efficiency in order to attain power. Thus, in regimes where corruption is rampant, blocking of reforms will be more pervasive. Thus our last proposition (also proven in the appendix):

NEW RESULT #4   A larger level of corruption reduces the efficiency of the political system.

16.4   Why the Reform Took Place

The process of monetary control seemed an unreachable target for the Radical government. Our previous setup has provided an explanation for why this was the case: the Radicals could not convince the voters that drastic fiscal adjustment was the solution to the inflation problem. We want to argue that several factors, both exogenous and endogenous to the Argentine economy were making the process of monetary reform increasingly likely over time. If the area of disagreement X is reduced, consensus is more likely. We thus envision an increased likelihood of reform as taking place, the smaller the area.

16.4.1   Exogenous Factors

16.4.1.1   Ideological Changes
Many authors have suggested that changes in the Soviet Union and China have triggered a compression of the political spectrum towards the right (see Cardoso 1992). Argentina has not been immune to those changes. Menem himself declared:

Countries with closed, protectionist economic systems that eliminate a free private sector can never rise from their prostration ... Look at how the Soviet Union ended because there was no freedom. (*Time*, 13 July 1992)

A similar mechanism is suggested from what are called "demonstration effects," the success of Mexico, Chile, and East Asia, for example, allowing to better assess the effects of economic reform.

In the context of our model this implies a reduction in polarization, i.e. a decline in the distance between a_R and a_L, and thus an increased consensus area from our simple result #3.

16.4.2 Endogenous Factors

16.4.2.1 Costs of Inflation
Hyperinflation led to widespread looting and social unrest. This unrest even put in question the survival of the country as a political entity. In such a context, politicians probably assigned less importance to implementing their preferred outcome and concentrated in implementing the socially optimal policies. In our model this implies a reduction in d_i/c_i ratio, which reduces the area of blocking of reforms. The model, in this way, may be interpreted as generating the usual result that increased costs of inflation generate the political support for inflation stabilization.

16.4.2.2 Inflation Dynamics
In period zero, $\theta^0 \in [\hat{a}_R, \hat{a}_L]$. If reform does not take place, inflation dynamics may lead to a deterioration of the situation. Dornbusch et al. (1990) discusses how inflation, if left unchecked, may become unstable over time. In our setup, in period 1 we have that $\theta^0 < \theta^1$ (because we associate a_R with fiscal restraint). This implies that $p(\theta^1 \in [\hat{a}_R, \hat{a}_L]) < p(\theta^0 \in [\hat{a}_R, \hat{a}_L])$. If reforms were blocked in period 0, they will be blocked with lower probability later on.[18]

16.4.2.3 Accountability
It has been argued that the instability of the political regime did not allow voters to properly understand the relation between macro-policies and inflation. How could voters assign responsibilities when civilian and military governments were pursuing completely opposite policies every odd-plus number of years? Nowadays, a stable democracy has allowed for a learning process to take place. The model can account for this learning by allowing the voter to observe the state of nature before the election. In this case, he will always be able to vote for the optimal policy.

16.5 Implications for the FCPEs

Our voting model stressed that the political process was an important determinant of the feasibility of inflation control. The importance of the political process was underscored by the risk premia data, which showed that political events significantly affected economic variables. Our model, based on informational asymmetries between voters and politicians, identified variables which were important in inducing a blocking of the reform process and explained why only the most unlikely candidate was able to implement monetary reform. Maybe, and this is just a hypothesis, the process of reform may follow a similar path in Eastern Europe, with ex-communists, rather than free-marketers actually carrying out reforms.

Among the most important conclusions (not all of them new), we have that

• Polarized political systems are very inefficient. Reforms are usually blocked and economic policy is not very flexible to economic events. In our model, polarization refers to economic policies rather than to other more "political" issues. However, as long as there is a correlation in divergence between all areas, the high degree of polarization present today in Russia and the Ukraine may not be conducive to economic reform.

• Ideological rigidity is a political liability. Reformers such as Gaidar, Balcerowicz, Lewandowski, and Bielecki were all ousted, because they had a very rigid approach to policy reform. Other politicians, such as Vaclav Klaus, which was willing to compromise on many areas, such as retaining rent controls and price ceilings for mass transit, have done much better.

• Political surprises may be very likely. Only the most unappealing candidate ex-ante may be able to implement reform. The moderation of inflation under Chernomyrdin in Russia may be due to his possibility of restricting subsidy demands.

• Extreme inflation may work as a catalyst for economic reform. Thus, a deterioration of the situation will improve the chances of stabilization.

• The transparency of the political environment, that is, the proper assessment by voters of the economic implications of different actions, increases the efficiency of the political system. This may be achieved by a "learning by doing" process as long as the democratic process remains strong and politicians are held accountable for their actions.

16.6   Appendix

16.6.1   A Two Period Model

In this specification, both politicians care about utility in both periods, and therefore behavior may be strategic in the first. As before we will solve the model by constructing a set of strategies and beliefs that conform a perfect Bayesian equilibrium. We will shown that the perfect Bayesian equilibrium for this game has the same properties as the equilibrium described in the text.

In our specification, we can identify the state of nature $\theta \in \mathcal{R}$ with a "type" of politician who chooses actions a_i in A. The voter chooses a voting rule v in $V = \{L, R\}$. (For simplicity we will concentrate only in pure strategy equilibria). A strategy for a politician prescribes an action a_i over actions in A for each type θ. A strategy for the voter prescribes an action v in V for each vector of actions a. The politician's payoff to playing a_i is given by

$$u_p(a_i, v, \theta) = u_p(a_i, v(a), \theta),$$

where the subindex p denotes a politician. Voters' *ex-ante* payoff to strategy $v(a)$ when politicians play a is

$$u_v(a, v(a)) = \sum_\theta \pi(\theta) u_v(a, v(a), \theta),$$

where the subindex v denotes voters and π the probability assessment. The strategy of the politicians may depend on their type. Call a_i^* this strategy. By knowing a^* and observing a, the voter can use Bayes's rule to update $\pi(.)$ into $\mu(\theta|a)$. A perfect Bayesian equilibrium requires that voters maximize their payoff conditional on a for each a, where the conditional payoff is

$$\sum_\theta \mu(\theta|a) u_v(a, v(a), \theta).$$

Then a perfect Bayesian equilibrium is a strategy profile a^*, v^* and posterior beliefs $\mu(\theta|a)$ such that

$$\forall \theta, a^*(\theta) \in \max_{a_i} u_p(a_i, v(a), \theta), \tag{i}$$

$$\forall a, v^* \in \max_v \sum_\theta \mu(\theta|a) u_v(a, v(a), \theta), \tag{ii}$$

$$\mu(\theta|a) = p(\theta) a^*(\theta) / \sum_{\theta' \in \mathcal{R}} p(\theta') a^*(\theta) \tag{iii}$$

if $\sum_{\theta' \in \mathcal{R}} p(\theta') a^*(\theta) > 0$, and $\mu(\theta|a)$ is any probability distribution on $\mathcal{R}$ if $\sum_{\theta' \in \mathcal{R}} p(\theta') a^*(\theta) = 0$.

Condition (i) states that politicians take into account the effects of voters, and (ii) that voters react optimally to the politicians' actions given their belief about θ. These beliefs are generated by Bayes's rule along equilibrium paths, and are unrestricted out of equilibrium.

Our model will be a special case of the above structure, where actions can take only two values: a_R and a_L. Furthermore, by restricting the first period voting to happen before any action is taken, the strategic considerations are only relevant for voting at the beginning of period 1.

The voting rule is a function which maps the expectation of the state of the world into voting behavior, i.e., it is a function $V : \mathscr{R} \to \{L, R\}$.

The voting rule is derived from preferences to be

$$V = \begin{cases} L & \text{if } |a_L - E_t \theta^t| < |a_R - E_t \theta^t| \\ R & \text{otherwise.} \end{cases} \tag{7}$$

Politician R's strategy is to play a_R if $\theta > \hat{a}_R$ and a_L otherwise. Similarly politician L plays a_R if $\theta > \hat{a}_L$ and a_L otherwise. The beliefs on θ are functions of the observed actions, thus the belief function $\mu : A \times A \to \mathscr{R}$. This belief function has the following properties:

$$\mu = \begin{cases} E\theta = E(\theta|\theta > \hat{a}_L) & \text{if } \{a_R, a_R\}, \\ E\theta = E(\theta|\theta \in [\hat{a}_R, \hat{a}_L]) & \text{if } \{a_R, a_L\}, \\ E\theta = E(\theta|\theta < \hat{a}_R) & \text{if } \{a_L, a_L\}, \\ E\theta = 0 & \text{if } \{a_L, a_R\}. \end{cases} \tag{8}$$

These are updated beliefs derived from the politicians' strategies. Notice that when actions are $\{a_L, a_R\}$ the voter does not know what to think, as these appear to contradict rationality. We assume that on this out-of-equilibrium path the voter just sticks to his original prior. Given our assumptions, the median voter votes for R in the first case, and for L in the following two.

If voters have voting rule (7) and beliefs given by (8), we now show that it does not pay for political parties to deviate from their strategies. In what follows, we denote intertemporal utility with a tilde. Consider first party L. Playing a_R in response to a_R gives utility $\tilde{u}^L = u^L(a_R) + \delta u^L(a_R)$. Playing a_L gives utility $\tilde{u}^L = \alpha u^L(a_R) + (1 - \alpha)u^L(a_L) + \delta u^L(a_L)$. It is clear that it is an optimal strategy to play a_L only if $\theta < \hat{a}_L$. Consider now party R. If she plays a_L rather than a_R, then utility will equal $\tilde{u}^R = u^R(a_L) + \delta u^R(a_L)$ if $\theta < \hat{a}_L$ and $\tilde{u}^R = u^R(a_L) + \delta(1/2)u^R(a_R) + \delta(1/2)u^R(a_L)$ otherwise. If she sticks to a_R she obtains $\tilde{u}^R = u^R(a_R) + \delta u^R(a_R)$ for $\theta > \hat{a}_L$, $u^R = \alpha u^R(a_R) + (1 - \alpha)u^R(a_L) + \delta u^R(a_L)$ for $\theta < \hat{a}_L$. Thus, it is optimal to play a_R as long as $\theta > \hat{a}_R$.

In conclusion, we have shown that voters' beliefs are rational given the optimal policy reaction to this voting behavior. In fact, the transmission of information allowed by this game is identical to that of the myopic model discussed above.

16.6.2 *Strategic Behavior*

The set of beliefs which supports the equilibrium are

$$
\mu = \begin{cases}
E\theta = E(\theta|\theta > \hat{a}_L^*) & \text{if } \{a_R, a_R\}, \\
E\theta = E(\theta|\theta \in [\hat{a}_R, \hat{a}_L^*]) & \text{if } \{a_R, a_L\}, \\
E\theta = E(\theta|\theta < \hat{a}_R) & \text{if } \{a_L, a_L\}, \\
E\theta = 0 & \text{if } \{a_L, a_R\}.
\end{cases}
$$

Consider now the decision of politician L on whether she should play a_R or a_L for $\theta > \hat{a}_L$ given the strategies of party R and that of the median voter. If she plays a_R, her utility equals $\bar{u}^L(a_R) = u^L(a_R) + \delta u^L(a_R)$, while if playing a_L her utility equals $\bar{u}^L(a_L) = \alpha u^L(a_R) + (1 - \alpha)u^L(a_L) + \delta u^L(a_R) + \delta h$. Thus, it is optimal to play a_L as long as $-(1 - \alpha)[u^L(a_L) - u^L(a_R)] < \delta h$. Because the left hand side is increasing in θ, it is clear that this inequality will hold only if h is large enough and that the larger is h the larger the set of θ for which it would be optimal to play strategically. In other words, $|\hat{a}_L^*| > |\hat{a}_L|$, and this difference increases with h.

Notes

Paper prepared for the conference "Economic Reform: Latin America and the FCPEs," Georgetown University, May 12–13, 1994. We thank Sebastian Edwards, Miguel Kiguel, Vincent Reinhart, Dani Rodrik, and an anonymous referee for useful comments. We also thank Gonzalo Sanhueza for able research assistance and Miguel A. Broda for data. The usual caveat applies.

1. For a review see Heymann (1991), Canavese and DiTella (1988), Kiguel and Liviatan (1991) and (1994), López Murphy (1991), and (1992).

2. The primary deficit figures are very reliable but still contain some problems. The surplus in the second quarter of 1989 is due to the sale of the Argentine Embassy in Tokyo. More substantially, because computed on a cash-flow basis, they do not include payments which were rolled over across periods.

3. Because our monetary indicators have a different base period the constant differs from theirs. But we obtain (in our estimation) the same semi-elasticity of $-.31$. The exercise was also carried through using the whole period 85.3–93.3 with similar implications.

4. The elections appear to have been good news, probably because the vote difference was so wide that any possibility of deadlock in the electoral college was ruled out.

5. We are puzzled about the fact that the risk premia peaked in February 7 rather than at the implementation of the plan (January 1).

6. This is even more unappealing as many of the relevant actors have recognized that they were aware of the main problems: see Gerchunoff and Cetrángolo (1989) and Machinea (1990). An explanation for this fact, suggested in Labán and Sturzenegger (1992), is that policy makers are "learning" about what has to be done in order to stabilize and that each failed attempt makes them update their prior beliefs about what is required for stabilization.

The story generates the prediction that (a) inflation has to increase to higher levels before a new stabilization is attempted and (b) stabilization efforts should be increasingly tougher. Thus, a cycle of increasing inflation cycles, can develop as the result of learning by policy makers.

7. See Labán and Sturzenegger (1994a, 1994b) for stories along this line.

8. A labor union leader even commented that he was happy with inflation because price increases were the government's fault, while nominal wage increases were to his credit. Don Patinkin (1993) reviews the evidence for Israel.

9. See Heyman, Navajas, and Warnes (1988), and Mondino, Sturzenegger, and Tommasi (1993).

10. See Rogoff (1990), Rogoff and Sibert (1988), Alesina and Cukierman (1990), and Harrington (1993) for similar models which allow, in addition, for uncertainty about the characteristics of policy makers.

11. Politicians may care about the welfare of the median voter because they are altruistic or because their constituency overlaps with the median voter.

12. This specification is used for simplicity. The degree of ideologization is different across parties and so is the reaction to shocks in θ. Thus, the riskiness of both politicians is different and this will, in general, skew the voter towards the more flexible politician. In this section we want to concentrate exclusively on how different degrees of ideologization affect the transmission of information, thus, by assuming risk neutrality for the median voter we effectively eliminate risk factors from the analysis.

13. In the following examples we describe one possible perfect Bayesian equilibrium. This does not mean that other equilibria do not exist.

14. Here is where the assumption imbedded in the utility function of the representative agent is important, assuming a quadratic utility function would have led the voter to choose party L, as it is less risky than party R. The assumption of risk neutrality could have been replaced by shifting the preferences of the median voter towards that of party R at a cost in terms of simplicity.

15. This result highlights the shortcomings of the model. The current setup implies that politician R will lose the following election with probability one. This cannot be an equilibrium outcome, and thus restricts the validity of the model to explain the long run dynamics of the political process. Nevertheless, in the short run, we believe the model properly captures the informational and strategy constraints faced by voters and politicians. To an important extent, the degree of flexibility assigned by voters to a given politician depends on history and political tradition, and is not completely under control of the relevant actors in the short run.

16. In an independent contribution, Cukierman and Tommasi (1994), also emphasize this point. Their model also relies on asymmetric information with politicians better able to identify appropriate policies. While their model has a unique policy maker, it is more general in that it identifies the conditions which have to be satisfied by preferences, timing and outcomes for transmission of information to take place as described in this chapter. They also find that "discrete" switches in policies are important in convincing voters on the need of certain actions.

17. It is difficult to provide hard evidence for this proposition. Anecdotal evidence, though, is available. In a commercial break shortly before the presidential election of 1989, in a prime

time political program (Tiempo Nuevo, with free market–oriented Bernardo Neustadt), Menem tried to convince the journalist not to attack him when on the air on the basis that he would implement his (Neustadt's) policy recommendations if elected.

18. It is clear that in this situation agents do not use (6) to assess where the state of nature will be. If $\theta^{t+1} = \theta^t + \alpha$, then α must be subtracted when updating expectations.

References

Alesina, A. (1989) "Macroeconomics and Politics," in *NBER Macroeconomics Annual*, edited by O. Blanchard and S. Fischer, Cambridge: MIT Press.

Alesina, A. and A. Cukierman (1990) "The Politics of Ambiguity," *Quarterly Journal of Economics*, CV(4): 829–850.

Alesina A. and A. Drazen (1991) "Why Are Stabilizations Delayed?" *American Economic Review*, 81(5): 1170–1188.

Canavese A. and G. Di Tella (1988) "Inflation Stabilization or Hyperinflation Avoidance: The Case of the Austral Plan," in *Inflation Stabilization: The Experience of Israel, Argentina, Brazil, Bolivia, and Mexico*, edited by M. Bruno et al., Cambridge: MIT Press.

Cardoso, E. (1992) "La Privatizacion en America Latina," in *Adonde Va America Latina?* Joaquín Vial editor, CIEPLAN, Santiago.

Cukierman, A., S. Edwards and G. Tabellini (1992) "Seigniorage and Political Instability," *American Economic Review*, 82(3).

De La Balze, F. (1993) "Reforma y Crecimiento en la Argentina," in *Reforma y Convergenica, ensayos sobre la Transformacion de la Economia Argentina*, Ed. Manantial, Buenos Aires.

Di Tella, G. (1991) "Comment to Description of a Populist Experience: Argentina 1973–1976 by F. Sturzenegger," in *The Macroeconomics of Populism in Latin America*, edited by R. Dornbusch and S. Edwards, Chicago: Chicago University Press.

Dornbusch, R., F. Sturzenegger and H. Wolf (1990) "Extreme Inflation: Dynamics and Stabilization," *Brookings Papers on Economic Activity*, 2: 1–81.

Downs A. (1957) *An Economic Theory of Democracy*, New York: Harper and Row.

Gerchunoff P. and O. Centrángolo (1989) Reforma Económica y Estabilización en Democracia Política, Examen de una Experiencia Frustrada, Mimeo, Buenos Aires.

Harrington, J. (1993) "Economic Policy, Economic Performance, and Elections," *American Economic Review*, 83(1): 27–42.

Heymann D. (1991) "From Sharp Disinflation to Hyperinflation, Twice. The Argentina Experience 1985–1989," in *Lessons of Economic Stabilization and Its Aftermath*, edited by M. Bruno and S. Fischer, Cambridge: MIT Press.

Heymann, D., Navajas F. and I Warnes (1988) "Distributive Conflict and the Fiscal Deficit: Some Inflationary Games." Working Paper, Instituto Torcuato Di Tella, Buenos Aires (in Spanish).

Kiguel, M. and N. Liviatan (1991) "The Inflation Stabilization Cycles in Argentina and Brazil," in *Lessons of Economic Stabilization and Its Aftermath*, edited by M. Bruno and S. Fischer, Cambridge: MIT Press.

Kiguel, M. and N. Liviatan (1994) "Stopping Three Big Inflations (Argentina, Brazil and Peru)," in *Stabilization, Economic Reform and Growth*, edited by R. Dornbusch and S. Edwards, Chicago: University of Chicago Press.

Kiguel, M. and A. Neumeyer (1992) "Seigniorage and Inflation: The Case of Argentina," (forthcoming *Journal of Money Credit and Banking*), Mimeo, July.

Labán R. and F. Sturzenegger (1992) "La Economia Politica de los Programas de Estabilizacion," *Coleccion Estudios CIEPLAN*, No. 36(Dic.): 41–66.

——— (1994a) "Distributional Conflict, Financial Adaptation and Delayed Stabilizations," *Economics and Politics*, 6(3): 255–274.

——— (1994b) "Fiscal Conservatism as a Response to the Debt Crisis," *Journal of Development Economics*, 45 (November): 305–324.

López Murphy, R. (1991) La Experiencia Argentina: Alta Inflacion, Hiperinflacion y Estabilzacion Fallida, Mimeo, Buenos Aires.

López Murphy, R. (1992) Planes de Estabilizacion, Mimeo, Buenos Aires.

Machinea J. L. (1990) Stabilization under Alfonsin's Government: A Frustrated Attempt, CEDES Buenos Aires.

———. (1991) "Comment to From Sharp Disinflation to Hyperinflation, Twice: The Argentina experience 1985–1989," in *Lessons of Economic Stabilization and Its Aftermath*, edited by M. Bruno and S. Fischer, Cambridge: MIT Press.

Mondino, G., F. Sturzenegger and M. Tommasi (1993) Recurrent High Inflation and Stabilization: A Dynamic Game, Mimeo, UCLA.

Patinkin, Don (1993) "Israel's Stabilization Program of 1985, or Some Simple Truths of Monetary Theory," *Journal of Economic Perspectives*, 7(2): 103–128.

Rogoff, K. (1990) "Equilibrium Political Budget Cycles," *American Economic Review*, 80(3): 21–36.

Rogoff, K. and A. Sibert (1988) "Elections and Macroeconomic Policy Cycles," *Review of Economic Studies*, 55(1): 1–16.

Sturzenegger, F. (1994) "Hyperinflation with Currency Substitution: Introducing an Indexed Currency," *Journal of Money Credit and Banking*, 26(3): 377–395.

Index